THE BOOK SMUGGLERS

THE BOOK SMUGGLERS

PARTISANS, POETS,

AND THE RACE TO SAVE

JEWISH TREASURES

FROM THE NAZIS

David E. Fishman

ForeEdge

ForeEdge
An imprint of University Press of New England
www.upne.com
© 2017 David E. Fishman

Manufactured in the United States of America
Designed by April Leidig
Typeset in Baskerville by Copperline Book Services

For permission to reproduce any of the material
in this book, contact Permissions, University Press
of New England, One Court Street, Suite 250,
Lebanon NH 03766; or visit www.upne.com

Library of Congress Cataloging-in-Publication Data
Names: Fishman, David E., 1957– author.
Title: The book smugglers: partisans, poets, and the race to save
Jewish treasures from the Nazis.
Description: Lebanon, NH : ForeEdge, an imprint of University
Press of New England, [2017] | Includes bibliographical references
and index.
Identifiers: LCCN 2017018923 (print) | LCCN 2017025877 (ebook) |
ISBN 9781512601268 (epub, mobi, & pdf) | ISBN 9781512600490 (cloth)
Subjects: LCSH: Holocaust, Jewish (1939–1945)—Europe. | Cultural
property—Protection—Europe. | Cultural property Europe—
Destruction and pillage. | Jewish libraries—Destruction and pillage
—Europe. | Art thefts—Europe.
Classification: LCC D804.3 (ebook) | LCC D804.3 .F585 2017 (print) |
DCC 940.53/18132—dc23

LC record available at https://lccn.loc.gov/2017018923

5 4 3

עליסאַן

"קום אַרויס צו מיר

מײַן טײַער זיס לעבן . . .

קום זשע אַרויס

כ'וויל מיט דיר צוזאַמען זײַן"

CONTENTS

Most of us are aware of the Holocaust as the greatest genocide in history. We've seen the images of concentration camps and piles of dead bodies. But few of us think of the Holocaust as an act of cultural plunder and destruction. The Nazis sought not only to murder the Jews but also to obliterate their culture. They sent millions of Jewish books, manuscripts, and works of art to incinerators and garbage dumps. And they transported hundreds of thousands of cultural treasures to specialized libraries and institutes in Germany, in order to study the race they hoped to exterminate.

This book tells the story of a group of ghetto inmates that resisted, that would not let their culture be trampled upon and incinerated. It chronicles the dangerous operation carried out by poets turned partisans and scholars turned smugglers in Vilna, the "Jerusalem of Lithuania." The rescuers were pitted against Dr. Johannes Pohl, a Nazi "expert" on the Jews, who was dispatched by the German looting agency Einsatzstab Reichsleiter Rosenberg to organize the destruction and deportation of Vilna's great collections of Jewish books.

The Germans used forty ghetto inmates as slave laborers to sort, select, pack, and transport the materials. In a nerve-racking eighteen-month project, the members of the slave labor group, nicknamed the "paper brigade," wrapped books around their torsos and slipped them past German guards. If they were caught, they faced death by firing squad at Ponar, the mass-murder site outside of Vilna.

After Vilna's liberation from the Germans, the surviving members of the "paper brigade" dug up the hidden cultural treasures from bunkers and hiding places. But they soon came to a stark realization: the Soviet authorities that ruled Vilna were just as hostile toward Jewish culture as were the Nazis. They needed to rescue the treasures again and get them out of the Soviet Union. But smuggling books and papers across the Soviet-Polish border was just as fraught with life-threatening danger as the operation in the ghetto.

This book tells the story of men and women who displayed unwavering devotion to literature and art, and who were ready to risk their lives for them. It pits men and women of letters against two of the most murderous regimes in history.

I have taken the liberty of imagining the feeling and thoughts of my protagonists at various moments, but the things they did are not imagined—they are based on extensive research and documentation. I have usually called the city where the events took place "Vilna," as Jews called it, but in certain contexts I have used the Lithuanian form "Vilnius" or the Polish one "Wilno."

At its heart, *The Book Smugglers* is a personal story: a story about people. Allow me then to tell one personal story. A few years ago, I gave a talk about the Vilna ghetto and mentioned in passing the bravery of the "paper brigade." After the program, an elderly man who moved with the assistance of a walker came over and said to me, "You know, I worked in that brigade for a few months. I slipped quite a few books and papers past the German guards myself." I was stunned. I didn't think any of the heroes of the "paper brigade" were alive by 2012. But as he answered my battery of questions, I could tell he was indeed a member of the group.

Ninety-three-year-old Michael Menkin now makes his home in an assisted-living facility in New Jersey. He is a soft and elegant man, a retired trader in gems and precious stones who is unpresuming about his successful business career. He enjoys the everyday pleasures that life affords him: the company of his son, daughter, six grandchildren, and many friends and admirers. Menkin is a staunch supporter of the State of Israel and remembers with pride how Menachem Begin, then the young leader of the Revisionist Zionists in Poland—and later the sixth prime minister of Israel—slept in his parents' home in Vilna. Michael was also one of the founders of the United States Holocaust Memorial Museum in Washington, D.C.

But back then, he was a tall and lanky eighteen-year-old inmate of the Vilna ghetto. The Germans ordered him to lug boxes of books to the loading dock—most of them destined for incinerators and "paper mills," and some for shipment to Germany. Poet Shmerke Kaczerginski took him under his wing and taught him the art of book smuggling.

Michael's activity rescuing books is one of the few happy memories he has from his years in the ghetto. His mother, two sisters, and a brother were executed in Ponar. "We were all certain we would soon be killed. So why not do a good thing and rescue some treasures? I don't remember the names of the books and manuscripts I 'stole' from work, but I often lie in bed at night and think to myself, *Who knows? Maybe I rescued something important.*"

He did. He rescued his humanity and ours.

Shmerke Kaczerginski. Age in 1942: 34. Born in Vilna, the "Jerusalem of Lithuania." Raised in an orphanage, he attended night school, worked in a printshop, and wrote poetry. Shmerke—everyone called him by his first name—joined the "Young Vilna" literary group and became its lively, upbeat heart and soul. He was a member of the underground Communist Party in Poland and the author of popular political songs. Street smart and independent, once the Germans invaded Vilna, he wandered the countryside for seven months disguised as a Polish deaf-mute. He decided to enter the Vilna ghetto in April 1942 and became its most popular bard.

Zelig Kalmanovitch. Age in 1942: 61. Born in Goldingen, Latvia. A scholar and intellectual to his bone, Kalmanovitch had a doctorate in Semitic philology from the University of Königsberg. A friend once remarked, "When Zelig walks into the room, I don't need an encyclopedia." A model of seriousness and integrity, he became codirector of Vilna's Yiddish Scientific Institute (YIVO) in 1928. Kalmanovitch embraced religious faith and Zionism in his midfifties, on the eve of World War II. In the Vilna ghetto, he called upon his fellow inmates to maintain their human dignity and moral stature, and was dubbed "the prophet of the ghetto."

Rachela Krinsky. Age in 1942: 32. Born in Vilna. She was a popular high-school teacher of history, with a master's degree from Wilno University and command of medieval Latin and German. In a scandal that shocked many of her friends, she had an affair with a wealthy married man, Joseph Krinsky, who eventually divorced his wife and married Rachela.

Joseph perished just a few weeks after the Germans invaded Vilna, and Rachela entered the newly created Vilna ghetto alone. She left her twenty-two-month-old daughter on the outside, in the care of her Polish nanny. In the ghetto, Rachela's greatest source of comfort and distraction from pain was reading poetry.

Herman Kruk. Age in 1942: 45. Born in Plock, Poland. A professional librarian, Kruk was director of the largest Jewish lending library in Warsaw. He was a dedicated democratic socialist, who believed that books were the means through which the Jewish workers would lift themselves up. Kruk fled Warsaw in September 1939 and settled as a refugee in Vilna. He could have immigrated to the United States in 1940 but stayed, in order to track down his wife and son, who were trapped in Nazi-occupied Warsaw. Once the Germans captured Vilna, in 1941, he became director of the ghetto library. A refined gentleman, he always polished his shoes and filed his fingernails—even in the ghetto.

Abraham Sutzkever. Age in 1942: 29. Born in Smorgon, Belorussia. Sutzkever spent his childhood during the Great War as a refugee in Siberia, a place he experienced as a snowy winter wonderland. The grandson of a rabbi, he was an apolitical aesthete who believed only in poetry. With his dreamy eyes and wavy hair, he was the poet laureate of the "Young Vilna" literary group. After the Germans invaded, he eluded death dozens of times, once hiding inside a casket at a mortuary. Sutzkever harbored a mystical belief that as long as he fulfilled his mission, and wrote exquisite poetry, he would survive.

 *Johannes Pohl.* Age in 1942: 41. Born in Cologne, Germany. An ordained Catholic priest turned Nazi book looter. Pohl pursued advanced biblical studies at the Pontifical Oriental Institute in Jerusalem, where he mastered biblical and modern Hebrew. Upon returning to Germany in 1934, he resigned from the priesthood and took a position as Hebraica librarian in the Prussian State Library. Diligent and aggressively obedient by nature, he became a loyal servant of Nazism and began publishing antisemitic articles on Judaism and the Talmud. In 1940, he joined Nazi Germany's agency for looting cultural treasures, the Einsatzstab Reichsleiter Rosenberg, as its Judaica expert. He arrived in Vilna in July 1941.

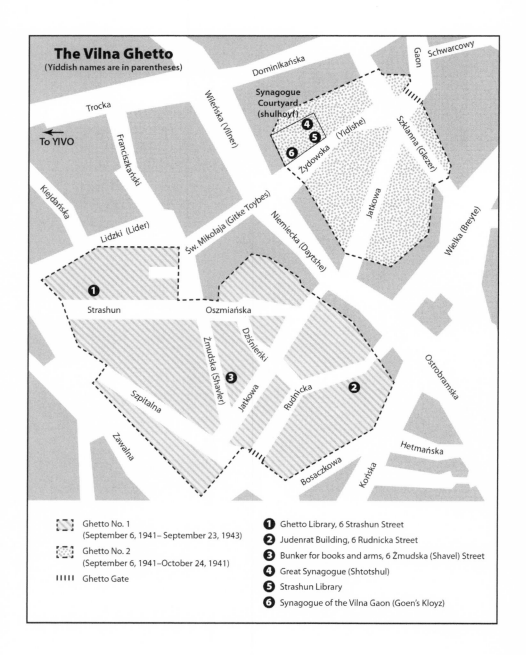

The Vilna Ghetto
(Yiddish names are in parentheses)

To YIVO

Trocka

Wileńska (Vilner)

Franciszkański

Kiejdańska

Lidzki (Lider)

Św. Mikołaja (Gitke Toybes)

Niemiecka (Daytshe)

Dominikańska

Synagogue Courtyard (shulhoyf)

Żydowska (Yidishe)

Gaon

Schwarcowy

Szklanna (Glezer)

Jatkowa

Wielka (Breyte)

Strashun

Oszmiańska

Żmudska (Shavel)

Dziśnieńki

Jatkowa

Rudnicka

Szpitalna

Zawalna

Bosaczkowa

Końska

Hetmańska

Ostrobramska

1

2

3

Ghetto No. 1
(September 6, 1941– September 23, 1943)

Ghetto No. 2
(September 6, 1941–October 24, 1941)

Ghetto Gate

1 Ghetto Library, 6 Strashun Street

2 Judenrat Building, 6 Rudnicka Street

3 Bunker for books and arms, 6 Żmudska (Shavel) Street

4 Great Synagogue (Shtotshul)

5 Strashun Library

6 Synagogue of the Vilna Gaon (Goen's Kloyz)

Central and Eastern Europe After World War II

FINLAND

NORWAY

Leningrad

ESTONIAN
SSR

RUSSIAN SOVIET
FEDERATIVE
SOCIALIST
REPUBLIC   Moscow ★

SWEDEN

LATVIAN
SSR

North
Sea

Baltic Sea

DENMARK

LITHUANIAN SSR

Vilnius ★

RSFSR

BELORUSSIAN SSR

Hamburg

NETH.   BRITISH
ZONE

Berlin ★

POLAND

Warsaw
★

BEL.

SOVIET
ZONE

Lodz

GERMANY

Hungen

LUX.

Frankfurt

FRENCH

UKRAINIAN SSR

FRANCE

AMERICAN
ZONE

CZECHOSLOVAKIA

ZONE

SWITZ.

AUSTRIA   HUNGARY   ROMANIA

The Germans shipped most of the books and cultural treasures that they looted in Vilna (Vilnius) to the Institute for Investigation of the Jewish Question in Frankfurt. After the war, Shmerke and Sutzkever dug up the material they hid from the Germans and smuggled part of it across the border to Lodz and Warsaw, Poland.

THE BOOK SMUGGLERS

Vilna, Nazi-occupied Poland. July 1943.

THE POET Shmerke Kaczerginski (pronounced Catcher-ginsky) leaves work to return to the ghetto. A slave laborer, his brigade sorts books, manuscripts, and art. Some will be shipped to Germany. The rest ends up in incinerators and paper mills. He works in the Auschwitz of Jewish culture, responsible for selecting the books that will be deported—and the ones that will be destroyed.

Compared to the work other slave laborers are doing across Nazi-occupied Europe, he is not digging fortifications to stave off the Red Army, clearing landmines with his body, or dragging corpses from gas chambers for incineration. Still, it's been a hard day, toiling away in the Vilna University Library's gray hall, stuffed to the ceiling with books. The brigade's brutish German master, Albert Sporket from the Einsatzstab Reichsleiter Rosenberg, had caught Shmerke and a few other workers reading a poem from one of the books that morning. Sporket, a cattle merchant by profession, burst into a shouting fit. The veins on his neck throbbed. He waved his fist at the workers and then flung the book across the room.

"You cheating thieves, you call this work? This isn't a lounge!" He warned them that if it ever happened again the consequences would be grave. The door slammed behind him.

The workers worked nervously all that afternoon. The cattle merchant treated them and the books like livestock—he would exploit them until it was time for their slaughter. If Sporket reported them to the Gestapo, their lives were over.

Shmerke's coworker and lover, Rachela Krinsky, a tall high school teacher with deep brown eyes, walked over to him.

"Are you still going to carry stuff today?"

Shmerke replied with his typical buoyant enthusiasm. "Of course. That madman might suddenly decide to send everything away. Or dump it all as wastepaper. These treasures are for our future. Maybe not for us, but for those who will survive us."

Shmerke wrapped an old embroidered Torah cover around his torso. Once it was snug, he stuck four little books inside his new girdle—old rarities published in Venice, Salonika, Amsterdam, and Krakow. Another tiny Torah cover swaddled him like a diaper. He buckled his belt and put on his shirt and jacket. He was ready to leave for the ghetto gate.

Shmerke had done it many times before, always with a mixture of determination, excitement, and fear. He knew the risks. If caught, he would likely face summary execution—like his friend, the singer Liuba Levitsky, who was found carrying a bag of beans on her person. At the very least, an ss man would give him twenty-five blows with a club or whip. As Shmerke tucked in his shirt, the irony didn't escape him. A member of the Communist Party and longtime committed atheist who hadn't gone to synagogue since childhood, he was about to risk his life for these mostly religious artifacts. He could smell the dust of past generations on his skin.

The line of returning workers was unusually long, twisting and turning for two city blocks before the ghetto gate. Word came back from the front of the line. ss Oberscharführer Bruno Kittel was personally inspecting people at the gate. Kittel—young, tall, dark, and handsome—was a trained musician and a natural, cool-headed murderer. He sometimes entered the ghetto to shoot inmates for sport. He'd stop someone on the street, offer the person a cigarette, and ask, "Do you want fire?" When the person nodded, he'd take out his pistol and shoot him in the head.

With Kittel present, the Lithuanian guards and Jewish ghetto police were more thorough than usual. From a block away, you could hear the shrieks of inmates being beaten for hiding food. The workers around Shmerke reached into their clothing. Potatoes, bread, vegetables, and pieces of firewood rolled into the street. They hissed at Shmerke, his puffed-up body obvious. In a landscape peopled with hungry, enslaved bodies, his inexplicably sturdy-looking torso could not have stood out more as he moved toward the inspection point.

"Dump it. Dump it!"

But Shmerke wouldn't unload. He knew it wouldn't save him. Even if he left the Hebrew books and Torah covers lying on the street, the Germans would trace them back to his team. Unlike potatoes, books had ex libris. Kittel might decide to execute the entire work brigade—including Rachela and Shmerke's closest friend, fellow poet Abraham Sutzkever. So Shmerke took his chances and tried to prepare himself for the blows that would follow.

Everyone else in line double-checked his or her pockets for coins or papers that might arouse Kittel's wrath. Shmerke began to tremble. As the line grew, it blocked traffic on Zawalna Street, one of Vilna's main commercial thoroughfares. Trolleys honked their horns. Non-Jewish pedestrians gathered across the street to watch the spectacle, some helping themselves to the discarded contraband.

Suddenly, voices called back into the crowd.

"He went inside the ghetto!"

"Let's go. Faster!"

Kittel, apparently tired of supervising the repetitious body searches, had decided to take a stroll through his fiefdom. The line surged forward. The guards, startled and relieved by Kittel's departure, turned to see where he was headed, making no effort to stop the rushing crowd. As Shmerke passed through the gate, the books pressed tightly against him, he heard jealous voices call out in his direction.

"Some people have all the luck!"

"And I left my potatoes on the street!"

They had no idea that he wasn't carrying food.

As his boots clanged against the cobblestones of the ghetto's Rudnicka Street, Shmerke started singing a song he had written for the ghetto youth club:

> Anyone who wants to can be young,
> Years don't mean a thing.
> Old folks can also, also be children,
> In a new, free spring.

In a secret bunker deep beneath the ghetto, a stone-floored cavern excavated from the damp soil, metal canisters were stuffed with books, manuscripts, documents, theater memorabilia, and religious artifacts.

Later that night, Shmerke added his treasures to the desperate depository. Before resealing the hidden doorway into the treasure room, he bade farewell to the Torah covers and old rarities with a loving caress, as if they were his children. And Shmerke, ever the poet, thought to himself, "Our present is as dark as this bunker, but the cultural treasures radiate with the promise of a luminous future."[1]

PART ONE

Before the War

CHAPTER ONE

Shmerke — The Life of the Party

FAMILY AND FRIENDS never dreamed that Shmerke Kaczer-ginski would grow up to be a writer. They expected him to become a porter, like his father, or some other kind of manual laborer. He was raised on one of Vilna's poorest streets, and when his parents both died of starvation in 1915, during the difficult first year of World War I, it looked as if the seven-year-old boy's fate was sealed. A porter. Perhaps a pickpocket or smuggler.

Shmerke did eventually become a smuggler but of a very different sort. As an inmate of the Vilna ghetto, he stole books from the repository where the Nazis held looted cultural treasures, in order to prevent them from being incinerated or shipped to Germany. He became so adept at book smuggling that he continued to practice this trade under the Soviets. But before he risked his life for books, Shmerke became a reader and then a writer, editor, and publisher.[1]

As a boy, the orphaned Shmerke (an affectionate Yiddish diminutive of his Hebrew name Shemaryahu) and his younger brother Jacob lived with assorted relatives, mainly with their paternal grandfather. But they spent most of their time on the streets. At age ten, he was admitted into the Vilna Jewish orphanage and moved into a dormitory that housed 150 children like him, who had lost their parents during the Great War. He was short, cross-eyed, and malnourished, with signs of rickets — a bloated stomach and a swollen head. During the daytime, he attended the Talmud Torah, the community-sponsored elementary school for orphans and indigent children, where he recovered from his illnesses and became a good student. Toward the end of his six years in the Talmud Torah school, he was reading works by the Yiddish essayist and philosopher Chaim Zhitlowsky.

But Shmerke's greatest skill wasn't scholastic. It was his ability to make friends and keep them. He had a winning smile, with boundless warmth and energy, and enjoyed giving to others the support and attention he hadn't received as a child. Shmerke loved to sing folksongs at parties and gatherings, and tell stories in hushed tones. Fellow students were drawn to him like bees to honey, and teachers spent extra time tutoring and mentoring him.[2]

In 1924, at age sixteen, Shmerke began working as an apprentice for Eisenshtat's lithography shop and moved out of the orphanage for a rented room. At night, he attended the I. L. Peretz Evening School, which offered a middle school education to working-class youths. The school was run by activists from the Jewish Workers' Bund, the main Jewish socialist party in Poland, and while there, Shmerke became involved in radical politics and the labor movement.[3] He wrote his first hit song at age eighteen, a political ditty called "Barricades" that imagined the workers' revolution as a happy family affair:

Fathers, mothers, little kids, are building barricades,
And workers are patrolling the streets in combat-brigades;

The kids all know — daddy isn't coming home,
He's busy in the street carrying his gun;

Chana tells her gang of kids there won't be dinner tonight,
Then she leaves the house to go help daddy fight;

The children build a barricade, there's no one in the house,
The kids are outdoors throwing stones at the police.

The song had a catchy tune and spread like wildfire to socialist meetings, demonstrations, and youth groups across Poland. While everyone sang it, most people didn't know its author's name.

Based on that poem, a few other pieces of verse, and a couple of articles, Shmerke joined a group of emerging Yiddish writers called Young Vilna in 1928. His main contribution to their gatherings, held around kitchen tables, was to sing folksongs and draw the members into lively group singing. One of the writers later remarked that Young Vilna didn't feel young until Shmerke appeared on the scene.[4]

His friend, the poet and novelist Chaim Grade, recalled, "He'd only nibble at a dish of food, but he'd belt out a song with all its melodic nuances, adding hand gestures and facial expressions. He'd repeat the song several times, until the group grew tired of the tune. Then he'd put the palm of his right hand to his ear, as if a tuning fork was vibrating inside, and wink his eyes: He's got it—and a different song would resonate. Everyone around him would happily catch the tune, as if they had been waiting for it all along."[5]

Shmerke didn't have any of the poses or affectations of a writer. With his short, trim frame, high forehead, and thick lips, he looked like your average worker—which he was. He wore round, black-rimmed glasses, a beret, and a disheveled jacket. And unlike most poets, he was street smart and a scrappy fighter. When a bunch of Polish teenagers attacked some friends and him one night while they were strolling down a dark alley, Shmerke eagerly joined the fight and beat up a few of the attackers. The rest ran away.[6]

The young poet was quite popular with girls. His charisma and warmth more than compensated for his short height, lazy eye, and unexceptional looks. His female friends were mostly newcomers to Vilna from surrounding small towns, whom he helped find work and a place to live. He intoxicated them with his singing and told them straight out, "Don't fall in love, or you'll suffer later." Everyone knew his flaw: if a girl stayed with him for more than a few months, he got bored and dropped her. But he was unfailingly devoted to his male friends, most of whom were poor workers and struggling writers. He lifted their spirits with jokes, songs, and stories. And when a few groszy fell into his hands, he took friends out to a café for tea or vodka.[7]

On weekend evenings, Shmerke walked down the streets of Vilna surrounded by a swarm of people, smiling and joking with everyone. But he'd be the first to notice an acquaintance approaching from a block away. He'd call out "How are ya?" and shake the person's hand with a wide motion as if he was going to slap it. They'd strike up a conversation, and the person ended up latching himself onto the gang, even if he had been rushing to an appointment.

Despite his easygoing, cheerful demeanor, Shmerke was serious about his politics. During his studies in the socialist-sponsored evening school, he joined the banned Communist Party. The twin plagues of poverty and antisemitism in Poland made the Soviet Union look, from across the border, like a haven of freedom and equality. His underground political activity—tying red banners to telegraph wires in the dead of night, printing up antigovernment proclamations and dropping them off in front of the local police station, or organizing an illegal street demonstration—led to several arrests and short prison terms.

Shmerke was under intermittent surveillance by the Polish security police and took precautions. He published his articles in New York's Yiddish Communist daily *Morning Freedom* (*Morgn-Frayhayt*) under a pseudonym and arranged for his pieces to be mailed out either by tourists or from a fictitious address in Warsaw. And he didn't talk to his literary friends about his political activity.[8]

But above everything, Shmerke was the heart and soul of Young Vilna, the life of the party (in both senses). He wasn't the group's most prolific or talented writer, but he was the guy who kept them together and soothed their competing literary egos. He was their organizer—manager, secretary, editor, and promoter—and thanks to him, the literary group became a fraternity, a fellowship of writers who helped and supported each other.[9]

His own writing was heavily political. His short story "Amnesty," published in 1934, described the grim living conditions of political prisoners in a Polish jail, whose only hope was that the head of state would pardon them. In order to get the story past the censors, Shmerke set it in a German prison, not a Polish one, but the purported location was belied by many details in the text. (Hitler didn't grant amnesties.) The story ended with the prisoners' realization that "no one will free us." They and the working masses would have to do it themselves.[10]

When a new poet named Abraham Sutzkever applied to join Young Vilna and submitted exquisite nature poems for the group's judgment, Shmerke warned him, "Abrasha, these are times of steel, not of crystal." Sutzkever's application was rejected, and he was only admitted into the group a few years later. He went on to become the greatest Yiddish poet of the twentieth century.

Personally and poetically, Shmerke and Sutzkever were opposites. Abrasha Sutzkever was the son of a middle-class merchant and the grandson of a rabbi. He was an aesthete—apolitical, pensive, and self-absorbed. He was a strikingly handsome young man, with dreamy eyes and a head of wavy hair. Having spent his childhood years during the Great War as a refugee in Siberia amid Kyrgyzians, Sutzkever was attuned to the beauty of snow, clouds, and trees, and to the exotic sounds of language. After the war, he settled in Vilna, attended private schools, and became well read in Polish poetry. Shmerke, who had received all his education in Yiddish, was not. But once Abrasha entered Young Vilna, the two of them became the closest friends in the group.[11]

The suppression of Communists intensified in late 1930s Poland, as the country tried to maintain good relations with its neighbor to the West, Nazi Germany. Shmerke's political activism led the authorities to suspect that his literary group was nothing more than a revolutionary cell. They confiscated most copies of the *Young Vilna* literary magazine, and in late 1936, Shmerke was arrested in his capacity as editor. He stood trial for threatening the public peace. His trial consisted of lengthy courtroom deliberations about the meaning of certain poetic lines. In the end, the judge reluctantly freed him from prison and released the magazine's latest issue from confiscation. As Young Vilna and Shmerke's friends celebrated their victory at a local café, with jokes and group singing, Sutzkever raised a toast: "Long live Shmerkism!" Shmerkism was the ability to prevail over any challenge with determination, buoyant optimism, and a sense of humor.[12]

Paradoxically, the outburst of the Second World War brought him yet another cause for celebration. While Poland was attacked from the West by Nazi Germany on September 1, 1939, and Warsaw came under German siege, the Soviet Union seized the eastern part of Poland, under the terms of a German-Soviet nonaggression pact. The Red Army entered Vilna. For most Jews, the Soviets were the lesser evil compared to the Nazis. But for Shmerke, the arrival of the Red Army was a dream come true—Communism in his beloved hometown. He and his friends spent the next Friday night singing, drinking, and dreaming.

But Shmerke's celebration was followed by disappointment just a few weeks later, when the Soviets decided to hand Vilna over to independent Lithuania, a capitalist and authoritarian country. He left for Bialystok, a city one hundred miles southeast of Vilna, which remained under Soviet rule, just so he could continue to live out his dream of building Communism. He lived there for close to a year, working as a teacher and soldier. When the Soviets seized Vilna a second time, and made it the capital of the Lithuanian Soviet Socialist Republic, in June 1940, Shmerke went home, full of confidence that the workers would become the managers of their own factories and that unemployment would be eliminated.

To everyone's surprise, Shmerke came back to Vilna a married man, with a wife who had fled from German-occupied Krakow. Barbara Kaufman was, like Shmerke, a dedicated Communist, but in other respects she was totally unlike him or his earlier girlfriends. Barbara came from a middle-class family, spoke impeccable Polish, and didn't know Yiddish songs or literature. Shmerke's gang didn't like her much—they thought she was stiff and cold—and she didn't like competing with all those friends for her new husband's attention.[13]

But Shmerke was happy. He was back home among friends, he was in love with a refined and beautiful woman, and he was a citizen of "the most just society in the world." Who could ask for more?[14]

———————————

Shmerke's rise from orphan to author wasn't typical—his younger brother became a locksmith and hardly read a newspaper—but his story wasn't exceptional in Vilna, the city nicknamed "the Jerusalem of Lithuania," where books and study were afforded the highest respect. Institutions such as the Talmud Torah and the Peretz Evening School converted many street children into avid readers. But in Shmerke's case, the bond with books went much deeper. He realized that books had rescued him from a life of crime and despair. The least he could do was repay the favor and rescue them from destruction when the need arose.

CHAPTER TWO

The City of the Book

S HMERKE KACZERGINSKI loved to show off his city to Jewish writers and intellectuals visiting from Warsaw and New York. He'd sometimes pop up unannounced at their doorstep or hotel room, with an offer to give them a tour of the sites. Vilna had 193,000 inhabitants, 28.5 percent of whom were Jews. Numerically, it was the fourth-largest Jewish community in Poland (After Warsaw, Lodz, and Lwów), but culturally it was the capital city of East European Jewry, "the Jerusalem of Lithuania."[1]

Legend had it that Vilna acquired that lofty title back in the 1600s, when it asked to become a member of the council of Lithuanian Jewish communities. The older communities of Grodno, Brest, and Pinsk refused to grant it a seat at the table, considering it to be a young upstart, small and undistinguished. In response, the heads of the Vilna community wrote an impassioned letter, noting that they had 333 residents who knew the entire Talmud by heart. The letter writers stressed the symbolic importance of the number. In Hebrew, the letters of the alphabet have numeric value (Alef is 1, Bet is 2, etc.), and 333 was the numerical equivalent of the word for snow, *sheleg*. Vilna, they wrote, was as pure and unblemished as a fresh coating of white snow.

The members of the council were awestruck and ashamed. Their communities had barely a dozen scholars who knew the Talmud by heart. One of the rabbis rose and declared, "Vilna must be admitted onto the council. It is the Jerusalem of Lithuania."[2]

Before starting his tour of the sites, Shmerke explained some basic history to his American guests: Vilna was situated between Warsaw and St. Petersburg (Leningrad), and had been ruled for the last four hundred years by either Poland or Russia. But back in the Middle Ages, Vilnius, as the city was then called, was the capital of the Grand Duchy of Lithuania, a large state that spanned from the Baltic to the Black Sea and included much of Belorussia, Poland, and Ukraine. The city's inhabitants were the last pagans on European soil, before they embraced Catholicism in 1387, and they spoke Lithuanian, a non-Slavic language related to Sanskrit.

Then Lithuania's neighbors started to expand and seize control. The Grand Duchy became part of the Polish state in 1569, leading to an influx of Polish language and culture. Vilnius became Wilno, the seat of a Polish university, and a center of Polish printing. The Russians conquered the region in 1795, in the final stage of the dismemberment of Poland, and the city became Vil'no, a provincial capital in the northwestern corner of the tsarist empire. The authorities imposed Russian as the sole language of instruction in schools and converted many Catholic churches into Russian Orthodox ones. After 125 years of Russian rule, when the dust settled at the end of World War I, the city reverted to Poland again.

But throughout all these shifts of power, Jews continued to call the region Lithuania; and Vilna, its Jerusalem.

Shmerke would start his idiosyncratic tour at the cathedral, the epicenter of town, situated near the banks of the Wilia River. The imposing structure stood on the spot where the Lithuanians embraced Latin Catholicism and baptized themselves in the river. They demolished their pagan shrine and built the cathedral on its ruins.

Shmerke would point out the figures of saints that adorned the cathedral's exterior, including a full-scale image of Moses with a long beard and horns, holding the Ten Commandments, which was set onto its facade next to the entrance. The unusual prominence of Moses at the front of the church gave rise to a legend among Vilna's Jews: The cathedral's Italian architect had been a convert from Judaism. After sculpting the figure of Moses, the artist announced that he planned to mold a final statue—an image of the Lord himself. But as he began working on the audacious figure, a sudden storm passed through the city and knocked the artist off his pedestal, plunging him to his death. The statue of Moses looked down at him in anger, its fingers pointing at the second commandment: "Thou shalt not make unto thee any graven image."[3]

In Vilna, even the cathedral had a Jewish story.

From there, Shmerke would take his guest down Wilenska Street, a busy commercial boulevard filled with Jewish and Polish businesses: appliances, knitwear, medical supplies, high-end tailoring, and dental offices. Along the way, he pointed out the Helios Theater, where the most famous Yiddish drama, S. An-Ski's *The Dybbuk*, was first performed in 1921, and the offices of the city's most respected Jewish newspaper, *The Day* (*Der Tog*).

Shmerke kept going until he reached Niemiecka Street and the narrow, crooked alleys of the old Jewish quarter that intersected with it. Jews first settled here in the early sixteenth century, and Polish king Sigismund Augustus II issued a royal charter in 1551 that specified three streets on which Jews were permitted to live. On one of them, called Żydowska Street ("Jews' Street"), they built a synagogue in 1572, which grew to become the Great Synagogue, or in Yiddish, the shtot-shul.

From the outside, the synagogue's edifice was unremarkable, especially when compared with the cathedral. It was only four stories high, because a royal decree stipulated that synagogues be shorter than local churches. But once you entered the building, you went down a set of stairs, and from the ground level visitors looked up and were bedazzled by the marble pillars, oak furnishing, ivory decorations, silver ornaments, and candelabra. The Holy Ark was covered by a satin curtain with gold embroidery.

It is related that Napoleon was left speechless when he visited the Great Synagogue in 1812, standing in wonder at its threshold.

The roof of the shtot-shul had a darkened spot, which, the story goes, dated back to the 1794 Kosciuszko uprising, a failed attempt to restore the Polish kingdom after most of its territory was seized by Russia. As battles raged on the streets of Vilna between the Russian conquerors and the Polish rebels, the Jews gathered in the Great Synagogue and prayed for God's protection. A cannonball hit the roof but failed to explode and remained lodged inside. More than a century later, the synagogue's congregants recited thanksgiving prayers annually on the day of that miracle.[4]

Then Shmerke took his guest for a stroll around the synagogue courtyard, the *shulhoyf*, and pointed out the dozen smaller houses of prayer and study, called *kloyzn*, which took up most of its space. One of the walls of the courtyard displayed a set of three clocks with Hebrew letters on their faces, which showed the times of morning prayer services, of Friday-night candle lighting, and the end of the Sabbath. "At the clocks" became a gathering place for congregants, passersby, and beggars, and the wall was plastered with public notices.[5]

While the Great Synagogue was Vilna's most famous Jewish landmark, it was not the most revered Jewish holy place. That distinction belonged to a house across the courtyard—the home and synagogue of the Vilna Gaon, or genius, Rabbi Elijah the son of Solomon Zalman (1720–97), who was the community's patron saint and cultural hero.

The reclusive Rabbi Elijah was known for his total immersion in the study of holy books, to the virtual exclusion of all other activities. He kept the shutters to his windows closed, to avoid being distracted by sights and sounds from the street. He slept very little and rarely left his home to venture outdoors. Although he lived just a few steps away from the Great Synagogue, he didn't attend services there. Instead, he established a private prayer house, a *kloyz*, in his home and invited a circle of disciples to worship with him. After his death, the disciples continued to study and pray there, and eventually passed on their seats to a subsequent generation of scholars.

Unlike any other synagogue in Vilna, the Gaon's kloyz did not have a women's section. And the services themselves were also peculiar, following a set of liturgical practices established by Rabbi Elijah that differed from the standard East European rite. When visitors were first allowed to attend its services, in the late nineteenth century, they were confused by the order of prayer.

The focal point of the Gaon's kloyz was the plaque along the southern wall, which marked the spot where Rabbi Elijah sat and studied Torah for forty years. Over the plaque, there hung an eternal light—an object usually found at the front of the sanctuary over the Holy Ark. But this synagogue had two eternal lights, one over the Ark, and the second over "the place of the Gaon" along the right-hand wall. Underneath the plaque, the wall protruded outward, in the rectangular shape of a lectern or pulpit, covering the spot where Rabbi Elijah had studied. The protrusion served not only as a monument but also as a barrier that prevented anyone from sitting in Rabbi Elijah's place.[6]

A local historian noted in 1918, "The Gaon's kloyz evokes fear and awe. When you enter and see the grey-bearded Talmudists, it seems as if the spirit of the Gaon is still hovering in the air." A guidebook added, "The Gaon's kloyz is the gem and crown of the Jerusalem of Lithuania."[7]

Rabbi Elijah symbolized the community's ethos: that the book was the supreme value of Jewish life. When European Jews imagined "the Jerusalem of Lithuania," they didn't think of a synagogue, statue, or memorial. They saw a large folio volume of the Talmud with the word "Vilna" on bottom of the title page in large bold letters. The Yiddish author Sholem Asch recalled that as a child, when he first studied the Talmud, he was certain that Judaism's ancient magnum opus had not only been printed in Vilna but also been written there.

By this point in the tour, after the cathedral, Great Synagogue, and Gaon's kloyz, Shmerke was probably a little tired of religious land- marks. He was anything but pious and never went to synagogue — except when he was showing them to visitors. So Shmerke was happy that the next stop was a place where he felt totally at home — the Jewish communal library.

The library was named after its founder, Matityahu Strashun, a wealthy businessman, scholar, and bibliophile, who bequeathed his pri- vate book collection to the Jewish community when he died, in 1892. It included five Hebrew incunabula (books printed before the year 1501), many sixteenth-century imprints from Venice (the first major center of Hebrew printing), and other rarities. After Strashun's death, bequeath- ing books to the community became fashionable among Vilna's Jewish elite, and the library grew by leaps and bounds.

The community board decided to construct a library building in the historic heart of Jewish Vilna — inside the *shulhoyf*, adjacent to the Great Synagogue. There was a message in their choice of location: the library was to be considered an intellectual sanctum. In another resonant act, the board decided to keep the library open seven days a week, even on the Sabbath and Jewish holidays. (According to library rules, one could not write or take notes in the reading room on those days.) Reading and study were integral to life; there were no "days off" from that activity.

By the 1930s, its collection had grown to forty thousand volumes.

The Strashun Library served as the intellectual hub of Jewish Vilna. There was often a line of people waiting for one of the hundred seats placed alongside the long rectangular tables. In the evening hours, younger readers sat on windowsills or leaned against the walls. The library was where the old and new trends in Jewish life met: bearded rabbis and young secular pioneers with blue or red neckerchiefs.

Shmerke spent many evenings after work reading Yiddish and world literature there. He wrote an article in honor of the library's forty-fifth anniversary called "Dust That Refreshes."[8]

Almost as famous as the library was its librarian, Chaikl Lunski, who was reference service, circulation desk, director of acquisitions, conservator, and janitor, all wrapped into one. The bearded Lunski was a fixture of Jewish Vilna, who bridged all the divides in the community. He was a religious man, who left work for afternoon prayers in the Great Synagogue, but he was also an aficionado of modern Hebrew and Yiddish literature, and treated every visiting poet as if he or she was a vip. Lunski was an avid Zionist, who dreamt of working for a library in Jerusalem some day, but he also had good friendships with socialists. During the early 1900s, he collected illegal revolutionary pamphlets for the library, such as the Bund's brochure "Down with the Autocracy!" and hid them in the bowels of the library stacks. When the tsarist police learned that the library held subversive literature, they threatened to close it down.

While Lunski wasn't trained in library science—there wasn't even a catalog until the late 1920s—he more than compensated for this deficiency with his erudition and personal warmth toward both the books and their readers. "He knew by heart the names of all the books in the library, and their place on the shelves, as someone remembers the home addresses of his personal friends," one reader recalled. People loved him, and called him "the guardian of the Jerusalem of Lithuania."[9]

After bidding farewell to the library, Shmerke would probably invite his tourist guest for a bite at Volf Usian's restaurant, popularly known as Velfke's. Located on the corner of the Niemiecka Street and Żydowska Street, Velfke's was a favorite meeting spot for Vilna's Jewish bohemia, because it was open all night. People used to quip that when the last Talmudists left the synagogue courtyard to go to bed, Velfke's started to wake up and get lively. The restaurant offered the best Jewish cuisine in town, with large portions: chopped liver, gefilte fish, boiled beef, and roast goose.

Velfke's had two dining rooms. The front room, with a bar, was used by droshky drivers, local toughs, and members of Vilna's Jewish underworld. The back room was frequented by couples and cultural types—actors, writers, intellectuals, and their VIP guests. Sometimes, when a poor writer didn't have enough money to pay his bill, an underworld type from the bar would pick up his tab.

The back room played music from the radio and had open space for dancing. The owner, Velfke, gave all of his clients a friendly welcome, as he floated between the front and back rooms.

Velfke's most celebrated regular customer was the flamboyant Yiddish actor Abraham Morevsky, who made his name playing the Hasidic rebbe of Miropol in *The Dybbuk*. Morevsky used to eat dinner here after every show. A large man with a big appetite—and an even bigger ego—he used to order five or six main dishes and attack them like a hungry wolf. People said that Morevsky paid for his meals at Velfke's by the hour, not by the dish.

If you visited Vilna and didn't go to Velfke's, you didn't know the city.[10]

After the break, Shmerke shifted gears to show off Vilna's modern Jewish cultural institutions. He walked down Niemiecka Street, turned right onto Rudnicka Street, and pointed out the Yiddish Real Gymnasium and the Jewish Musical Institute, which shared a large courtyard. The Real Gymnasium was Vilna's outstanding Jewish high school and one of the few schools in Poland that taught advanced chemistry and physics in Yiddish. The musical institute offered instruction in various instruments and vocal training with the focus on classical music. It organized Yiddish opera productions, including *La Traviata*, *Carmen*, *Tosca*, *Madama Butterfly* and *Aida*.

Then it was onward, across Zawalna Street to Kwaszelna Street and to the printshop and editorial offices of the Kletzkin Press—the most prestigious Yiddish publishing house in the world. Its founder and director, Boris Kletzkin, had been active in printing underground literature for the main Jewish socialist party, the Bund, back in the 1890s. He designed a print machine that could be hidden inside the frame of a specially constructed dining-room table. When freedom of the press was proclaimed in the Russian Empire in 1905, Kletzkin decided to go legal and turn commercial. But he never lost his idealistic commitment to books as a vehicle for improving the world. It helped that Kletzkin himself didn't need to worry about money: he made his fortune from real estate, forests, and a lumber business, which he inherited from his father.

The Kletzkin Press distinguished itself with high-quality sets, such as the collected works of I. L. Peretz, the father of modern Yiddish literature, in nineteen volumes. Kletzkin was the twentieth-century secular heir to Vilna's Romm Press, which published the classical twenty-volume edition of the Talmud known as the *Vilna Shas*. Kletzkin also issued the works of great European authors—Maxim Gorky, Charles Dickens, Thomas Mann, Knut Hamsun, and Romain Rolland—in high-quality translations. On top of that, there were works of scholarship: Simon Dubnow's classical history of Hasidism (translated from Hebrew) and Josephus Flavius's *Jewish Wars* (translated from ancient Greek).

In 1925, Kletzkin moved the headquarters of his publishing empire to Warsaw and converted the Vilna facility into a branch operation. But the press continued to call itself "the Vilna Publishing House of Boris Kletzkin," in an act of homage to its roots. Many lovers of literature got confused when they opened a book and saw both "Vilna Press" and "Warsaw" on the title page. But the oxymoron actually made sense. Vilna was a code word for high-quality Jewish culture. "Vilna Press" was shorthand for excellence.[11]

The last stop on Shmerke's tour was the building of the Yiddish Scientific Institute, YIVO, on Wiwulskiego Street. YIVO, the acronym for *Yidisher Visnshaftlekher Institut*, was a modern research academy that employed the methods of the humanities and social sciences to study Jewish life. Founded in 1925, the institute's organizational meetings were held in Berlin, but the resonance and centrality of Vilna virtually forced the founders to choose the city as its headquarters. Its branches were in Berlin, Paris, and New York.

The driving force behind YIVO was a brilliant scholar named Max Weinreich. A former activist in the Bund, Weinreich received his undergraduate degree from St. Petersburg University, where he studied history, languages, and literature. After dabbling in political journalism during the Russian Revolution of 1917, he went on for a doctorate in linguistics at the University of Marburg, Germany. Yiddish wasn't his native language—German was—but he became its greatest student and public champion. In his personal style, Weinreich mixed the formality of a German professor with the social commitment of a Bundist. He was also nearly blind in one eye, because of an injury he incurred from an antisemitic attack in 1931.

YIVO published more than twenty-four thousand pages of scholarship, in the fields of language, literature, history, folklore, economics, psychology, and education. The institute also devoted much energy to building its library and archive. Since it didn't have the funds to purchase rarities, YIVO appealed to volunteer *zamlers*, collectors, to send in materials from their local communities. By 1929, just four years after its founding, there were 163 YIVO collector groups across Eastern Europe and, indeed, the globe. They sent in folksongs, idioms, and folktales that they recorded from friends and family; handbills, posters, and theater programs that most people just threw away; and rare handwritten record books and documents that they found while rummaging in synagogue attics. Through encouraging voluntary collecting, YIVO engaged the masses as participants in the scholarly enterprise.

The institute's spacious building, built in 1933, was located at 18 Wiwulskiego Street, on a quiet, tree-laced avenue, removed from the hustle-bustle of the city center and from the grimy narrow lanes of the old Jewish quarter. The facility was clean, bright, and equipped with a state-of-the-art storage facility. Shmerke would have loved to study in YIVO's academic training programs, inaugurated in 1935, but he lacked the credentials—he didn't have a high school diploma.

YIVO was the national academy of a stateless people, the Jews of Eastern Europe, and Weinreich was president of the academy. The institute was a source of ethnic pride and self-validation for tens of thousands of Jews, in a country where they were widely despised. And because YIVO existed thanks to modest donations and a spirit of voluntarism, without any recognition or subsidy from the Polish state, YIVO was seen an expression of the Jewish people's will to survive in the face of adversity.[12]

Shmerke's tour of Vilna was over. Now it was time for some concluding reflections. He reminded his visitor that it was only a twenty-minute walk from the oldest to the newest embodiments of the Jerusalem of Lithuania—from the Great Synagogue to YIVO, 350 years in twenty minutes. He remarked upon the cultural distance between the two sites—a synagogue and a modern scientific research institute. But he also pointed out the underlying continuity. Jewish Vilna was devoted to the life of the mind. It was committed to the proposition that intellectual richness could grow in the midst of poverty and persecution, and could not only counteract them but also overshadow them.

Vilna Jews told a story about the Vilna Gaon and used its punch line as their slogan. A group of schoolchildren noticed Rabbi Elijah on the street, on one of the rare occasions that he left the confines of his home. When they began screaming "the Vilna Gaon!" "the Vilna Gaon!" Rabbi Elijah turned around and said to one of the boys, "Yingele, vil nor, vestu zayn a goen" (little boy, if you only will it [*vil nor*], you can become a gaon, a genius.) Vilna meant *vil nor.* The Jerusalem of Lithuania was about the ability of willpower to conquer adversity. Jewish greatness in the diaspora was possible "if you only will it." That, Shmerke concluded, is what the Jewish socialist leader Wolf Latsky Bartholdy meant when he declared during a visit to the Strashun library that "Vilna isn't a city; it's an idea."[13]

PART TWO

Under German Occupation

CHAPTER THREE

The First Assault

NOJEKH PRYLUCKI woke up on Sunday morning, June 22, 1941, to work on his book about the phonetics of the Yiddish language. He had gone to the theater the previous night, to attend the premier of Sholem Aleichem's comic drama *The Raffle Ticket*, and spent the evening in the company of Shmerke Kaczerginski, Abraham Sutzkever, and the writers of Young Vilna. The fifty-nine-year-old scholar was the most prominent Jewish intellectual in Vilna (now called by its Lithuanian name Vilnius)—despite the fact that he was a newcomer. He'd arrived in the city in October 1939, as a refugee from Nazi-occupied Warsaw.

When the Soviets incorporated Vilna into the USSR, in June 1940, they "Sovietized" the Yiddish Scientific Institute (YIVO) and appointed Prylucki as its director. Max Weinreich, YIVO's heart and soul, had been in Denmark in September 1939, in order to attend an international linguistics conference, and decided not to return to Eastern Europe once the war broke out. After seven months in limbo in Scandinavia, he settled in New York City in March 1940. The Soviets chose Prylucki to inherit his job.

Besides directing YIVO, the plump and goateed Prylucki also became the first incumbent of the newly created chair in Yiddish at Vilnius University. His inaugural lecture was a major Jewish cultural event in the city. Before the war, when Vilna belonged to Poland, the university was a hotbed of antisemitism, and the existence of a chair in any field of Jewish studies was unimaginable. There were no Jewish professors on the faculty, and Jewish students were required to sit on the left-hand side of lecture halls. (In quiet protest, they chose to stand in the back instead.) Prylucki's endeavors as professor, and as director of YIVO, embodied the hope that Jews and Jewish culture would flourish in

Soviet Vilnius "under the rays of the five-pointed star," as he put it in an interview.[1]

But those hopes were shattered on June 22, 1941, when the Germans attacked. Sirens began to sound at about ten in the morning, while Prylucki was sitting at his desk. At eleven, the Soviet foreign minister announced by radio broadcast that the USSR had been attacked by Germany. Aerial overflights of Vilna began at noon, followed by bombing. Prylucki and a group of colleagues rushed to the YIVO building on Wiwulskiego Street and began burying materials from the institute's rich archives, in order to conceal them from the advancing German invaders. They were particularly concerned about the records of the "Historical Commission" that Prylucki headed, which documented the ongoing Nazi atrocities against Jews in Poland. The "Historical Commission" recorded the testimony of over four hundred refugees who had escaped German-occupied territory and fled to Vilna. If the Germans found its papers, with detailed accounts of their crimes, they would undoubtedly execute the members of the commission.[2]

As the bombing persisted through Sunday night, Prylucki put on a confident face and told his friends, "With the first bomb that Hitler dropped on the Soviet Union, he dug his own grave. He will meet a swift and bitter end." But his wife Paula was more visibly worried. "We must run. Nojekh must not stay here for a second more. They will rip him to shreds."[3] She had good reason for concern: besides being a scholar of Yiddish language and folklore, Prylucki was a well-known Jewish political figure. He had headed the Jewish People's Party (*Folkspartey*) in Warsaw for some twenty years and had served as a member of the Polish parliament.

Prylucki was a Jewish nationalist and a Polish patriot, and a firm believer that the two were not contradictory. In the 1930s, he published scathing attacks on Nazi Germany on the pages of the Warsaw Yiddish daily *Moment*, of which he was editor in chief. After his escape to Vilna, he transformed himself into a staunch Soviet patriot, convinced that only the USSR could protect Jews—and the world—from Nazi aggression. In short, Nojekh Prylucki was just the kind of person that the Germans were sure to come looking for: an intellectual, a political leader, and an open enemy of the Third Reich. That is why Nojekh and Paula had fled Warsaw back in September 1939. But now, in June 1941, the Germans were catching up with them.

The Pryluckis made hasty plans to flee eastward again with a group of journalists and writers. But they were overrun by the German army, which entered the city on June 24, just two days after the outburst of hostilities. The Germans promptly sealed off all roads.

Trapped in Vilna, the couple took the only precautionary measure they could think of. They burned their personal papers in their kitchen oven, including documents from the "Historical Commission."[4]

Once the Germans took control, the living conditions of Vilna's seventy thousand Jews deteriorated quickly. On July 4, Lithuanian police loyal to the Germans and other armed groups began assaulting Jews on the streets; on July 7, Jews were ordered to wear armbands with a Star of David, so they were easily identified; and on July 10, 123 men were killed in a massacre on Szpitalna Street. A day later, a group of people were rounded up and sent to the outskirts of town, to a green, wooded place called Ponar, where they were lined up and shot dead. It was the first of many such mass shootings. Over the course of the month, thousands of Jewish men were seized off the streets and from their homes, and sent away, supposedly for work. No one ever heard from them again. There was no ghetto yet, but Jewish men did not go outdoors for fear of being seized in the "snatchings."

As Paula Prylucki suspected, the Germans came looking for her husband Nojekh, but for a different reason than she had anticipated. They didn't come to arrest or execute him but to exploit him as a slave-laborer scholar. The man who ordered his arrest was a Nazi Judaica expert named Dr. Johannes Pohl.

Pohl was a staff member of the Einsatzstab Reichsleiter Rosenberg (ERR), the German agency charged with looting cultural property across Europe. The ERR began its plunder in 1940 in France, by seizing books and artwork owned by Jews, but it soon moved on to stealing works on a much broader scale, from national museums, libraries, and private collections of all kinds.

One of the ERR's special interests was the looting of Judaica—books, manuscripts, and documents regarding the Jews' religion, history, and culture. These materials were considered valuable sources for the field of antisemitic Jewish studies called *Judenforschung*, which investigated the depravity of the Jews. Judenforschung legitimized in scientific terms the Nazi policies of persecution and later—extermination. For the Nazis, the "acquisition" of rare Jewish books and manuscripts was an important tool in the spiritual and intellectual struggle against Jewry. Pohl was in charge of that activity.[5]

Johannes Pohl was a devout Catholic turned Nazi. Born in Cologne in 1904 as the oldest son of a trucker, he used the priesthood as a means of upward mobility. Upon ordination, he became the vicar of the city of Essen, in North Rhine Westphalia, and went on to study Bible at the theological faculty of the University of Bonn. Pohl was never an outstanding student. But he was diligent and excelled at making connections that helped him move from one place to another. After Bonn, he studied at the Pontifical Biblical Institute in Rome, living in the Italian capitol for three years while the country was in the throes of Fascism. He concentrated on the Old Testament and wrote a dissertation on "Family and Society in Ancient Israel according to the Prophets" that received a low passing grade. From Italy, Pohl moved on to the Holy Land. He received a church stipend to pursue studies at the Pontifical Oriental Institute in Jerusalem and spent from 1932 to 1934 in its intensely pious environment studying Bible, archeology, and Hebrew. He even seems to have attended lectures at the Hebrew University, the Zionist movement's young institution of higher learning! During his stay in Jerusalem, the Nazis came to power in Germany, an event that Pohl supported enthusiastically. He and his German classmates used to sing "Deutschland über Alles" and other patriotic songs at night, sitting around the campfire.

In 1934, Pohl changed his life. He returned to Germany, resigned from the priesthood, and married a German woman he met in Jerusalem. Effectively unemployed, he decided to market himself to German state libraries as an Orientalist, specializing in Hebrew. Luckily for Pohl, this was a field with many openings, since Jews were being dismissed from the state libraries, and most Oriental librarians were Jewish. Pohl was hired as a Hebraica specialist by the Prussian State Library, the largest library in Germany, thanks to his language aptitude and political loyalty. He studied library science while on the job, in the evenings.

Pohl never realized his dream of pursuing an academic career. He applied to write a habilitation dissertation in Oriental studies at Friedrich Wilhelm University, Berlin's premier university, on ancient Israelite society. But his application was rejected, on the grounds that he didn't know any modern biblical scholarship. He reapplied, proposing to write on the relationship between Jewry and Bolshevism, a topic dear to Hitler and the Nazi Party, but the Oriental studies department demurred that the subject was more appropriate for political science. So Pohl remained a librarian and embarked on a side career as an antisemitic propagandist, publishing articles on the evils of the Talmud in, among other places, *Der Stürmer.* His book *The Spirit of the Talmud* became quite popular and went through two editions.

Pohl was an eager and obedient follower of the powerful institutions around him: first of the Catholic Church, and later of the Nazi German state. He developed his learned antisemitism during his Catholic studies and put it to use in the service of Nazism.

Pohl joined the Einsatzstab Reichsleiter Rosenberg as a Hebraica expert in June 1940. Nine months later, he was appointed chief librarian of the newly founded Institute for Investigation of the Jewish Question, in Frankfurt, one of the main centers of Judenforschung. His two jobs overlapped. He looted Judaica for the ERR and sent the looted materials to the institute, which quickly accumulated an extraordinarily rich Judaica library.[6]

Pohl came to Vilna just a week after the Germans seized control of the city, in early July 1941, accompanied by an instructor of Oriental and biblical studies at Berlin University, Dr. Herbert Gotthard.[7] The two Nazi scholars drove around the city wearing yellow-green uniforms with red armbands and black swastikas, accompanied by a retinue of soldiers.

They came prepared, with the addresses of Jewish cultural institutions and the names of their heads. Pohl stopped people on the streets of the old Jewish quarter and asked them where he could find Dr. Max Weinreich of YIVO, Professor Nojekh Prylucki of Vilnius University, and Chaikl Lunski of the Strashun Library. While Weinreich could not be found—he was in New York—Pohl tracked down Prylucki and Lunski and had them arrested. He ordered Prylucki to hand over YIVO's greatest treasures and prepare lists of its major holdings.

For the month of July 1941, Nojekh Prylucki was a prisoner scholar. A police escort took him on a daily basis from his home on Zakretowa Street to the YIVO building, where he performed his assigned work.[8] The same happened to Lunski, the storied head of the Strashun Library, and Abraham E. Goldschmidt, curator of the S. An-ski Museum of the Jewish Historical-Ethnographic Society. They were forced at gunpoint to hand over their institutions' greatest treasures to Pohl and Gotthard of the ERR.

This was a coordinated German assault on the written Jewish word. The fact that the operation took place just a few days after the German attack on the Soviet Union indicated that the seizure of Vilna's Judaica was a high priority.

After returning home from his first days of work, Lunski, the librarian, told his friends, "You wouldn't believe how well he speaks Yiddish, that German. How well he reads Hebrew, even cursive print. And he's familiar with the Talmud!"[9]

Besides ransacking YIVO, the Strashun Library, and the An-ski Museum, Pohl and a contingent of German soldiers raided the Great Synagogue, the shtot-shul, the pride and glory of Vilna Jewry. They found the synagogue's ritual administrator, the *shammes*, seized his ring of keys, and proceeded to remove the Torah scrolls and other ritual objects from the Holy Ark—silver Torah crowns, breastplates, and gold pointers. The *shammes* had, in anticipation of the raid, stored many scrolls and ornaments in a vault hidden behind a wall near the Ark. But the Germans discovered the vault, blew it open, and removed its contents. They then proceeded to plunder the other houses of prayer, the *kloyzn*, located in the synagogue courtyard.[10]

Then, on July 28, something changed. Prylucki did not return home from work and was taken to the Gestapo prison instead. His work in the YIVO building continued, but he was now shuttled between prison and YIVO. Paula visited him at work and brought him food and clothing. She reported that his face was drawn, his eyes were dark, and his body—bent over. It looked as if he had been beaten. Sometime in early August, the Germans put the three scholars—Prylucki, Lunski, and Goldschmidt—into a single cell in the Gestapo prison, from which they were taken daily to their respective workplaces. The three men reportedly spent their evenings in prison discussing Jewish literature and thought, including the works of Maimonides. Then in mid-August, Prylucki stopped going to YIVO. Witnesses reported seeing him in Vilna's central Lukishki Prison, badly beaten and bloodied, with a rag tied around his head. Lying beside him was the lifeless body of Goldschmidt and a dazed, disoriented Lunski.

Pohl, and his deputy, Gotthard, had concluded their mission to Vilna and left the three scholars in the custody of the Gestapo.

Nojekh Prylucki was executed on August 18, 1941. The Gestapo knew that he was the head of a Jewish political party and a member of the Polish parliament, and eliminated him as an enemy of the Third Reich. Goldschmidt expired in prison, apparently due to beatings. Lunski was the lucky one of the three. The Gestapo released him in early September—just in time for him to be herded into the newly formed Vilna ghetto.[11]

Vilna had been raped: the five incunabula from the Strashun library were gone, as were the oldest manuscripts and the most beautiful ritual ornaments from the shtot-shul. Pohl and his associates had shipped them off to Germany, along with eight crates of treasures from the Strashun Library and additional crates from YIVO and the An-ski Museum. The Germans had shown that they were serious, one might say dead serious, about "acquiring" Vilna's Judaica.[12]

Word about the ransacking of YIVO reached the well-known Polish-Jewish historian Emanuel Ringelblum, who was incarcerated several hundred miles away in the Warsaw ghetto. Using his connections in the Polish underground, Ringelblum sent a coded letter to a colleague in New York, to inform him of the catastrophe that had befallen YIVO. Ringelblum's letter began with the words "Yivush Wiwulsky died recently." This was his concealed reference to YIVO, located on Wiwulskiego Street. Then he continued, "You knew him well. He didn't leave behind any belongings. But in wartime people lose even more. You remember how much effort he put into his business. Now, all that's left is an empty house. His belongings were taken away by his debtors."[13]

Ringelblum's information was exaggerated. Only a small fraction of YIVO's holdings were hauled away in July 1941. Most remained behind. In fact, Pohl learned an important lesson from his brief foray into "the Jerusalem of Lithuania." Vilna housed too many Jewish cultural treasures, in too many locations, to seize all of them in a single raid. A long-term work group was needed to sift through hundreds of thousands of books and documents. When the ERR returned to Vilna in February 1942, it established such a group.

Meanwhile, German officials placed YIVO on their list of the top forty-three libraries in the occupied Eastern territories whose holdings were of greatest interest to the Reich. These libraries were targeted for "acquisition" on behalf of the planned megalibrary of the Nazi Academy, the Hohe Schule. A memo dated September 29, 1941, targeted three repositories in Vilna: the university library, the Wroblewski State Library (which was a regional branch of the Polish National Library), and YIVO, whose holdings were estimated at forty thousand books and seventy thousand archival units. The memo noted that libraries in Vilna were of importance to the Reich because they would enrich Germany's collections of Judaica, Hebraica, and Catholic literature.[14]

It was only a matter of time until the Einsatzstab Reichsleiter Rosenberg would return to Vilna to implement the memo's directive.

CHAPTER FOUR

Intellectuals in Hell

NOJEKH PRYLUCKI was one of several dozen refugee intellectuals from Warsaw who fled to the city in the fall of
1939: writers, journalists, educators, and political leaders.
But when it came to books, none of them equaled Herman Kruk, director of the Grosser Library, the largest Jewish lending library in Warsaw,
sponsored by an organization called Culture League. Kruk was the
most highly regarded Jewish librarian in all of Poland. He published
dozens of articles and brochures on bibliography and booklore, headed
the Culture League's library center, and edited its newsletter.

Kruk was a dedicated democratic socialist and a member of the
Bund. For him, libraries were the vehicle through which the workers
would lift themselves up and become class conscious, ready to forge a
just society.

After a month on the run during which he missed German bombs
and bullets by inches, and slept on the floor of blacked-out train sta-
tions, Kruk arrived in Vilna and went straight from the train station
to the Strashun Library and YIVO, to study their catalogs and methods
of operation. Only afterward did he find a place to live and a change
of fresh clothes.

Kruk stood out as a man of integrity and discipline, who naturally
elicited respect. "He had the gait of a corporal" (the rank he attained
during his service in the Polish military), "and with his head held high,
he seemed to be taller than he actually was." A refined and elegant
gentleman, he always polished his shoes and filed his fingernails, even
later on in the ghetto.[1]

Kruk came to Vilna together with his brother Pinkhas, who was a
leader of the Bund's youth movement, but without his wife and young
son, who stayed behind in Warsaw. The journey was too dangerous for

a child, and the organizers of the refugee group didn't allow anyone to take along family members. In Vilna, Kruk expended much of his energy trying to get information about his wife's whereabouts and sending letters to her via the Polish underground, to help her flee.

Kruk and his brother were lucky enough to receive American visas in the spring of 1940, thanks to the intervention of the Jewish Labor Committee in New York. Pinkhas left for the United States, but Herman kept delaying his departure, as he tried to track down his wife and son. When the Soviets reentered Lithuania and annexed it in June 1940, they cut back on issuing transit visas to Vladivostok, the only means by which to reach the United States. Soviet officials offered Kruk a deal. He could leave via Vladivostok if he agreed to serve as a Soviet agent abroad. (They used the word "friend," but the intent was clear.) He should enlist in the Polish Armed Forces in the West that operated under British command and send them information on its activities. They directed Kruk to a Polish recruitment center in Canada. Kruk refused to sign the agreement that the Soviet officials put on the table, and from that point on, he was trapped in Vilna.[2]

When the Germans attacked, on June 22, 1941, the forty-four-year-old Kruk didn't try to flee further east. He didn't have the energy to trek through forests and scavenger for food—for a second time. He stayed in his apartment and busied himself writing his diary. Over time, that diary grew into a monumental chronicle of the travails of the Jews of Vilna. Once he became director of the ghetto library (about which, more below), he spent two to three hours a day in his office dictating the text of his diary to his secretary, who typed it in three copies. If the Germans had ever discovered it, they would have executed him. But Kruk couldn't stop writing. It gave him a sense of purpose, a mission. He called the diary "the hashish of my life." In June 1942, the Vilna Ghetto Writers' Association awarded him a prize for his diary as a work of "underground literary journalism."[3]

Early entries recorded the march of the Germans' rein of terror: Jews were required to wear a yellow Star of David on their outer clothing, they were prohibited from walking on the city's main thoroughfares, and they had to stand on separate food lines during limited shopping hours. Kruk noted the roundups of Jewish men, allegedly for work, and the street massacre on Szpitalna Street, in which 123 men were executed. He described the reaction to the German decree to create a

Jewish Council, or Judenrat: most community leaders refused to serve but eventually relented in the hope that they would be able to ease the suffering of their brethren. Those hopes were dashed on August 6, when the deputy Gebietskommissar for Jewish affairs, Franz Murer, ordered the Judenrat to collect a five-million-ruble "contribution." When the Jews came up with only 3.5 million rubles, Murer had most members of the Judenrat summarily executed and ordered a new council to take its place.

Kruk was among the first to hear the "rumors" that mass shootings were taking place at Ponar, a green-forested area on the outskirts of town, but he rejected them as fear mongering. He considered the account by a Polish domestic servant who followed her employer to the shooting site to be either a lie or a hallucination. Then on September 4, he heard the firsthand testimony of survivors and recorded it "with trembling hands, and bloody ink." Two wounded girls, age eleven and sixteen, and four adult women had come to Vilna's Jewish hospital with gunshot wounds. Kruk interviewed them in person:

> They all recount: "They shot us with machine guns. In the ditch lay thousands of dead bodies. Before being shot, they took off their clothes, their shoes. . . . The fields reek with the stench of the dead bodies. . . . A few crawl out of there, and a few drag themselves to villages. . . . One woman dragged herself to a peasant and asked him to take her to the Jews. After what she saw, and after all of her loved ones were shot in front of her eyes, she considered her life worthless. But she wanted the Jews to know, and that's the only thing that led her to the peasant. Let the Jews know!!!"[4]

Kruk was shaken. He now realized that the thousands of "missing" people snatched off the streets during the past two months had been massacred in the pits at Ponar. He could only use apocalyptic language to express his emotions:

> Can the world not scream?
>
> If the heavens can open up, when should that happen if not today?
>
> If heaven is heaven, it should start pouring down lava. Let all living things be washed away once and for all. Let a greater world destruction than this one come—let a new world arise from the ruins!
>
> "Arise ye wretched of the earth!" [the first line of the International]

It is the darkness of Egypt in the middle of the day. Horror upon horror, dread upon dread!⁵

For Kruk, the news of Ponar was soon overtaken by the sudden decree of the ghetto. Word spread on September 5 that all of Vilna's Jews would be forced the next day into the narrow, rundown streets of the historic Jewish quarter, surrounded by a newly constructed wall. Kruk wrote hourly logs on what he called "the historic day."

> *9:00 a.m.*: Groups of Jews are being carried off. Everyone is padded; they wear several coats, they drag packs, they take things on baby carriages. The picture is awful. Dogs, as if they knew something, are barking and howling. Thus they take leave of their former masters . . .
> *2:00 p.m.*: People say that going into the ghetto is like entering a darkness. Thousands stand on line and are driven in a cage. People are driven, people fall down with their sacks, and the screams reach the sky. The mournful trek lasts for hours.⁶

The log broke off when Kruk himself was herded into the ghetto. The next days were too traumatic and disorienting for him to write. He resumed his diary on September 20 and reconstructed the events of the intervening weeks in retrospective entries.

The congestion was crushing. Forty thousand people were forced into a territory of eleven blocks that had housed six thousand residents before the war. Twenty-nine thousand people settled in the larger ghetto no. 1, and eleven thousand in the smaller ghetto no. 2. Much of the space of ghetto no. 2 was occupied by the Great Synagogue, the Strashun Library, and the kloyzn of the synagogue courtyard, all of which now became barrack-like residences. Kruk compared Strashun Street to an anthill, and its inhabitants to mice crawling out of holes. In an entry dated September 15 (but written later), he noted that nutrition was becoming a problem. There were reports of hunger and disease. But he also noted the efforts by Jewish doctors to minister to the ill and grassroots activity to smuggle, share, and distribute food.⁷

The new Judenrat, headed by engineer Anatol Fried, began to organize the ghetto's internal life. It established a hospital, sanitation services, schools, a police department, and . . . a library.

Kruk came to the attention of the Judenrat on the first night in the ghetto—Abraham Sutzkever, the poet, wrote that "the first night in the ghetto is like the first night in your grave." One of the local leaders of the Bund noticed Kruk wallowing through mounds of mud, pulling books out of the muck, and catching stray pages that were blowing in the wind. The Bundist was a member of the Judenrat and reported the scene to his colleagues. The next day, the council asked Kruk to direct the ghetto library.

———————

The existence of a ghetto library was largely the result of happenstance. The lending library of the Society for Jewish Enlightenment (*Hevrat Mefitse Haskalah*) found itself by coincidence within the territory that the Germans demarked for ghetto no. 1, at 6 Strashun Street. While located on Strashun Street, this was not the Strashun Library—by any stretch of the imagination. The Society for Jewish Enlightenment library held mainly fiction and educational literature, much of it in Russian and Polish. There were no rarities or treasures. It was a public-service lending library, with a collection of forty-five thousand volumes.[8]

Kruk found the collection in total disarray. The card catalogs had been carted away by Pohl. Kruk and his staff would need to recatalog everything from scratch. At first, he assumed that his task was to salvage the collection and serve as its custodian until the war was over. He didn't imagine that the throngs of frightened and confused people, looking for floor space to sleep and food to eat, would be psychologically capable of reading. But when the library began lending out select volumes on September 15, 1941, inmates "pounced on the books like thirsty lambs." "Even the horrible events they experienced could not stop them. They couldn't resign from the printed word." He called this "the miracle of the book in the ghetto."[9]

Kruk quickly staffed the library with the best professionals who were still alive: scholar Zelig Kalmanovitch, a deputy director of YIVO; Chaikl Lunski of the Strashun Library; Bella Zakheim, who ran Vilna's Jewish children's library, and her deputy, Dina Abramowicz; Dr. Moshe Heller, an instructor in the Yiddish Teachers' Seminary; and others.

Kalmanovitch, the YIVO scholar, became Kruk's deputy and a member of the library's three-person secretariat. (The third member was Kruk's secretary Rachel Mendelsohn.) The two men had sharply different worldviews. Kruk was a socialist; Kalmanovitch was not. After various ideological metamorphoses, he was now a Zionist and a religious man. But their personalities were similar, and their skills complemented each other. Kalmanovitch was a polymath who had studied in German universities, with a doctorate from Petrograd. (A friend once said of him, "When Zelig walks into the room, I don't need an encyclopedia.") Kruk, on the other hand, was a professional bibliographer and librarian. Beneath their ideological differences, both men were models of intellectual seriousness and commitment to public service on behalf of Jewish culture.

Chaikl Lunski, the legendary head of the Strashun Library, played a lesser role in the ghetto library. Badly shaken by his imprisonment and Prylucki's murder, he didn't have the psychological wherewithal to engage in intellectual work. Kruk retained him as a circulation librarian, who checked out books to readers.[10]

Kruk was a masterful organizer and administrator, driven and focused. Kalmanovitch was a man of deep moral passion who was called "the prophet of the ghetto." Together, they were totally committed to the library's mission of strengthening the spirit, dignity, and morale of the ghetto population.

And Shmerke Kaczerginski, the feisty bon vivant, troubadour, and leftist bard? Where was he in all of this? Shmerke and his wife Barbara participated in the debilitating march into the ghetto, padded with their winter clothing, bed linens, and kitchen utensils. They settled into a crowded apartment on Lidzki Street, together with Sutzkever, his wife Freydke, and several other intellectuals. But as soon as the Germans conducted their first raid, in which they seized and deported 3,500 inmates, on September 15, Shmerke decided that he must escape the deathtrap called ghetto. He would take his chances on the outside. Shmerke grew a mustache and removed his round-rimmed glasses, in order to look like a Pole or Belorussian, and together with the fair-haired Barbara, slipped out of the ghetto one sunny September morning, with a work brigade headed to a construction site. Once on the other side, they ditched the group and removed the Stars of David from their outer clothing. Shmerke could pass as a non-Jew—as long as he kept his mouth shut. But if he spoke a single word, the game was up. He had a thick Yiddish accent.

Shmerke and Barbara headed westward, toward the home of a Lithuanian friend who lived in the Zakret Forest. Once they arrived there,
they would plan their next moves. On the way through the thicket,
fearful of being detected as escapees from the ghetto, Barbara blurted
out at him, "If not for you, I—with my Aryan appearance and fluent
Polish—could easily pass as a Pole and save myself."

The words hit Shmerke like a ton of bricks. He had taken Barbara
in as a hungry, homeless refugee when she fled the Germans to Bialystok in the fall of 1939. He'd cared for her, fed her, brought her into
his circle of friends, and lifted her spirits—and now she openly regretted being with him. "If not for you, I could save myself." Shmerke
stopped in his tracks, took one glance at her, and without saying a word,
turned around, and started walking in the opposite direction back toward Vilna. Barbara didn't call to him, and he didn't look back. They
never saw each other again. Shmerke couldn't forgive Barbara for those
words, even after the Germans discovered her hiding place and sent her
to Ponar for execution, more than a year later. But he didn't talk about
that moment with anyone, other than with his closest friends.[11]

Shmerke headed to the address of a Polish woman in the city who, he
had heard, rescued Jews. He knocked on the door in the middle of the
night. At first, she told him he was mistaken but then she invited him
into her apartment, and in the darkness, he could make out silhouettes
sitting on the floor, people who had fled from the ghetto. The woman,
Wiktoria Gzmilewska, was the wife of a Polish military officer and
Shmerke's rescuing angel.

Gzmilewska's apartment was a transfer point. From there, the escapees were sent on to various addresses for hiding. But soon after Shmerke's
arrival, word reached her that the apartment was being watched by
spies, and she needed to dissolve her operation quickly. There was no
address to which to send Shmerke, who was the newest arrival and last
in line, so she arranged for him to receive forged "Aryan" papers that
identified him as a Pole named Waclaw Rodziewicz. Realizing that
Shmerke would expose himself as a Jew if he said so much as a sentence,
she ordered papers certifying that Rodziewicz was a deaf-mute, who
had suffered from a concussion as a soldier on the war front in 1939.

For the next seven months, the most talkative and gregarious person
in Vilna did not let a single word out of his mouth. He wandered from

town to town as a deaf-mute beggar, taking on odd jobs, and living in perennial fear that someone might recognize him. After all, "everybody" knew Shmerke before the war. So he kept his head down and covered it with his coat collar. In nighttime moments of solitude, in a forest or field, he would howl like a wild animal, just to hear the sound of his own voice.

Shmerke once found work as a cook for an old, abusive Polish countess. The woman kept yelling at him and insulting him, but Shmerke pretended not to hear whatever she said. Until one day she yelled at him, "You lazy good-for-nothing. You can't even catch a few Yids, take them to the Germans, and get a kilogram of sugar, like all the other peasants do." At that moment, he exploded, spit in her face and shouted, "You bitch, I'm gonna outlive you." The countess fainted, in shock that the deaf-mute had started talking, and Shmerke ran away.[12]

A few times, Shmerke stole himself into small-town ghettoes (in Michaliszki, Gluboka, Svir, and Kabilnik), just to spend a few days among fellow Jews. But he never stayed for long. He joined a brigade of thirty Jewish forced laborers on an estate near a town called Shumsk. One day, their boss, a Belorussian farmer, told the group that the auxiliary police had ordered him to send them to the district police station, for registration. "Don't go!" Shmerke told the workers, but they went. Two days later, the entire group—except for Shmerke—was shot.[13]

While Shmerke was wandering the countryside in disguise, the Vilna ghetto went through its bloodiest days.[14] The German raids into the ghetto that began in September intensified, and Jews built for themselves makeshift hiding places, called *malinas* in the local Yiddish dialect. On Yom Kippur, October 1, prayer services in the ghetto's packed synagogues were interrupted by Gestapo men who rounded up people "for work." Men in *taleysim* (prayer shawls) and their families fled to their *malinas*, but four thousand inmates were seized on that Yom Kippur day. They were sent to the Lukishki Prison and, from there, to Ponar for execution.

On October 24, the infamous "Aktion of Yellow Permits" took place. The Germans ordered the ghetto administration to issue new identification passes to all its inhabitants: 3,500 yellow work permits for "valuable specialists" and pink permits for their family members—a spouse and two children for each specialist. The bearers of yellow and pink permits, a total of fourteen thousand people, were protected against deportation. All other ghetto inmates received a white permit, the equivalent of a death warrant. Panicked men and women arranged fictitious marriages, in order to declare themselves the husband or wife of someone with a yellow permit. Herman Kruk received a yellow permit as director of the ghetto library and "married" the seventy-four-year-old pioneer of the Bund, Pati Kremer. He took two orphans off the street as his children.

After the bearers of yellow permits and their family members went to their workplaces outside the ghetto, German troops invaded its territory and rounded up five thousand people with white passes, who were sent to their deaths at Ponar. The month ended with the largest Aktion of all: on October 28–30, ghetto no. 2 was "liquidated," and nearly all of its eleven thousand inhabitants were sent to Ponar, which the Germans referred to sardonically as "ghetto no. 3."

Shmerke was outside the ghetto during this traumatic period of bloodletting, but his friend and pen colleague Abraham Sutzkever was inside. Abrasha had a long list of near-death experiences in just a few months' time. He survived one roundup by spending the night in a casket at the offices of the Jewish burial society. While inside the box, he wrote a poem about the experience. On another occasion, he escaped German soldiers who threatened to shoot him by jumping into a canister of quicklime. When Abrasha eventually stuck his head out, the mixture of blood from his forehead, quicklime, and daylight formed "the most beautiful sunset I have every seen." Later, Sutzkever stole himself into the second ghetto to find his mother, who was incarcerated there, and whisked her out to the first ghetto. A few weeks later, ghetto no. 2 was no more. What kept Abrasha going was a mystical faith in the power of the poetic word: as long as he would fulfill his life's mission and write poetry, he would survive.[15]

By the end of December 1941, the ghetto was a nervous and terrified mass of humanity. Kruk wrote, "None of us has been able to catch our breath. We all feel like we've been stabbed, with a rip in our heart. The last raid cost so many young lives. No one can collect themselves."[16] The librarian, the poet, and the scholar—Kruk, Sutzkever, and Kalmanovitch—were in a man-made hell.

CHAPTER FIVE

A Haven for Books and People

IT IS MIND-BOGGLING to think that a lending library functioned in the midst of Gestapo raids, deportations to Ponar, malnutrition, and unbearable congestion—but the ghetto library at 6 Strashun Street was not just open but also in high demand. The number of registered readers actually grew in October 1941, the ghetto's bloodiest month, from 1,492 to 1,739. The library lent out 7,806 books, or an average of 325 books per day. Meanwhile, behind the circulation desk, the staff cataloged 1,314 volumes.[1]

Herman Kruk noted the unbearable paradox of the ghetto library, as mass roundups were followed by spikes in book loans: "On Yom Kippur, October 1, three thousand Jews were taken away. And on the very next day, 390 books were exchanged. On October 3 and 4, masses of people were removed from the second ghetto, and the first ghetto was in an indescribable state of tension. But on October 5, 421 books were exchanged."[2] Reading was a means of coping, of regaining one's bearings.

In response to the high demand, Kruk opened a reading room on November 20, in space that had served as a storage room for duplicates before the war. The space was furnished with long tables and chairs that were smuggled into the ghetto on garbage trucks that came to collect trash. The walls of the reading room were lined with bookcases, filled with a reference collection of two thousand volumes that was divided into fifteen sections: encyclopedias, dictionaries, textbooks, and several subject areas such as philosophy and economics. The reading room also had glass showcases that displayed scrolls, Torah crowns, and other pieces of ritual art. These were sometimes referred to as the ghetto's museum.[3] The reading room emitted an atmosphere of normalcy, under conditions that were far from normal.

The library became an anchor of ghetto life during the so-called period of stability, which lasted for one and a half years—from January 1942 until July 1943. Large-scale *Aktionen*, roundups and deportations to Ponar, stopped, and life began to take on a routine for the remaining twenty thousand inmates (fourteen thousand of them registered and six thousand "illegals"). Work brigades left in the mornings for forced labor sites outside the ghetto, and the workers smuggled in foodstuffs under their clothing at the end of the day—if the circumstances allowed. The Judenrat preached the doctrine of a "working ghetto" as the key to survival: if the inmates were productive workers, and their labor was useful to the German military, the Nazis would keep them alive, as a matter of self-interest. Most inhabitants believed this was so, or at least wanted to believe it was so.

With the onset of the period of stability, cultural and social activity burst forth: a first concert was held on January 18, 1942; an Association of Ghetto Writers and Artists was founded the same month. A social aid committee was formed, as were a youth club, a lectorium, and various professional associations (of attorneys, musicians, and so on).[4] For all these groups, the library served as an invaluable resource.

The calm was broken by intermittent atrocities. On February 5, 1942, the Germans issued a ban on Jewish women giving birth, effective immediately. Many women were pregnant from before the ghetto. The lucky ones delivered their babies secretly in the ghetto hospital, whose medical staff predated the newborn babies' birth certificates. But most of the infants born after February 5 were murdered by the Germans, usually by means of poisoning. One of them was Sutzkever's infant son. His poem to his murdered baby exemplified his ability to write exquisite poetry in the midst of excruciating pain.

> I wanted to swallow you, child,
> when I felt your tiny body
> Cool in my fingers.
> Like a glass
> Of warm tea. . . .
> I wanted to swallow you, child
> to taste
> the future waiting for me.
> Maybe you will blossom again in my veins.

I am not worthy of you, though.
I can't be your grave.
I leave you
To the summoning snow.
This first respite.
You'll descend now like a splinter of dusk
Into the stillness
Bringing greetings from me
To the slim shoots
Under the cold.[5]

A few months later, On July 17, the Germans turned their murder machine against another vulnerable group: the elderly. Eighty-six aged ghetto inmates were rounded up and sent to a sanitarium, raising hopes that they would be cared for there. Ten days later they were all murdered.[6] And individuals and small groups were sent to Ponar to be executed for the slightest offense—such as breaking curfew or smuggling in foodstuffs.

But on most days, life was a grim struggle for survival, for dignity and hope, by a traumatized, frightened, and malnourished inmate population. The library was central to that struggle, and Kruk was its visionary.

Who were the readers, what did they read, and *why* did they read? In a report written in October 1942, after more than a year of operation, the sober and level-headed Kruk presented statistics and analysis. The library had 2,500 registered readers, more than twice as many as its prewar predecessor, the Enlightenment Society library. The readership was young: 26.7 percent of its borrowers were under age fifteen, and 36.7 percent were between fifteen and thirty years old. The ghetto inmates took out mainly novels: 78.3 percent of the books borrowed were fiction, 17.7 percent were children's literature, and only 4 percent were nonfiction.[7]

Dina Abramowicz, one of the ghetto librarians, recalled the different types of readers that passed through the circulation desk during the course of the day. In the morning, the "society ladies" came—women whose husbands had better work arrangements in the city and who were well-off by ghetto standards. With free time on their hands, these women wanted to read Russian sentimental novels. In the afternoon, children came straight from the ghetto's schools, in search of fantasy literature, such as Jules Verne's *Around the World in Eighty Days* and *Capitan Grande's Children*. In the late afternoons and on Sundays, laborers who worked outside the ghetto arrived. They were mainly interested in reading world literature in Polish translation.[8]

As to the psychology of reading, Kruk reported that readers' prime motivation was a desire to escape, to forget their immediate reality: "The ghetto has barely seventy centimeters of living space per person. [In the living quarters], everything is on the floor. There are no tables or chairs. Rooms are giant bundles. People are lying rolled upon their packages. . . . The book carries them over the ghetto walls to the wide world. Readers can at least in this way extricate themselves from their oppressive loneliness and connect themselves in their thoughts to life, to their lost freedom."[9]

Kruk noted with a mixture of dismay and forgiveness that the books in highest demand were crime stories and cheap novels. He explained that given the draining, distracting living conditions, most readers could not make the mental exertion to read challenging or demanding literature. He enumerated a long list of Polish and Russian works of pulp fiction that were popular among the ghetto inmates. As to Western literature, the most sought-after items were Edgar Wallace's crime novels, Margaret Mitchell's *Gone with the Wind*, and Vicki Baum's German romances. He lamented that there was no demand whatsoever for Flaubert and Gorky, and almost none for Dostoyevsky and Romain Rolland.

Reading, Kruk observed, was a narcotic, a form of intoxication, a device by which to avoid thinking. "It often seems to the ghetto librarian that he is a drug pusher. The aspect of, I wouldn't even call it reading, but self-intoxication, is so prevalent. There are people who on the most difficult days read incessantly but only cheap crime novels. Some intelligent readers won't pick up anything else." One ghetto inmate described her reading habits in similar terms: "I read crime novels until my head is numb. Now, when it's hard to get a cigarette, the little books are my narcotic. After reading three crime novels, my head is so stuffed that I forget about the world around me. I tried to read serious books, but I couldn't gather my thoughts."[10]

Children were among the most avid readers, ordering more items per capita than any other age group. Their reading needs were so intense that a few children broke into the library's closed stacks to steal books. The librarians had to call the ghetto police, who arrested the "thieves" and sent them home.[11]

But there was also a stubborn minority of "socially mature readers," who wanted to read books that shed light on their predicament. Such readers borrowed war literature. Tolstoy's *War and Peace* was borrowed eighty-six times in the first year of the ghetto library's existence, while in prewar times, it was borrowed an average of 14.8 times per year. Remarque's *All Quiet on the Western Front* was also in high demand. But by far the most popular European novel among the socially mature readers was Franz Werfel's *Forty Days of Musa Dagh*, based on the events in a town in Turkey at the outset of the Armenian genocide. Readers sensed that they were facing the same fate as had befallen the Armenians.

As for Jewish literature, sophisticated readers devoured Graetz's and Dubnow's volumes on medieval Jewish history that dealt with suffering during the Crusades and the Inquisition. The most popular work of Yiddish fiction was Scholem Asch's *Kiddush Ha-shem* (Martyrdom), a fictionalized account of the Khmelnytsky massacres in Ukraine in 1648–49.[12]

Besides the lending library, there was also the reading room, whose visitors had a more elite profile. Many of them were scholars and educators, for whom the library was their workplace—where they conducted research, prepared lectures, and wrote. Forty percent of the books given out in the reading room were nonfiction. It was one of the few places in the ghetto where you could read or write while sitting on a normal chair in front of a table.

The reading room was a place of refuge for people who were in need of quiet, repose, and dignity. Some of the visitors turned the pages of prewar newspapers and magazines, as they rested from a difficult workday and "pretended to read" (in Kruk's words). Library etiquette was enforced (Hush, no talking!), and the floors were washed daily. Schoolchildren were allowed into the reading room only during daytime hours and could not do their homework there.[13]

The ghetto library cultivated a culture of reading and an attitude of respect toward books. In the circulation area, near the card catalogs, there hung two notices:

Books are our only comfort in the ghetto!
Books help you forget your sad reality.
Books can transport you to worlds far away from the ghetto.
Books can still your hunger when you have nothing to eat.
Books have remained true to you, be true to the books.
Preserve our spiritual treasures—books!

Next to it, the library administration posted more prosaic instructions:

> Keep the books clean and intact; do not read while eating. Do not
> write in books; do not dampen them; do not fold pages or break bind-
> ings. If a reader has been ill with a contagious disease, he must notify
> the librarian upon returning the book.[14]

As the instructions indicate, one of the library's main problems was the
physical deterioration of its inventory, due to heavy usage. Under ghetto
conditions, most of the volumes could not be replaced with duplicates.
Kruk established a bindery on the premises, to repair damaged items.

The rules on borrowing were strictly enforced: Books were due three
days after they were withdrawn, and there were fines for late returns.
If a reader failed to return items after repeated reminders, his or her
name was forwarded to the ghetto administration, and deadbeat readers were sentenced to a one-day suspended prison term plus a stiff financial penalty.[15]

The library at 6 Strashun Street wasn't the only place where ghetto
inhabitants could read. Kruk established branch libraries in the ghetto's schools, at the youth club, and at a residential work bloc outside the
ghetto called "Kailis." There was even a branch library in the ghetto
prison, where inmates were sent by the Jewish ghetto police for offenses
ranging from violating curfew to theft. The prison library had a collection of one hundred volumes of fiction. Kruk recorded that the prison
inmates read an average of twenty volumes per month.[16]

On December 13, 1942, after fifteen months of operation, the library
held a program in honor of having lent out its one hundred thousandth
book. (The number included the use of books in the reading room.)
At the event, Dr. Daniel Feinshtein, an anthropologist and popular
lecturer, offered greetings in which he interpreted the outpouring of
reading in the Vilna ghetto: Reading was a tool in the struggle for
survival. It calmed one's strained nerves and served as a psychological

safety valve that prevented mental and physical breakdown. By reading novels, and identifying with their fictional heroes, one remained psychologically alert and emotionally alive.

Feinshtein used an image from Arabian literature as a metaphor: "We are physically cut off, like a man walking through the desert. The atmosphere is burning hot. We are yearning for a drink of life and freedom. And behold, our souls find what they are looking for in the artistic daydreams on the pages of the books. We feel refreshed, our vital energy and our lust for life grow. Our hope increases that we will survive this journey amid the desert sands and reach the oasis of freedom."[17]

In order to augment the collection at 6 Strashun Street, Kruk collected books from wherever they could be found. He arranged for the books of Vilna's premier Jewish high school, the Real Gymnasium on Rudnicki Street, to be transferred to the ghetto library, after the Judenrat took over the school building for use as its headquarters. Zelig Kalmanovitch, his deputy, discovered the warehouse of the Rosenkrantz and Shriftzetser Hebrew publishers and took control of its inventory. The ghetto library also issued an appeal to inmates to bring in whatever books they found. The hardest acquisitions job, from an emotional perspective, was collecting the books belonging to inmates who had been sent to Ponar and executed.[18]

The work of collecting, cataloging, lending, and reading inspired the ghetto's intelligentsia. The library became a symbol of the hope that Jewish culture would outlive this dark time, even if most inmates would not. Kruk recorded in his diary, "People come to me and say: 'I'm going crazy. I have nowhere to go. Give me work. I'm not asking for any money. Let me assist in your fine, painstaking effort.' Twenty volunteers are already working for me. New ones come and old ones often go away. Writers, journalists, doctors, and professionals work here. People bring books: 'Where should I dispose of them? Let them stay with you. With you, at any rate, they won't be burned. Maybe some of them will survive.'"[19]

Zamlen, collecting books and documents, became a passionate avocation in the ghetto library, as it had been before the war at YIVO. But now the activity had a more desperate feel to it, as if to say: something must remain after all this death and destruction; let it be the books.

From the outset, Kruk and Kalmanovitch knew that Vilna's cultural treasures were in peril. Johannes Pohl had stolen thousands of items back in July 1941. Kruk couldn't visit the buildings of YIVO and the An-ski Museum, since they were outside the ghetto, and he had no reliable information about the state of their collections. The Great Synagogue and Strashun Library were inside ghetto no. 2, but after that ghetto's liquidation at the end of October, and the deportation of all of its inhabitants to Ponar for execution, Kruk had no contact with the Strashun Library, even though it was just a few blocks away from the remaining ghetto no. 1.

As a first step to stop the cultural hemorrhaging, Kruk and Kalmanovitch prevailed upon the Judenrat to issue a decree ordering inmates to preserve "the remaining cultural treasures of our ghetto, works of art, paintings, sculptures, manuscripts and ritual objects." Inmates were obligated to report their existence and location to the ghetto library's administration.[20]

Next, Kruk and Kalmanovitch obtained authorization from the Judenrat to make an "expedition" to the building of the Strashun Library, located in the former ghetto no. 2, to retrieve as many volumes as they could put onto a hand wagon. Kruk visited the Strashun Library a second time, at his own personal initiative, in January 1942, when he was granted an extraordinary two-day travel pass to leave the ghetto. Instead of doing business in town, and stocking up on food, fur, leather, or gold, he spent his time selecting books from the Strashun collection. While in the eerily empty synagogue courtyard, he paid a visit to the kloyz of the Vilna Gaon, and retrieved its 180-year-old record book.[21]

Kruk also secured authorization to lead a small group of staff and volunteers on an excursion to the Great Synagogue, in search of ritual objects. One participant described the eerie scene upon entering the abandoned sanctuary: "It was steeped in darkness and melancholy. . . . Ruination was looking out of every corner. Only the marble pillars still stood proudly. Almost all the curtains to the Holy Arks were torn off their hinges and taken away. . . . The old wood-carved Holy Ark and the other arks stood half open and badly damaged. The most beautiful religious objects were desecrated."

The excursion yielded meager results. The sanctuary had already been ransacked and almost everything of value taken away. "Someone else had ruled in this place before we arrived and had made our task 'easier.' I took one last glance at the Great Synagogue: an abandoned, neglected ruin. Its grey walls looked mysteriously at us. There was thick dust and cobwebs. We left the synagogue with pain in our hearts and pushed our wagon. Who knows if we will ever return here again?"[22]

Thanks to all these efforts, Kruk amassed an extraordinary collection of cultural treasures. On January 7, 1942, he totaled up the new acquisitions in his possession. They included 126 Torah scrolls; 170 scrolls of the Prophets and Hagiographa (including scrolls of the book of Esther); twenty-six shofars; thirteen Chanukah menorahs; twelve candlesticks, made of silver, brass, and copper; seven memorial plaques with inscriptions from synagogue walls; twelve charity boxes; four Torah crowns (two silver, one tin, and one broken); twenty-one covers to the Holy Ark; 110 Torah covers; seventeen drawings; and two oil paintings. He had 2,464 books from the Strashun Library, twenty manuscripts, and eleven *pinkasim* (record books) of religious associations and synagogues.[23]

Some of the items that Kruk acquired leave us dumbfounded. How on earth did he remove and transport the inner walls of the Holy Ark from the Great Synagogue (which were 187 centimeters, or 6'2" long), the historic memorial plaque over the Vilna Gaon's seat in his kloyz (173 by 69 centimeters, or 5'7" by 2'3"), and the three clocks that hung in the synagogue courtyard, indicating the times of prayer and candle lighting?[24] Kruk received assistance from the ghetto administration to arrange their smuggling into the ghetto by truck.

As the acquisitions piled up, the ghetto library ceased being the repository for a middling collection of fiction and textbooks. It became the figurative and literal heir to the Strashun Library.

Kruk enhanced the library's public visibility and prestige by setting up several auxiliary institutions under its auspices: a *bookstore* that sold volumes of which there were multiple copies (mainly from the warehouses of publishers); an *archive*, charged with preserving copies of memos, minutes, and correspondence produced by the ghetto administration; a *statistical bureau* that generated reports on current trends in the ghetto in the areas of housing, employment, nutrition, health, and crime; and an *address bureau* that facilitated the reunification of families and friends.

There were also plans to create a *ghetto museum*, but the project was never completed.

Collectively, the library and its auxiliary institutions were referred to as "the agencies located at 6 Strashun Street," and the building was nicknamed the Culture House. It had a staff of eighteen employees.[25]

One of the ghetto's most popular institutions was located, by chance, just outside the library—the sports field. The ghetto administration decided to clear away the bombed-out building located next door and used the vacant space for gymnastics and team sports. The outer wall of the library building was covered with chalk-written slogans: "In a healthy body—a healthy spirit," and "a sporting person will find the hardest work easy." Just above the slogans were the images of people swimming and exercising.[26] The sports field was the only open space in the ghetto and served as a rendezvous spot for young people, especially young couples. Together, the sports field and library were a cry for life in the midst of mass murder.

It is no accident that the library occupied a central place in the Vilna ghetto and that collecting books and cultural treasures became a focus of activity among its inmate intellectuals. The traditions of the Strashun Library and YIVO lived on in the seven crowded blocks of ghetto no. 1. Even in its agony, Jewish Vilna did not forget that it was the "Jerusalem of Lithuania" and remained true to its inner self.

The Record Book of the Vilna Gaon's Synagogue

The Vilna Gaon's kloyz (house of prayer) was founded in 1757 and continued to function as a synagogue and house of study down until the German invasion in 1941. The wardens of the kloyz maintained a thick leather-bound record book containing its administrative decisions over a span of more than 150 years.

The Gaon's synagogue was located in the same house where the reclusive Rabbi Elijah resided and studied, just across from the Great Synagogue. He prayed at home on weekdays, Sabbaths, and holidays, with an exclusive group of disciples. The minyan (prayer group) was a by-invitation-only congregation, since praying in the presence of the great man was considered an honor. After Rabbi Elijah's death, in 1797, his disciples maintained the site as their house of study and prayer, and began to receive modest monthly stipends from the Vilna community to support their Talmudic studies, just as Rabbi Elijah had during his lifetime. Later, after the disciples died out, the wardens of the kloyz selected Talmudists who merited receiving a permanent seat and financial support. These Talmudists, called *prushim*, were expected to devote themselves full time to study and to lead a monastic life of purity and self-denial.

Eventually, in the mid-nineteenth century, the prayer services at the kloyz were opened up to the public. The space was renovated and expanded in 1866.

The record book (in Hebrew, *pinkas*) is a thick folio that looks from the outside like a volume of the Talmud. It contains handwritten entries beginning in 1768 and ending in 1924. Written in rabbinic Hebrew with ornate and sometimes minute lettering, most of the entries are of an administrative nature. They record donations of money and real property to support the kloyz, repairs to the facility, the selection of new wardens, the sale of seats, bequests of seats from fathers to sons, donations of religious literature, and so forth.

The record book was kept in the synagogue itself down until 1941 and was never sold or donated to the Strashun Library or to YIVO. The wardens kept it under lock and key as their prized possession and allowed just two modern scholars to examine it — one at the turn of the twentieth century, and one in the 1930s. Only since the end of World War II has the record book been freely accessible.

The *pinkas* reveals that for the first century of its existence, the Gaon's kloyz was not a fully independent institution. Like all other synagogues in Vilna, it was subordinate to the authority of the kahal, the city's officially constituted Jewish community board. The book's earliest entry, from 1768, was a decision by the Vilna community board authorizing the kloyz to hold services on weekdays, Sabbaths, and holidays. The authorization was contingent upon the Gaon continuing to live and study there. If he moved out, the synagogue was to be dissolved.[1]

Because the image of Rabbi Elijah and his circle of disciples is shrouded in folklore, legend, and hyperbole, the record book's early entries from the Gaon's lifetime are an invaluable source for historians. Here is a reliable, firsthand record of the people who prayed and interacted on a daily basis with Rabbi Elijah. The *pinkas* also reveals that upon the Gaon's death, there was a dispute between his children and disciples over who owned the facility and who should administer it. The matter went to the city's highest rabbinic court, which arbitrated a compromise and power-sharing arrangement.

Rabbi Elijah was a fierce opponent of the Hasidic movement, which grew and spread in his day. He was the driving force behind the writs of excommunication against Hasidim that were issued in Vilna in 1772, 1781, and 1796. His objections to the movement were theological and religious: he considered the Hasidic doctrine that godliness inhered in mundane objects to be heresy, and he also condemned the Hasidim for their ecstatic style of prayer and alleged denigration of Talmud study. "If I could, I would do to them what Elijah the Prophet did to the prophets of the Ba'al" (i.e., have them executed). After the Gaon's death, the wardens of his kloyz passed an ordinance (duly recorded in the record book) that no adherents of Hasidism would ever be admitted as congregants, stipend recipients, or officers. During the Gaon's lifetime, such an ordinance would have been unnecessary. It was unthinkable for a Hasid to set foot there.[2]

The record book also gives valuable glimpses into the operation of the kloyz in the early twentieth century, when it lost some of its luster: The wardens supported between twenty and thirty full-time scholars, the *prushim*, most of whom were ordained rabbis. The scholars delivered a daily Talmudic discourse to each other at noon, with instruction rotating within the group. Most of the kloyz's funds came from the rental of apartments that donors transferred to its ownership.[3]

In June 1916, during World War I, the kloyz was forced for the first time in its history to issue a public appeal for funds. The text, which was posted on the walls of the synagogue courtyard, was duly recorded in the *pinkas*. Famine and disease were widespread in the city, and the kloyz could barely collect any rental income. The better apartments were empty, because their inhabitants had left the city along with the retreating Russian forces in 1915, and the inhabitants of the simpler apartments were so impoverished that they couldn't pay rent. A group of nine businessmen responded to the appeal, with donations totaling three hundred German marks, a meager sum, but the best that could be done under conditions of war and famine.[4]

One of the record book's last entries, from 1922, recorded for posterity that the mausoleum of the Vilna Gaon at the old Jewish cemetery was rebuilt and expanded thanks to a generous gift by one of the Rabbi Elijah's descendants. The mausoleum had been in ruins since April 1919, when it had been attacked and damaged by Polish legionnaires during the pogrom that they perpetrated.[5]

Today, the original record book is displayed at the entrance to the YIVO Institute for Jewish Research in Manhattan.

CHAPTER SIX

Accomplices or Saviors?

O N THE COLD WINTER DAY of February 11, 1942, three
German officers from the Einsatzstab Reichsleiter Rosenberg (ERR) appeared at the ghetto gate and ordered the
Jewish policemen stationed there to take them to the ghetto library
at 6 Strashun Street. The surprise entry of Germans into the ghetto
provoked nervousness and commotion among the inmates, who feared
that it might be the beginning of an Aktion. The ERR team, headed by
Dr. Hans Muller, with Drs. Gerhard Wolff and Alexander Himpel by
his side, entered the library reading room and asked for Herman Kruk,
who came out of his office to meet them. "They behaved properly and
elegantly," Kruk wrote in his diary. They asked questions about his
work, about old books, and then asked him to introduce them to the
heads of the Strashun Library and YIVO. Kruk called over Chaikl
Lunski and Zelig Kalmanovitch. After a brief conversation, the Germans announced that they would like to invite the three of them for a
meeting in a few days' time. And they left.

The ghetto population heaved a deep sigh of relief. It was not an
Aktion. Or rather, it was the beginning of an Aktion of a different
kind—directed against books, not against people.[1]

The follow-up meeting took place in the new offices of the Einsatzstab Reichsleiter Rosenberg, at 18 Zigmuntowska Street, in what had
previously been the medical library of Wilno University. The spacious
rooms were filled with desks and typewriters, and staffed with secretaries, with Nazi banners hanging from the walls. It was clear that the
ERR had returned to Vilna for more than a quick looting spree. Muller
informed the Jewish scholars that from now on, they would work for the
ERR and collect Jewish books on its behalf. Kruk would be the head of
the work group, Kalmanovitch would be his deputy, and Lunski would

serve as expert bibliographer. Muller allowed Kruk to keep his other job as director of the ghetto library.

Their first assignment was to transfer the Strashun Library from its building in the synagogue courtyard, the *shulhoyf*, in the former ghetto no. 2, to designated space in the Wilno University Library. There, they were to sort the books, catalog them, and prepare the most valuable items for shipment to Germany. They would be assigned twelve workers for the menial labor of packing and moving the books.

Lunski gasped. He was being ordered to destroy the library he had built for more than forty years.

The Germans' plan was part merger, part plunder. It was a merger between the Strashun Library and the Wilno University Library, with the ERR taking "the best stuff" for itself. But the Germans presented their plunder as a form of rescue: they were "borrowing" the books, which would be safer in Germany, far away from the war front.

Kruk, who always seemed to keep his composure, was unnerved by the assignment. That evening, he wrote in his diary, "Kalmanovitch and I don't know if we are gravediggers or saviors. If we succeed in keeping the treasures in Vilna, it could be to our great merit. But if they take the library away, we will have been accomplices. I'm trying to insure myself for all cases."[2]

Kruk tried to keep as many books as possible in Vilna. He asked Muller for permission to transfer duplicate volumes from the Strashun Library collection to the ghetto library, and Muller agreed. Kruk also began stealing books behind the Germans' backs. He slipped volumes into his pockets and hid them elsewhere in the building of the university library. Finally, he created a hiding place inside the bowels of the ghetto library for the treasures he had collected. Kruk was the original book smuggler.

The Muller-Kruk relationship was complicated. On the one hand, Muller was the Aryan master and Kruk was his subhuman Jewish slave. But there was also mutual professional respect, as if between generals in two warring armies. Muller was a librarian and seemed to be sincerely interested in caring for the Jewish books. He was furious when he encountered a group of Lithuanians carting away wagons full of books from the former Lubavitch synagogue on Wilenska Street, to sell off as wastepaper. He stopped them in their tracks and seized the books from

Begin each day with a....

Aug — Taylor

17 - 24

ateful Heart

the looters. Muller related the incident to Kruk and reassured him that no harm would come to the volumes: "The books will come to me, and I will have them."[3]

After another meeting with the Germans, Kruk wrote in his diary, "Our reception was dignified, even cordial." Muller and his deputies engaged him, Kalmanovitch, and Lunski in a lengthy discussion about the question of Jewish languages: Why were Yiddish and Hebrew in conflict with each other? Why was Hebrew associated with Zionism? What was the Bolsheviks' attitude toward Hebrew? There seemed to be sincere curiosity, a desire to understand.[4]

When it came to protecting the physical condition of the Strashun Library's holdings, Kruk was more worried about what the twelve Jewish manual laborers might do to them than he was about the Germans. The laborers were a crude and uneducated group, who threw boxes of rare books around as if they were lumber, without the slightest appreciation of their value. One of the workers noticed an old illustrated Haggadah from the eighteenth century and, after looking it over, decided to take it aside and destroy it. When Kalmanovitch stopped him and asked him what on earth he was doing, the worker replied that the Haggadah has illustrations of Pharaoh's minions whipping the Jews, and he didn't want the Germans to see these images. It might give them ideas.

The collection's new facility at 3 Uniwersytecka Street consisted of rooms that had one year earlier, under the Soviets, housed the library of the university seminar on Marxism-Leninism. (Since the Nazis believed in a Judeo-Bolshevik conspiracy to rule the world, the Marxism-Leninism seminar room seemed like the most fitting place for the Jewish books.) Kruk was ordered to clear away the Marxist literature, to make space for the Strashun collection. The secretary of the university library, who knew Kruk from before the German invasion, quietly asked him not to throw away the Marxist books. Kruk did not need any prodding—he was a librarian, a bibliophile, and a committed socialist, who revered Marx (but not Lenin). He packed the collection into a nearby office.

The university librarian, in return, helped Kruk remove some Strashun volumes to a safe place elsewhere in the building, when the Germans weren't looking. It was a new kind of book exchange: you rescue my books and I'll rescue yours.[5]

Muller also gave Kruk a special assignment: to survey the university library catalog in search of Judaica and Hebraica. The volumes he discovered would either be added to the Strashun collection in the seminar room or be set aside for shipment to Germany. Kruk's dignified, restrained bearing in the catalog room impressed the staff of the university library. One of them turned to a colleague: "When this short Jew with the Yellow Star of David on his chest and back enters the library—we want to stand up and bow our heads to him."[6]

As the transfer of the Strashun Library to Uniwersytecka Street drew to a close, Muller announced to his Jewish slave laborers that the collections of YIVO, the An-ski Museum, and various synagogues would likewise be moved to the same facility. Now it was Kalmanovitch's turn to feel a stab of pain. The library of his beloved YIVO would soon be demolished. Muller also mentioned that he might ask them to assist in the processing of Polish and Russian libraries, museums, and archives.[7]

After less than a month of forced employment, Muller appointed Kruk "supervisor of work regarding the processing of Jewish books." The new title reflected the Germans' appreciation of his professionalism, and Kruk quipped in his diary that he was now a German "big shot." While the pay was negligible, the job came with a precious fringe benefit—an "iron-clad permit" that allowed him to exit the ghetto freely, without an escort, and to roam the city in search of Jewish books. It also granted Kruk the privilege of entering the ghetto without a body search at the gate—which made it a lot easier for him to smuggle in books and papers.

Over the course of several months, Kruk visited the addresses of former synagogues, schools, bookstores, publishing houses, scholars, and writers to retrieve the remnants of their libraries. The Polish house janitors were shocked to see a Jew walk up to their doorsteps in broad daylight and were even more stunned when he presented a letter stating that he was there on behalf of the German authorities.

For Kruk, it was a haunting experience to visit the places where Jewish life had pulsated just a short while ago and to enter the homes of his friends and colleagues, most of whom were now dead. He called his book excursions outside the ghetto "strolls over graves."[8] He handed some of his discoveries over to the ERR and smuggled the rest into the ghetto for safekeeping in the bowels of the ghetto library.

Kruk's book *malina* (hiding place) continued to grow. When inmates celebrated the Jewish holiday of Purim for the first time in the ghetto, on March 3, 1942, the only person in possession of scrolls of the biblical book of Esther was Herman Kruk, the secular socialist. The ghetto's synagogues borrowed the scrolls from his collection.[9]

Around Purim time, in early March 1942, Muller left for consultations in Berlin. When he returned, he announced that the ERR would expand its operations in Vilna. There would also be a change of venue: instead of transferring the collections of YIVO and the An-ski Museum to 3 Uniwersytecka Street, the Germans decided to convert the spacious YIVO building, with more than twenty rooms, into the main ERR worksite. The temple of Yiddish scholarship would become the headquarters for Nazi-German looting and plunder.[10]

During the first eight months on the German occupation, the YIVO building had been used as a barracks by Luftwaffe unit L.07449. As a military facility, it was out of bounds for Kruk to visit. When he, Kalmanovitch, and Lunski first entered their beloved shrine, on March 11, 1942, they found it in total disarray. The majestic entry hall, which once had a Yiddish map of the world indicating YIVO branches and affiliates across the globe, now had a German eagle and swastika with the inscription "Deutschland wird leben und deshalb wird Deutschland siegen" (Germany will live and therefore Germany will prevail). The collections and catalogs of the institute's various departments were thrown into the building's basement, where papers were piled a meter high. "It looked like after a real pogrom," wrote one member of the work brigade. The Luftwaffe unit had used some of the books, newspapers, and documents as fire paper. And it had shipped twenty crates of random material to paper mills for destruction, just to clear away space for their living quarters.[11]

Kruk went up the staircase to the exhibit hall on the second floor. It was empty. The display items from YIVO's 1940 exhibition on I. L. Peretz, the father of modern Yiddish literature, had been thrown into a nearby side attic. Pages from Peretz's manuscripts were lying amid mud and gravel. The documents, photographs, and artifacts were torn, crumpled, and muddy. Kruk, who revered Peretz as the symbol of modern Yiddish creativity, and who fondly remembered meeting the great author when he was a young dreamer, was shaken by the act of desecration. His first order to the work group was to clean up and arrange the items from the Peretz exhibit.[12]

As he waded through the mountains of books and documents dumped in the YIVO basement, as he passed by the large swastika on the entrance floor, and as he looked out at the filthy exhibit room filled with mud and dirt, Kruk found a new metaphor for his task. He and his colleagues were gravediggers, unwilling prisoner gravediggers, who were being forced to dispose of the dismembered remains of their own culture.

CHAPTER SEVEN

The Nazi, the Bard, and the Teacher

T
HE TWO CENTRAL players in the unfolding drama sur-
rounding the books returned to Vilna in April 1942: Dr.
Johannes Pohl and Shmerke Kaczerginski.

For Pohl, it was his first time in the city since his original looting spree
in July 1941. He was fresh off the heels of a major operation in Salonika,
where he had looted the library and archive of that centuries-old Jewish
community, which was called the "Jerusalem of the Balkans." Now he
was charged with organizing the expansion of the ERR operation in the
Jerusalem of Lithuania. As soon as he entered the YIVO building, it was
clear to Herman Kruk that Pohl was the man in charge.

> The "Hebraist" has come. He is a military man in a party uniform.
> A tall man with a Jewish appearance. He actually looks as if he's de-
> scended from Jews.
>
> His name is Pohl. He's a Doktor. He studied at the Hebrew Uni-
> versity in Jerusalem for two years. Published several works on the Tal-
> mud, etc. His behavior is courteous, even gregarious. But you can't
> get anything out of him. What will happen with his work in YIVO? We
> can't even guess. The issue is hanging in the air. No one knows what
> the "Hebraist" wants, or what his plans are.[1]

Pohl's Institute for Investigation of the Jewish Question had a slogan: "Judenforschung ohne Juden," study of the Jews without Jews. But
this slogan notwithstanding, Pohl knew from experience that the job
of cataloging and sorting the mass of Hebrew and Yiddish material in
Vilna could not be done by Germans alone. It would require Jews. One
of the ERR staff members, Dr. Alexander Himpel, estimated that if the
collections were shipped in their entirety to Germany and cataloged
there, the job would take ten years—after the war was over. There just

weren't enough qualified Judaica bibliographers and archivists in Germany.[2] Whether he liked it or not, Pohl needed to have a large group of Jewish intellectuals to sort through the material and catalog it.

Pohl instructed the head of the local team, Dr. Hans Muller, to increase the scholarly staff of the work group from three people (Kruk, Zelig Kalmanovitch, and Chaikl Lunski) to twenty and to increase the size of the total work brigade, including transport workers and technical staff, to forty people. Kruk did the hiring for the "intellectual brigade" (as the scholars were called), and the Judenrat's Labor Department provided the workers for the "physical brigade."[3] One of Kruk's very first hires was poet Abraham Sutzkever.[4]

The "intellectual brigade" segregated books based on their genre and century of publication. Pohl had a special interest in classical religious literature from his studies in Rome and Jerusalem, so he ordered the slave-labor scholars to make separate piles for Hebrew Bible, Mishna (the second-century code of Jewish law), Talmud (Judaism's magnum opus, edited in the sixth century), Maimonides (twelfth century), the Shulhan Arukh (the authoritative code of Jewish law composed in the sixteenth century), and prayer books. All other volumes were sorted into very broad categories: books printed between the fifteenth and eighteenth centuries, nineteenth-century imprints, twentieth-century imprints, periodicals, newspapers, and so forth. Each category of books had two piles: for shipment to Germany and for eventual transfer to Vilnius University.

Pohl's second-highest priority (after religious classics) was at the opposite end of the chronological and ideological spectrum: Soviet literature. The Bolsheviks were the greatest enemies of the Reich, alongside the Jews, and Jewish Bolshevism was a Nazi obsession. So he ordered that Soviet books in Yiddish, Russian, and other languages be sorted separately, apart from the other twentieth-century imprints.

The organization of nonbook material was rudimentary: newspapers and periodicals were arranged by title and year; manuscripts, by author; and archival collections, by provenance.[5]

In his reports to his superiors in Berlin, Pohl proudly surveyed his little "empire" in Vilna. In April 1942, when he came to organize the operation, he estimated that the ERR was in control of one hundred thousand Jewish books: forty thousand from Strashun, forty thousand from YIVO, ten thousand from synagogues and private collections, and ten thousand from the Lubavitch yeshiva and the Vilna Gaon's kloyz. Two months later, his estimate of the total number increased to 160,000 volumes.[6]

For "the Hebraist" (as Kruk called him), Vilna was a bibliographic gem, but it was still just one city among many. He was responsible for the looting of Judaica across all of eastern and southern Europe. His organizational visit in April 1942 lasted only a week, before he was off to his next destination. But he did find the time to examine piles of books and select 1,762 old imprints (from Altona, Amsterdam, Frankfurt, Lublin, Slawuta, Vilna, and other centers of Hebrew printing) for shipment to the Institute for Investigation of the Jewish Question. He estimated their value as half a million dollars.[7]

Pohl would return to Vilna frequently, to supervise the work at the YIVO worksite, usually en route to or from Belorussia and Ukraine.[8]

At about the same time as Pohl's first visit, Shmerke Kaczerginski smuggled himself into the Vilna ghetto, after seven exhausting months of traveling the countryside disguised as a Polish deaf-mute. The ghetto was now in its "period of stability." The mass Aktionen and deportations to Ponar were over, and Shmerke decided it was safe to return. He'd be freer in the sealed ghetto than in the open countryside. He wouldn't have to hide his face from every passerby who might detect his Jewish features. In the Vilna ghetto, he would be home, among familiar people and places, and he'd be able to open his mouth and talk. Shmerke's friends were glad he was alive and welcomed him warmly, although they couldn't quite understand why he was so happy to become a ghetto inmate.[9]

Shmerke moved in with Sutzkever, his wife Freydke, and several other intellectuals, in a crowded apartment at 29 Niemiecka Street. Kruk hired him to work alongside Sutzkever in the ERR work brigade. The two poets became like brothers, bound together not only by friendship, poetry, work, and home but also by the knowledge that they were the only members of "Young Vilna" who were alive—and in the Vilna ghetto. Most of their friends and colleagues had perished. A few, such as Chaim Grade, had managed to flee before the Germans arrived.[10]

The stability of ghetto life compared to life on the run meant that Shmerke could write again, after a seven-month hiatus. And his stifled muse burst forth. Sutzkever had already established himself in the intervening months as the Vilna ghetto's poet laureate; Shmerke became its bard. Sutzkever's verses inspired the ghetto intelligentsia. Shmerke's poems were set to music and were performed at concerts in the ghetto theater. Everybody sang them, not the least Shmerke himself.

Shmerke's poems vacillated between defiant optimism and lyrical mourning. His anthem for the ghetto youth club alluded to the mortal peril that young inmates faced, but it foresaw a brighter future for all of mankind:

> Our song is filled with grieving.
> Bold our step, we march along,
> Though the foe the gateway's watching,
> Youth comes storming with their song.
>
> Anyone who wants to can be young,
> Years don't mean a thing.
> Old folks can also, also be children,
> In a new, free spring.

His somber lullaby "Quiet, Quiet" began on a note of deep despondence:

> Quiet, quiet, let's be silent.
> Dead are growing here.
> They were planted by the tyrant.
> See their bloom appear.
> All the roads lead to Ponar now,
> There are no roads back.
> Father too has vanished,
> And with him our luck.

But even this dark song ended with a hopeful vision of a better day:

> Let your wellspring flow calmly,
> Be silent and hope . . .
> Father will return with freedom.
> Sleep, my child, oh sleep.
> The Wilia River—liberated
> The trees renewed in green
> Freedom's light will shine
> Upon your face, upon your face.[11]

Shmerke and Sutzkever were the only poets in the ERR work brigade. Its other members were a cross-section of Vilna's surviving Jewish intelligentsia: Israel Lubotsky, instructor of Hebrew at the Tarbut Hebrew High School; Dr. Daniel Feinshtein, an anthropologist and social scientist (the one who spoke about reading as an oasis in the desert of ghetto existence); Dr. Jacob Gordon, a scholar of modern Western philosophy from Spinoza to Bergson; Dr. Dina (Nadezhda) Jaffe, a historian of Jewish radicalism; Dr. Leon Bernstein, a mathematician who had studied in German universities; Uma Olkenicka, a graphic artist who had been curator of YIVO's theater museum; the educators Rachela Pupko-Krinsky, David Markeles, Ilia Zunser, Tzemach Zavelson, and Nadia Mats; and Akiva Gershater, a photographer and Vilna's foremost Esperantist.[12]

The "intellectual brigade" also included a number of bright young people whose university studies had been interrupted or obstructed by the war: Ruzhka Korczak and Mikhal Kovner, who were activists in the socialist Zionist "Young Guard" (Shomer Ha-Tza'ir); Avrom Zeleznikow, a young Bundist who was Kruk's protégé; and Noime Markeles, a Bundist turned Communist. (Noime and her father, the educator David Markeles, both worked in the brigade.)

The brigadier, who was responsible for all technical arrangements regarding both the "intellectual brigade" and the "physical brigade," was Tzemach Zavelson.[13]

Shmerke and Sutzkever's one close friend in the group was thirty-two-year-old Rachela Pupko-Krinsky. Before the war, she belonged to Shmerke's vast gang of friends and was an avid reader of Young Vilna's poetry and prose. She worked as a high school teacher of history in the Yiddish Real Gymnasium.

Rachela had the skills Kruk was looking for in a member of the "intellectual brigade." She had a master's degree in history from Vilna's Stefan Batory University, having written a dissertation on the diplomatic history of Poland-Lithuania in the early eighteenth century. She could read documents in Latin, German, Russian, and Polish with ease and was an aficionado of Yiddish literature.

An attractive woman, with an inviting smile and deep-set brown eyes, Rachela had a gaggle of young men around her in her youth. But she didn't show much interest in any of them. Instead, she had a two-year-long affair with a married man, the wealthy young businessman Joseph Krinsky. Krinsky ended up divorcing his wife and marrying Rachela, in a scandal that shocked many of her friends. He was a "parlor Communist," a man of means who supported the underground Communist party, and a donor to YIVO and other cultural causes.

The years between Rachela's wedding in 1936 and the German invasion in 1941 were happy ones: she taught in the best Yiddish school in town and was popular with students, parents, and colleagues. She lived in affluent comfort, enjoying the pleasures of fine clothing and custom-made furniture. And she gave birth to a daughter, Sarah, in November 1939. Because her husband had supported the Communist Party during difficult times, he was not arrested by the Soviets when they marched into Vilna at the outset of the war.

Her life fell apart quickly in 1941, in the course of two months. A Lithuanian "special squad" loyal to the Germans seized her husband at home on July 12, in one of the very first roundups of Jews. They ordered him to take along nothing but soap and a towel, and took him away to Lukishki Prison. He was shot at Ponar a few days later. In late August, Gestapo men walked into Rachela's house and summarily threw her out of her home. She left with Sarah in one arm and a single suitcase in the other, and moved in with relatives. Then on September 6, she, along with the Jews of Vilna, was ordered to march into the ghetto.

Rachela and her nanny Wictoria (Wikcia) Rodziewicz hastily decided that little Sarah, not even two years old at the time, should stay with Wikcia on the Aryan side. Her life would be safer and better. Wikcia moved to another part of the city and told everyone that the toddler was her daughter. The little girl, now called Irena, went to church every Sunday. Rachela went into the ghetto alone.[14]

Widowed from her husband, and bereft of her daughter, Rachela tried to find strength and solace in her friendships with Shmerke, Sutzkever, and surviving colleagues from the Real Gymnasium. Kruk kept a paternal eye out for her.

Everyone was now in place: the new ERR team headed by Pohl and Muller, and the expanded "intellectual brigade" of slave laborers led by Kruk and Kalmanovitch. The question was whether the Jewish intellectuals would be accomplices in carrying out the Germans' designs or the saviors of their threatened cultural treasures.

CHAPTER EIGHT

Ponar for Books

A s SOON AS the YIVO worksite began operation, disagreements arose between Herman Kruk and Zelig Kalmanovitch on what they should do. Kruk was an enthusiastic advocate of book smuggling. Kalmanovitch, his deputy, was not.

For Kruk it was easy. He had an "ironclad pass" that allowed him to enter the ghetto without a body search, and he had connections in the ghetto administration that facilitated his smuggling. The Judenrat organized large-scale smuggling of food products into the ghetto on vehicles that entered its territory with the Germans' authorization—to bring in the meager official rations of food and lumber, or to take out trash and remove snow. Kruk piggybacked off of the food-smuggling operations to bring in books.

He came up with clever schemes. The Germans once granted him permission to transport excess office furniture from the YIVO building to the ghetto library by truck—desks, file cabinets, and so on. He stuffed books and papers inside the furniture: textbooks, which he delivered to the ghetto schools, and rare imprints, manuscripts, and paintings that he took to his hiding place. After unloading the treasures, he diverted most of the furniture not to the ghetto library but to the ghetto administration for distribution as it saw fit. The library already had all the furniture it needed. The entire transport was a ruse to bring in books.[1]

Zelig Kalmanovitch couldn't employ such schemes, and he was by nature more cautious. While he harbored a ferocious hatred of the Germans, he thought that Hans Muller and Johannes Pohl were actually right about one thing: the cultural treasures *would* be safer in an institute in Germany than in war-torn Vilna. The allies would eventually win the war and find the treasures, wherever they would be. So he argued that the slave laborers should send as many books and papers as possible to Germany. Whether this was a rationalization of his fear of being caught smuggling or prophetic foresight is debatable, and was in fact hotly debated by his coworkers. But he was painfully consistent. When Kalmanovitch discovered an extremely rare eighteenth-century Yiddish booklet — an enlightenment manifesto and medical manual called *The Book of Remedies (Seyfer Refues)* — he didn't hide it or hand it over to Kruk. Instead, he showed the discovery to Pohl, who put it in a pile of items designated for Germany. Shmerke, Sutzkever, and other members of the work brigade were furious. Kruk was more forgiving.[2]

The stakes were raised and calculations changed in May 1942, when Muller and his team left for Kiev to set up Einsatzstab Reichsleiter Rosenberg (ERR) operations there. A new team, headed by Albert Sporket, replaced them. The fifty-two-year-old Sporket was no intellectual. He was a livestock businessman who owned and operated a leather factory in Berlin. He was also a hard-core Nazi who had joined the party in 1931, before Hitler's assumption of power. (Muller, on the other hand, had joined the party in 1937.) Albert Sporket was fluent in Polish and Russian, having conducted business in Poland before the war, but he knew nothing about Judaica. His deputy, Willy Schaefer, was a former Lutheran minister who was studying for his doctorate in the theological faculty of Berlin University. But he had only a sprinkling of biblical Hebrew. Another team member, Gerhard Spinkler, had excellent command of Russian but none of Hebrew or Yiddish.

Last but not least, there was Dr. Herbert Gotthard, who was the team's Judaica expert. A docent in Semitic languages at the University of Berlin, with a doctorate from Heidelberg, Gotthard was also the team's veteran. He had visited Vilna with Pohl to conduct the ERR's first looting spree back in July 1941. Now, he divided his time between Vilna and Riga, where he was the religion expert for the ERR's Main Working Group for Ostland. Gotthard was short and stout with a squeaky voice, leading Shmerke to nickname him "the little swine."[3]

Above all of these men, on the ERR's bureaucratic totem pole, stood Pohl. Everyone deferred to him — when he was in town.

The new ERR team treated its Jewish slave laborers much more harshly. Sporket was known for abusing and beating his workers. Rachela Krinsky recalled, "His yelling shook the YIVO building, and we were terrified of him. We tried to stay out of his sight as much as we could. But he used to go from room to room, and place himself next to each one of us. In such moments, everything would fall out of our hands." Kalmanovitch recorded in his ghetto diary, "The old man [his nickname for Sporket] beat a young worker today, when he discovered him smoking."[4]

Sporket and the ERR team members enjoyed wielding their power as Aryan "masters of the universe," acting on every whim and venting their frustration however they pleased. Sporket once ordered the wooden floors of the Wilno University Library torn open, on the suspicion that there were Jewish books hidden underneath. Nothing was found. Gotthard, "the little swine," was convinced that there was gold hidden somewhere in the YIVO building, and when he came across a safe, he ordered a locksmith to crack it open. Upon discovering nothing inside except for manuscripts and documents, he exploded, threw the papers on the ground, stomped on them, and left the room in a huff of anger.[5] Pohl set the tone. During an inspection, he smashed sculptures by the nineteenth-century Russian-Jewish master Mark Antokolsky, calling them "horrible." The Muller team had acted like gentlemen. The Sporket team acted like savage brutes.

But even more serious than the changed work atmosphere was the new policy to destroy "excess" books. The ERR headquarters in Berlin delineated the policy on April 27, 1942, in a memo to its field offices on the eastern front. The agency's first task was "the collection of material"; its second task was "the destruction of material." "One must take care that those spiritual weapons of our philosophic enemies which are not needed for the sake of the 'collection of material' be destroyed. In many cases, the destruction will need to be performed by other agencies, but the Einsatzstab must be involved in stimulating and guiding. This pertains to the detoxification of libraries, antiquarian book dealers, archives, art collections, and so forth, from those books, documents, manuscripts, pictures, placards, and films that may be used in the service of our philosophic enemies."[6]

The ERR office in Riga, which was in charge of the Vilna team, followed up with guidelines on how to treat various categories of "adversary writings." Hebrew and Yiddish materials, the Riga office wrote, "should be completely destroyed, to the extent that they do not qualify for shipment to the Frankfurt Jews' Institute." The only choice was between Frankfurt and incineration. There would be no more transfers to Wilno University Library.[7]

Pohl established a quota: no more than 30 percent of books and documents were to be sent to Germany. The remaining 70 percent or more were to be destroyed. Sporket, the businessman, made arrangements with local paper mills to receive shipments of *makulatur*, trash paper, from the YIVO building, in exchange for a payment of 19 reichsmark per ton. The mills melted the papers into a pulp and recycled them as new blank paper. The destruction of books became a small business venture, which covered the ERR team's pocket expenses.[8]

Sporket and his team generally left the sorting of materials, between those items designated for "collection" and those destined for "destruction," to the Jewish forced laborers themselves. This made the work brigade of Jewish scholars, educators, and writers responsible for life-and-death decisions about the fate of cultural treasures. On the rare occasions when Sporket and his team sorted Jewish material, they literally judged books by their covers and sent the volumes with attractive bindings to Germany.[9] Paradoxically, the harshest policy applied to Judaica books written in German, all of which were sent to destruction. "We already have an abundance of them in Riga; hundreds of thousands," Sporket barked.[10]

Kruk, the librarian, shuddered as he recorded the moment when the book dumping began, in early June 1942: "The Jewish laborers who are engaged in this work are literally in tears. Your heart breaks just looking at the scene." As someone who had built libraries, first in Warsaw and then in the Vilna ghetto, he recognized the full magnitude of the crime that was being perpetrated and the cultural catastrophe that was unfolding. He also noticed the parallel between the fate of Vilna's Jews and their books. "The death throes of the Yiddish Scientific Institute are not only long and slow, but like everything here, it dies in a mass-grave, along with scores and scores of others. . . . The mass grave, 'the trash paper,' grows bigger every minute."[11]

Pohl, on the other hand, was quite pleased with the efficiency of the Vilna operation. In a report to his superiors in Berlin, he boasted, "The objects are sorted by Jew labor. . . . The useless material is segregated as trash paper. . . . The sorting work at YIVO is efficient, because it obviates the need to send unnecessary material to the Reich."[12]

Religious objects met the same fate as books. The ERR team sold three hundred looted Torah scrolls to a local leather factory, which used the parchment to repair the soles of German army boots. The recycling idea was Sporket's. He was, after all, a livestock and leather industrialist.[13]

For Kalmanovitch, a religious believer, it was difficult to look at the scrolls destined for desecration: "How odd they appear in our time. Today I saw them in two different places—in all their ruination and degradation. They were leaning against the wall in the corner of the attic—tens of naked scrolls of the Torah and prophets, large and small, beloved and gentle—by order of the masters. What will be their end?"[14]

In perhaps the climactic act of destruction, Pohl sold the lead plates of the Romm Press's Vilna edition of the Talmud, weighing sixty tons in all, to smelting workshops, which melted them down into liquid form. The lead was then shipped to German armaments factories. The smelting workshop paid Pohl thirty-nine marks per ton for the lead.[15]

The destruction was not limited to Jewish materials. As Muller had foreseen, the Sporket team began processing not only Jewish books but also all sorts of "adversary writings" in Vilna. Russian and Polish books and archives started streaming into the building at 18 Wiwulskiego Street: Russian-language books from the Wroblewski State Library and Wilno University Library, books from the Tomasz Zan Polish public library, the research library of the Polish Society of Friends of Science, the warehouse inventory of the Józef Zawadzki Publishing House, and the library of the Wilno Evangelical Church—all were sent to YIVO for processing and sorting. The "Jew labor" (as Pohl called it) was responsible for making the "selection" of these materials as well.[16]

The ERR even sent Jewish forced laborers on special assignments to local churches and cathedrals, to process their collections. One such excursion stood out: Working under the supervision of a Polish professor, the group of ghetto inmates sifted through the 2,500-volume library of the Our Lady Gate of the Dawn Chapel (Polish: Ostra Brama), Vilna's most hallowed Catholic site. Not far from the icon of the Virgin Mary, which according to believers had performed numerous miracles, the work group "secured" five hundred volumes of Christian homiletics, exegesis, and theological literature, for shipment to Germany. It was probably the first time that a group of Jews paid an extended visit inside Ostra Brama.[17]

In later months, Russian manuscripts and archives from neighboring Belorussia began to arrive in the YIVO depot. In April 1943, a special train brought a vast collection of materials from the Smolensk museum and archives, which included chronicles from the sixteenth and seventeenth century, the diary of Peter the Great's chamber servant, and letters by Maxim Gorky and Leo Tolstoy. Soviet collections from the Vitebsk archives were also transferred to Vilna, en route to Germany.[18]

Sporket was an efficient administrator. He divided the "intellectual brigade" into departments, each of which was located in a different room of the YIVO building. Sutzkever recalled the building layout and the staff assignments as follows:

First floor: *Sovietica books*—Paturksy, Spinkler, and Sporket; *Judaica books*—Mikhal Kovner and Dr. Daniel Feinshtein; *Polish books*—Dr. Dina Jaffe, Tzemach Zavelson; *Card catalog room*—Hirsh Mats, Brayne As.

Second floor: *Manuscript room*—Abraham Sutzkever, Rachela Krinsky, Noime Markeles; *Youth studies*—Uma Olkenicka; *Pedagogical department*—Ruzhka Korczak; *Hebrew department*—Israel Lubotsky, Shmerke Kaczerginski; *Lithuanian department*—Benjamin Lamm; *Translation department*—Zelig Kalmanovitch; Dr. Jacob Gordon.

Third floor and basement: *Newspapers department*—Akiva Gershater, David Markeles.[19]

Three out of the eleven departments dealt with non-Jewish materials. Sporket himself worked on sorting Russian books.[20]

Shortly after the destruction of material began, Sporket announced to Kruk that he had orders to "remove and process" the ghetto library. Kruk was horrified. The ghetto library was the apple of his eye, his greatest cultural achievement, and the single most important support to the ghetto's morale. He launched into action and came up with a scheme to annul the decree, by playing different Nazi-German agencies off against each other.

Kruk approached Jacob Gens, the head of the ghetto police, who was by that point, in June 1942, the effective head of the ghetto. He asked Gens to secure an order from Franz Murer, deputy Gebietskommissar for Jewish affairs, that duplicate books from the ERR worksite should be handed over to the ghetto library. Gens, who had recently deposed engineer Anatol Fried as head of the Judenrat, was eager to gain popularity among the ghetto intelligentsia. So he was glad to do Kruk a favor. Murer, the deputy Gebietskommissar, was eager to strengthen Gens's new position of supremacy in the ghetto and acceded to his request. So he issued a written order to the ERR to hand over Judaica duplicates to the ghetto library. When Sporket received the order, he took it as a sign that Murer, the top German official for all Jewish affairs in Vilna, was interested in preserving the ghetto library. Sporket had no choice but to give up his plan to "remove and process" the ghetto library.[21]

It was a small consolation, in an ocean of book destruction. Meanwhile, Kruk took the one precaution of transferring most of the contents of his book *malina* (hiding place) from the ghetto library to a new location, a cellar in the center of town, outside the ghetto.

After July 1942, Kruk's diary rarely mentioned the ERR operation at YIVO. What was happening there was too painful to describe—the physical extermination of an entire culture. But scholar Zelig Kalmanovitch kept a ghetto diary of his own and provided a chronicle of the destruction process in short entries:

> August 2, 1942: "Actions have been taken which cannot be undone—all the libraries have been dismantled. The books are thrown into the basement like junk. Our master announced that he will obtain vehicles to take the 'paper' to the mill. The basement must be emptied to make room for a new transport."
> November 19, 1942: "The nearby paper mill has closed down. The paper from the basement is being sold to a mill that is at a distance of tens of kilometers."
> January 24, 1943: "They are constantly removing trash paper. Our master is dumping more and more trash paper."
> July 5, 1943: "The remnant of the YIVO library has gone to the mill."
> August 26, 1943: "I sorted books all week. I sent several thousand books to their destruction with my own hands. A mound of books is lying on the floor of the YIVO reading room. A cemetery of books. A mass grave. Books that are victims of the War of Gog and Magog, along with their owners."

While the transports to the paper mills were frequent, the shipments to Germany began later. They required supplies (crates), coordination (with the military and railway administration), and approval from Berlin. The first shipment to Germany, consisting of archival documents, took place at the end of October 1942. On November 16, fifty crates of books were sent to Germany, and in February 1943, there was a shipment of thirty-five crates, containing 9,403 books. There were two main destinations: the ERR headquarters in Berlin and the Institute for Investigation of the Jewish Question in Frankfurt. Soviet publications were usually sent to the nearby ERR Main Working Group for Ostland in Riga. The last major shipments to Germany took place in June and July 1943, and consisted of approximately ten thousand Yiddish and Hebrew books.[22]

The materials sent to Germany were the "fortunate" minority. For most of the books, manuscripts, and documents, the YIVO building at 18 Wiwulskiego Street was their Ponar, the last stop on their way to the paper mills.

CHAPTER NINE

The Paper Brigade

AMONG GHETTO INMATES, the ERR was considered an easy work brigade. It didn't require strenuous physical labor and it didn't include demeaning tasks, such as cleaning toilets. All you did was sort books and papers, fill out catalog cards, and make inventories of archival files. And you didn't have to worry that the Germans would replace you with a Pole who was stronger or better skilled, as was the case in factories and workshops. The ERR was the only all-Jewish worksite outside the ghetto.

With a touch of mockery, the Jewish guards at the ghetto gate nicknamed the group *di papir-brigade*, "the paper brigade," to suggest that there was no substance to their work. They were just pushing papers. The name spread and stuck. Some took the joke a step further and called them *di papirene brigade*, "the brigade made of paper," which meant the brigade of weak-bodied intellectuals.

The YIVO building at 18 Wiwulskiego Street was a peaceful and safe place to work. Beatings were not commonplace, and most of the German masters, with the notable exception of Sporket, spoke calmly. "They are refined gentlemen," Shmerke wrote with bitter sarcasm. The building was maintained in good condition, there was light and heating, and the slave laborers received a daily meal at work (tea, bread, and either an egg or a potato), prepared in the basement.[1]

Best of all, the Germans didn't spend more than a few hours per day in the YIVO building. They arrived late, left early, and took a long lunch break. Sporket and the ERR team spent more time in their offices on Zigmuntowska Street. When the Germans were out, a Polish civilian guard named Virblis watched over the site. Johannes Pohl wanted to maintain a "civilized" work environment and did not allow the use of military guards. The only other living soul in the vicinity was an old

75

Polish woman who had been YIVO's caretaker before the war and who lived in a hut at the edge of the building's grounds.

Despite these advantages, the YIVO building wasn't a particularly desirable workplace. Unlike a factory or a warehouse, there were no goods to steal and then sell. There were only books, for which there was no buying market. And there were no Christian coworkers, from whom you could buy food in exchange for money or an object of value. Shmerke recalls a friend from a different work brigade chiding him, "We get beaten every now and then at work. But it's easier to endure a blow from a rifle butt or boot on a full stomach, than to work while starving, with your head and stomach spinning."[2] Many of the physical laborers, who did the lugging and packing, asked the Labor Department of the ghetto administration to transfer them to more promising worksites.

And the members of the paper brigade, all of them book lovers, paid an emotional price for their work: they felt responsible for sending thousands of volumes to their destruction, and for dismantling YIVO, an institution they loved dearly. When Herman Kruk first offered Rachela Krinsky the opportunity to work there, she hesitated, because she wasn't sure she could endure the experience of seeing books treated like trash. Kruk himself was deeply disturbed by the scene, even a half a year after the book destruction began: "Your heart bursts with pain at the sight. No matter how much we have become used to it, we still don't have enough nerves to look at the destruction calmly."[3]

Each morning, the paper brigade would assemble near the ghetto gate at 9:00 a.m. and march in rows of three, led by their brigadier, Tzemach Zavelson, through the streets of the city—literally through the streets, since it was forbidden for Jews to walk on the sidewalks. There were no German or Lithuanian escorts to or from work, but the members knew that if anyone disappeared, there would be severe repercussions for the entire work brigade. The route to the YIVO building took fifteen to twenty minutes on foot and passed by Rachela Krinsky's pre-ghetto home. She could see the sign that still hung on the gate to her house, with her family's name on it: Krinsky. Whenever she saw it, she felt she was reading the epitaph on her tombstone.[4]

The YIVO building was located in a quiet, green residential area, far from the noise of the city center and from the crowded grime of the ghetto. The daily workload assigned by Sporket was easy and could actually be filled in two or three hours' time. The ERR masters and their Jewish slaves had a mutual interest in not performing their work too quickly. The Germans didn't want to leave Vilna for a new station closer to the front. Some of them had girlfriends in Vilna who worked as secretaries and assistants for the German military, civil administration, and other agencies. Shmerke wrote in a diary, "Schaefer's only desire is that we make a commotion when guests or other strangers appear, to show them that there is work going on."[5]

Most mornings passed uneventfully. Things got more interesting once the German officers left the building for their long lunch break. The Polish guard, Virblis, would disappear to take care of his own affairs, and the laborers were left on their own. They turned to other activities: in warmer weather, they lounged on the lawn in front of the YIVO building. They took a fresh shower in the basement, or just chatted.[6]

One of the most enjoyable lunch-hour activities was reading. Each slave laborer hid his or her own secret stash of reading material buried in a corner or pile. Rachela Krinsky later recalled the intensity of the reading experience in the YIVO building and the bond between reader and book: "Who knows? These might be the last books we ever read. And the books were also, like us, in mortal danger. For many of them, we were their last readers."[7]

At lunch, the members of the paper brigade often gathered in one of the rooms, to listen to Sutzkever and Shmerke hold forth. Sutzkever would recite works by his favorite Yiddish poets: H. Leivick, Aaron Glants-Leyeles, Yehoash, and Jacob Glatshtein. Shmerke told jokes and stories, and recited his own newest poems, often while standing on a table, with the group gathered around him. He was still the life of the party. Krinsky listened as she knitted a sweater. She later recalled, "Thanks to the poetry, we had many hours of forgetfulness and consolation." In quieter moments, Shmerke and Sutzkever wrote their "ghetto poems" in the YIVO building—which was, strictly speaking, outside the ghetto.

There were other activities: Dr. Daniel Feinshtein, a popular lecturer, prepared the notes for his talks; Uma Olkenicka, the artist, drew illustrations, including draft stage sets for performances by the ghetto-theater; Ilia Zunser, who was responsible for cataloging YIVO's music collection, read sheet music, which he said he could "hear" as clearly as if he were at a concert.

Rachela later remembered her work in the German-occupied YIVO building as a kind of lost paradise—the only part of her wartime experience in which she retained some joy, humanity, and dignity. It was the only place where she could see the sky and the trees, and could, thanks to poetry, remember that there was beauty in the world.[8]

Also during the unsupervised lunch hours, members of the work group received visitors, Christian friends who gave them food and moral support, and shared news about the outside world. They included Wiktoria Gzmilewska, the wife of a Polish military officer who had helped Shmerke and dozens of other Jews hide outside the ghetto; Ona Šimaite, a librarian at Vilnius University, who repeatedly entered the ghetto under false pretenses, ostensibly to collect overdue books but in fact to lend aid and support to friends; and Shmerke's young Lithuanian friend Julian Jankauskas, who hid Shmerke's wife Barbara for several weeks, after the couple separated angrily in the forest.

On one or two occasions, Rachela Krinsky had a very special visitor: her little daughter Sarah. At the time of the march into the ghetto, in September 1941, Rachela decided to leave her twenty-two-month-old girl on the outside, in the care of her Polish nanny, Wikcia Rodziewicz. More than a year later, Wikcia brought the toddler for a ten-minute rendezvous in the front yard of YIVO. Rachela, terrified that the Germans might return at any minute, said a few words to the girl, now called Irena, who did not know that the woman speaking to her was her mother. Rachela gave her a flower, and the girl turned to Wikcia, the nanny, and said "Mommy, this lady is nice; I'm not afraid of her." They then parted.

On other occasions, Wikcia just strolled down Wiwulskiego Street with Sarah, so Rachela could catch a glimpse of her daughter from afar.[9]

The non-Jewish visitors took a calculated risk that the Germans wouldn't return soon, and on one occasion, it almost ended in catastrophe. The embittered old lady who had been YIVO's caretaker before the war decided to "teach them all a lesson" and locked the gate to 18 Wiwulskiego during the lunch hour, with all the visitors inside the grounds. "I'll give the key to the Germans when they arrive," she said. The guests were alarmed, especially Wikcia Rodziewicz, who had already been arrested once before by the Gestapo. But Shmerke came to the rescue. Having grown up on the streets, he knew how to use his fists. Without a moment's hesitation, he went over to the woman, grabbed her arm, and shouted in his heavily accented Polish: "Before the Germans come back, I'll give you such a beating that no doctor will be able to help you. Give me the key right now!" As he twisted her arm, she knew he wasn't bluffing. He liberated the frightened visitors and went off into a corner of the building.[10]

Since the YIVO building had a large front yard, and many windows facing the front, the members of the paper brigade could easily see if the Germans were coming and quickly resume work. During the extended lunch hour, the slave laborers designated one member of the group to act as lookout and call out the code word "apple" when a German was coming.

According to the protocol established by Sporket, whenever an ERR official entered a workroom, the Jewish forced laborers were required to rise. It was Sutzkever's idea that whenever one of them saw a German approaching the building and called out "apple," they would all resume work in a standing position, so as not to rise when he entered. It was a form of quiet resistance, an affirmation of their human dignity and equality.[11]

Over time, the paper brigade bonded into a tightly knit fellowship, setting aside their political differences and personal accounts. The Hebraist and Zionist Israel Lubotsky became close friends with the socialist and anti-Zionist Daniel Feinshtein. Zelig Kalmanovitch developed a fatherly affection for Uma Olkenicka, the artist, despite the fact that he wasn't on speaking terms with her husband, Moshe Lerer. Lerer, a former YIVO staff member and a fanatical Communist, had deposed Kalmanovitch as acting director of YIVO when the Soviets took over the institute in June 1940. The five Yiddish educators on the brigade stayed close to each other, sharing food and words of encouragement. And the members of Shomer Ha-tsa'ir, the Young Guard socialist-Zionist organization, were a tight but secretive clan.

A paper-brigade romance developed between Shmerke and Rachela Krinsky. Both were recently widowed, having lost their spouses to the German death machine. Rachela's husband was seized from their home and sent to Ponar for execution in July 1941, even before the creation of the ghetto. Shmerke's wife Barbara, who hid in the city disguised as a Pole, was discovered and executed in April 1943.

It was more than just loneliness and proximity that drew the two coworkers together. Rachela adored Shmerke's warmth, humor, and optimism, and admired his street smarts.[12] Shmerke was touched by her love of poetry and by her quiet dignity in the face of her personal tragedies. He was impressed by her broad culture and erudition. While Rachela had a master's degree from Wilno University, he had never finished high school.

The Shmerke-Rachela romance was a quiet affair between friends and colleagues. They didn't move in together, and people didn't consider them a couple. But the affection between them was real and was strong enough that after the war, he asked her to marry him. (She was tempted but turned down his proposal.)

The relationship also inspired Shmerke to write a poem about Rachela and her daughter called "The Lonely Child." It spoke of a girl whose father was "snatched by the terrible giant" and who was now separated from her mother. The pained mom would someday, after much wandering and many restless nights, find her daughter and sing her a lullaby:

One day, when you'll be a mommy,
Tell your children of the agony,
That your parents endured from the enemy,
Remember the past, and tell it to posterity.

The poem was set to music, performed in the ghetto theater, and became a popular hit.[13]

Among the groups' difficult moments were the shipments of books and documents to Germany. The shameless looting and theft infuriated the younger coworkers. Kalmanovitch tried to reassure them that the shipments were a blessing in disguise. "The Germans won't be able to destroy everything. They're retreating now. And whatever they remove will be found at the end of the war and taken from them." Uma Olkenicka, the artist, said the same: "If the Germans don't destroy the material, if they sell it or hide it in an archive, then it'll be alright. We'll find it." But the deep sadness on her face belied her words, as she gracefully moved her arm across the room, as if surveying the treasures.

There was a good measure of wishful thinking in Kalmanovitch's and Olkenicka's remarks.[14]

Kalmanovitch tried to hide his pain from his coworkers, but he was more tormented than they realized. His emotions once burst forth at a literary program in the ghetto where he was the featured speaker. When the chairman introduced him as "the guardian of YIVO in the Vilna ghetto," Kalmanovitch jumped out of his seat and cut him off: "No, I'm not a guardian; I'm a gravedigger!" Members of the audience were upset by the outburst and began protesting, but Kalmanovitch continued to call out: "Yes, I am YIVO's gravedigger. I helped build a cultural building, but now it's being laid to rest!"[15]

The vagaries of ghetto life also weighed on the work group's mood. When Franz Murer announced the Aktion to round up the elderly, on July 17, 1942, several older members of the paper brigade feared for their lives. Kalmanovitch hid overnight in the ghetto hospital. The next day, the brigade gathered as usual at the ghetto gate, at 9:00 a.m. Security was heightened. The Germans checked the work permits of everyone who left the ghetto and shouted orders at the top of their lungs. The paper brigade arranged itself in rows of three and began to march, as usual. The group was silent, immersed in thoughts about the Aktion that had taken from them close to a hundred inmates. Suddenly, Kalmanovitch started gesticulating and raised his voice at his neighbor, Dr. Jacob Gordon. "I'm not afraid of them, I'm not afraid. They can't hurt me!" Gordon responded in disbelief, "What do you mean, Kalmanovitch, you're not afraid of them?" Everyone's ears lit up, to listen to Kalmanovitch's words, proclaimed on the streets of Nazi-ruled Vilna. "They can't hurt me. I have a son in the Land of Israel."[16]

CHAPTER TEN

The Art of Book Smuggling

A S SOON AS THE destruction of books and documents began, in June 1942, Herman Kruk started enlisting members of the paper brigade to smuggle materials out of the worksite. Many agreed on the spot, thinking to themselves, "I'm not going to live much longer anyway. Why not do a good thing and rescue some materials?"[1]

Kruk was pleased with the responses and early results: "People are trying to rescue and are doing much. The risk to their lives for every piece of paper is awesome. Every scrap of paper endangers their head. Nonetheless, there are idealists who do it skillfully."[2]

It wasn't hard to set aside the material for eventual smuggling. The whole building contained piles upon piles of books and papers. All you had to do was stick the valuable book or manuscript inside a pile when Albert Sporket and his team members weren't looking and pick it up later for removal. You could even create a separate "for smuggling" pile on the floor, if the Germans weren't in the room.

Each slave laborer made thousands of spur-of-the-moment decisions about what to set aside for rescue. While there wasn't time for deliberation, they did have a few rules of thumb.

- Books: Set aside just one copy for smuggling. Duplicates may be sent to Germany or the paper mills. Since the paper brigade processed numerous libraries, multiple copies were commonplace.
- Books: Small-format books and pamphlets are easier to smuggle inside clothing than large folios of the Talmud or albums. Larger items need to be set aside in the YIVO building, until transport by vehicle into the ghetto could be arranged.
- Manuscripts: Shmerke and Sutzkever gave high priority to liter-

ary manuscripts, and letters by famous writers. Both men were poets and appreciated the importance of preserving literary legacies. Letters, poems, and short stories were also not too voluminous and could be hidden on one's body with relative ease.

- Archives: A big problem. Archival collections were too large for on-body smuggling. Nor was it feasible to pick out one "gem" document among the thousands of pages of a collection. The paper brigade designated most archives for shipment to Germany. A few fragments were set aside for smuggling by vehicle.
- Works of art (paintings and sculptures): smuggling by vehicle.

The group believed that the safest hiding place for books and papers was *inside* the ghetto, among fellow Jews. But the Germans considered smuggling materials into the ghetto to be a severe offense — on two accounts. First, they were stealing property from their workplace. Johannes Pohl and Sporket made it absolutely clear that there were only two destinations for all the books and papers in the building: Germany and the paper mills. Second, there was a blanket prohibition on bringing books or papers into the ghetto, by anyone from any worksite.

Toward the end of the workday, they would wrap papers around their bodies and stuff items inside their clothing. The long, cold winter months were best suited for smuggling, when the laborers wore heavy coats and several layers of garments. They also created girdles and diapers and filled them with books and papers.

But in order to load themselves up, they needed to retrieve their coats from the small wooden hut near the worksite, which was inhabited by their nemesis, YIVO's former caretaker. The woman sometimes noticed the laborers stuffing paper into their coats and denounced them to Virblis, the guard on duty. Luckily, Virblis didn't take her accusations too seriously — she was a bitter woman who was known to concoct stories about people — and he didn't bother to pass on her denunciations to the ERR officials.[3]

As the brigade left YIVO for the ghetto, the question on everyone's mind was, who would be manning the gate for inspections? If Jewish ghetto policemen and Lithuanians were at the gate, there would usually be no problem. Their inspections were not particularly strict, especially when it came to patting down the members of the paper brigade. The guards knew full well that these people were just carrying paper — and not food products, a more serious offense. Some ghetto policemen even asked members of the work brigade to bring them an interesting novel the next time they returned from work.

But if Germans, such as Martin Weiss, head of the security police; Franz Murer, deputy Gebietskommissar for Jewish affairs; or ss squad leader Bruno Kittel, were stationed at the gate, all bets were off. The Germans mercilessly beat inmates discovered carrying any form of contraband. Murer showed up frequently to conduct surprise inspections. When he found a returning worker with bread or money under his or her coat, he stripped them naked, whipped them, and threw them into prison. If Murer sent the offender to the ghetto prison, they would probably survive. If he sent them to Lukishki Prison, their next stop would be Ponar.[4]

"Who is at the gate?" was a life-and-death question.

While marching back from 18 Wiwulskiego Street, the slave laborers would ask other work brigades that had just left the ghetto for the night shift about the situation at the gate. If there were Germans at the gate, the paper brigade had a number of options: They could make a detour and circle various blocks, in order to buy time until the Germans left. Or they could drop off the material, at least temporarily, with Jews who lived in the "Kailis" labor bloc, which was located not far from YIVO. But there were cases when the group arrived too close to the gate to turn back without being detected and had to pass through German inspection.[5]

Shmerke's audacity was breathtaking. He once carried a huge, worn volume of the Talmud up to the gate in broad daylight and explained to the armed German guard, "My chief, Sporket, ordered me to take the book into the ghetto and to have it rebound in the bindery of the ghetto library." The Gestapo man couldn't imagine that this short Jew would concoct a blatant lie that could cost him his life, so he let Shmerke through.[6]

Sometimes the book smugglers were just plain lucky. Murer discovered a silver wine-cup inside Rachela Krinsky's pocket, and everyone was sure that her life was over. But Rachela told Murer that she had brought the silver cup for him as a personal gift, and she threw in a pair of expensive leather gloves for his wife. Inexplicably, the deputy Gebietskommissar accepted the story, or at least the bribe, and let her through unscathed. He was in a good mood that day.[7]

Sutzkever had boundless creativity as a book smuggler. He once obtained written authorization from Sporket to take a few bundles of wastepaper into the ghetto, to burn in his household oven. He displayed the document to the guards at the gate, with the bundles of wastepaper in his hands. The "wastepaper" consisted of letters and manuscripts by Tolstoy, Gorky, Sholem Aleichem, and Bialik; drawings by Chagall; and a unique manuscript by the Vilna Gaon. On another occasion, he managed to smuggle sculptures by Mark Antokolsky and Ilya Gintsburg, and paintings by Il'ia Repin and Isaak Levitan, underneath a transport vehicle, with the help of some well-connected friends.[8]

Not all stories ended as happily: there were cases when Shmerke and others were beaten at the gate, either by Germans or by the ghetto policemen when the latter were under orders to "tighten up" their inspections. But no one was deported to Ponar. They were lucky.[9]

Despite the risks, Rachela Krinsky recalls that just about every member of the paper brigade participated in the smuggling—including many of the transport workers from the "technical brigade," the ones who made the boxes and cartons and packed and lugged them. One of the technical workers had a toolkit with a false bottom and transferred books and papers in a secret compartment underneath his hammer, wrench, and pliers.[10]

Zelig Kalmanovitch reversed himself and joined the operation. He knew that, given the 30 percent quota on shipments to Germany, many valuable items would be destroyed if they weren't smuggled. He considered the group's activity an affirmation of the spirit, a form of moral resistance, and he blessed the book smugglers as a pious rabbi: "The workers are rescuing whatever they can from oblivion. May they be blessed for risking their lives, and may they be protected under the wings of the Divine Presence. May the Lord . . . have mercy on the saving remnant and grant us to see the buried letters in peace."[11]

Shmerke later recalled, "Ghetto inmates looked at us as if we were lunatics. They were smuggling foodstuffs into the ghetto, in their clothes and boots. We were smuggling books, pieces of paper, occasionally a Sefer Torah or mezuzahs." Some members of the paper brigade faced a real moral dilemma whether to smuggle in books or foodstuffs for their family. There were inmates who criticized the work brigade for occupying itself with the fate of papers in a time of a life-and-death crisis.

But Kalmanovitch replied emphatically that books were irreplaceable; "they don't grow on trees."[12]

Once the materials had passed through the gate, they needed to be hidden somewhere. The simplest arrangement was to hand them over to Kruk, who put the rarities in his book *malina* (hiding place) and added the nonrarities to the ghetto library's collection. Kruk kept a card catalog of the cultural treasures in his possession, and recorded their provenance. The items "stolen" from the ERR worksite were listed as coming "from that institution." Writing "from Einsatzstab Reichsleiter Rosenberg" would have been incriminating evidence of theft, if the inventory cards ever fell into the Germans' hands.[13]

But no one could be sure that the ghetto library or Kruk's book *malina* would survive intact. What if the Germans raided the building and sequestered its inventory? It was wiser to distribute the treasures among many hiding places. Sutzkever recalled that there were ten hiding places and remembered the addresses of seven: 29 Niemiecka Street (in the building where he, Shmerke, and Dr. Daniel Feinshtein lived); 6 Strashun Street (the ghetto library); nos. 1, 8, and 15 Strashun Street; on Sw. Janska Street; and at a bunker at 6 Shavel Street (in Polish: Żmudska).

Two of the most precious items to be rescued from the Germans' clutches were the diary of Theodor Herzl, the father of modern Zionism, and the record book of the Vilna Gaon's kloyz (synagogue). Sutzkever discovered them early on, smuggled them into the ghetto, and kept them in two separate hiding places.[14]

But there were other solutions. Shmerke and Sutzkever gave many items to Polish and Lithuanian friends who visited them during the lunch hour. Ona Ŝimaite, the librarian at Wilno University, picked up a bundle of manuscripts by I. L. Peretz and arranged with colleagues to hide them in the university library. The Lithuanian poet Kazys Boruta hid packages of materials in the Literature Institute of the Lithuanian Academy of Sciences.[15] Sutzkever handed over valuable materials to Wiktoria Gzmilewska, who was connected with the Polish underground. When he gave her a document signed by the eighteenth-century Polish freedom fighter Tadeusz Kosciuszko, she knelt and kissed the name on the page. She later reported that upon delivering the document to a local group of the Polish resistance, its members reacted as if a spark had been thrown into a pile of gunpowder.[16]

But as the shipments to the paper mills intensified, it became clear that the paper brigade was winning small battles but losing its war. Only a tiny fraction of the treasures were being rescued. In the spring of 1943, Sutzkever thought up a new tactic. He would create a hiding place, a *malina*, inside the YIVO building itself. This would open up a new rescue avenue and perhaps eliminate the need for smuggling altogether.

Upon examining the building's architecture, Sutzkever found large cavities underneath the beams and girders in the attic. All that was needed was to distract the Polish guard, Virblis, so that Sutzkever and others could whisk materials up to the attic during the lunch hour. Fortunately, Virblis regretted that the war had interrupted his formal education and eagerly accepted an offer by two members of the work group, Drs. Feinshtein and Gordon, to teach him mathematics, Latin, and German while the Germans were out. As the teachers and their student were engrossed in study, other members of the paper brigade transferred materials to the attic.[17]

It is worth pausing for a moment to ask a basic question: why? Why did these men and women risk their lives for the sake of books and papers? Basically, they were making an existential statement and performing an act of faith. The existential statement was that literature and culture were ultimate values, which were greater than the life of any individual or group. Since they were sure they would soon die, they chose to connect their remaining lives, and if necessary their deaths, with the things that truly mattered. For Shmerke, books had saved him as a youngster from a life of crime and despair. It was time for him to repay the favor and rescue them. Abrasha Sutzkever harbored the mystical faith that poetry was the animating force behind all of life. As long as he remained devoted to poetry—writing it, reading it, and rescuing it—he would survive.

The book smugglers were also expressing their faith that there would be a Jewish people after the war, which would need to repossess its cultural treasures. Someone would survive and would retrieve these items, in order to rebuild Jewish culture. In the darkest hours of the Vilna ghetto, it was far from clear that any of this would ever come to pass.

Finally, as proud citizens of Jewish Vilna, the members of the paper brigade believed that the very essence of their community lay in its books and documents. If volumes from the Strashun Library, documents from YIVO, and manuscripts from the An-ski Museum were saved, the spirit of the Jerusalem of Lithuania would live on, even if its Jews would perish. Kalmanovitch put it quite sharply: "Perhaps there will be Jews in Vilna after the war, but no one will write Jewish books here ever again."

Sutzkever affirmed his faith in the work of the paper brigade in a poem called "Grains of Wheat," written in March 1943. He portrayed himself running through the streets of the ghetto with "the Jewish word" in his arms, caressing it like a child. The pieces of parchment cried out to him: "Hide us in your labyrinth!" While burying the materials in the ground, he was overcome with despair. But he composed himself when he recalled an ancient parable: An Egyptian pharaoh built a pyramid for himself and ordered his servants to place some grains of wheat in his coffin. Nine thousand years passed, the coffin was opened, and the grains of wheat were discovered and planted. A beautiful bed of stalks blossomed forth from those grains. Someday, Sutzkever wrote, the grains he was planting in the soil of the Vilna ghetto—planting, not burying—would also bear fruit.

> Efsher oykh veln di verter
> dervartn zikh ven af dem likht—
> veln in sho in basherter
> tseblien zikh oykh umgerikht?
>
> Un vi der uralter kern
> vos hot zikh farvandlt in zang—
> veln di verter oykh nern,
> veln di verter gehern
> dem folk, in zayn eybikn gang
>
> Perhaps these words will endure,
> And live to see the light loom—
> And in the destined hour
> Will unexpectedly bloom?
>
> And like the primeval grain
> That turned into a stalk—
> The words will nourish,
> The words will belong
> To the people in its eternal walk.[18]

One of the paper brigade's sources of strength and encouragement was their knowledge that YIVO and its prewar director, Max Weinreich, were alive and well in America. Weinreich had settled in New York in 1940 and transformed the institute's New York branch into its headquarters. Kruk and Kalmanovitch were overcome with joy when they heard bits of news about the reconstituted YIVO in America. The news came, surprisingly, from Pohl himself.

Pohl was a regular reader of the *Yiddish Daily Forward* and clipped out items that demonstrated to his mind the Jews' moral depravity and hatefulness. (He considered anything decrying the persecution of the Jews as an example of anti-German "hatefulness.") While perusing an issue of the *Forward*, he came across an article on the YIVO convention in New York on January 8–10, 1943, and after reading it, showed it to Kalmanovitch. The article reported on lectures by several of Kalmanovitch's prewar friends and colleagues, refugee scholars from Warsaw and Vilna. It also mentioned that the convention passed a resolution formally transferring YIVO's headquarters to New York. As emotions welled in Kalmanovitch's heart, he rushed to the ghetto library to share the news with Kruk. The two men embraced, and tears of joy rolled down their cheeks. Kruk observed in his diary,

> You have to have been in the Vilna ghetto, to have gone through what we have, and to have seen what has become of YIVO here, to understand what it means for us to get regards from the American YIVO, and especially from all those who are alive there, and rebuilding the trunk of Jewish scholarship. . . .
>
> Kalmanovitch and I wished each other that we may survive and be able to tell the world about everything we have gone through, especially the chapter called YIVO. While fate has been so cruel to us as to make us bear the burden of this particularly tragic ghetto, we are full of joy and satisfaction to know that Jewishness and Yiddishism live and carry on our common ideals.[19]

The members of the paper brigade felt assured that the "Jerusalem of Lithuania" had not been totally destroyed. Its surviving remnant lived on in New York. The remnant of scholars would someday inherit the remnant of books and documents. The thought was a ray of hope in the darkness.

Herzl's Diary

Theodor Herzl (1860–1904), the legendary father of modern Zionism, spent his adult life in Vienna, as a journalist for the "Neue Freue Presse" and as president of the World Zionist Organization. How did his handwritten diary from the years 1882–87, when he was a Viennese law student and struggling writer, end up in the Jerusalem of Lithuania? That itself is a story.

Herzl never published or disclosed the contents of his youthful diary during his lifetime. It was first discovered in 1930, in the estate of his wayward son, Hans Herzl, whose life ended in suicide.

Hans was a thirteen-year-old boy at the time of his father's death. The scene of the youngster reciting kaddish at Theodor Herzl's graveside left an indelible impression on all who attended or read about the funeral of the Jewish national leader. Hans was raised in England and attended Cambridge University but was unable to find his place in life. He resented being known only as Theodor Herzl's son and was haunted by a sense of failure. He fell into depression and into debt. In 1924, at age thirty-three, he converted to the Baptist Church, in order, he said, to establish his independence from his father. He later converted to Catholicism. The Zionist movement and the British Jewish community dissociated themselves from him and cut off all ties. Hans was lonely, impoverished, embittered, and desperate. His sister Pauline was his last anchor in life. Then she fell ill and died. On the day of her funeral, he committed suicide.[1]

Hans, who received the diary from his father, stipulated in his will that it should be sold for the price of a few dozen pounds, in order to pay off one of his debts. The executor of his will was the Anglo-Jewish journalist Joseph Leftwich, one of the few members of the community who had stayed in touch with him after his conversion. Leftwich was also an avid reader of Yiddish literature and a friend of YIVO. He later became the first major English translator and anthologist of Yiddish literature. As it happened, one of YIVO's leaders, Zalmen Rejzen, passed through London shortly after Hans's suicide, on his way back to Vilna from a fundraising trip to the United States. Rejzen met with Leftwich, who told him about the diary. Excited about the find, and by the prospect of enhancing YIVO's prestige, Rejzen jumped out of his seat, and exclaimed, "The manuscript must belong to YIVO!" He offered to purchase it immediately at the price specified in Hans's will—and didn't even bother to consult with his colleagues back in Vilna. Leftwich agreed, and Rejzen signed an agreement, paid a deposit, and took the Herzl diary back to Vilna in his coat pocket.

Then controversy erupted. Zionist leaders from Vienna were furious that the diary had fallen into the hands of a Yiddishist organization, whose heads were either cool or hostile toward their movement. They wrote letters to YIVO claiming that Hans did not have the right to sell his father's diary. The notebook belonged to Theodor Herzl's literary estate, whose executor was the Viennese banker Moritz Reichenfeld. The Vienna Zionists threatened to sue YIVO in a court of law. But YIVO refused to give up its acquisition, unless a court ordered it to do so.

After threats did not yield the intended results, the Zionist movement resorted to diplomacy. The movement's central offices in Vienna asked local Zionist leaders in Vilna to meet with YIVO's heads and use their powers of persuasion. At the meeting, the Vilna Zionists, led by Dr. Jacob Vigodsky, argued that it was preferable for all of Herzl's diaries to be located in one place. The notebook should be united with the other Herzl diaries held by the Hebrew University in Jerusalem. They also suggested that Theodor Herzl wasn't really a topic related to YIVO's area of scholarship. The Vilna Zionists presumably offered a sum of money to compensate YIVO for its expenses, and perhaps to sweeten the pot.

But YIVO responded that all Jewish affairs, including Theodor Herzl, were of interest to the institute. And they didn't hide the fact that YIVO considered possession of the diary a matter of institutional prestige. It put their young institute (founded in 1925) on the map as a major Jewish repository. After one and a half years of intermittent meetings, the Zionists gave up.[2]

The diary, which was mainly a journal of the books Herzl read, offered a fascinating glimpse into the mind of the man who went on to make history. It revealed just how assimilated and, indeed, assimilationist Herzl was in his younger years. The future father of the Jewish state considered himself a proud German. He harshly criticized French literature, including Emile Zola's novels, as "bordellotristic literature" (a combination of bordello and belletristic), remarking that "we Germans write better."

Herzl was outraged by Eugen Dühring's antisemitic treatise "The Jewish Question as a Racial, Cultural and Moral Problem," which argued that Jews were irredeemably depraved and needed to be removed from all spheres of public life — education, the press, business, and finance. The young Viennese law student drew the very "un-Zionist" conclusion that Jews needed to blend fully into the majority society. If there were no differences between Jews and Germans, no one would be able to detect Jews and discriminate against them. "The blending of the Western races with the so called Eastern races on the basis of a common civil religion — this is the desired solution!" he wrote in an early entry.

The Herzl that emerged from the pages of the diary was an insecure young man, especially when compared to the regal and domineering leader of the Zionist movement a decade or so later. "I am not one of those who will attain a visible position among the great minds of our time. . . . I do not have any illusions about myself," he brooded. "Today, I am twenty-two years old! And I have accomplished close to nothing. Without denying my talent, I feel that I do not have a great book in me." The feelings expressed in these passages were similar to the dejection and depression later felt by his son Hans. "There is no love in my heart, no yearning in my soul, no hope, no joy," Herzl wrote on April 13, 1883.[3]

The diary complicated the image of the man who became a myth and a legend. The author of the slogan "if you want it, it is not a fantasy" (in Hebrew: 'im tirtsu eyn zu agadah) wrote that he had no yearning in his soul. The diary showed what an unlikely candidate Herzl was for his future role as leader of the Jewish national movement. When Weinreich offered to publish its text in the New York *Yiddish Daily Forward*, its editor, Abraham Cahan, turned him down. Cahan, a long-standing socialist, had become a supporter of labor Zionism after his 1925 visit to Palestine. The Herzl of this early diary was not the Herzl that Cahan wanted his readers to know.

CHAPTER ELEVEN

The Book and the Sword

I T DIDN'T TAKE LONG for the work of the paper brigade to
come to the attention of the ghetto underground, known as the
United Partisan Organization or FPO (in Yiddish, Fareynikte
Partizaner Organizatsye).

The FPO was born on New Years' Eve of 1942, at a gathering of members of various Zionist youth movements, where Aba Kovner, head
of the Young Guard (Shomer Ha-Tza'ir) read a proclamation calling
on Jewish youth to engage in armed resistance against the Germans:
"Hitler has conspired to destroy all the Jews of Europe. It is the fate
of the Jews of Lithuania to be the first. Let us not go like sheep to the
slaughter! Yes, we are weak and defenseless, but the only response to
the murderers is self-defense. Brothers! It is better to fall as free fighters
than to live at the mercy of the murderers. Let us resist, resist until our
very last breath."[1]

Three weeks later, the organization was formally founded. Its objective was to perform acts of sabotage against the enemy and prepare
the ground for a popular ghetto uprising. Itzik Vitenberg, head of the
Communist Party organization in the ghetto, became commander in
chief, and Kovner was elected his deputy. The FPO was an interparty
organization, and representatives of the Revisionist Zionists, General
Zionists, and Bund also joined the command.

The organization's greatest challenge was obtaining arms. Kovner
held talks with the Polish nationalist underground in Vilna, but after
some hopeful early contacts, the Polish group received orders from
headquarters in Warsaw not to provide any assistance, and certainly
not arms, to the Jewish fighters. (Headquarters doubted the Jews' Polish patriotism and suspected that they would someday use the arms to

secure the Soviet conquest of Eastern Poland.)[2] This left the FPO with no choice but to purchase weapons on the black market and smuggle them into the ghetto — an expensive and difficult enterprise. As it built up a rudimentary arsenal, the organization began to train its members in the handling of weapons and established an infrastructure: units and lines of command, codes and protocols, secret meetings and news bulletins.

Initially, the ERR worksite wasn't of interest to the FPO. Its inventory wasn't very useful: no arms, no metallic objects, just books.

Their attitude changed in June 1942, when the FPO command decided upon its first act of sabotage. It would blow up a German military train using a homemade mine. The plan was absolute lunacy — no one in the FPO had any background in pyrotechnics. How would they construct a mine? They needed to get their hands on a munitions manual and follow its instructions carefully. But where could one find such a manual? They could find it in the YIVO building, which now stored tens of thousands of Soviet books!

At the time, there were two FPO members in the paper brigade: Mikhal Kovner, Aba Kovner's younger brother, and Reizl (Ruzhka) Korczak, Aba's party comrade and close friend. Mikhal and Ruzhka started looking for Soviet munitions manuals in YIVO, in absolute secrecy — not only from the Germans but also from their Jewish co-workers. When Albert Sporket and his ERR team were out for lunch, and the other workers were preoccupied, the two picked the lock to the sealed room for Soviet literature. But they couldn't find the kind of books they were looking for. After several fruitless break-ins, they finally came across a set of small grey booklets with red letters engraved on their covers: "Library for Military Commanders, Published by the Defense Commissariat." The booklets had everything the FPO wanted: Instructions on how to make mines and lay them, how to assemble and use hand grenades, and how to maintain and repair weapons.

Over the next few days, Mikhal and Ruzhka smuggled the booklets into the ghetto, without telling anyone. When their coworkers asked them to take in rare Hebrew books and documents, they refused, to their colleagues' shock and dismay. Members of the paper brigade were furious that the two young Zionists had abandoned the group's lofty cause. The Hebrew teacher Israel Lubotsky sighed and shook his head in disappointment: "Today's young people! They have no feeling for cultural treasures! What do they understand about such things? We were different when we were their age."[3]

Using those manuals, a group headed by Aba Kovner prepared the mine. Three FPO members, Vitka Kempner, Moshe Brause, and Izia Mackowicz, left the ghetto in the dark of night, on July 8, 1942, and placed the mine on railway tracks seven kilometers southeast of Vilna. They returned before dawn in a state of exhaustion and elation. In the afternoon, news reached the ghetto that the mine had destroyed the engine and freight cars of a German train and knocked it off its tracks. It was the first major act of anti-German sabotage in the Vilna area, and a cause for celebration. Everyone in the city assumed that it was the work of Polish partisans. No one even suspected that Jews in the ghetto were behind the landmine, let alone that it was constructed thanks to a booklet stolen from the YIVO worksite.[4]

In the following months, Mikhal and Ruzhka recruited other members of the paper brigade to join the FPO: Shmerke and Sutzkever; the young Communist Noime Markeles; Mendl Borenshtein, a carpenter from the "physical brigade"; brigadier Tzemach Zavelson; and Bundist Avrom Zeleznikow. Once inside the highly secretive underground, they began attending clandestine nighttime meetings, where they were trained in the handling of weapons. Most laborers in the paper brigade had no idea that some of their coworkers were active in the ghetto's armed resistance.

As the ties between the paper brigade and the FPO grew, the leaders of the underground decided to extend their support to the book-smuggling operation. How? The FPO had "moles" in the ghetto police, and some of the guards at the gate were "their" people. On days when the paper brigade planned to smuggle in particularly precious treasures, they notified the FPO, which arranged for guards belonging to the organization to be on duty and "inspect" them at the gate. There were no guarantees, because the guard details were mixed (FPO and non-FPO), and no one knew when Germans would show up. But from that point on, smuggling through the gate became less perilous.[5]

The FPO also shared its best storage facility with the paper brigade: the bunker at 6 Shavel Street. The cavern descended more than sixty feet underground. One entered through the sewage system and climbed down ladders two levels, to a facility that had its own ventilation system, electricity drawn from wires outside the ghetto, and a tunnel leading to a well on the Aryan side. The bunker was built by a young construction engineer named Gershon Abramovitsh in order to store arms caches for the FPO, and also as a hiding place for his paralyzed mother. Beginning in the spring of 1943, crates of books lay alongside the crates of arms.[6]

In appreciation of the FPO's assistance to the paper brigade, Herman Kruk, the librarian, extended help to the resistance organization. He created a hiding place for arms inside the ghetto library. With weapons kept in a central public location, the organization would be able to mobilize much more quickly in case of an emergency. Behind a bookshelf with copies of Josephus's *Jewish Wars* (which described the rebellion by the Maccabees against the Greek Empire), there was a secret compartment that stored Degtyarev machine guns. In the dead of night, FPO members entered the room one by one and, after pulling down the shades, an instructor gave them lessons on how to handle the weapon, while the shelves full of library books looked down at them. Once the lesson was over, the group of aspiring modern Maccabees returned the weapons to their place and dreamed of the next Jewish war.[7]

Helping store arms was a good thing, but procuring them was even more important. Since the ERR worksite was poorly supervised by the Germans, it was an ideal location for meeting Poles and Lithuanians to purchase arms. The conduit for those purchases was none other than Shmerke Kaczerginski.

In May 1943, FPO commander in chief Itzik Vitenberg summoned Shmerke for a face-to-face meeting, in total violation of the organization's conspiratorial protocol, which stated that there be no direct contact between its rank-and-file members and the commander in chief. Until then, Shmerke only knew the commander's code name, Leon. After being escorted through a maze of hiding places, he was stunned to meet the commander, who was none other than his old friend Itzik Vitenberg. They had worked together in the Communist Party.

Once Shmerke rebounded from his discovery, Vitenberg stunned him again with an order to obtain arms for the organization through his Lithuanian friend Julian Jankauskas. Jankauskas had hidden Shmerke's wife in the desperate days of September and October 1941, and was a frequent visitor in the front yard of the YIVO building, during lunchtime.

At their next lunchtime meeting, Shmerke told Jankauskas about the FPO and its plan for armed resistance. The rest of the conversation went as follows:

> Shmerke: We have arms, but we need more. And you need to help us. If you'll need money, we'll get the money.
> Jankauskas: I can't say anything now. I need to think about it. I'll bring you an answer tomorrow.
> Shmerke: Your answer should be in the form of the first pistol.
> Jankauskas: Maybe it will be.

The next day, Jankauskas arrived during the lunch hour, his face flaming red and his eyes sparkling. Shmerke went out to meet him amid the bushes and trees in front of the building.

> Shmerke: I hope your answer will come not from your mouth but from your pocket.
> Jankauskas: And if it comes from between my pants, you won't accept it?

With those words, Jankauskas pulled a six-shot revolver out of his pants. Shmerke jumped for joy, embraced Jankauskas's neck, and affectionately bit him on the cheek. Shmerke went back into the YIVO building and buried the pistol underneath a pile of newspapers in the basement.

That night, he reported his acquisition to Abrasha Chwoinik, the Bundist member of the FPO command who was in charge of arms purchases. Chwoinik was pleased but spoke with playful disappointment. A six-shot revolver was a good present for your girlfriend, and was a nice weapon for a duel, if you didn't want to kill your opponent. But the organization was short on arms and would accept the piece. He informed Shmerke, "Tomorrow afternoon, shortly before you leave work, a ghetto policeman will come calling for you at the YIVO building. When he says the code phrase 'Berl is waiting for you,' give him the gun."

The next day, the handoff went smoothly. Ghetto police sergeant Moshe Brause used the code phrase, Shmerke retrieved the pistol from its hiding pace, and Brause left with the weapon, wishing him, "May it be a good beginning!" It was.[8]

From then on, the meetings became a routine. Every second or third day, Jankauskas brought arms during the lunch hour—a handgun, grenades, and bullets—and Brause came at the end of the day to pick up the weapon and deliver money for payment. Ruzhka Korczak and Mikhal Kovner were in on the scheme and checked the incoming weapons to make sure they were operational, and evaluated their worth. In a month's time, Shmerke acquired an arsenal of fifteen handguns, each of which cost between 1,500 and 1,800 German marks.

It was crucial that the handoffs of arms and money be performed quickly, without drawing the attention of coworkers who were not members of the FPO. Many in the paper brigade worried that one of their work colleagues was an informer.[9]

Besides Sergeant Brause of the ghetto police, the paper brigade also used a second channel to smuggle the weapons into the ghetto. Mendl Borenshtein, a carpenter who belonged to the "physical brigade," carried ammunition and small weapons in the false bottom of his toolkit.[10]

The paper brigade also helped pay for weapons with its own inventory. Among the items that poured into 18 Wiwulskiego Street from the An-ski Museum, there were dozens of silver kiddush cups, Torah pointers, and other ritual objects made of gold and silver. Kovner, Ruzhka, and others smuggled these items into the ghetto and handed them over to the FPO, which melted them down. The organization then sold the gold and silver on the black market and used the money to purchase their much-needed arms.[11]

The smelting operation inspired Sutzkever to write one of his most famous ghetto poems, "The Lead Plates of the Romm Printers." In it, he imagined Jewish fighters melting down the lead plates used by the Vilna Romm Press to print the Talmud, in order to make bullets to fight the Germans. As letter after letter dripped into liquid, Sutzkever sensed that he and his fellow fighters were like the priests in the ancient temple, filling the menorah with oil. The Jewish genius, that had for centuries expressed itself in religious study and worship, now needed to express itself in armed combat.

> Liquid lead brightly shining in bullets so fine,
> Ancient thoughts—in the letters that melted hot.
> A line from Babylonia, from Poland a line,
> Boiled, flooded together in the foundry pot.
> Jewish valor, hidden in word and in sign,
> Must know explode the whole world with a shot![12]

Sutzkever's poem was a powerful metaphor, and an inspiring dream. In fact, it was the Germans who seized the lead plates of the Romm Press and melted them down. But the poem was based on a different real-life FPO melting operation: one that boiled down metallic kiddush cups and Torah pointers to purchase arms.

One day, Chwoinik of the FPO command asked to meet with Shmerke. "You're doing excellent work. The merchandise is good. But we won't be able to fight only with handguns. You need to get us rifles, and most important of all, machine guns." Shmerke let out a nervous chuckle. When he regained his composure and military discipline, he replied obediently, "Yes, sir!"

The next day, when Shmerke met Jankauskas, he raised the subject of machine guns, and to his utter amazement, his friend wasn't surprised. "I'll see what I can do."

Jankauskas didn't show up for their next scheduled meeting. He disappeared for several days, and Shmerke was worried he'd been arrested. If so, the Germans would come looking for him, for Shmerke, next. So he slept at different ghetto addresses for the next few nights.

Then, on a rainy day, toward the end of the lunch break, when the Germans were soon expected back, Jankauskas opened the gate to the YIVO grounds carrying a viola case. Shmerke rushed down to meet him.

Shmerke: What happened? You've taken up viola playing?
Jankauskas: It's a viola that shoots. Take it.

Shmerke grabbed the heavy case and lugged it down to the basement. He informed Mikhal Kovner, Ruzhka, and Sutzkever about the acquisition. They decided to dismantle the machine gun immediately and conceal its parts in different rooms, just in case a curious laborer, who had seen the viola case through a window, decided to come down and take a look at the musical instrument.[13]

As soon as they dismantled the machine gun and hid its parts, the Germans arrived—not in one vehicle but in two. They had guests. Willy Schaefer walked into the building with high-ranking visitors in uniform. The FPO members' hearts beat loudly, as Schaefer decided to give the visitors a tour of the worksite, room by room, showing off its treasures. The Germans entered the art room where the barrel of the machine gun lay underneath three paintings and began examining different pieces of art: Chagall, Minkowsky, and others. Sutzkever, who was in charge of the art department, and who was working in the adjacent room with Rachela Krinsky, was beside himself. Schaefer picked up one painting and then another; he was just one painting away from discovering the barrel of the gun. Sutzkever's face turned white as chalk, and he ran out to tell Shmerke that catastrophe was imminent.

Rachela Krinsky detected her friends' agitation and sensed that something was seriously wrong. She wasn't a member of the FPO and wasn't "in the loop" about the arms-smuggling operation, but she had figured out a long time ago that Jankauskas was giving Shmerke more than just bread during his lunch-time visits. Without a second to lose, she decided to create a diversion. She went over to the doorway from the connecting room and called out to Schaefer, "Mr. Chief, Mr. Chief, I've found an important manuscript." The Germans turned to her and came over to look at the item she held in her hands: a document from the Polish uprising of 1830. After examining it, they left the room.[14] The diversion succeeded, and the catastrophe was averted.

Shmerke took equal pride in his activities as book smuggler and FPO fighter. He saw them as complementary forms of resistance. In his memoirs, he recounted a folktale: When the Lord created the first Jew, the biblical patriarch Abraham, the Almighty gave him two presents for his life journey—a book, which Abraham held in one hand, and a sword, which he held in the other. But the patriarch became so fascinated reading the book that he didn't notice how the sword slipped out of his hand. Ever since that moment, the Jews have been the people of the book. It was left to the ghetto fighters and partisans to discover the lost sword and pick it up.[15]

CHAPTER TWELVE

Slave-Labor Curators and Scholars

I N EARLY JULY 1942, Albert Sporket, the ERR team's brutish chief, gave the paper brigade an unexpected assignment: to prepare an exhibit on Jews and Bolsheviks, using materials located at the worksite. He envisioned the exhibit as a vehicle for the political education of German troops, to instill in them hostility toward the two greatest enemies of the Reich. Sporket wanted to showcase the ERR's work in Vilna to higher-ups in the German command, to show just how important its looting was for Nazi "science."

There was just one catch: Sporket and his colleagues were totally ignorant of Jewish affairs, and his Judaica expert Herbert Gotthard wasn't interested in curating an exhibit. So Sporket left the exhibit preparation to the Jewish slave laborers themselves, on the assumption that anything they put together would constitute an "exposé" of the vile and degenerate nature of Jewry and Communism. What emerged in the end was an odd hybrid of a sympathetic, objective, and antisemitic presentation.

The exhibit, which was put on display in the YIVO exhibition hall (where the Yiddish institute had once mounted its exhibition on I. L. Peretz, the father of modern Yiddish literature), was divided into two parts: the Jewish section on the right-hand side and a Soviet section, fittingly, on the left. Portraits of the Vilna Gaon, Matityahu Strashun, and other rabbis were on one wall, and photographs of Stalin, the members of the Soviet politburo, and Marshal Voroshilov hung opposite them. The two groups of dignitaries stared across the room at each other.

The Jewish section consisted of items from the An-ski Museum, whose entire collection was hastily transferred to the YIVO building for sorting. On display were sculptures and paintings by various Jewish artists, old rare books (including a tiny pocket siddur from the seventeenth century), and manuscripts. There was a glass case with the illustrated title pages of modern Hebrew and Yiddish books. A Torah scroll was situated in the center, surrounded by silver ritual objects, and a Hasidic satin caftan (Yiddish: *kapote*) hung on a makeshift mannequin.[1]

The caftan became the subject of a crisis, when it disappeared one night, apparently lifted by a chimney sweep. (Chimney sweeps had total freedom of movement from one rooftop to another in the city and engaged in smuggling and theft. Some of them helped smuggle arms for the FPO.) Sporket's deputy, Willy Schaefer, accused the members of the paper brigade of stealing the caftan, a valued exhibit item, and threatened to inform the Gestapo unless they returned it the next day. The slave laborers' protests that they knew nothing about the whereabouts of the stolen item only infuriated Schaefer even more. The group decided they would need to find a substitute *kapote* in the ghetto after work that evening, but they couldn't find a single Hasidic caftan in the ghetto of Vilna, which was historically a non-Hasidic and anti-Hasidic community. So they replaced the original with a "forgery": Shmerke's black raincoat with the lining let down. Luckily, Schaefer didn't notice the difference and was placated.

The exhibit's Soviet section, decorated with red ribbons, included editions of Lenin's works in numerous languages and sample volumes of writings by Stalin. In a corner, there was a display case entitled "Incitement" with publications against Nazi Germany in Russian, Yiddish, and other languages. The exhibit culminated with a glass display case of Nazi literature—brochures, newspapers, and magazines, and several issues of the *Stürmer*—that revealed "the truth" about Jews and Bolsheviks.

In the middle of the room, between the Jewish and Soviet sections, there was a bookcase marked "Karaitica," dedicated to the sect that split off from Judaism in the ninth century. It displayed Karaite books, photographs of individuals and groups, and a large portrait of the Karaite cleric of Vilna, Seraya Szapszal. Inclusion of the sect in the Judeo-Bolshevik exhibit was probably Zelig Kalmanovitch's idea, since he was convinced that the Karaites were of Jewish origin and was researching their history at the time.[2]

Herman Kruk was quite pleased with the outcome of his colleagues' work as slave-labor curators: "The exhibition is designed so that everything Jewish is really Jewish and none of us needs to be ashamed of it. Everything Bolshevik is a fine Bolshevik corner, with no tones of anti-Bolshevism. And the Germans think that the Jewish workers are helping them with everything as much as possible. The wolf is satisfied and the lamb is whole." Kalmanovitch was even more effusive: "The exhibit testifies to the cultural strength of the Jewish people. It is like the biblical Balaam, who intended to curse, and against his will ended up blessing."[3]

In advance of the exhibit's official opening, the YIVO building was cleaned up and looked, in Kruk's words, like "a small town Jewish philanthropic institution on the eve of a visit by the American 'Joint Distribution Committee.'" Several of the workrooms were filled with crates, and signs were hung up with the word "transport"—all to make an impression that this was a very busy shipping dock. Gebietskommissar Hans Hingst and numerous German and Lithuanian officials attended the exhibit's opening reception.

A few days later, a rave "review" of the exhibit appeared in *Wilnaer Zeitung*, the local organ of the German authorities. The article heaped praise on the ERR: "The political-military struggle against Jewry and Bolshevism is now being followed up by something else: struggle on the level of scientific research. We must not only fight our opponents, we must know their essence, their intentions and objectives. . . . The men of the Einsatzstab are the shock troops of science. . . . These men have made numerous discoveries that are of importance for the understanding of Jewry and Bolshevism—some of which are of direct practical political importance."[4] The article pointed out Vilna's position as the historic "headquarters of Jewry" and the Jews' "second Jerusalem." "Vilna offers a truly enormous selection of important and interesting documents on World Enemies no. 1 and no. 2—the Jews and the Bolsheviks."

The correspondent for *Wilnaer Zeitung* hailed the exhibit as an important educational achievement: "It displays the cunning, cruel faces of Jewish 'greats' from the nineteenth century, the stuttering attempts of modern Jewish artists. . . . On the other side, there is a special collection of photos from the 'Soviet Paradise' that speak more than any words can of the wretchedness and backwardness of Soviet Man."

The article informed readers that the exhibit could be viewed by appointment by all interested individuals and groups. It concluded,

"Whoever views it will have a rough notion of the importance and scope of the work that is quietly being performed by the men of the Einsatzstab."

During the course of its "run" at 18 Wiwulskiego Street, the Judeo-Bolshevik exhibit was viewed by several visiting delegations. (Plans to send it on tour to cities in the German Reich were never implemented.) Kalmanovitch noticed that the German visitors avoided making eye contact with the Jewish slave laborers in the building, and he mused in his diary that eye contact might lead them to sense a common humanity with their victims and arouse feelings of compassion. The visitors found such feelings impermissible.[5]

A high-ranking commission from Berlin, with a staff person from Heinrich Himmler's office, came to inspect the exhibit. They were not pleased. They considered the exhibition ideologically deficient, and one member even called it "Communist propaganda." After their visit, Sporket ordered the inclusion of more explicitly antisemitic and anti-Bolshevik material. In its final version, the exhibit displayed falsified photographs, ostensibly showing Jewish Bolsheviks tormenting Lithuanian peasants. In fact, the photos were of Jews being tortured by Germans and Lithuanian collaborators.[6]

Dr. Herbert Gotthard, the Judaica expert on the ERR team, had more serious projects in mind than an exhibit, which to his mind was nothing more than a publicity stunt. "The little swine," as Shmerke called him, had big ambitions to make the Vilna ERR into a center of Judenforschung, antisemitic Jewish studies. He decided to exploit its forced laborers as the authors of studies on Jewish topics, which he would rewrite in an antisemitic spirit and submit to the ERR's analytic department in Berlin.

Gotthard started by giving modest research assignments to Zelig Kalmanovitch, the YIVO scholar with a doctorate from the University of Petrograd. Upon seeing the quality of his work, Gotthard put Kalmanovitch in charge of an entire group of slave-labor researchers and of an associated translation group, which rendered prewar studies into German. The researchers (Dr. Moshe Heller, Rabbi Abraham Nisan Ioffe, and others) were based in the ghetto library, where reference literature was readily available, and the translators (Dr. Jacob Gordon, Akiva Gershater, and others) were situated in the YIVO building. Kalmanovitch "floated" between both locations.

Kalmanovitch was outraged by his new job as slave-labor scholar and disgusted that his work would be exploited to spread antisemitic canards. But he kept his feelings to himself and vented them in the privacy of his diary. "They want to uncover our 'secrets,' to reveal our 'hidden affairs.' What imbeciles! Their crudeness and fraudulence rule. But I must be dumb with silence — until the danger passes."[7]

On some level, Kalmanovitch must also have welcomed the challenge to engage in intellectual activity during the long workday. He probably wanted to prove to himself that he was still the scholar he had been before the war, even after nine months of incarceration in the ghetto, at the age of sixty-one.

His first major assignment was to compile a bibliography and translate studies on the Karaites, the sect that had broken away from Judaism in the ninth century. Since the early nineteenth century, Karaites in Eastern Europe and Crimea argued that they were a Turkic group, who spoke a Turkic language and practiced a distinct religion of their own that was only distantly related to Judaism. The Russian tsars accepted this argument and did not apply their restrictive laws regarding the Jews to Karaites. Nazi Germany followed the tsarist tradition and didn't consider the group to be racial Jews. But German scholars described their religion as "Jewish" or "Judaism without the Talmud," which made them an odd group: racial Turks with a Jewish religion.[8]

Once the war broke out, the on-the-ground treatment of the Karaites varied. Not everyone "got the memo" that the members of this tiny sect were not Jews, and military commanders in the field made snap decisions. In Ukraine, the swiftly moving German murder machine didn't distinguish between Jews and Karaites, and two hundred Karaites were killed at Babi Yar, on the outskirts of Kiev, as part of the great massacre that mowed down thirty-three thousand people on September 29–30, 1941. In France, on the other hand, the Karaites were registered as Jews but were not deported to the death camps, on explicit orders from Berlin. In Crimea, the Karaites' greatest numeric center, they enjoyed favorable, even privileged, treatment. The Germans recognized them as a Turkic people related to the Tatars and not only protected them but even cultivated a positive relationship.[9]

There were about two thousand Karaites in Vilna and the nearby town of Troky. Dr. Gerhard Wunder, head of the ERR's analytic department in Berlin, ordered his subordinates in Vilna to study them. He explained the importance of the topic as follows: "There have recently been unfortunate cases in which the Karaites were mistaken for Jews. I consider it our task to offer instruction on this peculiar ethnic group. . . . Our work will prevent mistakes in the future, such as those that have taken place in the past."[10] Those "mistakes" had been fatal for hundreds of Karaites in Ukraine.

Besides compiling a bibliography and supervising the translation of studies on the Karaites from Hebrew and Yiddish, Kalmanovitch wrote a review of the scholarship in which he pointed out that there was a general consensus that the group was descended from Jews and practiced a form of Judaism. This was the very opposite of what Wunder, the head of the analytic department in Berlin, wanted to hear.[11]

To counteract Kalmanovitch's opinion, Gotthard commissioned the Karaite *hakham* of Vilna, Seraya Szapszal, to compose a study on his community's racial origin, religion, and culture. And he ordered Kalmanovitch to translate the manuscript from Russian into German. The two men worked in tandem; Kalmanovitch translated as Szapszal wrote. In the privacy of his diary, the Jewish scholar mocked the Karaite author and his magnum opus: "How narrow is his horizon! His genius is in delineating his Turkish-Tatar descent. But he knows more about caring for horses and handling weapons than he does about the teachings of his own religion!"[12]

The project led to a personal acquaintance between the two men. Szapszal visited the YIVO building on several occasions to examine its Karaite-related materials, and Kalmanovitch visited Szapszal at his home—he was taken there by German military escort—to discuss certain points in his study.

There could be no mistaking that the status of the two scholars was entirely different. The Germans referred to Szapszal as "Professor," paid him an honorarium of one thousand reichsmark and promised to distribute his study among German government agencies. Kalmanovitch, his learned translator, had no name in ERR memos; he was just "Judenkraefte" (Jew labor). He was paid the standard slave laborer's wages—thirty reichsmark per month. At most, he received a loaf of bread from his ERR masters to thank him for a job well done.[13]

The Karaite project culminated with an arranged debate between Szapszal and Kalmanovitch on the group's descent, held in the presence of the ERR team and other officials. During the debate, Kalmanovitch reversed himself and conceded that the Karaites were racially unrelated to the Jews. He did so not out of conviction but out of compassion: to help the Karaites avoid persecution.[14] Kalmanovitch's reversal was an act of moral magnanimity. Szapszal had never helped Jews and had, in fact, assisted the Germans in capturing them.

During the first months of the German occupation, several hundred Jews lived outside the ghetto with forged papers identifying them as Karaites. Since Karaite males were circumcised, this was a plausible way for Jewish men to avoid discovery. And dark-haired, brown-eyed Jewish women also had a better chance of passing as Karaites than as Poles or Lithuanians. Szapszal reportedly provided the Germans with a list of the names and addresses of authentic Karaites in Vilna, in order to facilitate the arrest of the "frauds," who were rounded up and sent to Ponar for execution.

Months later, after the large-scale deportations to Ponar had stopped, Szapszal wrote a letter to the Germans to inform them that he was receiving requests for certificates of Karaite ethnicity from people who were in fact Jews. He offered his services to resolve all dubious claims of Karaite descent, and the Germans gratefully accepted. The Reich Office for Genealogical Research (Reichstelle fun Sipenforschung), which was responsible for investigating cases of uncertain racial origin, used Szapszal as a consultant.[15]

But at the debate, Kalmanovitch did not repay Szapszal or his community in kind.

In August 1942, the ERR analytic department issued a new assignment: it ordered working groups in Ostland (Riga, Vilna, and Minsk) to submit studies on the Jewish ghettos in their regions, both in the past and in the present. Since in German the word "ghetto" could mean Jewish community, the order from Berlin was rather vague and open-ended. Almost anything about the local Jews could be submitted.

Gotthard handed the assignment over to Kalmanovitch and asked him to prepare some studies. Kalmanovitch was struck by the bitter irony—first the Germans exterminated the Jews; now they wanted to study them. "They want to know the height of the mountain that they have leveled," he remarked sardonically in his diary.[16]

Kalmanovitch's research group prepared five studies. Two of them were penned by Kalmanovitch himself: a historical overview on Lithuanian Jews since the Middle Ages and an analysis of the Jewish community in independent Lithuania between 1918 and 1940. Two other studies were on topics that were of greater interest to Kalmanovitch than to the Germans: a catalog of Vilna's 114 synagogues by Rabbi Abraham Nisan Ioffe and an analysis of the history and art of the Zarecha Jewish cemetery, including the transcription of scores of historic tombstones. Kalmanovitch decided to take advantage of the ERR's ambiguous order to prepare these studies on Vilna's Jewish heritage sites, fearing they might not exist much longer. (He was right.) Fifth and last, there was a report on the contemporary Nazi-imposed Vilna ghetto written by Dr. Moshe Heller.[17]

For Gotthard, the ERR Judaica "expert," the studies by Kalmanovitch and his research group were raw material that he edited, altered, or simply ignored, as best suited his purposes. Most of the time, he used their information, while interjecting antisemitic comments and observations into the text.

For instance, he brought Kalmanovitch's statistical table on the occupational breakdown of Lithuanian Jews and then added his own interpretation: Jews didn't work in heavy industry because they were weak bodied, lazy, and undisciplined. They preferred tailoring, shoemaking, and other crafts that allowed them to drop their work whenever an opportunity arose to make a quick profit from huckstering and brokering.[18]

Gotthard threw out Kalmanovitch's survey on Jewish political movements in Vilna and wrote instead a new section with his own conclusion: Jews were Bolsheviks and enemies of the Reich. "The entire population of Wilno is of the opinion that the Jewish masses welcomed the Bolsheviks with enthusiasm. In contrast, the Christian population shunned the Soviet-Russian army. . . . The Communist Youth League was made up entirely of Jews."[19]

Gotthard mastered the craft of transforming Jewish scholarship to Nazi *Judenforschung* and passed it on to his younger colleague Willy Schaefer. Schaefer rewrote the study on "Jewish Cemeteries and Tombstones in Vilna," transforming it into a virulently antisemitic work. "Hardly any creative elements can be detected in Jewish tombstone art,

and in Jewish visual art in general." Synagogue art and architecture
lacked any aesthetic value; they were "primitive," "repetitive," "impoverished," and "devoid of style." As for Jewish cemeteries, "when one stands
before them, one can see the petrified chaos of the Jewish racial soul."[20]

The combination of detailed research and antisemitic interpretation
impressed ERR officials in Berlin, who singled out the Vilna team for
praise. "The work provided by Dr. Gotthard is excellent. It is the most
extensive and reliable. Especially his studies on the ghetto."[21]

Toward the end of 1942, Kalmanovitch began working on topics
from classical Jewish literature and culture: the birth of Moses in the
Jewish tradition and the history of the Star of David. Schaefer, who
was a doctoral student of theology at Berlin University, even proposed
to his faculty in Berlin that he'd write a dissertation on the image of
Moses in rabbinic legend with the assistance of "Jew labor." But the
faculty rejected his proposal and noted that "a dissertation must be the
product of original research, and not be based on the work of others,
all the more so the work of Jews."[22]

The Germans came to realize they had a goldmine on their hands: a
contingent of scholars and researchers who could produce high-quality
papers on demand, about virtually anything, free of charge. By early
1943, the ERR team was using the research group to prepare studies on
non-Jewish topics as well: "Masonic Lodges in Lithuania" and "Portraits of Cultural Institutions in Vilna (museums, theaters, fortresses,
churches)." Kruk took on the latter assignment, because researching
Vilna's cultural institutions gave him a new pretext to make "excursions" outside the ghetto. He met with Catholic priests and museum
curators to collect information for his study, and some of them agreed
to provide hiding places for smuggled books and papers.[23]

For Kalmanovitch, working as a slave-labor scholar was deeply of-
fensive. It violated all his youthful hopes and ideals. As a young man, he
had studied in Germany, at the universities of Berlin and Königsberg,
to master the methods of critical scholarship. But now, the Germans
had betrayed and perverted the ideal of *Wissenschaft* (science) to advance
a barbaric racial theory and justify mass murder. Before, as a leader
of YIVO, he had believed that modern scholarship would elevate and
strengthen the Jewish people. But now, the Nazis exploited his very own
scholarship in order to justify the extermination of the Jews.

CHAPTER THIRTEEN

From the Ghetto to the Forest

IN MID-JULY 1943, the Germans learned of the existence of the ghetto's United Partisan Organization (FPO) from a captured Polish Communist who cracked under torture. They knew that Itzik Vitenberg was the organization's commander and demanded that Jacob Gens, the ghetto chief, hand him over. Vitenberg went into hiding, and Gens gave a speech to inmates warning that if he wasn't captured, the Germans would exterminate the entire ghetto. It was one life or twenty thousand lives. After a desperate manhunt by agitated ghetto inmates, Vitenberg surrendered himself to the Germans and died in Gestapo custody on July 17, apparently by suicide.

Shmerke Kaczerginski, the bard of the ghetto, memorialized those fateful events in a ballad, which concluded with a soliloquy by the martyred hero and a call to arms:

> Then spoke up our Itsik
> With words like lightning
> "I must heed this edict, that's clear.
> I'll not forfeit your lives,
> To the tyrants' cruel knives."
> To death he goes without fear.
>
> Again, somewhere the enemy
> Lurks like a beast;
> My Mauser is alert in my hand
> Now, my dear Mauser,
> Be you my liberator
> I'll follow your every command![1]

The song's bravado notwithstanding, the situation was bleak. Now that the Germans had discovered the FPO, they would either launch a military attack to crush the resistance organization or liquidate the Vilna ghetto altogether and deport its inhabitants. In either case, the ghetto's days were numbered.

On July 19, two days after Vitenberg's death, Albert Sporket instructed Herman Kruk to write a final report on his work for the Einsatzstab Reichsleiter Rosenberg (ERR), covering the entire one-and-a-half-year period of his slave labor. This was a sign to the members of the paper brigade that their employment, and probably their lives, was approaching the end.[2]

The premonition was confirmed by their work assignment. Ten members of the brigade were sent to Uniwersytecka Street, to "finish the job" with the Strashun Library. The group, which included Shmerke, Sutzkever, and Rachela Krinsky, performed their final "selection" of books and bid a sad farewell to the legendary library collection. Shmerke smuggled a few last items into the ghetto.[3]

Then the group returned to YIVO for a final cleanup. Sutzkever rummaged through the building one last time, looking for treasures that he could whisk off to the attic. He came across YIVO's leather-bound guest book, signed with dedications by prominent personalities: writers, scholars, politicians, and communal leaders. As he and his friends turned its pages, memories of prewar YIVO rushed through their minds: classes with Max Weinreich, research in the library, conversations with staff and graduate students.

The group decided to add their own dedications on the guest book's final page and to hide the album in the attic. Perhaps someone would find it after the war, when they would no longer be alive, and it would serve as a monument to their activities. Sutzkever inscribed the last stanza of his poem "A Prayer to the Miracle" ("A tfile tsum nes"), an insistent petition for rescue:

Death is rushing, riding on a bullet head,
To tear apart in me my brightest dream.
One more second—and I'll be lead,
If you don't catch up, be a rein.
Catch up! If not, you will regret.
A miracle must also have a moral sense.

Rachela Krinsky's inscription was much gloomier: "Morituri vos salutant" ("Those who are about to die greet you"). It was the phrase used by the ancient gladiators when they addressed the emperor before entering the arena.[4]

Back in the tense and nervous ghetto, Zelig Kalmanovitch called on inmates to keep their hope and faith. At a meeting of the Association of Ghetto Writers, the man they called "the prophet of the ghetto" took out a copy of a Hasidic book smuggled from the YIVO worksite and recited a passage to the assembled: "A person must not fall into sadness, because sadness is the nullification of existence." Kalmanovitch interpreted the passage as a Hasidic rebbe who held forth at a festive meal: "Sadness is the nullification of existence, and that is what the Germans want to achieve. They not only want to kill us; they want to nullify our existence *before* they kill us. To spite the Germans, and no matter how hard it may be, let us remember not to fall into sadness!"[5]

On August 1, 1943, the ghetto was sealed off. From that day on, no work brigades were allowed to leave for labor sites on the outside. The members of the paper brigade were officially dismissed from their positions.[6]

On August 6 and 19, Aktions by German forces and Estonian police, with the assistance of the Jewish ghetto police, rounded up thousands of inmates for deportation to labor camps in Estonia. Whether those captured were actually sent to labor camps or to their deaths was unknown at the time. Anxiety rose to a new peak, despite Gens's reassurances.

Sensing that the end was near, Kruk decided that the moment had come to bury the ghetto archive in metal canisters. The archive was a documentary kaleidoscope of ghetto life, with thousands of letters, memos, reports, and requests written or received by the departments of the ghetto administration. He also hid all three copies of his diary. He placed his greatest hopes in the copy he hid in the attic of 19 Small Stephanowa Street (Polish: Kwaszelna Street), outside the ghetto, and used his "ironclad pass" to take his secretary there, to show her the spot where it lay. Perhaps she would survive. He buried the second copy in metal canisters in Gershon Abramovitch's bunker on Shavel Street. And he gave his third copy to a Polish priest whom he had befriended while writing portraits of Vilna's churches for the ERR.[7] It seemed that Kruk's life endeavors—preserving books, smuggling printed matter and manuscripts, and recording the agony of Vilna's Jews—had reached their end.

Then, after everyone in the paper brigade was resigned to dying, either in deportation or in battle, there was a surprise return to the Yiddish Scientific Institute (YIVO). Sporket managed to extract his work brigade for a final week of cleanup at the end of August. The slave laborers made piles of the last books and newspapers destined for shipment to Berlin and Frankfurt. And Kalmanovitch wrote in one of his last diary entries, on August 23, "Our work is reaching its conclusion. Thousands of books are being dumped as trash, and the Jewish books will be liquidated. Whatever part we can rescue will be saved, with God's help. We will find it when we return as free human beings."[8]

During the lunch hour of their final day at YIVO, several members of the brigade met in Rachela Krinsky's room and began to write their last wills and testaments. Shmerke looked around as they put pen to paper and bid farewell to the world: At age thirty-five, he was the oldest person in the room.

A blond-haired twenty-year-old named Rokhele Trener, who had joined the work brigade just a few months earlier, asked Shmerke what she should write. "Well, you must have relatives somewhere." Trener listed her relatives: "I've got a sister and an aunt in New York, four cousins in the Land of Israel, two more cousins in South Africa, an uncle in Cuba. I've got a sister and a husband in the ghetto, and . . . I've got my parents and my two brothers in Ponar." As Trener began writing, something happened to Shmerke, the cheerful friend, the happy-go-lucky joker, and the ironclad optimist, that had never happened before: an unstoppable well of tears broke through his eyes.[9] Shmerke, the author of the upbeat youth hymn ("Everyone Who Wants to Can Be Young") realized that the youth of the Vilna ghetto would not live to see "a new free spring."

On the morning of September 1, Germans and Estonian police surrounded the ghetto and sent in forces to round up anyone who appeared on its streets. The Germans demanded that three thousand men and two thousand women appear for deportation to Estonian labor camps—a third of the total remaining population.

The FPO, now under the command of Aba Kovner, considered the Aktion the beginning of the ghetto's liquidation and ordered a general mobilization. The organization transferred its operational headquarters to 6 Strashun Street, to the building of the ghetto library. One of its largest arms caches was inside the library, and another was underneath the adjacent sports field. The fighters stationed themselves alongside the bookshelves, ready to make their last stand. If the Jerusalem of Lithuania would fall, it would fall amid books.

Other groups of FPO fighters were stationed up and down Strashun Street. The organization issued an appeal to the ghetto population to join in a general uprising, but relatively few heeded the call. The inmates did not believe that they faced imminent death. They had received reports and letters from deportees to Estonia that they were alive and working. The remaining ghetto population preferred deportation to labor camps, with a chance of survival, to a suicidal battle against the German military.[10]

Later that day, the Germans sent a military detachment into Strashun Street to seize people for Estonia. A group of FPO fighters at 12 Strashun Street opened fire, and the group's commander, Yechiel Sheinbaum, was killed in the brief firefight. Then, as evening drew near, the Germans decided not to advance in the direction of the library at number 6 Strashun Street and left the ghetto, to avoid engaging in street warfare in the dark of night.

Shmerke was among the FPO fighters stationed inside the library, awaiting the final battle. As he stood guard at his station, he read to his comrades-in-arms sections of Franz Werfel's novel *The Forty Days of Musa Dagh*, which told the story of the Armenian genocide, through the lens of an Armenian town that resisted Ottoman forces.[11] It was like reading a dark prophecy of their own experiences.

During the following days, the Germans rounded up three thousand inmates for Estonia, with the help of the ghetto police, but they did not return to Strashun Street. They wanted to avoid full-blown combat with the FPO for the time being. But the ghetto fighters were cornered. There were Germans on the adjacent streets, and the inmate population had not responded to their call for a general uprising. The underground feared that in the event of an armed conflict with the Germans, fellow Jews might actually fight *against* them.

The FPO command came to the bitter realization that there would be no Vilna ghetto uprising as there had been in Warsaw. The FPO had no choice but to retreat and regroup. On September 4, Kovner and the other members of the command decided to send groups of fighters out to the forests, where they would join up with the Soviet-led partisan movement.

Shmerke, Sutzkever, and his wife Freydke left the ghetto on September 12, 1943, as part of the second group of departing FPO fighters. They were eager to join the battle against the enemy, but as they prepared to leave, there was a tug of anxiety; they were leaving the books and cultural treasures behind, in a dozen hiding places: Theodor Herzl's diary, the record book of the Vilna Gaon's kloyz, a painting by Chagall, and letters and manuscripts by Tolstoy, Gorky, Sholem Aleichem, and Bialik. Would they ever see them again? Had all their work been in vain?

An FPO officer gave final orders to the group of twenty men and six women leaving for the forest: "Once you leave these walls, you are no longer ghetto fighters; you are partisans. Do not disgrace Vilna, and remain Jews!" The group tore their yellow Stars of David off their clothing and set out in the dead of night, in ones and twos, to a side gate of the ghetto on Jatkowa Street that was used only by the Gestapo and the ghetto administration. Somehow, the FPO had a copy of the key. Most members of the departing group were armed with pistols, but some had nothing but their bare hands. Sutzkever carried a six-shot Belgian revolver in his pocket, which he shared with Shmerke, who had purchased it from his friend Julian Jankauskas.[12]

The Germans liquidated the Vilna ghetto eleven days later, on September 23, 1943. They sent most of the inmates to labor camps in Estonia. Several thousand were sent to the Treblinka death camp. The elderly and infirm were finished off nearby, at Ponar.

Shmerke's and Sutzkever's group set out for the Narocz forest, some two hundred kilometers northeast of Vilna, where they hoped to join the Soviet partisan forces of Colonel Fyodor Markov, organized into the Voroshilov brigade. A few months earlier, Markov had sent emissaries into the ghetto to recruit FPO fighters for his brigade. But the FPO refused at the time to abandon the ghetto and its inhabitants. Now that the ghetto front was hopeless, the FPO fighters were fleeing to the forest and looking for Markov.

During the two-week journey to Narocz, they plodded through thick forests and muddy swamps, while avoiding towns and villages where someone might spot them and inform on them to the Germans. The group traveled only at night and rested during the daylight hours in the forest.

The most perilous part of the journey was crossing train tracks, bridges, and rivers—places that were patrolled by the Germans. The group lost one of its members early on; he was shot dead at the first set of train tracks.

After forty kilometers of walking, many in the group had torn their shoes and boots to shreds, and walked the rest of the journey barefoot, trying not to pay attention to their bloodied and bruised legs. They drank muddy swamp waters and ate whatever grew in the forests. When they were lucky, they stole a few vegetables from the edge of a field or garden.

When the group finally crossed the Wilia River, at a point 150 kilometers northeast of Vilna, they entered a new world, the "partisan zone," where Germans rarely dared appear and the local peasants were not hostile toward Jews. A pair of partisan horsemen rode up to them in broad daylight and took them to an encampment that housed Jews from the vicinity. As they rested and recovered, Shmerke fell in love with the fields and forests around him. After sixteen months in the suffocating, grimy ghetto, the forest was for him a fantasyland, a "green legend." He felt like a wild animal that had been let out of its cage and could now roam the jungle.[13]

But Shmerke's mood soon changed. He was shocked by the way he and the other Jewish new arrivals were treated by Colonel Markov and the command of the Voroshilov brigade. The partisan brass considered them an excess burden. Markov rejected most of the group members outright and told them to leave, to go wherever they wanted. Only a few young men who came with their own arms and who were sized up as being fit for combat were taken in as fighters. Shmerke, Sutzkever, and many others were neither rejected nor allowed to fight. Instead, they were assigned to a support unit in the rear. Their dream of engaging the enemy in combat was quickly stamped out.

Major General Klimov, who headed the brigade's Communist Party organization, complained to Shmerke: "If you didn't have arms, why did you come here?" Shmerke couldn't restrain his anger and shouted back: "Comrade Klimov! Dozens of Ukrainians who fought with the Germans against the Soviet Union recently deserted their units and arrived in the forest. They too came to you without arms, but they were inducted into fighting units!" Klimov barked and turned away.[14] He had no answer for the naked truth: former Nazi collaborators were welcomed into the brigade, but former ghetto fighters were not.

One of Markov's deputies registered those Jews who were inducted and announced that they should donate their silver watches and leather coats to the Fund for Defense of the Fatherland. The newcomers were surprised by the request but wanted to make a good impression on their new commanders. So they reluctantly parted with their valuables. The next day, they saw the watches and coats being worn by Markov's deputy, the deputy's wife, and other partisan officers. It was a humiliating shakedown.

In October, the Voroshilov brigade received intelligence information that the forest was encircled by thousands of German troops, who planned to clear it of partisans in an extended operation. The brigade's detachments scattered in different directions. Shmerke and Sutzkever's support unit was left without a commander and without guidance. In the midst of the confusion, Shmerke gave Sutzkever his prize possession —his revolver. "If only one of us can save his life, it should be you, Abrasha. You are the greater poet; you'll be of greater service to the Jewish people."[15]

They set out for an island in the depths of the forest that was surrounded by marshlands. It was nicknamed "America," since it was far away and across the water. The unit hoped that the Germans wouldn't discover America.

Shmerke, Sutzkever, and his wife Freydke hid together in the overgrown swampy waters. They heard the sounds of approaching gunfire and knew that the Germans were nearing. At that moment, the three of them sealed a death pact: if Germans troops surrounded them, they would use the last bullets in their revolver to kill themselves. After some argument back and forth, it was agreed that Sutzkever would shoot Freydke first, Shmerke second, and himself last.[16]

The Germans discovered "America," but fortunately they didn't sweep through it thoroughly. Instead, they engaged in sporadic shooting across the island, in the hopes of hitting partisans that were hiding there. When the Germans left, they set fire to the dry lands on the other side of the island. Shmerke, Sutzkever, and Freydke stayed in "America" for a few more days, eating the bark of trees for nourishment.

Once the German assault on the Narocz forest was finally over, its consequences became painfully evident. Hundreds of partisan fighters had been killed, including Joseph Glazman, a member of the FPO command, and Mikhal Kovner, Aba Kovner's brother and a member of the paper brigade. Mikhal was the one who found the munitions manuals among the Soviet books. The Voroshilov brigade had survived, but its capacity was serious compromised.

Shmerke and Sutzkever's support unit reestablished itself on a base deep in the forest. Part of their job was to expropriate food from peasants at gunpoint, demanding flour, grits, peas, salt, pork, and other items. Such raids, called "economic operations," were the unpleasant dirty work necessary to feed the brigade. Back at the base, the unit's members cooked, baked, and built temporary structures. The unit also had tailors, shoemakers, and tanners. Shmerke called it a shtetl in the forest. They spent their evenings around the campfire, with Shmerke leading communal singing and Sutzkever reciting his latest poems.[17]

In December, Colonel Markov summoned the two partisan poets to his hut at brigade headquarters and gave them a new assignment: they were to write the history of the Voroshilov brigade. "It would be a great loss for the partisan movement if all the achievements of our brigade were lost to history. All you need to do is watch, listen, and write." Markov wanted his brigade's exploits recorded for posterity, and he happened to have two writers under his command who were perfectly suited for this task. Since they weren't top fighters and they weren't tailors, why not make them historians?

Shmerke and Sutzkever were transferred to brigade headquarters, where they were given ideal living and working conditions. They had a private earthen hut of their own, with a horse, wagon, and coachman at their disposal to travel from one partisan base to another. They had a translator, who rendered their Yiddish texts into Russian, and an artist, who served as their surrogate photographer.[18] They met hundreds of fighters—Jewish, Russian, Lithuanian, and Belorussian—and heard their stories over mugs of coffee and vodka. Shmerke did most of the history writing, and both of them wrote poetry on the side.

Shmerke took a special interest in the stories of Jewish fighters, who were living refutations of the canard that Jews were cowards. Twenty-one-year-old Boris blew up an approaching German train and almost killed himself in the process. Avner of Gluboka single-handedly captured a group of Red Army deserters and persuaded them to go over to the partisan side. A mother and son team, Sarah (age forty) and Grisha (age twenty), fought side by side in the same partisan brigade to avenge her husband's murder—until Sarah fell.[19]

The travel was exhilarating, and the stories were inspiring. There, in the depths of the Narocz forest, while living in his earthen hut, Shmerke celebrated the exploits of Jewish partisans in a poem he set to a Soviet melody:

From the ghetto prison walls
To the forest free,
I've thrown the chains off of my hands,
And carry a gun on me.
My new friend caresses me
When I'm on a mission.
My gun and I have over time
Grown in unison.

We are few in number,
But we're as bold as millions.
We can blow up hills and dales,
Bridges and echelons.
The Fascist shakes in his boots,
Doesn't know what hit him.
We come storming from under the ground,
Jewish partisans.

The word "revenge" means a lot
When in blood it's written,
For the sake of the new dawn,
We are out here fighting.
No, we'll never be the last of the Mohicans,
The sunshine brightens up the dark,
—The Jewish partisan.[20]

CHAPTER FOURTEEN

Death in Estonia

ELIG KALMANOVITCH and Herman Kruk decided not to flee to the forest. The sixty-two-year-old Kalmanovitch didn't have the energy for life on the run, after nearly two years of physical and emotional depletion in the ghetto. Instead, he decided to join a transport to Estonia, voluntarily, after ghetto chief Jacob Gens gave him personal assurances that the living conditions there were good. Kruk, the librarian, was younger, forty-five, in better shape, and could have weathered life in the forest, but he decided to stay in the Vilna ghetto and chronicle its history until the very end. Ever a man of principle, he felt it would be treasonous to abandon the twelve thousand remaining inmates to save his own skin. He was ready for whatever fate would bring.[1]

Kalmanovitch "settled" in a camp in Narva, in the far northeastern corner of Estonia, after stops in Vaivara and Ereda. Gens had lied to him. Food rations were a starvation diet — coffee and bread in the morning, a watery soup for lunch, and nothing for dinner. Kalmanovitch worked loading and lugging sacks for the camp's textile factories, located ten kilometers away from the barracks.

But even under the debilitating conditions of the Narva camp, he continued to serve as a prophet of consolation. He participated in nighttime literary-artistic programs in the men's block, giving lectures and talks. At a Chanukah evening attended by three hundred inmates, he gave a half-hour talk on the holiday, offering words of encouragement that the light of Judaism would continue to shine on.[2]

While in Narva, Kalmanovitch reconciled with his former archenemy, Moshe Lerer, a hard-core Communist who had worked in YIVO's archives. When the Soviets marched into Vilna in June 1940, Lerer seized control of the institute, deposing Kalmanovitch and purging the staff of non-Communists. He removed all "anti-Soviet literature" from the YIVO library and covered the building's walls with slogans glorifying Stalin. For the next three years, Kalmanovitch didn't forgive Lerer for the personal humiliation and, even more so, for the political defilement of YIVO. (Kalmanovitch was a lifelong anti-Communist and opposed subordinating scholarship to politics.) Even in the ghetto, the two men did not speak to each other. They worked in nearby rooms in the ghetto library—Kalmanovitch as deputy director, and Lerer as curator of the ghetto archive and museum—but did not exchange words. At work, Lerer reported to Kruk.[3]

But in Narva, they became close friends, sleeping in the same plank bed and spending long nights in conversation.[4] When Lerer fell ill with dysentery, Kalmanovitch cared for him and shared his bread ration with him. When Lerer died, Kalmanovitch, the believer, recited kaddish, the Jewish prayer for the dead, in memory of his friend, the Communist.

Kalmanovitch's own body gave way to illness just a few weeks later. Inmates bribed a camp official to assign him to easier work that didn't require him to go outdoors in the bitter cold—cleaning the toilets in the barracks. During the weeks that he performed this work, he is reported to have said to his blockmates: "I am happy that I have the privilege of cleaning the excrement of these holy Jews."[5]

Some say that Kalmanovitch died quietly in his plank bed. Others report that a German medical review team ordered him killed. According to the latter account, his final words, as he was dragged away, were the ones he had once said to his paper-brigade colleagues on the street: "I laugh at you. I have a son in the Land of Israel." This time, it was a taunt. His body, like that of others who died at Narva, was burnt in the camp's large basement ovens, which served as a crematorium.

A fellow inmate reported that Kalmanovitch had one prized possession in the Narva camp: a tiny Bible that he managed to hide from the Germans, either buried in the barracks or secreted on his body. How tragically fitting that one of the leaders of the paper brigade perished carrying a smuggled book on his body. His death was like that of the second-century martyr Rabbi Chaninah Ben Tardion, who was burnt alive by the Romans holding a Torah scroll.[6]

Kalmanovitch didn't live to see the fulfillment of the words in the final entry of his ghetto diary: "We will find the rescued books when we return as free human beings."

———————

Herman Kruk remained in the ghetto until the very end. He outlived Gens, who was executed by the Germans on September 14, 1943, ostensibly for maintaining contact with the FPO underground. A few days after Gens's execution, the Germans stopped sending their starvation-diet food rations into the ghetto.

At 5:00 a.m. on September 23, SS Oberscharführer Bruno Kittel entered the ghetto's territory with a retinue of soldiers and spoke from the balcony of the Judenrat offices reading the order: the Vilna ghetto was hereby liquidated. All its inhabitants were being "evacuated" to labor camps in northern Lithuania and Estonia. The inmates were to assemble at the ghetto gate on Rudnicki Street at 2:00 p.m. for deportation. They should bring along a bucket, pots, and other kitchen utensils, because such items would not be distributed at their destination. Inmates were allowed to take as many belongings as they could carry by hand.

Many of the famished and weakened inmates assumed that it was all a ruse and that they were headed to Ponar. Kittel tried to ease their fears and tensions, because desperate people might take desperate measures—like rebelling.

Kittel also stressed that there was no point in hiding. After the liquidation, the Germans would close down the water and electricity in the area of the ghetto and detonate its houses. Whoever hid would die of thirst or be crushed by the collapsing buildings. Whoever came out of their hiding place would be shot on the spot.[7]

At 2:00 p.m., several hundred Lithuanian and Ukrainian auxiliary police invaded the ghetto and stationed themselves on all of its streets. Thousands of inmates proceeded quietly to the gate, where Kittel, Martin Weiss, and other SS officials stood, and counted heads as they left. The crowding and hysteria at the gate were unbearable. Parents lost their children; children, their parents. After leaving the ghetto, the exhausted and frightened throng walked down the long winding Subocz Street, which was lined with soldiers in full battle gear—helmets, hand grenades, loaded rifles, and machine guns. Barking military dogs kept watch for anyone who tried to escape. Many weakened inmates dropped their bundles in the middle of the street, making movement more difficult.

The Germans conducted their first "selection," separating the men from the women, children, and elderly. They sent the men ahead, to a holding pen in a swampy valley off of 20 Subocz Street, while the others were stopped from moving forward and were forced into a large church courtyard. Cries and wails filled the street as couples and families bid farewell for the last time.

The sun set, and it was nighttime. The Germans shone portable strobe lights onto the men's valley, which they surrounded with barbwire, and onto the women-and-children courtyard, which they surrounded with soldiers. The inmates were blinded by the lights. Then the Germans began playing jazz music through loudspeakers, for their own nighttime listening enjoyment. The detained women, children, and elderly either sat or lay on the ground of the churchyard. They stayed there overnight, without any rations of food or water — congestion, filth, crying children, groans by the elderly, hunger, and thirst. Some inmates expired right there, while under street arrest.

The Germans lined up the men in the valley in rows for a second selection. This time an ss officer walked through the rows, pointing his finger at those inmates who were too old, too young, or weak looking and ordered them removed from the crowd. The weaker men started to hide behind able-bodied ones, but the officer was thorough. In the end, he chose one hundred inmates, who were sent off in vehicles to Ponar for execution. A similar selection took place among the women.

Several members of the paper brigade perished in those selections. One of them, the artist Uma Olkenicka, went to Treblinka of her own free will because she wasn't willing to abandon her elderly mother.

The crowd of men was then exposed to a spectacle. The Germans built four gallows in the valley holding pen, with ladders leading up to platforms and nooses. An ss officer stepped forward and announced, "We will now execute people who resisted us and tried to flee to the partisans. This is to show you all what should be expected if you resist."

They brought forward four captured FPO fighters, who were caught while leaving the ghetto. As a thirty-year-old woman named Asya Big walked up to the gallows, she called out to the crowd, "Death to the German murderers! Long live the FPO avengers of the blood of the

Jewish p——!" Before she could finish the sentence, the noose was around her neck, and the ladder was removed. Her body shook on the gallows and fell limp within a minute.[8]

A few members of the paper brigade chose to go into hiding, rather than march to the ghetto gate. Sixty-two-year-old Chaikl Lunski, the legendary librarian of the Strashun Library, joined a group of people who hid in the cellar of 5 Strashun Street. The Germans discovered their hiding place on October 4, eleven days after the ghetto's liquidation, and sent everyone to the Gestapo prison on Mickewicz Street. Lunski and the others spent the night in cell number 16, "the death cell." They all wrote their names on the wall, as their surrogate tombstone. Many, including Lunski, added an inscription: "We are going to Ponar. Avenge our blood!" Chaikl Lunski was executed, quietly, at Ponar on October 6.[9]

Herman Kruk participated in the march out of the ghetto down Subocz Street and survived both "selections." He spent most of the next year in a camp called Klooga, near Estonia's northern coast. Klooga became one of the German's main industrial complexes in the East, producing reinforced concrete and lumber for the military. Kruk called it "the metropolis of Jewish camps."

The contrast between Klooga and the Vilna ghetto was like between night and day. Beatings and whippings were ubiquitous, as were other forms of physical abuse. Inmates were forced to stand at attention for hours in the bitter cold for roll call, at the beginning and end of the workday. They were subjected to punitive gymnastics, during which those who fainted or collapsed were taken away and shot.[10]

Kruk worked mainly at paving roads and constructing barracks. He was also active in the camp underground, an organization called the PG (Partisan Group). This organization functioned first and foremost as an aid committee, which secretly provided food and medicine to the sickest and neediest. The PG also organized clandestine cultural events, including Kruk's own political talks on Sundays. And it assembled a hidden collection of pistols, for use in an envisioned uprising if the end—either by massacre or by liberation—seemed imminent.

For a full year after his deportation, Kruk continued to write: diary entries, stories of fellow inmates, and vignettes of camp life. Everything went into tiny notebooks that he stole from a storage room and kept hidden in his barracks. When one notebook filled up, he started another one. His handwriting verged on the illegible. "I write on my knees, in constant fear of an unwelcome guest, either in the tailors' workshop or while mixing cement and pouring concrete, or at night on my hard night chair."[11] Despite Kruk's physical and psychological deterioration, he never stopped writing. Camp doctors urged him to rest during the evenings after work, but Kruk replied that writing was more valuable to him than life itself. His notes, he said, would outlive Hitler and would be a treasure for future generations.[12]

The biggest problem in Klooga was hunger. Scores of inmates died daily from starvation. Kruk wrote a powerful essay on the new type of hunger he encountered in the camp. "Thirty-three decagrams of bread is neither enough to live on nor enough to die on. . . . The majority, who cannot help themselves, eventually starve and expire. . . . The more energetic ones try to get potato peels. They sort them out and take the thicker ones. Consumers often get stomach cramps from them. But the stomachache passes and hunger returns. So they chase after a turnip, moldy pieces of bread, and stuff their bellies with poison, with aches, just to drive out the hunger, the worm that gnaws and gnaws and won't stop."[13]

When inmates expired, the Germans piled the bodies on top of wooden logs, poured them with gasoline, and set them on fire. The officer who supervised the burning was dressed in his best uniform. In the words of one surviving inmate, he was like a pagan priest bringing an offering to his deity.

Kruk knew that the Red Army was near. On July 14, 1944, he recorded in his notebook that Vilna had been liberated. "Vilna is liberated and here we groan under the yoke, crying over our lot. The Vilna FPO is surely now marching victoriously through the alleys of the ghetto, searching and looking. I hope they also try to save my materials."[14]

Kruk and five hundred other inmates were suddenly transferred on August 22, 1944, to a camp called Lagedi, where conditions were much worse than Klooga: They lived in low-lying wooden shacks built on the bare ground and ate one "meal" a day: a watery flour soup. There were no beds, blankets, or bathrooms. It was a doggish existence. The only ray of hope was the proximity of the war front. One could hear shooting from aircraft and bombs dropping nearby. Tartu, Estonia's second city, had been liberated by the Red Army.

Because the transfer of the inmates from Klooga to Lagedi was a surprise operation, Kruk didn't have the time to take along his hidden notebooks. They were lost, or so he assumed.

Lagedi was the final stop for Kruk and the other inmates. They were murdered on September 18, 1944—on Rosh Hashanah, the Jewish New Year.

The Germans carried out the slaughter with shrewd cynicism. A top ss officer came to the camp, reprimanded the director for the inmates' deplorable living conditions, and ordered him, within earshot of the inmates, to transfer them to a better location. Trucks drove up and delivered a meal of bread, margarine, jam, and sugar. This was all a deception, to lead them to believe they were indeed being transferred to a better location and life would improve.

The trucks were loaded up with fifty inmates and left at half-hour intervals to a prepared execution site. This was done to prevent the inmates from knowing what was going on—until it was too late.

The method of execution was a variation of the one used at Klooga. The Germans tied together groups of ten to twelve people, ordered them to walk onto a log platform, and shot them in the back of the head. Then, a second platform was placed on top of the bodies, and another group of inmates walked onto it and was shot. After the entire fifty-inmate truckload was executed, the Germans doused the platforms and corpses with gasoline, and set them on fire. The Lagedi execution lasted from 11:00 a.m. until the evening.

The Red Army arrived the next day, September 19, and discovered hundreds of charred bodies—and two survivors.

On the day before Kruk's execution, a secret courier brought him a small package with his notebooks from Klooga. Kruk was overcome with joy. He decided to bury his writings and did so in the presence of six witnesses in the hope that at least one of them would survive and retrieve them. One of them did.[15]

As a cover note for posterity, he included a prose poem he had written in Klooga, which opened with the following lines:

Neighbors in Camp Klooga often ask me
Why do you write in such hard times?—
Why and for whom? . . .

I know I am condemned and awaiting my turn.
Although deep inside me burrows a hope for a miracle.
Drunk on the pen trembling on my hand,
I record everything for future generations.
A day will come when someone will find
The leaves of horror I write and record.[16]

CHAPTER FIFTEEN

Miracle from Moscow

ABRAHAM SUTZKEVER'S personal miracle—the one he had summoned in his inscription inside YIVO's guest book—came in March 1944. Fyodor Markov received a cable from Moscow that a Soviet military airplane would be sent to collect the poet Sutzkever and his wife. The partisan commander arranged for armed guards and a horse-drawn sled to take them to a partisan airstrip. It took two attempts to perform the private airlift—the first plane was downed by German artillery, but the second plane retrieved its human cargo, and the next day Abrasha and Freydke Sutzkever were in Moscow, sitting in the general headquarters of the Lithuanian Partisan Division.[1]

The extraordinary private airlift was arranged by Justas Paleckis, the titular head of the Lithuanian Soviet government in exile. Paleckis was a well-known poet before he became president and befriended Sutzkever at a meeting of Lithuanian and Yiddish writers in early 1940. An opponent of the authoritarian Lithuanian regime of Antanas Smetona, he reportedly picked up Yiddish in prison, where he served time for antistate activity alongside Jewish inmates.

Paleckis joined the Communist Party in June 1940, when Stalin incorporated Lithuania into the Soviet Union. A few months later he was appointed president, as a gesture by the new rulers to reach out to the Lithuanian intelligentsia. The position of president was largely symbolic.[2]

Paleckis evacuated to Moscow at the time of the German invasion, in June 1941. When he received a letter from a partisan field commander informing him that the poet Sutzkever was alive and writing in the Narocz forest, the head of state intervened with the Soviet military command. The next thing, Sutzkever was on that plane.[3]

The abrupt change in Sutzkever's life was almost surreal. For two years, he and his wife Freydke had been animals of prey in the ghetto, and for most of the last six months they had slept outdoors or in earthen huts. Now, after one quick plane ride, they lived in the luxurious "Moscow" hotel, wore fresh changes of clothing, and walked freely down the streets of a modern city. They had rejoined human civilization after a nearly three-year absence.

Sutzkever's arrival in Moscow was a sensation in literary circles. At age thirty-one, he was already recognized as one of the greatest Yiddish poets of his time. While still incarcerated in the Vilna ghetto, he had sent a few of his poems by partisan courier to Moscow, where they were read at a meeting of writers with bated breath and amazement. A few days after his miraculous airlift, the Yiddish section of the Union of Soviet Writers held a reception in his honor in the Moscow Writers' House. The poet Peretz Markish, a laureate of the Stalin Prize for Literature, chaired the program, and introduced Sutzkever: "People used to point at Dante: 'This man was in hell!' But Dante's hell is like a paradise compared to the inferno from which this poet just rescued himself."[4]

Sutzkever's arrival was an event not just for writers. He was the very first ghetto inmate to reach the Soviet capital and to report firsthand on the German extermination of the Jews. He was invited to speak at a large anti-Nazi rally, held on April 2 in the Pillar Hall of the House of Trade Unions, just across from the Kremlin. The event, sponsored by an organization called the Jewish Anti-Fascist Committee, attracted more than three thousand people who listened to speeches by the most prominent Jews in the Soviet Union—military heroes, writers, the chief rabbi of Moscow, and Sutzkever. He was the only speaker who had actually survived a ghetto.

In brief staccato paragraphs, Sutzkever portrayed the mass executions, the ghetto's spiritual and armed resistance, and the escape of the FPO to the forests. He concluded, "Let the entire world know that in the forests of Lithuania and Belorussia, hundreds of Jewish partisans are fighting. They are proud and courageous avengers of the spilt blood of their brethren. On behalf of those Jewish partisans, and on behalf of the surviving remnant of Vilna's Jews, who are in forests and caves, I call upon you, fellow Jews everywhere, to fight and take revenge."

Sutzkever's public appeal for Jewish solidarity in fighting the Germans was not unusual in Moscow in 1944. Stalin had relaxed the bans on nationalism and religion, in order to exploit such sentiments for the war effort. The Jewish Anti-Fascist Committee was a brainchild of the Soviet state to unite Soviet and foreign Jews in the struggle against Nazi Germany. It was chaired by the famed Yiddish actor Solomon Mikhoels, director of the Moscow State Yiddish Theater.

Sutzkever's speech was unusual not for what it said but for what it omitted. He was the only speaker that did not invoke the name of Joseph Stalin. Even the Moscow rabbi fawned over the Great Leader and proclaimed that "in the land of Stalin's constitution, the brotherly friendship between peoples is deeply rooted." The rabbi concluded that "the heroic Red Army, under the leadership of the commander-in-chief Marshal Stalin is ceaselessly beating the enemy." Sutzkever refrained from such paeans. As he later put it, the flames of the ghetto had burnt out of him the fear for any ruler. He had already been killed so many times that he could speak freely.[5]

In Moscow, Sutzkever's fame rose meteorically. On April 15, the *New York Times* ran an article about him: "Poet-Partisan from Vilna Ghetto Says Nazis Slew 77,000 of 80,000." And on April 27, *Pravda* published a half-page portrait of him penned by Ilya Ehrenburg, the most prominent wartime writer in the USSR. Ehrenburg, who fled from his Jewish roots before the war, now openly embraced them. He was deeply moved by his encounter with a Jewish poet, ghetto inmate, and partisan.

The article, called "Triumph of a Human Being" opened by introducing Sutzkever to the readers of *Pravda* as the man who had rescued cultural treasures from destruction. "He brought with him letters by Maxim Gorky and Romain Rolland—letters that he rescued from the Germans. He rescued a diary by a servant of Peter the Great, drawings by Repin, a painting by Levitan, a letter by Leo Tolstoy, and many other extremely valuable Russian cultural relics."

The article recounted the Jews' suffering and heroism in the Vilna ghetto, as told by Sutzkever. It was one of very few times during the war that *Pravda* offered a detailed description of the Holocaust. But Ehrenburg closed by circling back to Sutzkever's rescue of cultural treasures and by bringing together his different personae into a single image: "He held in his arm a machine gun, in his head—lines of poetry, and in his heart—letters by Gorky. Here they are, pages with faded ink. I recognize the well-known handwriting. Gorky wrote about life, about the future of Russia, about the power of a human being. . . . The rebel of the Vilna ghetto, poet and soldier, saved his letters, as a banner of humanity and culture."[6]

Ehrenburg presented Sutzkever not just as a fighter, not just as a poet, but first and foremost as a savior of culture.

Jews throughout the Soviet Union read the article with pride. Dozens of people wrote letters to Sutzkever to express their admiration—Red Army soldiers, refugees in Central Asia, and intellectuals. After its publication, Sutzkever became a celebrity and was invited to parties and gatherings by Russian literati. He had a private meeting with Russia's greatest poet, Boris Pasternak, where the two writers recited their works to each other. Pasternak—who did not consider himself Jewish—still remembered some Yiddish from his childhood.[7]

While Sutzkever basked in the recognition and fame, Shmerke Kaczerginski continued to tough it out in the forest, as the lone historian of the Voroshilov brigade. The more he talked to Jewish fighters, the more he reached the bitter conclusion that the Soviet partisan movement was infested with antisemitism. He wrote in his diary, "If a non-Jewish partisan committed a transgression, he was punished with a few days of arrest, while a Jewish partisan would be shot for the same act. Jewish fighters often had to be careful, while out on combat operations, not to be shot in the back by one of their own. Jews [who had escaped from ghettos] were often shot dead on charges of being . . . German spies."[8]

Shmerke asked himself, was it conceivable that the Soviet government, the Communist Party, the general staff of the partisan movement, didn't know how Jews and other ethnic minorities were being treated in the forests? No, it was not. They either tolerated it, supported it, or ordered it. These were Shmerke's first gnawing doubts about the Soviet system.

On June 2, 1944, Shmerke transferred out of the Voroshilov brigade to the Lithuanian "Vilnius" brigade, where half of the fighters were Jewish. (The other half was mixed—Lithuanian, Polish, Belorussian, and Russian.) The next six weeks were the happiest ones in Shmerke's career as a partisan. He served in a sabotage unit that blew up trains, railway tracks, and storage facilities, and downed telephone lines. He passed through towns and villages in Belorussia that he had visited two and a half years earlier, disguised as a Polish deaf-mute. Now he was a proud Jewish partisan, armed and fighting.[9]

Shmerke was in a village near Polotsk, Belorussia, on June 7, 1944, when he learned that the Americans and British had landed in Normandy. He and his unit danced with joy. Victory was near.[10] A few weeks later, he and his unit fought to liberate Svientsian (Lithuanian: Švenčonys), a city forty-two miles northeast of Vilna. Once there, he appealed to his commanding officer for permission to leave in the direction of Vilna, to participate in its liberation: "I can't bear it any more; I must go." The commander consented and gave him a vehicle and a group of partisans to accompany him.

The night before his departure, Shmerke tossed and turned, unable to sleep, and wrote in his diary, "Vilna, my dear city, what do you look like now? Did the wild beasts destroy *you* as they destroyed Svientsian? Just thinking of such a possibility makes me dizzy and ill. Whom will I find there? Will I find the amazing cultural treasures that we secretly stole from the Germans and buried?"[11]

The literary group Young Vilna. Sitting in the center: Shmerke Kaczerginski; to his right: Abraham Sutzkever. Shmerke was the group's manager, editor, and life of the party. Sutzkever was all poet. Photograph from YIVO Institute for Jewish Research.

The Strashun Library, Vilna's Jewish communal library, and behind it, the Great Synagogue. Together, the two buildings formed the intellectual and spiritual heart of Jewish Vilna. Drawing by artist Zigmund Czajkowski, 1944. Photograph from Vilna Gaon State Jewish Museum, Vilnius.

The reading room of the Strashun Library. Standing on the right is assistant librarian Isaac Strashun, grandson of its founder Matityahu Strashun. Photograph from YIVO Institute for Jewish Research.

The building of the Yiddish Scientific Institute, YIVO, at 18 Wiwulskiego Street. YIVO was the national academy and national library of Yiddish-speaking Jewry worldwide. The sign welcomes delegates and guests to its 1935 conference. Photograph from YIVO Institute for Jewish Research.

(*Left*) Max Weinreich, director of yivo in Vilna and, from 1940, in New York. He combined the formality and rigor of a German professor with the public engagement of a socialist. Weinreich was nearly blind in his right eye, due to an antisemitic attack before the war. Photograph from yivo Institute for Jewish Research.

(*Right*) Herman Kruk, director of the Vilna ghetto library and head of the "paper brigade." A refined gentleman, even in the ghetto he polished his shoes and filed his fingernails. Photograph from yivo Institute for Jewish Research.

Zelig Kalmanovitch, codirector of yivo before the war and deputy head of the "paper brigade." Dubbed "the prophet of the Vilna ghetto," he reassured his coworkers: "Whatever they remove will be found at the end of the war and taken from them." Photograph from yivo Institute for Jewish Research.

The gate to the Vilna ghetto with German and Lithuanian guards. Smuggling foodstuffs or books into the ghetto could cost an inmate his or her life. Genrikh Agranovskii and Irina Guzenberg, *Vilnius: Po sledam litovskogo yerusalima.*

Dr. Johannes Pohl, chief Judaica expert for the Einsatzstab Reichsleiter Rosenberg (ERR), Nazi Germany's agency for looting cultural treasures. A former Catholic priest, Pohl studied Hebrew and Bible in Jerusalem between 1932 and 1934. After resigning from the priesthood, he embraced Nazism and pursued a career as a Hebraica librarian, antisemitic author, and looter of Jewish books. Photograph from Dr. Paul Wolff & Tritschler, Historisches Bildarchiv.

A Jewish slave laborer sorting books in the YIVO building, which the Einsatzstab Reichsleiter Rosenberg converted into its main worksite in Vilna. According to the quota set by the Germans, 30 percent of the materials were sent to Germany and the rest were sent to paper mills for destruction. Photograph from YIVO Institute for Jewish Research.

The transport of books, manuscripts, and documents at the Vilna train station. Non-Jewish materials were sent from Soviet Smolensk and Vitebsk to Vilna for processing. Leyzer Ran, *Yerushalayim de-lite ilustrirt un dokumentirt.*

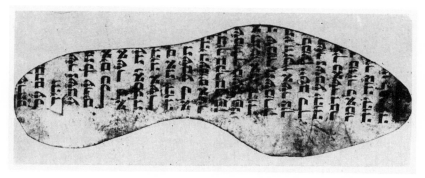

A piece of a Torah scroll from Vilna, made into a boot insert. The Germans sold three hundred Torah scrolls to a local leather factory, which used them to repair the soles of German army boots. Leyzer Ran, *Ash fun yerushalayim de-lite.*

Shmerke Kaczerginski and Abraham Sutzkever on the porch of their apartment in the Vilna ghetto, July 20, 1943. The poets led the smuggling operation from the Einsatzstab Reichsleiter Rosenberg (ERR) worksite. "Ghetto inmates looked at us as if we were lunatics. They were smuggling foodstuffs into the ghetto, in their clothes and boots. We were smuggling books, pieces of paper, occasionally a Torah scroll or mezuzahs." Photograph from National Library of Israel.

Shmerke, Sutzkever, and their "paper brigade" coworker Rachela Krinsky, in the Vilna ghetto, July 20, 1943. A high school history teacher and lover of literature, Rachela read poetry during the lunch hour, when the Germans were out. She later recalled, "Thanks to the poetry, we had many hours of forgetfulness and consolation." Photograph from National Library of Israel.

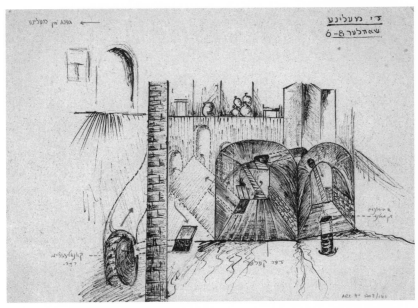

Diagram of bunker at 6–8 Shavel Street, sixty feet underground in the Vilna ghetto. It stored books smuggled by the "paper brigade" and arms acquired by the ghetto's United Partisan Organization (FPO). Red arrows mark the entrance path via the sewage system. Photograph from National Library of Israel.

Shmerke Kaczerginski and Abraham
Sutzkever as partisans. They left the
Vilna ghetto for the forest just two weeks
before the ghetto's liquidation, when all
remaining inmates were deported to
labor and death camps. Kaczerginski
photo: *Shmerke kaczerginski ondenk-bukh*.
Sutzkever photo: Leyzer Ran, *Yerushalayim de-lite ilustrirt un dokumentirt*.

Abraham Sutzkever (left) and Gershon Abramovitch (right) with a wagon of recovered newspapers and artwork, including a bust of Leo Tolstoy, July 1944. Photograph from YIVO Institute for Jewish Research.

Shmerke Kaczerginski among rescued sculptures, paintings, and newspapers, 1944. Shmerke Kaczerginski, *Khurbn vilne.*

The Jewish Museum, in Soviet Vilnius. It was founded by Shmerke and Sutzkever on July 26, 1944, under the auspices of the Commissariat of Education of the Lithuanian Soviet Socialist Republic.

The courtyard of the Jewish Museum, 6 Strashun Street. The museum was located in buildings that had served as the ghetto library and ghetto prison. The courtyard had been the ghetto sports field. The museum staff used the former prison cells as their offices, since they were the only rooms in usable condition. Photograph from Ghetto Fighters' House, Israel.

Museum volunteers unload potato sacks stuffed with documents that were retrieved from the Shavel Street bunker. Shmerke wrote in his diary, "The Polish inhabitants are constantly calling in policemen and other officials. They think we are digging for gold." Leyzer Ran, *Ash fun yerushalayim de-lite*.

Jewish books and papers in the yard of the Vilnius Trash Administration, 1944. The Germans didn't manage to send tons of materials to the paper mills before they retreated from the city. Shmerke Kaczerginski, *Khurbn vilne.*

Sutzkever beside the ruins of the YIVO building during his last visit to Vilna, April 1946. He made arrangements with the Zionist underground to smuggle suitcases full of documents across the border to Poland. Photograph from YIVO Institute for Jewish Research.

Rachela Krinsky with her daughter Sarah in Poland, late 1945. At the time of the Jews' forced resettlement in the ghetto, Rachela arranged with her nanny Wikcia Rodziewicz to hold on to the twenty-two-month-old child and raise her as a Polish girl. Mother and daughter reunited after four years of separation. Courtesy of Alexandra Wall.

From left: Shmerke Kaczerginski, Abraham Sutzkever, Yitzhak Zuckerman (leader of the Warsaw ghetto uprising), and Chaim Grade (a surviving member of Young Vilna), in Warsaw, November 1946, on the eve of the writers' departure for Paris. When Shmerke and Sutzkever left Poland, they needed to smuggle the books and papers across yet another Communist-controlled border. Photograph from National Library of Israel.

The Offenbach Archival Depot, in the American zone of occupied Germany. It held three million Nazi-looted books, half of them Judaica. The US government returned most to their country of origin and redistributed the rest. It considered sending YIVO's books back to Soviet Lithuania or Poland. Photograph from Yad Vashem, Israel.

Leaders of the New York–based YIVO examine the crates of books and documents from Vilna that were returned to the institute by the US government. The photo was taken in the New Jersey warehouse of the Manischewitz Matzo Company, which initially stored the materials. Photograph from YIVO Institute for Jewish Research.

Antanas Ulpis, standing second from left, with a group of staff members at the Book Chamber of the Lithuanian Soviet Socialist Republic. During the years of Stalin's antisemitic campaigns, Ulpis, the director, hid thousands of Jewish books and documents in St. George's Church, which served as the Book Chamber's storage facility. He joked that "some day they will erect a monument for me in Israel, for rescuing the remnants of Jewish culture." Photograph from Martynas Mažvydas National Library of Lithuania.

Eighty-six-year-old Rachela Krinsky examines documents that she helped rescue in the Vilna ghetto, upon their return to YIVO in 1996. Why did she risk her head for the sake of books? "I didn't believe at the time that my head belonged to me. We thought we could do something for the future." Photograph from YIVO Institute for Jewish Research.

PART THREE

After the War

CHAPTER SIXTEEN

From under the Ground

ON JULY 10, 1944, Shmerke Kaczerginski entered Vilna's city limits, along with a mixed unit of partisans. The Soviet army was already engaged in street battles against the Germans. Shmerke's group came from the south and, to the sound of heavy gunfire and bombardments, passed through narrow lanes and alleys toward the city center. As they approached the train tracks near Torgowa Street, they were met with a hail of machine-gun fire. Two Polish fighters from his unit were killed, and the group decided to stop its forward movement. It took two more days of fighting until German forces retreated from the city, with some surrendering and taken prisoner. As Shmerke reached the center of Vilna, on July 12, he saw dozens of bodies of dead German soldiers on the streets. "I recalled their brutality and only regretted that they met such an easy death."

Some of the city's main avenues—Mickiewicz, Wielka, and Nemiecka—were in ruins and in flames. As he walked down those familiar streets, amid fire and rubble, Shmerke was in a confused and overwhelmed daze. He wrote in his diary, "I didn't know where to go, but my feet took me somewhere. They knew where I should go. They took me uphill. . . . Suddenly I saw myself at the foot of my dear Wiwulskiego Street, and—woe is me—the YIVO building! It was unrecognizable, a ruin. It seemed as if no other building in the entire city was as ruined as it was." Shmerke felt a rush of pain, as if his body was about to burst. His heart contracted, twisted, and shriveled up, as he realized that the Yiddish Scientific Institute, YIVO, was destroyed—and that all the materials he and his colleagues had hidden in its attic were now soot and ashes.[1]

In his anguished stupor, Shmerke's next destination was 6 Shavel

(Żmudska) Street, inside the territory of the ghetto—the site of the sixty-foot-deep bunker, where the FPO stored arms and the paper brigade hid books. When he reached the spot, he could tell it had recently been inhabited by people seeking shelter from the bombing. He used his flashlight to pierce the bunker's darkness and began clearing away sand from the earthen floor with his bare hands. Suddenly, pieces of paper sparkled before his eyes, and Shmerke felt a sense of joy and relief. The materials here were safe. But his joy did not last long. A minute later, as he left the bunker and was blinded by the sunlight, he thought to himself, "So much sunshine, but the world has never been darker for me than now."[2] There was no sign of any Jews on the streets.

The city was officially liberated by the Red Army the next day, July 13. The Jewish partisan brigade "Avengers," headed by Aba Kovner, Vitka Kempner, and Ruzhka Korczak, entered Vilna and assembled in the empty ghetto, where they met Shmerke and other Jewish fighters from the "Vilnius" brigade. Their joy was mixed with heartrending pain: Vilna was liberated, but it was a different city; it wasn't the Jerusalem of Lithuania any more.

Also entering Vilna on liberation day was Ilya Ehrenburg, the Soviet Union's most illustrious war correspondent, and the author of the article in *Pravda* about Sutzkever. Ehrenburg was moved by the sight of ghetto survivors with machine guns on their shoulders, and embraced them. The Jewish fighters' spirits were lifted by their warm reception from a prominent Soviet personality and by the regards he gave them from Abrasha back in Moscow.[3]

Over the next week, Jews began appearing. Some had been hiding underground in the sewage system; others, in the basements of Polish and Lithuanian homes. People who had hidden in surrounding towns or in the forests began to stream into the city.

Because Shmerke was a partisan, the Soviet command gave him a fully furnished three-room apartment on the city's main thoroughfare, Mickiewicz Street, now renamed in Lithuanian Gedimino Street. The apartment had been the residence of a high-ranking German official before he fled in haste, leaving behind food and clothing. For the first time in ten months, Shmerke slept in a bed.[4]

On the day of Vilna's liberation, July 13, Sutzkever found himself in a rustic writers' sanitarium in Voskresensk, outside of Moscow. His reaction to the news, splashed across the front page of *Pravda*, was similar to Shmerke's: "I can't stay here in a sanitarium now that Vilna has been liberated. I must go to my home city and see our destruction." He left for Moscow and went straight to Justas Paleckis, the president-in-exile of Soviet Lithuania who had extracted him from the Narocz forest. This time Sutzkever asked for help with transportation in the opposite direction, back to Vilna, as soon as possible. Paleckis, who was himself on the verge of returning home, replied, "Alright Abrasha, we'll ride or fly together."

They rode, and on the night of July 18, Sutzkever and Paleckis arrived in Soviet Vilnius aboard a military vehicle. As they traveled down the highway, the road was filled with the reeking corpses of German soldiers. "But this odor was more pleasant to me than any perfume," Sutzkever wrote in his diary. He then added pensively, "If not for the hidden cultural treasures, I don't know if I would have had enough strength to return to my home city. I knew that I wouldn't find my dear ones. I knew that everyone had been executed by the murderers. I knew that my eyes would be blinded with pain as soon as I saw the Wilia River. But the Hebrew letters that I had planted in Vilna's soil sparkled at me from a thousand kilometers away."[5]

Upon his arrival, Sutzkever was astonished to be surrounded by his comrades from the FPO—Shmerke, Aba Kovner, and others—who were now wearing military fatigues instead of yellow Stars of David. He moved in with Shmerke in his apartment at 15 Gedimino Street. For the next two years they would work closely again, for the forth time— after Young Vilna, the paper brigade, and the forest.

The next morning, the group of partisans set out for 18 Wiwulskiego Street, and Sutzkever laid eyes on its decimated structure for the first time. That is the moment when he realized that his Vilna, the capitol of Yiddish culture, was gone. The group vowed to retrieve and recover the surviving remnants of the Jewish cultural treasures. Shmerke gave a painfully honest assessment: the vast majority of the books and documents had been destroyed in the paper mills, a minority had been shipped off to Germany, and only "a minimal part" had been rescued by the paper brigade.[6] But it was their moral duty to posterity, and to their murdered colleagues, to retrieve that tiny part.

The fate of their colleagues from the paper brigade weighed heavily on Shmerke and Abrasha. Zelig Kalmanovitch had perished in Narva. Dr. Jacob Gordon, who worked in the translation group, perished in Klooga; Uma Olkenicka, the graphic artist and YIVO theater archivist, was deported to Treblinka; and Dr. Daniel Feinshtein, the social scientist who gave lectures in the ghetto, was murdered just two days before the city's liberation.[7] Dr. Dina Jaffe, who performed translations, met her death in Treblinka; the teacher Israel Lubotsky, who worked sorting Hebrew books, perished in an Estonian labor camp. David and Chaya Markeles (Noime Markeles's parents), both teachers, were shot in Ponar.[8] Ilia Tsunzer, who worked sorting musical materials, died of typhus in the Narva camp in Estonia. Rabbi Abraham Nisan Ioffe, who participated in the research group, was discovered by the Germans in a hiding place at the time of the ghetto's liquidation, and was shot in Ponar.[9] Mendl Borenshtein and Mikhal Kovner, both FPO fighters, escaped the ghetto only to be killed in the German sweep of the Narocz forest.[10]

In all, six surviving members of the paper brigade returned to Vilna after its liberation: Shmerke, Sutzkever, Ruzhka Korczak, Noime Markeles, Akiva Gershater, and Leon Bernstein. Two others were interned in German concentration camps: Herman Kruk and Rachela Krinsky. Kruk perished in Lagedi in September 1944, and Krinsky survived—but never returned to Vilna. The six survivors in Vilna were now joined by Aba Kovner, the former commander of the FPO, who agreed with them that retrieval of the books and documents was a solemn duty and urgent priority.[11]

The group's initial survey of the ten hiding places known to them yielded mixed results: The *malinas* (hiding places) at 1 Strashun Street and 8 Strashun Street were intact, as was the bunker at 6 Shavel (Żmudska) Street. But the hiding place at 29 Niemiecka Street, Sutzkever and Shmerke's ghetto address, was unreachable, covered by the ruins of a building that had collapsed on top of it. The book *malina* inside the ghetto library at 6 Strashun Street had been discovered by the Germans shortly before their retreat. They removed all its materials and set them on fire in the courtyard.[12]

Shmerke and Sutzkever approached Henrik Ziman, a member of the Central Committee of the Communist Party of Lithuania, and asked him for official support for an operation to retrieve the treasures. Ziman was well known to them from the forest, where he was the deputy commander of the Soviet Lithuanian partisans. Before the war, he had been a teacher in Jewish schools in Kovna, but as partisan commander, he adopted the Lithuanian code name Jurgis and claimed to be a Lithuanian Communist only. Not everyone in the forest knew he was Jewish. In keeping with his internationalist posture, Ziman responded to Shmerke and Sutzkever's request with demonstrative disinterest: the newly restored Soviet Lithuania had more important things to deal with.[13]

It isn't clear how Sutzkever made contact with Juozas Banaitis, head of the Arts Administration of the Peoples' Commissariat of Education, but somehow Sutzkever persuaded him to support the project. On July 25, Banaitis issued him a handwritten document authorizing him "to collect and transport to 15 Gedimino Street apartment twenty-four valuable items of Jewish culture and art, which were scattered and hidden throughout the city during the time of the German occupation."[14]

Sutzkever, Shmerke, and Kovner met the next day, July 26, to establish the Jewish Museum of Culture and Art. They called themselves the museum's "initiative group" and sent a memorandum to the authorities requesting official sponsorship. They knew that in the Soviet Union, cultural institutions had to belong to a ministry, a commissariat. There was no such thing as an independent, private museum in the USSR. Banaitis issued a temporary certificate to Shmerke that he was a staff member of "the Jewish Museum that we are in the process of creating."[15]

Shmerke, Sutzkever, and Kovner conceived of the museum as a continuation of both the paper brigade and the FPO. It was their objective to collect and preserve prewar Jewish cultural artifacts, but they would devote special attention to collecting documents from the ghetto and material on the crimes committed by the Germans. The three of them resolved to find the records of the Gestapo, which would have extensive information on the perpetrators of the mass murder. They also decided to prepare a questionnaire for survivors who were witnesses to crimes. Finally, the initiative group agreed that once the museum secured an official status, it would ask to be affiliated with the Vilnius Extraordinary State Commission for Investigating the Atrocities of the

German-Fascist Invaders and Their Accomplices. The "Extraordinary State Commissions" were Soviet state agencies that collected testimony and documentation, and referred cases for prosecution. In sum, the initiative group intended to use different types of material (the ghetto archive, Gestapo archive, and survivor testimony) to ensure that murderers would be brought to justice and punished.[16] They saw the Jewish Museum as a framework for continuing the battle against the German murderers and their local collaborators, with trials and evidence instead of guns and landmines.

The museum set to work immediately. Sutzkever was chairman; Shmerke was secretary and chief administrator; and Kovner headed the collection and retrieval operation. But the division of labor wasn't firm, and their roles and titles changed repeatedly over the next few weeks.

The initial work focused on the bunker on Shavel Street, which was an underground labyrinth of cellars, passageways, and compartments. Shmerke described the operation in his diary: "On a daily basis, sacks and baskets of treasures are transferred from the bunker—letters, manuscripts, and books by famous Jewish personalities. . . . The Polish inhabitants of the courtyard are constantly calling in policemen and other officials; they think we are digging for gold. They can't understand why we need the dirty pieces of paper that are stuffed amid feathers inside pillows and blankets. None of them realize that we have found letters by I. L. Peretz, Sholem Aleichem, Bialik, and Abraham Mapu; the handwritten diary of Theodor Herzl; manuscripts by Dr. Solomon Ettinger and Mendele Mokher Seforim; and parts of the archives of . . . Max Weinreich, Zalmen Rejzen, and Zelig Kalmanovitch."

The work at 6 Shavel Street went on for weeks. Some of the cultural treasures were packed in crates or canisters, while others were simply buried under the ground without any covering. In the middle of the project, Gershon Abramovitsh, the engineer-architect of the bunker, appeared on the scene to help out.

Some members of the retrieval team had shovels; other used their hands. The partisans in the group worked with machine guns hanging over their shoulders. The materials they unearthed represented the full range of Jewish, Russian, and world culture: the record book of the Vilna Gaon's kloyz (synagogue); posters of the earliest Yiddish theater performances by Abraham Goldfaden, the father of Yiddish theater;

letters by Gorky, a bust of Tolstoy, Russian chronicles from the seventeenth century; and . . . a portrait of a British statesman painted in Bombay. (The latter items originated from the Smolensk museum.)[17]

As Sutzkever and his comrades dug up artwork and sculptures buried in the bunker, they hit upon a sculpture of King David by the nineteenth-century Russian Jewish master Mark Antokolsky. An arm extended from under the surface, and Sutzkever grabbed it, thinking it was another work of art. He shuddered when he realized that the arm was made of human flesh, not clay. A group of Jews had hidden in the bunker after the ghetto's liquidation, and one of them died there, underground. After recovering from his initial shock, Sutzkever and his friends continued their excavation of the sculpture. He found poetic symbolism in its proximity to the corpse. "Hitler's victim lies under the ground, but the mighty King David, with a sword in his hand, now stands above the ground. He has set himself free, to take revenge."[18]

The newly founded museum was located in Shmerke and Sutzkever's apartment at 15 Gedimino Street. The two poets decided to hang up a sign in Russian and Yiddish near the street entrance to their building, even before the institution was legally recognized.

Besides the Shavel Street bunker, materials were discovered in numerous other locations. Shmerke recorded in his diary on August 5, "We are bringing in Torah scrolls that are lying scattered across the city. I brought in an enormous amount of valuable books that were kept by the Polish woman Marila Wolska, who received them from her friend Moshe Lerer."

Meanwhile Kovner looked for the documentary traces of the FPO partisan organization that he had headed. In a pile of trash in the courtyard of 6 Strashun Street, he found a copy of the organization's last appeal, "Jews, Prepare for Armed Resistance!" dated September 1, 1943. "I read it, and just like then, my eyes turned bloodshot. Not because it was my writing or because it was my command, my voice. Nor because I just plucked *my life* out of the ashes, but because I felt the petrified pain of those days slash into my face again. A kind of pain that no one will ever completely fathom."[19]

Shmerke and Sutzkever's apartment on 15 Gedimino was filling up quickly with material. A newspaper correspondent who visited them described the scene: The room was full of packages of leather-bound volumes, blackened by dampness and aging. There were Torah scrolls lined against the wall, piled up in rows. The floor was covered with piles of manuscripts, and on the desk table there stood a caste-clay statue, scratched, with one of its arms broken off. There was hardly space for Shmerke and Sutzkever to sleep.

The rooms had an eerie feeling at night, in the dark. It was as if you were sleeping in a cemetery, amid tombstones and open graves.[20]

CHAPTER SEVENTEEN

A Museum Like No Other

FOR THE FIRST FEW months after Vilna's liberation, the museum in Shmerke and Sutzkever's apartment served as a surrogate community center for survivors, returnees, and Jewish Red Army soldiers. People gathered in the evenings to tell their stories, share their hopes, and exchange advice and information. There was no other Jewish address in town. For native Vilners, the city felt empty. Shmerke remembered the hoards of friends that used to surround him as he walked down Zawalna Street on weekends. Now he walked down that thoroughfare without recognizing a single soul. He started keeping lists of his dead friends, with their biographies and the dates and circumstances of their deaths.[1]

The museum arranged with the postal service that it forward all incoming letters addressed to unknown Jewish names to the museum. (Most of the intended recipients had perished.) Noime Markeles, the museum's secretary, hung the letters up on a bulletin board, so that survivors could find relatives or friends, and sent confirmation of their receipt to the letter writers. The museum even served as the distribution point for free meals. The initiative group (Shmerke, Sutzkever, and Aba Kovner) planned to hand over these functions to a municipal Jewish committee once it was approved by the authorities. Meanwhile, rumors spread that there *was* a Jewish committee in town, located in Shmerke and Sutzkever's apartment.[2]

On August 2, the initiative group organized a meeting of some sixty Jewish partisans, to enlist them as collectors for the fledgling museum. It was the first public Jewish gathering in post-Nazi Vilna. Sutzkever spoke emotionally:

This is a gathering of the last remaining Jews, the survivors. The eyes of the whole world are now turned to our city. The Vilna ghetto is known all across the world. . . . Ilya Ehrenburg is writing about Itzik Vitenberg, and Russian poets have composed poems in his honor. . . . In order to justify Vilna's power of attraction, in order to justify our lives, we must be creative while sitting on top of the ruins. A group of us have undertaken the first task: to bring together the remaining cultural treasures, to gather the remnants. Before we begin to ask others to help, let every one of us search among our belongings and in our immediate environment for the remains of our murdered lives.

Kovner followed and addressed the partisans who had been under his command in the ghetto, giving them new orders. The armed resistance of the FPO and the spiritual resistance of the paper brigade were one and the same: "In the bunker at 6 Shavel Street, thirty crates of valuable YIVO materials were hidden. And that is also the place where the FPO hid its machine guns. This symbolizes the great importance of our work. We must rescue whatever remains. We must document our struggle and transmute it into a political force. The destruction of our cultural treasures is perhaps a greater tragedy than the tragedy of our blood."[3]

In the meeting's aftermath, grassroots support for the still-unauthorized museum mushroomed. Its volunteer staff grew from six in mid-July to twelve in mid-August and twenty-nine in early September. The retrieval operation became a movement.[4] In response to Sutzkever's plea, survivors mulled around the ruins of their prewar homes and schools, as well as their ghetto addresses and workplaces—discovering old photographs, school notebooks, copies of the *Ghetto News* newspaper, bread-ration card, and much more. They donated "the remains of their murdered lives" to the Jewish Museum.[5]

Pages from Jewish books surfaced in unexpected places: in one of the city's open-air markets, the saleswomen wrapped herring and other food products in pages from the Vilna edition of the Talmud. When an outraged Jewish partisan yelled at the market women for their callousness, they replied that they didn't know the pages were from the *zhids'* holy book. The partisan told Shmerke about the situation, and the street-smart poet went to the marketplace to solve the problem.

Waving his fists at the saleswomen, he threatened to beat them up and inform the Soviet police that they had looted Jewish property under the Germans if they didn't hand over all the pages from Jewish books immediately. Seeing that Shmerke was serious, the market women acquiesced.[6]

A Polish woman walked into their apartment one day and delivered a handwritten letter with the heading "A Plea to Our Jewish Brothers and Sisters." It was a bombshell. The letter was written by two women, who threw it out of the vehicle that took them to Ponar. It was dated June 26, 1944, just two weeks before Vilna's liberation, and described how they had hidden from the Germans for nine months after the ghetto's liquidation, in a group of 112 people, including thirty children. Only one Polish woman knew of their hiding place and provided them with food. In return, she extorted from them furs, silk, and tens of thousands of German marks. When the group could no longer meet her increasing demands (she wanted five kilograms of gold), the woman denounced them to the Germans.

The letter described in detail how the Germans and Lithuanian police tortured them for four days. It related how eight-year-old girls were raped in the presence of their mothers and how adult men were sexually mutilated with pins and needles. The letter concluded with a call for revenge:

> If Jews will kill at least one of them, as retribution for what they did to the 112 of us, they will have performed a great service for their people. With tears in our eyes, we plead: Revenge! Revenge! I am writing in Polish, because if someone finds a Yiddish letter, they will burn it, but a good and honest person may read a letter in Polish and hand it over to the Jewish police. May the latter do something to the bestial woman who is responsible for so much blood. Our thirty children died; may her three children—her two boys and girl—die along with her.

The letter gave the name and address of the extortionist and informer: Marisia the widow, 34 Wielka Pohulanka Street, on the left side of the courtyard. It concluded, "We bid farewell to you and to the world. We call for revenge!"[7]

As soon as the letter fell into the Jewish Museum's hands, Aba Kovner and his partisan comrades began to investigate. They tracked down

Marisia the extortionist and informer. She was living as the mistress of a high-ranking officer in the Soviet security police. Due to the officer's position, there was no possibility of having her arrested and put on trial. The Jewish partisans decided to take justice into their own hands. They ambushed the woman on the streets of Vilna and killed her.[8]

For Shmerke, Sutzkever, and Kovner, retrieving Jewish cultural arti- facts was an obvious, self-evident need, a precondition for the resump- tion of Jewish life, wherever or however it would happen. They were driven by an elemental sense that a self-respecting people couldn't abandon its printed and documentary legacy, any more than it could leave behind its surviving children in Polish or Lithuanian homes. But other museum activists were interested exclusively in the documents on the Germans' crimes and in using them for political, judicial, and educational purposes. The Bundist Grigorii Yashunsky argued at a general staff meeting, "We aren't collecting for the sake of collecting. These materials are historical arguments that are of current political significance." Other volunteers agreed; the museum's main objective should be to unmask the Germans' brutality and to demand justice on behalf of the Jewish people.[9]

The tension between retrieving cultural heritage and unearthing Holocaust documentation was of little practical consequence. Both types of materials were buried in the same hiding places, and one couldn't make distinctions in the retrieval process. But it highlighted the fact that for the museum activists, recent events overshadowed the previous 450 years of Jewish life in Vilna, even though the volume of prewar books and papers was infinitely greater.

To make up for the paucity of Holocaust documents, the museum began almost immediately to record the testimony of survivors. Sutz- kever and Shmerke's apartment was a beehive of activity, with volun- teer staff members sitting at tables interviewing former ghetto inmates from Vilna, Kovna, and Shavel.[10] Staff member Dr. Shmuel Amarant, who had been the director of Vilna's Hebrew Teachers' Seminary be- fore the war, developed a comprehensive questionnaire, divided into twenty sections, which served as the basis for survivor interviews.[11]

The museum also collected first-person essays on everyday life under the Nazi occupation. These included "Song and Music in the Ghetto,"

"The Ghetto High School," "How I Created an Underground Printing Press," "The Official German Bordello on Subocz Street," "The History of Sports in the Ghetto," and "The Ghetto's Burial Department."[12]

As retrieval work intensified, the museum's most pressing issue was to find an appropriate facility, a building. The collection had outgrown the capacity of Shmerke and Sutzkever's apartment. At first, the initiative group considered basing the museum in the Choral Synagogue, which had survived intact. The Choral Synagogue, not to be confused with the Great Synagogue, had been the congregation of Vilna's Jewish haute bourgeoisie. It was located on Zawalna Street (now renamed Pylimo), outside the Nazi-imposed ghetto, not far from the train station, and the Germans used it as a warehouse. But Shmerke and Sutzkever dropped that idea when they learned that Vilna's surviving religious Jews wanted to use the building as a synagogue again.

The initiative group then turned its designs to the building of the Ramayles Yeshiva, Vilna's largest Talmudic academy, on Novigorod Street. It too was located on a major thoroughfare outside the ghetto and had been used by the Germans as a grain warehouse. But the yeshiva building was already in use by the Office for State Grain Trade, which refused to relinquish control.[13]

On August 11, the founders decided to accept an offer from the Vilnius municipality to relocate the museum to the empty buildings at 6 Strashun Street, inside the abandoned and burnt-out ghetto. It was a difficult decision.

For former inmates, 6 Strashun Street was an emotionally charged address that evoked a rainbow of associations and memories. It had housed the offices of the first Judenrat, most of whose members were murdered by the Germans when they couldn't come up with more than 3.5 million marks out of a 5-million-mark contribution. What's more, 6 Strashun Street was the site of the ghetto library, the hub of the ghetto's cultural and intellectual life. In front of the library building, there was the sports field, which was used for gymnastics and team sports.[14] And next to it was the ghetto bathhouse, which inmates were required to visit every two weeks, by German decree, for delousing and disinfection. Underneath the bathhouse, there were deep cellars, which were used as an FPO safe house, to stockpile weapons, train partisans, and hold secret meetings. (The bathhouse administrator was none other than Itzik Vitenberg, the commander of the FPO.)

Off from the sports field, the adjacent one-story building that led onto Lidzki Street was the ghetto prison, which held people arrested for various offenses: violating the curfew, smuggling food, theft, or "spreading false rumors." The Germans took many of its prisoners to their deaths in Ponar. The arrestees knew full well the fate that awaited them and covered the prison walls with farewell graffiti: "Tomorrow we'll be taken to Ponar"; "Take revenge for the innocent blood"; "Truth will prevail"; and "Down with Gens!"[15]

The entire history of the Vilna ghetto was encapsuled in this one address, 6 Strashun Street: the intense cultural life, the striving for normalcy, the forced degradation, the heroic armed resistance, and the inescapable conclusion, deportation to Ponar to be executed.

Some museum activists objected to the location, arguing "we must not go back to the ghetto." They argued that new Jewish life could not be built on the very streets that reeked of death. Some survivors had a visceral aversion to those streets and avoided them on the way to work or errands. But Shmerke argued in favor of 6 Strashun Street. The site was itself a piece of history, which needed to be preserved for future memory. Otherwise it would become another nondescript Soviet office, like the building of the Ramayles Yeshiva.

Shmerke prevailed, and 6 Strashun Street became the museum's base of operations. The buildings were badly damaged, some were in ruins, and others were filled with mountains of rubble and trash. The only rooms that were in useable condition were the prison cells, whose tiny windowsills were covered by bars. The museum's staff members worked in the prison cells. As they identified and sorted the remnants of Vilna's Jewish treasures, the handwritten graffiti on the walls looked down at them as eerie reminders of the community's tragic denouement.

One wisecrack called the institution the Ghetto Prison Museum.[16]

With the problem of space officially resolved (although repairs and reconstruction would take years), the museum's main problem was its ambiguous legal status. The Arts Administration reversed itself and withdrew its sponsorship. Instead of a Jewish museum, Juozas Banaitis, the head of the Arts Administration, proposed that the institution become the Jewish department of the Lithuanian National Museum. But Sutzkever, Shmerke, and Kovner objected vigorously. They wanted to have a distinct and independent institution. Sutzkever went looking for a sponsoring government agency. He arranged for the Lithuania

Academy of Sciences to take the institution under its wings, as its Jewish Division. But the academy withdrew its support after two and a half weeks, with the explanation that none of the staff members were scholars or had academic credentials.[17] The museum was in legal limbo, without a sponsor.

By late August, the three founders were frustrated and angry. Kovner recorded in his notebook,

> Sutzkever has been running around for six weeks and cannot get the legal approval for a Jewish museum or scientific institute. Across the city, precious Venice imprints, manuscripts, and unique items are being ripped apart, trampled upon, and used to heat ovens, and we are not given the opportunity to save these treasures. For two years, we risked our lives to hide them from the Germans, and now, in the Soviet Union, they are being destroyed. No one is interested in helping us. Sutzkever and I have had dozens of meetings with ministers, the Central Committee of the Communist Party, and other important persons. They all promise, but no one helps.[18]

Just at this moment of infuriated despair, Banaitis reentered the picture with a creative solution: the institution would be called the "Commission to Collect and Process Documents of Jewish Culture." As a commission, it would not require an official budget line or approval by higher-ups, and it could begin functioning immediately. The eleven-member commission was formed on August 26, 1944, by order of the commissar of education, Juozas Ziugzda, with Sutzkever as its chairman.[19]

That was the good news. The bad news was that the commission didn't have a budget. Ziugzda paid salaries on an irregular basis, in varying amounts, from an unknown source. There were no funds for transport, supplies, or repairs to the museum's buildings. (Everyone still called it a museum, even after it became a commission.) Most commission members worked on a volunteer basis.

Undeterred, the commission began to furbish its buildings. Shmerke recorded the outpouring of aid in an August 28 entry in his diary: the director of a local factory donated tables and chairs; others brought paper, ink, and lamps. Shmerke himself found a source for pens and paperclips. When someone donated file folders, envelopes, an eraser, and nails, Shmerke was overjoyed, and wrote, "We are getting richer."

One of the most pressing needs was for transport vehicles, to take the cultural treasures discovered all over the city to 6 Strashun Street. Someone who worked in a trucking operation occasionally "lent" one of its trucks to the museum—without his boss's knowledge. But more often than not, the activists resorted to wooden handwagons.[20]

In early September an enormous mountain of materials was found in the courtyard of the Vilnius Trash Administration (*Soyuzutil*). The Germans had disposed of scores of tons of Jewish materials as trash, for shipment to the paper mills. But several tons never left the Trash Administration. Isaac Kovalsky, who discovered the trove, which was the largest one after the bunker at 6 Shavel Street, brought in a sample package of materials to the museum. When Shmerke opened it, the first item on top was a manuscript by the early nineteenth-century Hebrew Enlightenment author Joseph Perl. Underneath it were newspapers, pedagogical materials, and small sculptures. The transport and processing of the treasure trove from the Trash Administration preoccupied the museum's staff for more than half a year.[21]

News of the cultural retrieval operation in Vilna spread to Moscow, and the response among Soviet Jewish intellectuals was one of excited enthusiasm and admiration. The premier Yiddish novelist Dovid Bergelson wrote to Sutzkever: "There was recently an article in *Unity* [the main Soviet Yiddish newspaper] about the great work you are performing in Vilna. It is truly great work. I don't know whether anyone is doing anything more important for our culture than you are." Shakhna Epshtein, the executive secretary of the Jewish Anti-Fascist Committee, wrote to Sutzkever in a similar tone: "We are following your activity with the greatest interest. Your achievements are truly historic. May your hands be strengthened!"[22]

Sholem Aleichem's Letters

Sholem Aleichem (1859–1916), whose work "Tevye the Dairyman" served as the basis for the Broadway hit *Fiddler on the Roof,* was the most popular and prolific of all Yiddish writers. His works were read aloud by families after their Friday-night Sabbath meal. The standard edition of his collected works is twenty-eight volumes long, and it is far from complete.

Besides his published works, Sholem Aleichem was a prolific and talented correspondent. In his younger years, he numbered his letters sequentially, and in the single year of 1889, he composed more than a thousand letters.[1] There were many reasons for the outpouring of correspondence: He lived in Kiev, while most of his colleagues were in Odessa and Warsaw. After immigrating to New York, he continued to publish his works in Eastern Europe. He spent many months each year at resorts in Italy and Switzerland, far away from family and friends, attending to his fragile health. So he needed to write letters to stay in touch. But the main reason was that he loved letter writing, as well as epistolary novels.

Shmerke and Sutzkever rescued fifty-three letters by the great Yiddish author and humorist, out of the close to two hundred letters held in YIVO's archive.[2] The earliest rescued gem was written in Kiev in 1888 and was addressed to two colleagues in Warsaw, asking them to contribute to the Yiddish literary almanac *The Jewish People's Library* (*Yidishe folks-bibliotek*). The almanac, edited and financed by Sholem Aleichem, was an époque-making literary event that brought together the greatest talents of the day, including S. J. Abramowicz and I. L. Peretz, the grandfather and father of modern Yiddish literature.

The last Sholem Aleichem letter in the Sutzkever-Kaczerginski bundle was a typewritten piece from August 15, 1915, sent from his home at 110 Lenox Avenue in Manhattan, to a young English translator. It concerned the translation of his novel *The Bloody Joke*—a tragicomedy in which two university students, one Russian and one Jewish, decide to exchange identities and live under the other's name. Ivanov becomes Rabinovitch and learns firsthand that "it's hard to be a Jew"—the name that Sholem Aleichem gave to the popular stage version of his novel. The English translation was intended as a device to draw attention to the plight of Russia's Jews through humoristic literature.

Sholem Aleichem was very interested in making a larger name for himself in America, through English translations of his works—in print, on the stage, and in silent films. All of his attempts to break through to the American audience failed during his lifetime. Only fifty years later, with the success of *Fiddler*, did Sholem Aleichem become a household name.

Here is one of the more wistful letters rescued from the ERR worksite by the poetic duo. It was written in 1906, when Sholem Aleichem was in Lemberg, in the Habsburg Empire (today: Lviv, Ukraine) en route to America. He was fleeing Tsarist Russia in the aftermath of the wave of bloody pogroms that struck in the fall of 1905, including the pogrom in Kiev that he narrowly escaped by hiding in a hotel. The letter, addressed to an unnamed friend and admirer, dealt with the topic of his own mortality.

Dear Friend,

As you can see, my Torah portion "Get Thee Out"* is not close to its end. I'm still in the early part. Until I get to the happy, blessed land of America, it'll be a lo-o-o-o-ng way.

You write that you're willing to go through fire and water for my sake. That's very kind and nice of you. If you want to do me a big favor, an act of true kindness, I'll tell you what to do: Once my 120 years on this earth will be over (you might imagine that it could be a little sooner), and I'll move on to the place from which you can't send telegrams or even write letters, I imagine that the people of Israel will finally want to do something for its folk writer, now that he's in the world-to-come. They will probably want to put a proper tombstone on his grave. I'd like to ask that they inscribe on the

---

*An allusion to Genesis 12:1 in which the Lord says to Abraham "Get thee out of thy country . . . unto the land that I will show you."

stone the following epitaph, which I recently composed while at a banquet in my honor. Others were drinking wine, celebrating, singing songs, and offering toasts. This person sat down and wrote the following epitaph.

> Excuse me mister, what's your rush?
> You're needed, sir, my dear.
> Sholem Aleichem, I'm sure you know,
> Is buried over here.
>
> He was a simple Jew,
> Wrote Yiddish-German for the women,
> And for the plain folks he—
> Here lies a "Jargonist,"* a writer.
>
> He scoffed at all of life,
> And laughed at all the rest.
> His readers chuckled o-so much,
> And he? So much distress!
>
> And precisely when the public
> Laughed and clapped in revelry,
> He cried—as only God knows,
> In secret, no one should see.

If you don't like the word "Jargonist," I give you permission to replace it with "humorist." The main thing—pay attention to the spelling, because one should always write correctly, even on a tombstone. Besides that, may you be healthy, happy, write lots of letters, and send my warmest regards to everyone.

Sholem Aleichem
February 1906, Galicia[3]

The letter contains the earliest draft version of Sholem Aleichem's epitaph. He subsequently made small modifications, deleting the first stanza and changing "Jargonist" to "humorist." The final version is inscribed on Sholem Aleichem's tombstone in the Mount Carmel Cemetery in Queens, New York.

---

*Detractors of Yiddish referred to it as "Jargon."

CHAPTER EIGHTEEN

Struggling under the Soviets

A s JEWISH REFUGEES began streaming into Vilna from all
directions, a Jewish community of sorts began to emerge.
A religious congregation was established in mid-August,
headed by Rabbi Yisroel Gustman, the only surviving member of the
Vilna rabbinate. It employed a ritual slaughterer, two gravediggers, a
religious administrator, and a secretary. It also took over the responsi-
bility for posting and replying to letters in search of relatives.[1]

On September 18–19, 1944, Rosh Hashanah services were held in
the partially ruined building of the Great Synagogue. Only half of the
structure's roof remained, and a light rain fell on the worshipers' heads.
Only four people wore *taleysim* (prayer shawls).[2] On Yom Kippur, services moved to the Choral Synagogue, whose structure was safe from
the elements. It became the permanent home of the Jewish religious
community.

A committee was formed to care for Jewish orphans, who wandered
about the city without proper housing, food, medical care, or education. The committee was headed by Tzivia Vildshtein, an educator
who had graduated from the pedagogical faculty of Wilno University.
Shmerke, Sutzkever, and Aba Kovner joined as members.

In late September, the authorities granted permission for the committee to establish a Jewish school, kindergarten, and orphanage, all
in a single building that was called the "Jewish Children's Combine."
The school followed a Soviet curriculum with Yiddish as the language
of instruction. There were no religious subjects or observances, but it
did teach Yiddish literature. The museum donated copies of textbooks
and children's literature to the "Children's Combine."[3]

By the fall of 1944, the two thousand Jews in Vilna had a modest
institutional infrastructure: a synagogue, a secular school, and a mu-

seum. But there was no municipal Jewish committee, as Shmerke and Sutzkever had envisioned. The authorities nixed that idea.

The three institutions faced restrictions, harassment, and outright hostility from local officials, many of which were holdovers from the previous administration, under the Germans. The synagogue was prohibited from receiving a shipment of clothing sent to it from America. And it could not host Sabbath meals, or offer religious classes. In the USSR, places of worship could engage *only* in worship, not in philanthropy, social gatherings, or religious instruction. And since Saturdays was a workday, attendance at Sabbath services was modest. The Jewish Children's Combine was forced to relocate twice during its first year, as the authorities repeatedly assigned its facility to other schools. The Commissariat of Education even closed the school down midyear but reversed that decision after receiving a protest telegram from the Jewish Anti-Fascist Committee in Moscow.

And the museum limped along as a commission that had no budget.[4]

Beyond that, Jewish life was hamstrung. Shmerke and Sutzkever appealed to the authorities to allow publication of a weekly Yiddish newspaper. Initially, the first secretary of the Communist Party of Lithuania, Antanas Snieckus, replied via Henrik Ziman (the only Jew in the party leadership) that it was premature to talk of a newspaper, but there would be support for a literary almanac. Then Snieckus changed his mind—the idea of an almanac was "not timely." Meanwhile, newspapers and periodicals began to appear not only in Lithuanian and Russian, the state languages, but also in Polish, the language of another ethnic minority. Why could the Polish population have a newspaper but Jews could not? The question was left hanging.[5]

No one even asked the authorities to fund a standing Yiddish theater or a Jewish workers' club, the Soviet equivalent of a community center.

Shmerke, the seasoned activist and perennial optimist, found some cracks in the system. He gave weekly lectures for parents at the Jewish school; he persuaded the leadership of the Lithuanian Writers' Union to establish a Yiddish writers' section, and became its chairman; he organized Yiddish concerts (of recitations, song, and music) in the Vilnius municipal theater "Lutnia," under the auspices of the Yiddish section of the Writers' Union.[6] But even with these initiatives, Jewish life in the liberated Soviet Vilnius was clearly struggling against bureaucratic strangulation.

The city's Jews clung together in circles of friends that met in private homes in the evening. No one could ban that. Shmerke had his circle—a motley crew of former ghetto inmates who survived in hiding, in the forests, or miraculously, in the Estonians camps, plus a few discharged Red Army soldiers and refugees who returned from central Asia. Like Shmerke, they were all in their late thirties. Couples started getting engaged and married, and at the dinner parties to celebrate those occasions, Shmerke was the first to strike up a tune and bang out the song's beat on the table. But everyone bore their searing pain just underneath the surface—they were all young widows and widowers, many of whom had lost children.

Shmerke was still buoyant and energetic when in the company of these friends, but deep down he was lonely. Sutzkever left for Moscow in early September, and no one in Shmerke's circle belonged to his prewar gang. It wasn't Young Vilna. The women weren't like Barbara (his murdered wife) or Rachela Krinsky (who, from what he heard, was languishing in a German labor camp).

In his spare time, Shmerke collected and wrote down the songs that inmates sang in the Vilna ghetto. He compiled a draft manuscript with forty-nine songs, some from the ghetto theater and some written by martyred poets. In a short introductory essay, he argued that the victims should be remembered in their own words—the words of the songs in which they expressed their determination and fear, hope, and despair.[7] Those songs now became a part of his repertoire. But even the defiant and optimistic ones, such as his own "Youth Anthem" and his marching song "Jewish Partisan" now had a bittersweet flavor.[8]

The Commission to Collect and Process Documents of Jewish Culture faced a new jolt when Sutzkever decided to leave for Moscow shortly before the High Holidays, on September 10. The poet was eager to return to his pregnant wife and to his literary projects, now that the retrieval operation was in full gear and the museum (or commission) had a building.[9] Sutzkever asked Kovner to take over as chairman of the commission, with Shmerke as his deputy. Everyone assumed that Sutzkever would return in a month or two, but he ended up staying in Moscow for close to a year.[10]

Before he left, Sutzkever drafted the text of a promotional brochure about the commission's work, which listed some of its unearthed treasures: letters by (and to) the early nineteenth-century mystic Rabbi Eliyahu Gutmakher ("the only Hasidic master in Germany"); the manuscripts of early Yiddish theater plays by the father of Yiddish theater, Abraham Goldfaden; writings by S. J. Abramowicz, the grandfather of Yiddish literature; ten *pinkasim* (record books), including the record book of the synagogue of the Vilna Gaon; rare sixteenth-century Hebrew books published in Venice, Cremona, Cracow, and Lublin; sculptures by Mark Antokolsky; and the Vilna ghetto archive, with the records of the ghetto administration, placards, diaries, and photographs.[11]

Not mentioned in the draft brochure was one of the commission's most important discoveries: the handwritten diary of Theodor Herzl from the 1880s. In the Soviet Union, possession of a document by the founder of political Zionism wasn't something to publicize or boast about. Lenin had vilified Zionism, and the movement was banned in the USSR since the 1920s.[12]

But the absence of the Herzl diary from the brochure ended up not mattering. Because the brochure never appeared. The Censorship Bureau referred its text to the Central Committee of the Communist Party, which refused to approve publication.

As soon as Sutzkever left, Shmerke and Kovner began feuding. Shmerke resented the fact that Kovner was titular head of the commission, while he, the person who had risked his life smuggling the treasures, and who had been the first to retrieve them, was his subordinate. Shmerke also loathed Kovner's lengthy absences from the museum to engage in other activities—rebuilding the Shomer Ha-Tza'ir movement, organizing acts of revenge against known Nazi collaborators, and planning illegal emigration to Palestine. What kind of museum director was that?

Ideological factors also fueled the tensions: Shmerke was a Communist who, in the fall of 1944, still put his faith in the Soviet system. Kovner was a socialist Zionist who rejected the prospect of rebuilding Jewish life in Vilna, in the USSR, or for that matter anywhere in Europe. And Shmerke was jealous of Kovner's cool air of authority, and . . . his success with women.[13]

But the retrieval work continued as before, and in October, Shmerke made a monumental discovery: he found Herman Kruk's ghetto diary in the bunker on Shavel Street. (Sutzkever had discovered a few dozen pages back in August and taken them with him to Moscow, but Shmerke found several hundred more.) Kruk, the librarian, had hidden three copies of his great chronicle in different parts of the city, but only the copy buried in the Shavel Street bunker survived the ravishes of war.

The typescript was in total disarray. Kruk had placed it in a sealed metallic canister, but the people who lived in the bunker after the ghetto's liquidation opened the canister in search of valuables. The diary's pages were strewn across the bunker, crumpled and torn, amid papers of all kinds. It took weeks to gather the pages and reassemble the diary.[14]

Even more miraculous was the discovery of Kruk's notebooks from the Klooga camp in Estonia. Kruk had buried them in a little ditch at Lagedi in the presence of six witnesses, on the day before he and four hundred other inmates were executed. One of those six witnesses, Nisan Anolik, survived. He returned to Lagedi after the liberation, recovered the notebooks, and handed them over to the Jewish Museum.

Kruk's dream that his writings would survive for future generations came true.[15]

The diary eventually reached YIVO in New York, which published the original Yiddish text, with copious notes and indexes, and a lengthy biographical introduction by Kruk's surviving brother Pinkhas. When the Kruk diary appeared in English translation, it was hailed by historians as "one of the world's great wartime memoirs" and "a one-person Ringelblum archive about the Vilna ghetto, which is simultaneously a literary masterpiece." The dean of Holocaust historians, Yehuda Bauer of the Hebrew University in Jerusalem, called it "one of the essential documents from that tragic era." Shmerke and Sutzkever made sure that the words of the murdered head of the "paper brigade" would live.[16]

Just as Shmerke was savoring his Kruk discovery, an existential crisis burst forth. In late October 1944, an institution in Moscow known as the Personnel Policy Commission rejected the application by the "Commission to Collect and Process Documents of Jewish Culture" for state funding; it ordered the commission dissolved. The consequences were felt almost immediately. The staff's privileges—food rations and exemption from the military draft—were revoked, and their identification cards were invalidated.

Kovner and Shmerke joined forces, their mutual hostility notwithstanding, to rescue the commission, or as they still called it, the museum, from destruction. Kovner went straight to Juozas Ziugzda, the commissar of education, and did not mince words: Moscow's decision was the direct result of the Lithuanian authorities' failure to support the Jewish Museum. He warned Ziugzda that once news of this decision would spread outside the USSR, it would be interpreted as an antisemitic act by the Lithuanian government.

Kovner shot off a letter to Sutzkever with urgent instructions: ask the Jewish Anti-Fascist Committee to intervene; Ilya Ehrenburg must help; and meet with the top Lithuanian leadership (Snieckus, Justas Paleckis, and others) who were reportedly in Moscow. "You must demand that they preserve this Jewish cultural institution and not aid the destruction of that which the Germans didn't manage to destroy!"[17]

Meanwhile, Kovner decided to up the ante. In a memo to the authorities, he demanded that the commission be reconstituted as the Institute for Jewish Culture of the Lithuanian Academy of Sciences. There was such an institute in Soviet Kiev, and before the war there had been one in Minsk, so why not also in Vilnius? Kovner asked for a staff register of twenty employees.[18]

Kovner met with Ziugzda three times, but the minister's position hardened with each meeting. He was firmly opposed to the museum's revival, whether as a commission, museum, or institute. The documents in its possession could be forwarded to Lithuanian archives; the books to the state library; the works of art to the national museum; and scholarly materials to the Academy of Sciences. Kovner characterized Ziugzda's position in evocative terms, especially for a ghetto survivor: "He wants to turn us into ashes."[19]

Kovner and Shmerke assumed that the Lithuanian authorities were responsible for the commission's dissolution, as well as for the ban on Yiddish publishing and the harassment of the Jewish school. What they didn't know was that the Lithuanian leadership was under severe pressure from Moscow to take these steps and more. The man who was responsible for the pressure was Stalin's special emissary to Vilnius, Mikhail Andreievich Suslov, the head of the Lithuanian Bureau of the Central Committee of the Communist Party of the USSR.

Suslov, as coldhearted and brutal a Soviet official as there ever was, virulently opposed the existence of Jewish cultural institutions in Lithuania, or for that matter, anywhere in the European USSR. He insisted that the Jews could either assimilate or migrate to Birobidzhan, the miniscule Jewish Autonomous Region in the Russian Far East, near the Chinese border. In Birobidzhan, which was home to ten thousand of the 2.2 million Jews in the Soviet Union, Yiddish was an official language. Elsewhere, Suslov pressed, Jewish cultural activity should be considered "nationalism," a dirty word in the Soviet lexicon.

When a representative of the Vilnius Jewish school met with him to ask for state resources on the school's behalf, Moscow's man threw the representative out of his office and accused him of being an agent of Jewish nationalism.[20]

Inspired by Mikhail Andreevich's position, officials in the Central Committee of the Communist Party in Moscow wrote a formal memorandum to their top boss, Georgy Malenkov, blaming the Lithuanian Communists for their "improper approach to the Jewish question." They attacked the Lithuanian leaderships for "acceding to the demands of the Jewish community" and approving the establishment of a separate Jewish school and museum. The authors complained that Jewish Communists in Vilnius "are . . . not explaining to the Jewish population the falseness and harmfulness of creating special Jewish organizations. They are in fact actively defending these institutions and are essentially their organizers." This was a broadside at Shmerke and others like him.[21]

Suslov and his followers took the extreme position that Jewish cultural institutions should be prohibited in Lithuania, at a time when there were many such institutions in Moscow: the Jewish Anti-Fascist Committee, the Yiddish publishing housing The Truth (Der Emes), the Moscow State Yiddish Theater, the newspaper *Unity* (*Eynikayt*), the literary journal *Homeland* (*Heymland*), the Yiddish department of Moscow Radio, and so forth.

The party leadership in Vilnius responded to the sharp criticism from Moscow by withdrawing their initial support for the Jewish Museum.

Kovner warned the Lithuanians that liquidation of the museum would have political repercussions. It "will awaken an unpleasant feeling throughout the world and is likely to be misinterpreted."[22] Translation: It would reinforce the view that Lithuania was thoroughly infested with antisemitism, even under Soviet rule. This was an image that Snieckus, Paleckis, and others wanted to avoid.

But when the storm quieted down, and Suslov turned to other more pressing issues, the Lithuanian authorities found a clever device by which to sneak the museum past the gray eminence from Moscow. On November 9, the Council of People's Commissars of the Lithuanian SSR issued an order opening thirty-four museums. Buried in the list as number eighteen was the Vilnius Jewish Museum.[23] In reality, the thirty-three other museums were opened on paper only. They had no staff, no facilities, and no activities. The memo was a statement of intent and a ploy to give the Jewish Museum a legal standing.[24]

Shmerke and Kovner celebrated. Shmerke, the party member, was appointed director and wrote to Sutzkever in Moscow that he was keeping the director's seat warm for him until he returned. The other staff positions were two conservators (Avraham Ajzen and Shmuel Amarant), a graphic artist (Kovner), a secretary (Noime Markeles), a bookkeeper named Rubinshtein, and two maintenance workers (Kaplan and Vitka Kempner).[25]

From Shmerke's perspective, the title Jewish Museum was just a name. He didn't intend for the institution to follow the norms and practices of the museological profession. Only a tiny part of its collection consisted of art and artifacts, and there were no plans to mount exhibits. Amarant and Ajzen weren't actually working as curators, and Kovner wasn't a graphic artist. The Jewish Museum was a library, an archive, and, perhaps in the future, a research institute. Above all, it was a monument to the memory of the lost Jerusalem of Lithuania.

Shmerke still hoped that the museum, with its eight-member staff register, would be a temporary holding pen until the authorities approved the establishment of an institute for Jewish culture. "I am sure that we will be made equal with others," he wrote to Sutzkever. This was yet another dream of Shmerke's that did not come true.[26]

Even with the new official status, everyday work was difficult and frustrating. There were no allocations for transportation and refurbishing the building. Shmerke wrote to Sutzkever, "You understand my dear Abrasha. In order to get three meters of glass [to install windows], I need to go request it twenty times. And that's only if *I* go. If someone else went, he wouldn't get anything."[27]

The months between July and November 1944 were a war of nerves between stubborn Vilner determination ("if you only will it, you can be a Gaon") and Soviet bureaucratic obstructionism and inertia. But in November 1944, the Vilners prevailed. The Jewish Museum was an official reality.

CHAPTER NINETEEN

Tears in New York

I T WAS MAX WEINREICH's good fortune and heavy burden to be the only member of the Vilna YIVO's leadership who was spared from the ravages of the war. He was en route to a linguistics conference in Denmark on September 1, 1939, and remained stranded in Copenhagen for the next few weeks. When his close friend and YIVO colleague Zalmen Rejzen was arrested by the Soviets on September 18, Weinreich decided not to return home. Rejzen was never heard from again. He died in Soviet detention.

With the outburst of war in Europe, the American branch of YIVO became the institute's temporary headquarters, and its first act was to arrange for Weinreich's immigration to the United States. He arrived in New York on March 18, 1940, became director, and began to rebuild.

Almost surreally, he set up everything the way it was back in Vilna: he divided the institute's scholarly work into the same four sections (historical, philological, psychological-pedagogical, and economic-statistical); he reestablished the *aspirantur* graduate-training program; and he edited the institute's journal *YIVO bleter*. Volume 14 appeared in Vilna in 1939, and volume 15 was published in New York in 1940. Seamless continuity.[1]

As Weinreich went about the business of solidifying the institute on American soil, the unfolding catastrophe in Europe was never far from his mind. The featured lecture at YIVO's January 1942 annual conference was entitled "How Do Polish Jews Live in the Ghettos?" It was given by Shloime Mendelsohn, a Bundist educator and member of YIVO's board of directors, who escaped Poland via Vilna in 1940.[2]

On February 14, 1943, YIVO celebrated the grand opening of its building at 535 West 123rd Street, a modern three-story facility near Columbia University, just behind the Jewish Theological Seminary of

America. The opening signaled YIVO's entry into the mainstream of American academic life. The 123rd Street site would replace Wiwulskiego Street, at least for now, and perhaps forever.

The inauguration featured an exhibit of documents that belonged to YIVO's collections before the war and that had been whisked out of Europe before the Germans could get their hands on them. Its 195 display items included a decree on the legal status of the Jews in Poland from 1634; notebooks with writings by the Lubavitch "middle" rebbe, Dovber Shneuri (1773–1827); a notice by the rabbis of Genoa from 1852; testimony by the survivors of the 1919 pogrom in Proskurov, Ukraine; and letters by the Russian writer Vladimir Korolenko. The catalog noted with solemn resolve, "This exhibit is more than a 'remembrance of the destruction.' It is also a call for continuity, in the hope that everything that YIVO possessed will in due time return to it."[3]

Like so many families, YIVO was torn apart by the war, with the American side hoping against all odds that it would eventually reunite with its European relatives.

But such hopes were slim. Weinreich's keynote address at the institute's 1943 conference was entitled "YIVO in a Year of Extermination." Before the war, he had fought to keep YIVO apolitical and derided those who demanded that it issue protest resolutions. Now, he organized a petition to President Roosevelt on the plight of European Jewry and collected the signatures of 283 professors from 107 American colleges, universities, and research institutions. "We appeal to you to take measures that have not yet been undertaken to rescue the millions of European Jews who have been sentenced to death by the enemies of civilization."[4]

The YIVO staff divided its energy between engaging in scholarship, institution building, and a grim deathwatch, as news reports trickled in. The institute held a program in memory of Simon Dubnow, the dean of Jewish historians and a member of YIVO's academic board, on October 17, 1943, soon after word reached the West that he had been murdered in the Riga ghetto. Everyone worried most about Zelig Kalmanovitch.[5]

Weinreich's heart sank when he received a coded letter from Emanuel Ringelblum, an eminent historian and communal leader, written in hiding on the Aryan side of Warsaw, and smuggled out by the Polish underground. It was dated March 1, 1944, after the Warsaw ghetto was no more, and it mentioned in passing: "In 1941 and 1942, we were in touch with Zelig Kalmanovitch in Vilna, who under the supervision of the Germans arranged YIVO's materials and hid a large part of them. Today, there are no more Jews in Vilna. That great center of Yiddish culture and of modern scholarship is totally destroyed." It was Ringelblum's last letter. His hiding place was discovered by the Gestapo five days later.[6]

As soon as Vilna was liberated by the Red Army, on July 13, 1944, Weinreich jumped into action. He wrote to the State Department and asked it to ascertain through diplomatic channels the condition of YIVO's building in Vilna and the location of its library and archive. The Special War Problems Division responded with a polite brush-off. "As the area in question is still a military zone, the department is not in a position to undertake the desired inquiry." It suggested that YIVO contact the Soviet Embassy in Washington, since the USSR was in control of Vilna, but Weinreich thought that was a bad idea. It would only alert the Soviets to the importance of the institute's collections and prompt them to claim the materials as "Soviet property."

He found a more sympathetic ear at the American Commission for the Protection and Salvage of Artistic and Historic Monuments in War Areas, known for short as the Roberts Commission. Its special adviser, John Walker, urged patience. "Difficult legal and diplomatic questions are involved." But patience was one thing Weinreich didn't have much of. YIVO was his child, and he was the sole surviving parent.[7]

With little concrete information about the condition of the Vilna YIVO and its collections, Weinreich's hopes were lifted by a surprise envelope he received from Abraham Sutzkever.

Sutzkever had taken bundles of documents from the Shavel Street bunker to Moscow. He was so emotionally invested in the retrieval operation that he needed to hold on to some of its rescued gems. Shmerke and Aba Kovner asked him to send them back, or at least send back copies, but he never did.[8]

Out of the clear blue, Sutzkever found an opportunity to send documents to Weinreich in New York. In December 1944, he was interviewed by a journalist for the *New York Post* in Moscow, Ella Winter. In the interview, he told Winter about YIVO, the Einsatzstab Reichsleiter Rosenberg , the heroic work of the paper brigade, and the recent excavations in Vilna. Noticing her intense reaction, Sutzkever asked Winter, who was about to leave for New York, to take an envelope of materials for Max Weinreich, who was, he explained, YIVO's sole surviving director and who had rebuilt the institute in America. Winter agreed.

Sutzkever packed the envelope with a document from the archive of Simon Dubnow, an issue of *Ghetto News* (*Geto yediyes*), the official newsletter of the Vilna ghetto administration, and a few other items. Not knowing Weinreich's address or telephone number, he gave her the following instructions: "Take the package to 183 East Broadway, the editorial offices of the Yiddish newspaper *The Day* (*Der Tog*), and someone there will give you Max Weinreich's telephone number. Call him from there and wait. Do not give the package to anyone else, or even mention it to anyone else. Just call and wait, and may God bless you."⁹

Winter followed Sutzkever's instructions, and Weinreich reacted exactly as he had expected. He told her to stay where she was; he would come immediately. Weinreich collected the envelope and, with it, a short note from Sutzkever: "I send you regards from our destruction. Your wife's mother lived in the ghetto almost the entire two years of its existence. In August 1943, she died in her own bed, the greatest joy for a ghetto-person. . . . I rescued a part of your archive and library. Not everything was preserved in the ground. It's hard to write. My heart is on the verge of bursting."¹⁰

The letter reestablished the bond between the two men, who had once between teacher and student. Weinreich had headed the Yiddish scouting movement *Di Bin* (The beetle), where Sutzkever had been a member, and a few years later, Weinreich taught him Old Yiddish so he could write poems in "Shakespearian" Yiddish. Now, one Holocaust later, the student reported to his teacher that he had hidden his private library and papers in the ghetto, and that he had kept an eye on his mother-in-law, Stefania Shabad. But Sutzkever concealed her true fate, probably out of compassion for his reader. Stefania Shabad did not die in her bed in the ghetto. She was deported to the Maidanek death camp.¹¹

Weinreich knew from press reports that parts of YIVO's collections had been rescued in Vilna. But now, in January 1945, he held a few fragments of its archive in his hands. Upon returning to the YIVO building on West 123rd Street, he invited three members of its leadership into his office: chief librarian Mendl Elkin, historian Jacob Shatzky, and the chairman of YIVO's academic board, educator Leybush Lehrer, all of them immigrants from Eastern Europe. He unraveled the package, and the four men touched the pages that were, in Sutzkever's words, "a bloodied reflection of their souls." They bowed their heads and broke down in tears.

Weinreich did not respond to Sutzkever's note. He knew that writing to him in Moscow would only alert the Soviet security services to the fact that the celebrity poet from Vilna was in touch with Americans. That could cause serious problems for Sutzkever. So Weinreich did the hardest thing of all, under the circumstances. He was silent and waited.

As the fog of war began to clear, devastating news started to flow into YIVO from survivors of the Vilna ghetto. The institute's entire staff had been murdered. No one, literally no one who had worked for YIVO and had been in Vilna when the Germans marched in was alive. Weinreich was the only man left standing. It was a chilling realization.

Weinreich dedicated the first postwar issue of *YIVO bleter* to the memory of YIVO's murdered scholars, staff members, *zamlers* (collectors), graduate students, and board members. The sixteen-page memorial section was called "Yizkor," the name of the Hebrew memorial prayer for the dead. "Amidst the destruction of our people, YIVO mourns its own calamity. The community of East European Jews, whose needs gave rise to YIVO, is almost no more. Gone are almost all of YIVO's thousands of correspondents from hundreds of cities and towns, who served as the foundation of the YIVO structure. Gone are almost all of the people who built YIVO through their daily efforts and imbued it with their body and soul." "Yizkor" gave biographical portraits of thirty-seven individuals with deep love and pain.

> Zelig Kalmanovitch: "This name must stand at the top of the list of the YIVO martyrs who perished at the Germans' hands. Since 1929, when he returned to Vilna after a hiatus of fifteen years, he was a member of YIVO's Executive Committee. In 1931, when *YIVO bleter* began publication, he was its editor in chief. But no enumeration of his institutional positions can give a portrait of his radiant personality. You had to know this man, who at age sixty held on to the passion and modesty of his youth. His erudition of the Jewish past and present, of Hebrew and Yiddish, was as vast as his general knowledge. . . . If he was fond of you, you could lean on him like an old oak tree. And he was fond of everyone in whom he saw truthfulness and honesty. Those were his distinguishing characteristics. . . . He had endless love not only for the Jewish people but also for individual Jews. He showed this in the last stage of his life, in the death camp in

Estonia, from which he and his wife Riva never returned. There he cared, with loving devotion, for a sick person who had hounded him just a few years earlier. The world exists due to the merit of people like Zelig Kalmanovitch."

Mark Idelson: "An engineer by profession, and an instructor in the ORT Polytechnic Institute in Vilna, he devoted his free time to YIVO. From the beginning of our institute until the end of our Vilna, he worked in the archives without receiving a penny for his labors."

Uma (Fruma) Olkenicka: "She came from a well-to-do family where more Russian was spoken than Yiddish. But it was she who built YIVO's Yiddish theater museum. An artist, she didn't realize the dreams of her youth. Instead she invested her fine artistic taste into arranging the paintings and photographs on the walls, writing the plaques and signs in the YIVO building, and designing the title pages to YIVO's publications."

Meir Bernshtein: "He was YIVO's accountant. But besides that, he was a supporter and admirer of every Yiddish institution in the city. Reb Meir, as he was called, was the first to donate for a communal cause, even though he made a very meager living."

Chana Grichanski: "She was a quiet librarian. When YIVO's reading room first opened, she worked at the circulation desk. But interacting with the people who ordered books was too much for her. She felt more at home making catalog cards."

Ber Shlosberg: "YIVO was his entire life. For him, carrying boxes was as much a holy labor as reading page proof or translating. When he was asked to write something, he approached the task like a Torah scribe who needs to immerse him in a ritual bath beforehand. Conscientiousness was his most striking trait. His scholarship was only beginning to blossom. He was murdered by the Germans together with his wife and baby."[12]

The list went on and on.

Adding to the sense of devastation was the news that the YIVO building on 18 Wiwulskiego Street, the shrine of modern Yiddish culture, was now a pile of rubble. One ardent Vilner who survived the war, Leyzer Ran, sent an envelope to New York with a small pouch of ashes from its ruins. He began the accompanying letter with the words, "On

November 20, 1945, I sat *shiva* at what was once the Yiddish Scientific Institute in Vilna." The ashes were put on display in a glass case near the entrance to the building on 123rd Street.[13]

The realization that the Vilna YIVO was no more only added to Weinreich's urgency to retrieve the remnants of its collections, wherever they could be found.

Besides his deep pain and resolute determination, Weinreich felt something else: burning anger at Germany, the country where he had lived and studied from 1919 to 1923, and the culture he had admired. He had once seen German *Wissenschaft* (science) as a model and hoped to instill its methods in the Jewish community through YIVO, a Yiddish-speaking academy. But *Wissenschaft* had betrayed him. It had betrayed basic human values and turned itself into a criminal weapon. Hundreds of professors had put their scholarship in the service of Nazism, and the German academic community had actively participated in the vilification and dehumanization of the Jews. This raised deep existential questions for him. How had that happened? Had he placed too much faith in the value of science for society?

In response to these questions, Weinreich did the only thing he knew how to do. He decided to study the topic. He threw away his linguistic research on the history of Yiddish and, for a year, delved into reading German antisemitic scholarship. The result was a book-length indictment, *Hitler's Professors: The Part of Scholarship in Germany's Crimes against the Jewish People*. Weinreich became the world's foremost expert on Judenforschung (antisemitic Jewish studies) and knew everything one could know about the Institute for the Investigation of the Jewish Question in Frankfurt. He read its newsletter and studies; he researched the biographies of its staff. And the more he read, the more he suspected that YIVO's looted collections were there.

Weinreich never gave up on scholarship as a force that could—and should—ennoble humanity. But he did give up on Germany, totally and absolutely. He avoided contact with German scholars, at least until they gave him a complete reckoning of their activities during the war. He rejected invitations to lecture at German universities. As a linguist, he expressed his quiet fury most profoundly in the sphere of language: for the rest of his life, Weinreich, a native German speaker with a doctorate from Marburg, refused, with rare exceptions, to speak or write in German.[14]

CHAPTER TWENTY

The Decision to Leave

J UST AS THE Vilna Jewish Museum secured its legal status, it began to collapse, as its staff members rushed to leave the country.

The first one to go was Ruzhka Korczak, Aba Kovner's close party comrade, and a member of the paper brigade. In October 1944, Kovner sent her on a special mission, to find an opening in the Soviet border with either Poland or Romania for illegal emigration to Palestine. Ruzhka found that all the border crossings were tightly controlled, and once she finally succeeded in getting to the other side, she decided that it was too dangerous to return. She continued onward and reached Haifa port in December—one of the very first survivors from Nazi-occupied Europe to reach the Land of Israel. From there, she wrote excited letters to her friends and comrades back in Vilna.[1]

Using Ruzhka's guidelines and precautions, other museum staff members and volunteers from the Young Guard ("Shomer Ha-Tzair") circle left Vilna for the border—including Dr. Shmuel Amarant and Zelda Treger.

In November, emigrationist fever exploded among the Jews of Vilna. The catalyst was the murder of the lone surviving Jewish family in the town of Ejshishok. This event was followed by a spate of murders of Jews who had returned to their hometowns in search of their relatives and property. When the victims' corpses were brought to Vilna for burial, people found notes in their pockets with the words, "You will all meet a similar fate."

The security agencies responded with indifference. The commissar for state security met a Jewish delegation and contemptuously dismissed their demand for protection: "What do you want me to do, station a policeman in front of every house?" Fear and worry spread among the Jewish population.[2]

At about the same time, official notices appeared on the streets announcing that individuals who had been citizens of the Polish Republic before 1939 could register for "repatriation" to Poland. While the Soviet-Polish agreement concerned mainly ethnic Poles, it also applied to Jews. This meant that native Vilner Jews, who had been Polish citizens before the war, could legally "return home to Poland" and leave for Warsaw or Lodz. Knowing that the Soviet Union did not allow free emigration, hundreds of surviving Vilner Jews jumped at this rare opportunity, including most of the museum's staff and volunteers. Before long, Avraham Ajzen, Leon Bernstein, Grigorii Yashunsky, and Dr. Alexander Liro were gone. The institution was in a downward spiral.

All of this was topped off by Kovner's own surprise departure in the dead of night. Ever since the October crisis, when the Commission to Collect and Process Documents of Jewish Culture was dissolved and it looked as if the museum might actually be closed down, Kovner had been removing materials from the premises in order to transfer them to Eretz Israel. He lifted a large stash of FPO documents, including the organization's most famous appeal "Let us not go like sheep to the slaughter." He took out a piece of Herman Kruk's diary and issues of *Ghetto News*, and set his eyes on the most precious prize all—Herzl's diary—but was unable to remove it. Shmerke had locked it up in his office.

Kovner did all of his lifting behind Shmerke's back. The two men, who couldn't stand each other, had made an agreement back in August not to remove museum materials from the premises. But Kovner had changed his mind when the crisis erupted. As a fervent Zionist, he believed that Jewish culture had a future only in the Land of Israel. From his perspective, the gathering-in of exiled cultural treasures was an important act of nation building. Shmerke, on the other hand, was committed to building Jewish culture in Soviet Vilnius.

One evening in late December, Kovner received reliable information from a former Jewish partisan who worked in the Vilnius police that he would be arrested the next day. Someone from the museum— apparently it was Shmerke—had denounced him for stealing museum property. Kovner left Soviet Lithuania immediately, disguised as a Pole who enlisted in the First Polish Army. He hopped onto a military train bound for Bialystok.[3]

Shmerke vented his anger at Kovner in a letter to Sutzkever in Moscow: "Before leaving, Aba and Amarant took (read: 'stole') certain items without my knowledge. In doing so, Aba broke his promise to me and to you."[4] As director, Shmerke had good reason not only to be angry but also to be scared for his own skin. He would be held responsible. And indeed, a few weeks later, an NKVD agent visited the museum and angrily reprimanded Shmerke for the fact that one of his staff members, Dr. Amarant, had been detained at the Soviet-Romanian border with museum documents in his luggage. The agent warned Shmerke that if such instances continued, he would pay for his lack of "Soviet vigilance."[5] If Shmerke was the one who denounced Kovner to the authorities, as seems likely, he did it to protect both himself and the museum.

Once Kovner was on the other side of the border, he tried to downplay the seriousness of the matter. From Poland, he wrote to Sutzkever in Moscow: "Abrasha, write to Shmerke on my behalf and tell him not to take to heart the minor misunderstandings that arose between us at work, and to remember the great thing that the three of us accomplished together."[6]

After Kovner's escape, there was another unexpected loss: Noime Markeles, the museum secretary, who was both a member of the paper brigade and a founder of the museum. Her departure was a sign of the changing mood. In the ghetto, Markeles was an ardent Communist, but after much soul-searching she decided to leave for Palestine. For her, the decision wasn't ideological. She needed to build a new life, and all of her friends were leaving for Palestine. Her parents were dead, and she wanted to be among friends. Many of the men around the museum had crushes on the brunette with wavy hair and dark brown eyes, and were sad to see her go.[7]

Shmerke was committed to staying and building. He found a valuable new recruit for the museum in the person of Shloime Beilis, one of the original founders of the Young Vilna literary group. In the 1930s, Beilis was a highly regarded Yiddish journalist. Under Soviet rule in 1940–41, he served as managing editor of *Vilna Truth* (*Vilner Emes*), the only local Yiddish newspaper. As soon the Germans attacked, he enlisted in the Red Army.

Beilis had more administrative experience and years of memberships in the Communist party than Shmerke, and he looked down on the impulsive and emotional poet who was now his "boss" at the museum.[8] Beilis also didn't think very highly of former inmates of the Vilna ghetto, who in his eyes had failed the supreme test of mounting a full-fledged ghetto uprising, as they had in Warsaw. He had fought the enemy, while poets like Shmerke wrote songs that accomplished nothing. Shmerke and Beilis didn't like each other, but they shared a strong commitment to rescuing the remnants and put that cause ahead of their animosities. The two men were also bound together by their prewar memories of Young Vilna and a common very personal pain: both of them had a wife who lay somewhere in the mass graves at Ponar.[9]

But Beilis could hardly make up for the shrinking staff, as the mountains of materials in the courtyard of 6 Strashun Street kept growing. The bundles and potato sacks of books and papers in the yard were exposed to mice and water damage. The roof of one of the museum's wings had holes so large, you could count the stars at night from inside the building. Most of the window frames still lacked glass.[10] But the Lithuanian Soviet bureaucrats just let the cultural treasures rot. As the mountains grew, so did Shmerke's frustration. The authorities had banned a Yiddish newspaper, books, and theater, and were hounding the one and only school. He was at his wits end.

In an act of desperation, Shmerke decided to go to Moscow in March 1945. If officials there sent clear-cut instructions to Vilnius to stop the obstructionism, it would stop. Shmerke spent three weeks in the Soviet capital, his first visit there ever. If the circumstances had been different, he would have been an excited pilgrim to the citadel of Communism. Instead, he was angry and frustrated. He spent many hours with Sutzkever, weighing various plans of action. And thanks to efforts by famed journalist Ilya Ehrenburg, he had an audience with an official at the Central Committee of the Communist Party of the USSR — the head of the Department for Cultural Affairs of National Minorities, Comrade Arfo Arfetisovna Petrosian.

Petrosian was sympathetic. As she listened to his litany of complaints, she grew increasingly angry herself. "This is absolutely unacceptable! What does comrade Suslov say about this? We sent him to Lithuania to direct the work there. I am going to write to Suslov that this is an important political matter and that he should receive you. I believe everything will be corrected, unless . . ." She paused pensively and added with uncertainty, "unless the Jews of Lithuania need to be sacrificed for the good of our overall cause."[11]

Shmerke was shaken by Comrade Petrosian's final words: perhaps the Jews of Lithuania needed to be sacrificed for the good of the overall cause. But he still held on to a sliver of hope that the Central Committee would instruct Mikhail Andreievich Suslov to back the museum and support Jewish culture.

As soon as he got off the train, he proceeded to the museum and found the staff deeply distraught. The Trash Administration had decided that it could not wait any longer for the museum to retrieve the remaining tons of paper that were piled in its courtyard. (The museum had no space in its own courtyard and no transportation to move the tons of papers.) During Shmerke's absence, the Trash Administration had cleared its yard and sent the mountains of material—some thirty tons—to the train depot, for shipment to a paper mill in the Ivanovsk Oblast of Russia. The train wagons to Ivanovsk would be loaded any day now.

Shmerke dashed to the train platform and found the materials wrapped in balls, the size of hay bales, ready for shipment. He started grabbing items out of the balls—a script of a Yiddish drama, a book from Chaikl Lunski's library, and an autobiography from a YIVO youth-autobiography competition. He then rushed from one bureau to another to stop the shipment. He appealed to the director of the train station not to send the papers, but the latter replied that Shmerke had no standing. The "scrap paper" wasn't his; it belonged to the Trash Administration. Since time was of the essence, Shmerke contacted the highest Lithuanian official he knew, Henrik Ziman, even though the latter was always cool toward Jewish concerns. Ziman did the bare minimum: he dispatched an inspector to the train depot, who wrote up a report. But the inspector did not order the shipment stopped. Shmerke called Ziman again the next morning, but the member of the Lithuanian Central Committee barked at him to stop wasting his time and slammed down the phone. When Shmerke returned to the train depot later that morning, the balls of paper were gone.

Shmerke rushed off three letters to Moscow, to the Jewish Anti-Fascist Committee, to Ilya Ehrenburg, and to Sutzkever, pleading with them to stop the transport. "Intervene with the paper factory in Aleksandrov, Ivanovsk Oblast, or with the Central Office of the Trash Administration in Moscow, 6 Bolshaia Cherskaskaia Lane, Moscow, director: Vayner. I am sure that your immediate intervention will rescue these treasures from destruction," he wrote to the Anti-Fascist Committee. He was more candid with Ehrenburg. The story of this transport was indicative of the attitude of the Lithuanian authorities toward the museum: "I still have not received any moral or material support for the museum from the Commissariat of Education, and it is because of these moral and material reasons that many Jewish cultural treasures are destroyed, annihilated, and lost."[12]

While waiting for news from Moscow, Shmerke was called in to the chief of the Lithuanian Censorship Bureau, who reprimanded him for insubordination. If there was a problem, Comrade Kaczerginski should have contacted the Censorship Bureau, which had broad authority over printed matter, the chief told him. Instead, he had gone over his head and appealed directly to Moscow. When Shmerke asked the chief of the Censorship Bureau to telegraph his superiors to stop the shipment, the chief told him that it was too late. Nothing was left of the papers.

Upon hearing those words, Shmerke sat down and put his head in his hands. He was speechless. He thought to himself, "Everything destroyed, as if sent to the crematorium."[13]

The fact that the Soviet state apparatus had sent tons of Jewish cultural treasures to their destruction was a devastating blow to Shmerke. That's when it hit him: the Soviets were continuing the work of the Germans. Mikhail Suslov was no better than Johannes Pohl.

And the news was equally dismal regarding other aspects of Jewish communal life. The Yiddish concerts in the "Lutnia" theater that Shmerke had initiated were now blocked by administrative fiat. The Jewish school was informed by the Commissariat of Education that it would not be allowed to grow beyond the fourth grade. After that, students would have to attend Russian or Lithuanian schools.[14]

Shmerke's faith in the Soviet Union, and in the prospect of building Jewish culture there, was shattered. Five to six months after the departure of Ruzhka, Amarant, and Kovner, all of whom were Zionists, he, the Communist, began to think seriously about leaving.[15]

The last straw was the appearance of NKVD agents in the museum. While requesting materials relevant to their investigations of war criminals, they also reminded Shmerke that none of the museum's books were to be made available to the general reading public without prior review by the Censorship Bureau. When he asked them whether the Lithuanian Censorship Bureau had any censors for Yiddish and Hebrew books, they answered no. One of the NKVD agents asked Shmerke to lend him copies of German, Lithuanian, and Polish newspapers that appeared during the German occupation. Shmerke complied and never saw the newspapers again.

Shmerke described his moment of epiphany in his memoirs, written just a few years later: "We, the group of museum activists, had a bizarre realization. We must save the treasures *again* and get them out of here. Otherwise they will disappear and perish. In the best of cases, they will not see the light of day in the Jewish world."[16]

The paper brigade had rescued the cultural treasures from extermination under the Germans, but in "liberated" Vilna, they were locked up in a Soviet prison camp. Only half a year ago, he had complained about Kovner, and probably informed on him, for stealing materials from the museum. Now, after a cascade of disappointments, he was contemplating doing the very same thing that Kovner had done.

For Shmerke, the decision to remove materials from the museum and smuggle them abroad was the product of a deep internal struggle. He had to make three painful decisions: to give up on the Soviet Union —his political hope and inspiration since he was a teenager; to give up on Vilna, his home city, which he loved deeply; and to give up on the Jewish Museum, the institution that he had built with his own willpower and perseverance.

Sutzkever reached the same conclusion as Shmerke—the treasures must be removed—but with much less agonizing. He had never been a Communist, and as a lover of the Yiddish word, it was clear to him that the treasures' legitimate home was the Yiddish Scientific Institute, YIVO, now in New York.

Shmerke and Sutzkever knew what they needed to do. But smuggling the materials out of Soviet Vilnius would be no less dangerous and life threatening than it had been to smuggle them out of the ERR worksite. The operation needed to be done with great care and caution. They needed time to plan it and carry it out.

CHAPTER TWENTY-ONE

The Art of Book Smuggling — Again

S HMERKE KACZERGINSKI began the difficult emotional process of "letting go." His dreams would not be realized; he needed to start thinking differently. The Jewish Museum was a deathtrap for Jewish books and documents. He needed to rescue whatever he could.

Shmerke told only a few close friends of his plans to leave for Poland. In late April 1945, he wrote to Sutzkever in code: "I'm going to travel to Aunt Lola in five to six weeks from now." Aunt Lola was a codename for Lodz, the main destination of Jewish repatriates to Poland.[1] But his time frame was totally unrealistic. As a first step, before even applying to leave, he tendered his resignation as director of the Jewish Museum, with the pretext that he wished to devote himself entirely to his literary projects. (As long as he was director of a state museum, he would not be allowed to emigrate.) But the commissar of education, Juozas Ziugzda, refused to accept his resignation until he found an appropriate replacement. Shmerke asked the Yiddish writers Hirsh Osherovitsh and Yankl Yosada to take the job, but both declined.[2] In June 1945, he finally found the right man: Yankl Gutkowicz.

Gutkowicz was a childhood friend of Shmerke's from the Vilna Talmud Torah and, later, from the underground Communist Party. He spent the entire war, from June 1941 until May 1945, in the ranks of the Soviet army and proceeded home to Vilna as soon as he was discharged. The moment Shmerke bumped into him on the street, they embraced, and Shmerke said, "It's good that you're here. You'll take over the museum." Gutkowicz started working at the museum immediately, and the formal transfer of leadership took place on August 1, 1945.[3]

Shmerke remained on the staff of the museum after August 1 but no longer as director. Sutzkever also had an official position and worked

there during his periodic visits to Vilna. But unbeknownst to Gutkowicz and Shloime Beilis, both Communist believers, the former members of the paper brigade began to work not so much *for* the museum
as *against* it. They secretly removed items from the premises and set
them aside in hiding places, either on the museum's grounds or in their
apartment on Gedimino Street.

Shmerke's first step was to remove the hundreds of Torah scrolls that
he and the group of museum volunteers had found across the city. He
remembered how Zelig Kalmanovitch had been pained and saddened
by the sight of the lonely, naked scrolls lying in the ERR-controlled YIVO
building. He recalled how Johannes Pohl had destroyed scores of them
by sending them off to a leather factory. Shmerke couldn't leave them in
the museum, a Soviet state museum, where they might be confiscated
or shipped off as trash. They deserved better than that. But he also
couldn't take the scrolls out of the country—they were too large and
bulky, and there were just too many of them. Shmerke decided to transfer them gradually and quietly to the synagogue. Gutkowicz and Beilis
didn't object and turned a blind eye to their gradual disappearance.

The scrolls were eagerly received by the Jewish religious community,
then headed by Rabbi Isaac Ausband, a former student in Lithuanian
yeshivas who replaced Rabbi Gustman after the latter departed for
Poland. Upon examining the scrolls, Ausband realized that most of
them were damaged and ritually unfit. Many were mere fragments or
sections of the Torah. He decided to organize a public funeral for the
scrolls and pieces of parchment, in keeping with Jewish religious tradition. It was, in effect, a funeral to mourn the demise of the Jerusalem
of Lithuania, the Jewish city of the book.

The ceremony was held on May 13, 1945, the first day of the Hebrew
month of Sivan, just a few days after V-E day, when Nazi Germany
was vanquished. It was the most powerful commemoration ever held
in Vilna by its Holocaust survivors.

A black casket stood on the Bimah of the Choral Synagogue, filled
with tattered pieces of Torah parchment. The casket was covered with
a torn prayer shawl marred by dried bloodstains. The cantor recited
the memorial prayer "El Male Rahamim" ("God who is full of mercy")
for the martyred Jews of Vilna and its environs, and Rabbi Ausband
gave a eulogy. The Torah was read in honor of Rosh Hodesh (the first
day of the Hebrew month), and the entire congregation said the bless-

ing "Ha-gomel," traditionally recited when someone survives danger or peril, to mark their survival from Nazi extermination.

After the Torah reading, fragments of parchment were distributed to all those present, and they lined up to throw their fragments into the open casket. The leaders of the religious community then lifted the casket onto their shoulders and carried it out of the synagogue and through the streets of Vilna.

A procession of several hundred people marched to the ghetto, stopping momentarily at the site of the ghetto gate, where many had lost their lives due to smuggling, and then at the building of the Judenrat, where Jacob Gens had presided. Non-Jewish pedestrians were deeply impressed by the scene and moved quietly onto the narrow sidewalks. The procession halted at the *shulhoyf*, in front of the damaged Great Synagogue and the ruins of the Vilna Gaon's kloyz. There, waiting for them were vehicles filled with desecrated Torah scrolls, and the black casket was loaded onto one of them. Standing on the rubble of the Vilna Gaon's kloyz, a survivor of the Vilna ghetto recited the blessing said by mourners at a funeral: "Blessed art Thou, Lord our God, King of the universe, who is the true judge." A survivor from the nearby town of Niemiencin performed the ritual rending of his garments, and educator Michael Rajak spoke. "How fortunate are Vilna's Torah scrolls compared to its Jews. The scrolls will have the privilege of receiving a proper burial. They will rise up before God's throne of glory and testify as witnesses. They saw everything that the evil ones did to us."

The trucks with the scrolls, followed by the procession, moved slowly in the direction of the Zarecha Cemetery, Vilna's second-oldest Jewish cemetery. Once there, each participant took a scroll or fragment out of one of the vehicles and placed it into the open grave. As the ceremony approached its conclusion, a man came running with a large object wrapped in a prayer shawl. It was the body of his daughter, who had been murdered by the Germans. He had kept her corpse in the underground hiding place where he had survived, and now he decided to bury her with the Torah scrolls. The entire assembly recited kaddish.

A journalist who reported on the funeral noted, "All those who were present erupted into sobs and tears, and the sound of their crying carried far beyond the cemetery. That sound will remain forever in the broken hearts of those who were there on that day."[4]

With the funeral, the surviving remnant of Jewish Vilna bid farewell to its violated Torahs. This "proper burial" was made possible by Shmerke, the Communist Party member. But in order to avoid drawing attention to himself and his "illegal" role in the transfer of the Torahs, Shmerke stayed away from the event.

———————

Removing other museum objects behind the back of his childhood friend and successor, Gutkowicz, was difficult both logistically and emotionally. Gutkowicz suspected something but couldn't bring himself to confront Shmerke. The tense scene was described by Young Vilna writer Chaim Grade, who heard about it from Shmerke himself:

> Every day, Gutkowicz would walk into Shmerke's office and complain that according to the list that he, the former director, had put together, important manuscripts and rare books were missing. Shmerke shrugged his shoulders and told him to look for them in the mountains in the courtyard. Gutkowicz went to look for them and came back the next day with the same complaint, that he couldn't find anything.
>
> "As long as I work here, I'm still in charge of my own office," Shmerke said and didn't let go of the key to his room. Meanwhile, he preferred to work in the museum at times when the new director was somewhere else — either in a government office or at home for lunch. . . .
>
> One day Gutkowicz walked into Shmerke's office without the list of missing treasures, so as not to appear as if he suspected something. He spoke in an intentionally indifferent voice: he had gone through mountains of books and documents and still couldn't find the letters by Abraham Mapu, Dr. Herzl's diary, and the manuscripts by Dr. Ettinger. Maybe Shmerke remembered where he had put them? . . . This time Shmerke got angry, and he turned to his friend: "Don't worry about it. What's the difference if there's one book more or one book less? What do you care, anyway? You didn't risk your neck to save them from the Germans." . . .
>
> Gutkowicz didn't want to ruin his time-tested friendship. So he didn't even answer back that the Soviet State Committee could demand of him an accounting for the missing manuscripts. After a long silence, Gutkowicz replied, "I didn't mean anything in particular. I

just asked if perhaps by chance you saw the materials." And he quietly left Shmerke's office.[5]

All the while, Shmerke told no one except for his closest friends that
he planned to leave for Poland. He put up a public front of being a loyal
Communist and Soviet patriot. In June, he composed an end-of-year
play for the children of the Jewish school, which began with the Soviet
anthem and ended with expressions of thanks to Comrade Stalin. In
August, he signed a contract with the "Emes" publishing house in Moscow to publish his collection of ghetto songs. As late as mid-October,
the Moscow Yiddish poet Itzik Feffer wrote to him: "I want to break
away from here and come visit you."[6]

As Shmerke accumulated a treasure chest of books and manuscripts
in his apartment, he started giving small packages to people who were
"repatriating" to Poland and asked them to take the items across the
border in their luggage. They were happy to comply. They felt they
were taking a little bit of the Jerusalem of Lithuania with them, as they
bid farewell to the city. Shmerke told them to hold on to the packages
in Poland until he arrived or sent them further instructions.[7]

In July 1945, Shmerke sent a package of materials with emigrating
friends to Rachela Krinsky, his former colleague and lover from the
paper brigade, who had survived the concentration camps and was
living in Lodz. The package included Theodor Herzl's diary and other
rarities. In the accompanying letter, he gave Rachela very strict orders:
she was not to tell anyone about the package, and she should not hand
over its contents to anyone, unless the person presented a note from him
with the code phrase "Shweik has requested." (Shweik was an acronym
for Shmerke Kaczerginski.)[8]

Shmerke left Vilnius suddenly, in late November 1945, without so
much as saying good-bye to Gutkowicz. According to Chaim Grade's
account, staff member Shloime Beilis intimated to Shmerke that he
should leave the country immediately or face arrest. He walked into
Shmerke's office, shook his hand, and said to him, "Have a good trip.
You're leaving today, right?" When Shmerke answered that he had no
such plans, Beilis remarked that Gutkowicz had just been summoned to
the Ministry of Culture to give a detailed accounting of the museum's
manuscripts and rare books. He then added suggestively, "I am sure
that comrade Ziman of the Central Committee is mistaken in his as-

sessment that you are an enemy of the Soviet Union." Shmerke got the message: the authorities had marked him for arrest. He left Vilna the same day for another part of the country, to shake any "tails" that were following him. After a few days, he crossed over into Poland.[9]

Shmerke, like Aba Kovner a year beforehand, was forced to leave suddenly in order to avoid arrest. He wasn't able to take with him most of the cultural treasures he had hidden. It remained for Sutzkever to collect them and get them out.

Sutzkever visited Vilna twice in 1946, after Shmerke had left.[10] During those visits, he had a twofold mission: to excavate materials *on behalf* of the Jewish Museum and to extricate materials *from* the museum. Shmerke sent him a letter by courier from Poland with specific instructions on where certain items were located: "In the courtyard of the Jewish Museum, under the stairwell, where the religious books are piled, I buried Kruk's diary. Be sure to find it."[11]

Sutzkever left for Poland in May 1946. Exactly how he smuggled materials across the Soviet-Polish border is unclear. In letters to Max Weinreich, he only related that the operation involved "countless difficulties and life-threatening dangers." Shmerke was equally cautious not to disclose details, presumably to protect people who were still in Soviet Vilnius. In his memoirs on his Soviet experiences, Shmerke wrote laconically that "there will come a time when this chapter of Jewish heroism and self-sacrifice will need to be described in detail."[12] But that time never came. So we can only speculate.

It is likely that the Bericha, the underground Zionist operation to smuggle Jews across Europe to Palestine, helped move the books and documents across the border to Poland. The materials were simply too voluminous to be carried out in one or two suitcases.[13] The Bericha ran an underground railroad all across Europe that moved Jews from one country to another and placed them on unregistered ships to Palestine. In the Soviet Union, the movement's operations were based in Vilna and run by two members of Shomer Ha-tsa'ir, Shmuel Jaffe and Yaakov Yanai. The two men managed to whisk 450 Soviet citizens out of the USSR illegally in the first six months of 1946. They had help from a former Belorussian partisan officer, who worked as the Soviet representative to the repatriation commission in Baranovici, near the Soviet-Polish border. It is likely that Sutzkever's suitcases with books and documents crossed the border via the Baranovici checkpoint.[14]

CHAPTER TWENTY-TWO

Rachela's Choice

RACHELA KRINSKY's story after the dissolution of the paper brigade was a string of nightmares. At the time of the final liquidation of the ghetto, in September 1943, the high school teacher was deported to the Kaiserwald camp near Riga, where her head was shaved, her body sprayed with disinfectant, and she was issued a concentration-camp uniform. She worked piling lumber and digging pits in the bitter cold. Slackers were executed on the outskirts of the camp, but Rachela was a hard worker and survived.

From Kaiserwald, the Germans sent her on to the Stutthof camp near Danzig, where she was interred for more than a year. Rachela was one of the lucky Stutthof inmates who did not die of typhus and who were not gassed in the camp's gas chamber. While it was originally a labor camp, Stutthof began doubling as a death camp in 1944, when Auschwitz was working at full capacity. The Germans sent the overflow of Hungarian Jews to Stutthof, where they went straight to the gas chamber. Every night, Rachela watched the smoke rise from the camp crematorium and asked herself when her turn would come. When the Red Army started approaching the vicinity, the Nazis dissolved the Stutthof camp and drove the remaining inmates on a death march up the Baltic coast in the bitter winter cold. Stragglers and the infirm were shot dead without warning. But Rachela survived. She was liberated by the Soviets on March 13, 1945.

After recovering her strength, she made her way eastward, from Germany to Poland, to Lodz, the main gathering place for surviving Polish Jews.[1]

Once there, Rachela reestablished contact with her nanny back in Soviet Vilnius, Wikcia Rodziewicz, and learned that her young daughter Sarah, whom she had left in Wikcia's care three and a half years earlier, was alive and well. The mother in Rachela was happy, but she was guilt-ridden that she had abandoned her child. She shared her private pain in letters to Shmerke and Sutzkever: Wikcia had been a wonderful mother to Sarah during the war years, and "there is not much justice in the fact that I've survived." She was depleted, depressed, and confused. Her life in the camps, she wrote, had been a never-ending hell. "I experienced my own death hundreds of times, only to remain alive—to await even worse things."

Rachela wrote that now, after the liberation, she could not rediscover joy. "I simply cannot catch the rhythm of this new life. I imagined that it would be different, that the miracle would have a moral sense" (a phrase from Sutzkever's ghetto poem "A Prayer to the Miracle"). "I miss beauty so very much. I've had a tremendous shortage of it for the last two years." She remembered fondly, even nostalgically, Sutzkever's recitation of Yiddish poetry in the ERR-controlled building of YIVO. In fact, the only joy she could find in her new life was in reading poetry.[2]

Rachela wasn't sure of her future. Confused and depressed, she didn't even bother writing to her brothers and sister in America for several months after her liberation. She didn't think it was important. Sutzkever informed her American family of her survival.[3]

But Rachela did do one thing: she asked Wikcia to "repatriate" to Poland with Sarah, or as everyone now called her, Irena. She wanted to reunite with her daughter, whom she had left behind as a twenty-two-month-old, who was now six and didn't even remember her. Rachela confided to Sutzkever, "Perhaps reuniting with my daughter will help me. Not that I'll help her, but she—me." Sutzkever replied from Moscow:

> Rachela. I can feel (I used to think that I couldn't feel anything) how your heart is contorted with pain. But I don't believe that life deserves to be taken so seriously. . . . We must accept reality as it is. We must learn to discover the chemical formula for transforming sorrow into joy. Otherwise, it is impossible to live. . . . I reject resignation. The aircraft that came to collect me from the forest, to take me across the front to Moscow, was burnt to a crisp in the sky, before my very eyes. I waited and waited until a second aircraft came.

And if you have lost faith in humanity, then the world *beyond* humanity is still so beautiful! No one on earth can rob me of that eternal beauty.[4]

Shmerke likewise urged Rachela to put her painful thoughts aside. He wrote to her from Vilnius in July 1945: "I very much want you to crawl out of the past and forget it as much as possible. I want you to be at least the way you were in your little room in YIVO: someone who understands everything without asking, a warm person, and a real friend. All of these things together are more than each one separately. You'll see that everything will be much better than you think."

Then Shmerke suggested rather coyly that he and Rachela consider marrying each other. He asked her to send him an official letter of invitation to immigrate to Poland, in which she named him as her husband. This would help him leave more easily. Whether the word "husband" would be a legal fiction or a reality, he left for her to decide. Shmerke didn't hide from her that he had a girlfriend in Vilna, but he wrote that he didn't love her and would leave her. He wanted to be with Rachela. "I believe that if we were together, you would feel much better."

At this point, the letter turned romantic: "I want to see you, talk to you, be silent together, and be together. I'm ashamed to talk a lot and say a lot, and even to write a lot to you—because I feel that you're looking at me, and I must drop my eyes. I hope you'll wait for me, and that you won't move elsewhere for the time being. But if you must, then it's lost. Then I hope I'll chase after you in your thoughts."[5]

Rachela didn't send an invitation designating Shmerke as her husband. She made no promises and no commitments. As she wrote in one of her letters to Sutzkever, she couldn't imagine remarrying. "It seems comical to me when people talk about love. I really can't feel anything."

When Shmerke arrived in Lodz, the first thing he did was look for Rachela. He found her living in an apartment with her daughter, nanny, sister-in-law, and a close friend. She was engaged in the difficult work of rebuilding her life and her relationship with a daughter who called the nanny "mama" and referred to her as "the lady."

The romance between Shmerke and Rachela rekindled immediately. For Rachela, reuniting with Shmerke was her first experience of simple joy, while the reunion with her daughter was mixed with guilt and frustration. Both Rachela and Shmerke had other romantic partners in Lodz, as their erotic energies came roaring back to life. (One survivor commented that Shmerke "went from woman to woman like a bee from flower to flower.") But the love and understanding between them were deep. Among the survivors in Lodz, it was a foregone conclusion that "the bard will marry the teacher."

But the romance created a new challenge for Rachela. She found it difficult to balance satisfying her own reawakening desires with meeting the needs of her daughter. She wrote to one of her admirers, "Here I am sitting on the sofa, with Shmerke kissing my eyes out, with little Sarah looking on, and with me thinking about you." Close friends warned her that if she continued to make passionate love in front of the child, she would lose her daughter.

There were also tensions between Rachela and Wikcia, the nanny, who felt that she knew better what the child needed and found it difficult to relinquish her maternal role.[6]

And on top of it all, Rachela struggled with bouts of depression. She wrote to Sutzkever in Moscow:

> I pretend to be alive. I go to the cinema, theater, or café. But I often look at myself from the outside and see prisoner number 95246, according to the Stutthof register. The register that also recorded how many gold teeth each of us had, so they would know from which corpses to extract teeth. I'm listening to music, my "date" tells me something, and I don't even hear what he's saying, because I'm seeing other images. I just want to scream. . . . In the mornings, I'm too lazy to wake up and begin living. But I put up appearances, and probably no one would believe me, that I'm only pretending to be alive.[7]

Rachela was right about one thing. The relationship with her daughter helped her, as the two gradually bonded. After a few months of living together, she wrote to Sutzkever, "The little one and I are already very good friends. I am her mother again."[8] But there was one problem: six-year-old Sarah didn't like Shmerke, the "short cross-eyed man" who visited them often. She complained to her mother that "he sings songs to you, not to me. And I'll be taller than him in a year."

Sarah clearly preferred to play with another man who visited her mother from time to time, Abraham Melezin. A former instructor of geography at Wilno University, Melezin had lost his wife and young son at Majdanek and, like Rachela, was a survivor of the Stutthof camp. He was drawn to little Sarah, in part because she filled the void of his murdered son, and she, in turn, adored him. She told her mother straight out: "Lady, why don't the two of you get married? I want him to be my daddy!"

As the months passed, Rachela came to realize that Shmerke would never be the father Sarah so desperately needed. He was too light-hearted, too self-absorbed, and too busy. With her family in America beckoning, she decided to join them, alone, without marrying Shmerke.

Wikcia also stayed behind in Poland.

Rachela and her daughter left Poland in April 1946, for Sweden, where she awaited the American visa that was arranged by her brother Chaim in New York. Before she left, Shmerke wrote her a farewell poem:

> You brought me springtime
> When all around was autumn,
> In the darkness of night
> You caressed and soothed my roar.
>
> My roar, like that of a wolf in the forest,
> You rocked to sleep with your breath,
> And my loneliness disappeared with the darkness,
> As you adorned my mood with joy.
>
> Now, when loneliness gnaws at me
> I roar like that wolf and look for your limbs,
> My dream flies around and whispers at your door:
> . . . I am alone.[9]

Shortly after Rachela's departure, Shmerke married his girlfriend from Vilna, Mary, who had repatriated to Poland.

Rachela Krinsky settled in New York, in her brother's apartment. A few months later, the man who had played so nicely with her daughter, Abraham Melezin, arrived in New York as well. Without a home or relatives, he stayed with Rachela in her sister's apartment. Upon seeing him, little Sarah jumped for joy. Rachela was more reserved and conflicted, but after a few weeks of hesitation, she decided to marry Melezin. She chose the man who would be a good father to her newly regained daughter, over the greatest love of her life. She sacrificed herself for Sarah.

The paper-brigade romance was over.[10]

CHAPTER TWENTY-THREE

The German Discovery

A s THE WAR in Europe drew to a close, Max Weinreich decided to renew his efforts to recover the remnants of the
institute's collections. On April 4, 1945, he sent a letter to
assistant secretary of state Archibald MacLeish, asking for US government assistance. According to the information at YIVO's disposal, he
wrote, its books and archives were held by the Nazi Institute for the
Investigation of the Jewish Question in Frankfurt. Weinreich asked US
forces to seek out and locate YIVO's treasures, which might be buried
under the ruins of the bombed-out German city.[1]

A month later, on May 7, Weinreich and Sol Liptzin, the secretary
of YIVO's academic council, and professor of German at City College,
met with State Department officials in Washington. The latter listened
carefully to their case and referred them, surprisingly, to the Commerce Department. Since YIVO was an American institution, incorporated in the state of New York, this was a case of retrieving American
property looted by the Germans. So Weinreich and Liptzin jumped
into a cab and met with the head of the Division of Economic Security
at Commerce, Seymour J. Rubin. Rubin was so impressed by YIVO's
claim that he cabled US Military Headquarters in Germany (SHAEF)
immediately and requested that it "find out what has been saved from
the collections of the Rosenberg Institute, and whether property of the
YIVO was found among them."

After the meetings in Washington, YIVO sent Rubin and the State
Department a review memo with one new piece of information: the
address of the Institute for the Investigation of the Jewish Question, 68
Bockenheimer Landstrasse, Frankfurt. YIVO's materials might be there.

A copy of the YIVO memo landed in the Berlin office of General

Lucius Clay, the deputy supreme Allied commander in Europe. General Clay ordered a military detachment to go examine the building at 68 Bockenheimer Landstrasse and take along an officer from the Monuments, Fine Arts, and Archives Department, a "Monuments Man."[2]

They found a lot more than they expected. Beneath a building that was badly damaged by allied bombing, there were cellars with crates containing one hundred thousand books. The detachment couldn't identify them because they were in Hebrew letters. us military headquarters in Frankfurt dispatched Corporal Abraham Aaroni to the site since he was a Hebrew scholar. Aaroni visited the building on June 19 and 20, 1945, and determined that the books included parts of three well-known Jewish libraries: yivo of Vilna, the Ecole Rabbinique of Paris, and the Rabbiner Seminar of Amsterdam.[3]

yivo learned about the discovery with lightning speed, not from the us government, but from Aaroni, who was friends with a yivo staff member in New York, Shlomo Noble. On the day he examined the crates of books in the cellar, Aaroni sent a letter to his wife Celia in Brooklyn with the news:

> Darling,
> You may call Noble and tell him that I found part of the yivo library. It is not 200 boxes of books from all over the world that I found, but about 1,000. Which means about 100,000 volumes. . . . It would take a staff of about 20 men a year to sort all of this. . . . My primary job today is to convince Military Government authorities [of] the importance of removing all this priceless treasure to a more appropriate place. I foresee a fight.
> Bright morning to you. Yours, A.[4]

Aaroni's wife called Noble, who informed Weinreich. It was all so straightforward and easy. Give them the address, and they'll find your books. Weinreich found out about the discovery before the State Department did.

He wrote to the Office of Economic Security Controls at State and urged the United States to move the Jewish cultural treasures, including yivo's property, out of the crumbling building of the Nazi institute to a secure facility. Weinreich quoted a letter he had received from a soldier stationed in Germany: "There is a wholesale redistribution of property here, and many items which should make their way into museums or archives are becoming souvenirs."

Weinreich also asked the State Department to assist YIVO in sending a representative to Frankfurt "to complete the identification of YIVO property and arrange for its return to the United States." He offered to travel to Frankfurt himself. But the State Department assured him that there was no need for a representative. The books and papers were being protected, and it would take time to sort out the matter of their final disposition.[5]

The discovery in the cellars of 68 Bockenheimer Landstrasse was only the beginning. There were reports that many more Jewish books were stored in Hungen, a town thirty miles north of Frankfurt. The US military dispatched a Monument's Man to investigate, and he discovered a trove ten times as large as the one in Frankfurt. The cache was located in this innocuous provincial town, because the heads of the Institute for the Investigation of the Jewish Question had decided to transfer most of its looted collections out of Frankfurt in early 1944, when the allies began bombing the city and struck their building. The Germans, who had devoted extensive manpower and resources to amass the greatest Judaica collection in the world, were intent on keeping it, even in the face of allied bombing. This was a priority, even as they were going down in defeat.

In Hungen, looted books and archives were held in numerous scattered locations: in a cave, a castle, a school, a barn, and in cellars and offices belonging to commercial enterprises. The total number of books was estimated at one million. The Monuments Man reported to his direct superior: "[They] include historical materials of great importance, including Jewish materials removed by the Germans from the occupied territories, including the Yiddish Scientific Institute at Vilno."[6]

US forces transferred the books from the cellars of Bockenheimer Landstrasse and Hungen to the building of the Rothschild Library in Frankfurt. That facility had housed the extraordinary library of the Rothschild family, which specialized in literature, art, and music. (It was opened for public use in 1895 and was transferred to municipal control in 1928. The Nazi authorities removed the Rothschild name and de-Judaized its collections in the 1930s.) But the Rothschild Library proved to be too small, especially after deposits of books were discovered in other locations in the American zone of occupied Germany.[7]

The books and papers from Vilna were mixed up with the other collections. The US authorities needed to sort the books, put them in order, and resolve the question of their ownership.

But the actions taken by the US military government after they assumed control of the books were not encouraging. They hired twenty German librarians to catalog and arrange the books. While the librarians were "carefully screened" to excluded Nazi Party members, none of them knew Hebrew or Yiddish, and they worked with no supervision or guidance. Unsurprisingly, they made virtually no progress.

And on the restitution front, things looked even worse. In response to a letter by Rabbi Judah Nadich, General Eisenhower's advisor on Jewish affairs in Europe, who urged the return of YIVO's collection to its headquarters in New York, the Civil Affairs Division of the War Department wrote that it could not make any commitments. Standard restitution policy required that looted property be returned to its country of origin. "Since the library was removed from Vilna, and since this city is in the USSR, the question arises as to whether our policy concerning the restitution of Nazi looting will permit its transfer to New York." The matter would need to be reviewed by the State Department.[8] The news that the United States might "restitute" YIVO's collections to the Soviet Union made Weinreich's blood boil over. Was this what Zelig Kalmanovitch and Herman Kruk had died for? He put his scholarship on hold and, for the next year, made retrieving YIVO's collections his top priority.

While YIVO couldn't take control of its books, the American Jewish Joint Distribution Committee (JDC) wanted to distribute some of them among the survivors, who were desperately in need of reading material. There were hundreds of thousands of Jewish "displaced persons" (DPs) living in transit camps in Germany who wanted to resume the normal life activities of reading and schooling. The "Joint" (JDC) led a large-scale educational program in the camps. Rather than ship books across the ocean, which would cost a lot of time and money, the organization asked the US military for permission to borrow twenty-five thousand volumes from the Frankfurt book-collection point. Mindful that some of the best Yiddish books belonged to YIVO, the JDC reached out to YIVO with a request to borrow several thousand YIVO volumes held in

Frankfurt for distribution in the DP camps, primarily textbooks for use by the JDC-run schools.

Weinreich was torn. He, the institute's sole surviving director, could not examine his own rescued library. The War Department had turned down his request to travel to Frankfurt to review the collection. But another organization wanted to select items from the remnants of the YIVO library, without any guarantee that they would be returned undamaged.

On the other hand, for whom were these books rescued, if not for living Jews? How could YIVO turn its back on the surviving Yiddish readers and put its institutional interests ahead of the dire human needs of the victims of Nazism?

Weinreich cabled back to the JDC on December 4, 1945:

IN VIEW OF THE EXTREME IMPORTANCE OF YOUR EDUCATIONAL PROGRAM, WE DECIDED TO PUT ASIDE BOTH SCHOLARLY AND EMOTIONAL CONSIDERATIONS WHICH WOULD IMPELL US TO PRESERVE IN TACT THAT PART OF OUR LIBRARY SAVED FROM NAZIS STOP. WE AUTHORIZE YOU TO INSPECT OUR LIBRARY NOW IN FRANKFURT AND DRAW FROM ITS TEXTBOOKS.

Of course, Weinreich had certain conditions: The JDC should select, first and foremost, textbooks published in the United States, Western and Central Europe. "NO BOOKS PUBLISHED IN SOVIET UNION STOP." These were bibliographic rarities. The JDC must maintain a full list of the borrowed books and send a copy to YIVO. It should also advise the individuals and organizations who received the books to treat them with the utmost care. But in the final analysis, Weinreich acted on trust and out of love for the remnants of East European Jewry.[9]

In February 1946, the US authorities decided to transfer the book-collection point from the overcrowded Rothschild Library to a depot in Offenbach, just across the river from Frankfurt. The facility was the confiscated headquarters and warehouse of I. G. Farben, the vast German chemical conglomerate. There was much irony here. Farben was the manufacturer of Zyklon-B, the poison gas used to murder more than a million people in Auschwitz and other death camps. The company's spacious five-story building now became the site for the Offenbach Archival Depot, billed in internal memos as "the largest collection of Jewish material in the world." The depot stored 1.5 million looted

Jewish books, and an equal number of other books, which the Germans had stolen from major libraries across Europe.

The man put in charge of the Offenbach depot was a young lieutenant from Chicago named Seymour Pomrenze, who had been trained as an archivist before being inducted into the army. Pomrenze was a short, bright man, with a strong will and a sharp tongue. He took the inert and moribund Offenbach collection point, with a staff of six Germans, and turned it into a large, efficient operation, with 176 workers. As an observant Jew with knowledge of Hebrew and Yiddish, he cared about the fate of the books more than his steely military demeanor let on. Pomrenze's most important decision was *not* to catalog the books but to sort them by country, based on their ex libris and markings, in preparation for their return to their owners and countries of origin. Instead of making catalog cards, the Offenbach depot made piles.

Identification was easy when it came to books belonging to general libraries and Judaica collections from France, Holland, and Germany. Their stamps and ex libris were written in the Latin alphabet. But Jewish books from Eastern Europe had stamps and markings in Hebrew and Yiddish, and general libraries from the Soviet Union had stamps in Russian and Ukrainian. No one on staff could read those languages. And the US military was not about to transfer dozens of soldiers with specialized language skills to Offenbach, for a bibliographic mission.

So Pomrenze came up with an ingenious system: a human conveyor belt for the visual examination of stamps. He photographed the images of all the stamps found inside the Jewish and Cyrillic books, and hired scores of Germans as sorters. Each German employee was responsible for knowing the exact shape and appearance of a limited number of stamps, usually ten to twenty. Each German examined the book, and if it had a stamp that matched one of his photographic images, he set it aside and sent it to a corresponding numbered box. If he didn't recognize the stamp, he passed the book on to the next sorter, and to the next, until it matched someone's stamp.

In April 1946, Pomrenze had 176 employees at the Offenbach depot, all of them Germans, 63 of whom worked in the sorting department. Using this system, Pomrenze was able to identify the ownership of more than half of the 1.5 million Hebrew and Yiddish books, without a single employee being able to read the Hebrew alphabet.[10]

The depot soon began shipping out collections for restitution to Holland and France. These included the Bibliotheca Rosenthaliana from Amsterdam, one of the world's greatest collections of rare Hebrew manuscripts and imprints, and the archive of the Paris-based Alliance Israelite Universelle, the world's first international Jewish aid organization. General library collections, of non-Jewish books, were returned to ten different countries. Foremost among them were Holland (328,007 items restituted in 1946), France (328,181 items), and Italy (224,620 items).[11]

The YIVO books were identified, segregated, and packed in crates that were marked "JIVO." Pomrenze didn't need to be told what YIVO was. His older brother Chaim was a member of YIVO's board of trustees. Weinreich was delighted that the military officer responsible for custody over YIVO's books was a friend of the institute. Weinreich wrote his letters to Pomrenze in Yiddish.

On the matter of the books' ultimate disposition, Weinreich's greatest fear was that "by intention or by mistake, the YIVO library may be sent to Russia, in which event it probably would never be recovered and returned to YIVO, its rightful owner. This loss would be a terrific and irreparable one, not alone for YIVO itself, but also for Jews interested in research on problems and aspects of Jewish community life throughout the world." Weinreich scrutinized every shred of information coming from Offenbach from this perspective, to prevent that nightmare scenario from happening. When the depot listed the YIVO library in its first monthly report and indicated its country of origin as "Vilna, USSR," Weinreich hit the roof. Later reports listed the YIVO books without a country of origin.[12]

Weinreich exploited whatever political connections he had to advance YIVO's claim to its books and papers. The executive vice president of the American Jewish Committee, John Slawson, wrote to secretary of state James Burnes; Rabbi Judah Nadich wrote directly to General Eisenhower; and the Jewish Welfare Board, which ran the Jewish military chaplaincy and had good ties to the War Department, also became involved. But the American Jewish Committee was the most active and fruitful channel of communication.

Weinreich not only pressed for the return of the books with YIVO stamps inside but also claimed that there were collections with non-YIVO markings that belonged to the institute. The great Jewish historian Simon Dubnow had donated a part of his library to YIVO during his lifetime and bequeathed the rest to YIVO in his will. But the only stamps on his books were "Simonas Dubnovi, Riga," which meant that the Offenbach staff would put them in a pile marked "Riga, Latvia." Weinreich compiled a list of twelve such "YIVO associated libraries" that he claimed as YIVO property. Foremost among them were the Strashun Library and the An-ski Museum, both of which, he contended, merged with YIVO in October 1939 in the hope of transferring their collections to the safety of the United States. This meant that YIVO laid claim to thousands of additional books, documents, and manuscripts.

Weinreich's assertion that the Strashun Library and An-ski Museum merged with YIVO on the eve of the German occupation was rather dubious. There was no documentary evidence to support it, and almost all the trustees of the Strashun Library and An-ski Museum perished during the war, meaning that there was no one alive to confirm this version of events. (The only trustee who could have corroborated Weinreich's story, chief rabbi Isaac Rubinshtein, who escaped Vilna in 1940, died in New York in 1945, before the caches of books were discovered.) Weinreich may have fibbed in order to obtain more books. He definitely believed that YIVO had a moral right to these collections, since it was the sole surviving Jewish institution from Vilna. Pomrenze accepted Weinreich's version of events and packed the "associated collections" in the YIVO crates or, in the case of the Strashun Library, in separate crates that were placed next to the YIVO ones.[13]

But even with Pomrenze's support, the matter of final disposition was stuck in a bureaucratic logjam. The State Department was in favor of returning the books and papers to New York, but the Office of Military Government, United States (OMGUS) in Germany, part of the War Department, was opposed, or at least hesitant. Robert D. Murphy, the political head of OMGUS, explained his reservations in a cable to the State Department on April 12, 1946:

> Proposed action [shipment to New York] runs counter to restitution directives and quadripartite decisions, which stipulate that restitution to be made to the governments of the countries from which the property was removed. In no case is restitution made to individuals, business establishments or other organizations. . . . Feel that difficult precedent established if restitution made to Institute rather than gov-

ernment. If Department feels the circumstances surrounding case warrant restitution to United States rather than Poland, we suggest the possibility of designating Library of Congress Mission now in Germany as interim custodians. . . . Suggest desirability of clearing with Polish Government before taking proposed action.

Murphy.[14]

Until that point, Weinreich feared that the books would be sent to the Soviet Union. Now a high-ranking official of the US military government in Germany stated that since Vilna had belonged to Poland before the war, restitution to Poland should be considered. At the very least, he recommended that the United States clear the matter with the Polish government.

Weinreich received the discouraging news from Major L. B. LaFarge, the head of the Monuments, Fine Arts, and Archives Department, who told him rather bluntly that this was a governmental matter, not a YIVO matter. "We wish to draw your attention to our basic policy on restitution, which states that this headquarters will deal only with nations, through their accredited representatives, and not directly with individuals or institutions from such nations."

LaFarge added, "Inasmuch as the restitution of YIVO material now in our custody presents an extremely complicated problem from the international point of view, we have referred it to higher authority for clarification and instructions."[15]

The "complicated problem" was that the YIVO case did not fit easily into established international law and practice. YIVO was a refugee institution that had fled Europe and transferred its headquarters to New York in 1940. While the headquarters had moved, the library and archive had stayed behind in the institute's Vilna branch and were subsequently looted by the Germans. Established policy required that the books be returned to their country of origin—either the Soviet Union or Poland. But that meant that YIVO, the refugee owner, whose entire staff had been murdered by the Germans, would be robbed of its property yet again. And the party responsible for the second robbery would be none other than the US government.

CHAPTER TWENTY-FOUR

Parting Duties

W HEN SHMERKE KACZERGINSKI left Vilnius suddenly and unexpectedly, to avoid arrest, he left behind a large volume of valuable treasures. It was left to Abraham Sutzkever to get as much of it as he could out of the country, by whatever means at his disposal. Sutzkever's emigration deadline was the end of June 1946, when the repatriation treaty between the USSR and Poland would expire. As a former Polish citizen, he was allowed to leave until that date. Sutzkever arranged his personal documents, with all the necessary stamps and permits, but received an unexpected invitation that changed his plans. Soviet officials asked him to serve as a witness at the Nuremberg tribunal of major Nazi war criminals. The prosecutors designated him as the witness who would speak about the suffering of the Jews. Sutzkever dropped everything and flew to Nuremberg to perform his duty.

Sutzkever gave his testimony on February 27, 1946. He spoke of the roundups, massacres, and deportations to Ponar for execution; he told of his discovery of one of his mother's shoes in a wagonload of shoes from Ponar; and he recounted the murder of his newborn child in the ghetto hospital. His testimony lasted thirty-eight minutes. Unlike other witnesses, he refused to sit in the witness stand. He gave his entire testimony standing upright, as if the act was too solemn, too holy, to perform sitting down.[1]

Sutzkever's notes in preparation for his testimony show that he intended to speak at length about the looting and destruction of cultural treasures by the Einsatzstab Reichsleiter Rosenberg (ERR). He planned to cite specific acts: Johannes Pohl sold the lead linotype plates of the Vilna Romm Press's edition of the Talmud to a factory that smelted them down into liquid form; Albert Sporket sold five hundred Torah scrolls to a leather factory for conversion into raw leather; and Pohl personally demolished sculptures by Mark Antokolsky and paintings by Il'ia Repin, shouting that they were "horrible."[2] But the Soviet prosecutor, Lev Smirnov, took his questioning in other directions and concluded his examination of the witness before Sutzkever could mention the subject.

Sutzkever managed to allude to his recent retrieval of documents in the surprise coda to his testimony. When Smirnov finished his questioning, and the witness was told that he may leave the stand, Sutzkever volunteered to Judge Geoffrey Lawrence, president of the tribunal, that he had a document he had discovered after the liberation that he believed would be of interest to the court. Smirnov was unprepared for this spontaneous offer by the witness and interjected that he was not familiar with the document. Lawrence was intrigued and asked Sutzkever to read the document. It was all of one sentence in German: "To the Gebietskommissar for Vilna. At your order, our institution is currently disinfecting the old Jewish clothes from Ponar and will hand them over to the Vilna administration."

The hall shuddered at the image. The Germans had a system for disinfecting and redistributing the clothes of the people they murdered. Judge Lawrence asked Sutzkever exactly where and when he had found the document. Sutzkever replied that he had found it in the former offices of the German Gebietskommissar in Vilna. Lawrence asked Sutzkever to read the document again, and it was accepted into evidence as exhibit URSS-444.[3] It was the first time that a victim of Nazi persecution had submitted documentary evidence at Nuremberg.

Sutzkever savored the moment. He had used one of the fruits of his searches and excavations to help bring the chief mass murderers to justice. This had been one of the original goals of the Jewish Museum—to use the documents in courts of law. He had done it, and not in just any court, but in Nuremberg. Sutzkever's dramatic submission of the document was reported by *Pravda* in its dispatch from the tribunal.[4]

Sutzkever also used his visit to Germany to send another envelope of rescued materials. This time, he found a courier who was a personal acquaintance of Weinreich's: Benjamin Wald, a translator for the American delegation. Sutzkever gave him three letters by Sholem Aleichem, a notice of a school program in the Vilna ghetto, and a few other items. He appended a short letter. "I carried these letters through the ghetto, through fire and swamps, underground and in the air. The school program from the ghetto was discovered at Ponar. Please hold on to it at home, until I can pick it up in person. . . . Warm regards to the entire staff of YIVO."[5]

Upon returning to Moscow, Sutzkever gave a public lecture on his trip to Nuremberg, sponsored by the Jewish Anti-Fascist Committee. So many people filled the hall, the foyer, and the surrounding streets that the featured speaker had a hard time getting inside.

Solomon Mikhoels, chairman of the Anti-Fascist Committee, introduced Sutzkever by remarking that his testimony was the greatest act of revenge against the murderers of the Jewish people. Sutzkever followed, speaking passionately and without notes for two hours. Looking for a way to end, he found himself concluding, to his own surprise, with the following words: "Comrade Mikhoels said that my testimony was a great act of revenge. But what pleasure can I take in such revenge, when my mother is burnt at Ponar and the Jerusalem of Lithuania is without Jews? That is why I believe that the greatest revenge against the murderers of our people will be when we will secure our own free Jerusalem. It was the martyrs' dream that Jewish life be rebuilt in the Land of Israel."

There was a moment of stunned silence in the electrified hall. Sutzkever had just broken one of the greatest political taboos in the Soviet Union—he had publically affirmed his attachment to Jerusalem and the Land of Israel. Zionism had been outlawed in the USSR for twenty-five years, and association with the movement, which was branded as a tool of British imperialism, was punishable with a one-way ticket to the gulag. Yet Sutzkever stood in a packed hall and said aloud that "it was the martyrs' dream that Jewish life be rebuilt in the Land of Israel." Mikhoels, bewildered and alarmed, rose to cut him off and announce that the program was over. But even before he could say those few words, the audience exploded in a stormy ovation that drowned out the chairman's voice, and went on and on.

Later, Professor Yakov Etinger, a prominent medical scientist from Moscow, approached Sutzkever and thanked him. "For thirty years, the word Jerusalem was hidden in our hearts, like a pearl on the bottom of the sea. With your mentioning the city by name, you awakened that pearl with a magical spell, and it flowed out of our eyes."[6]

Sutzkever made one last wrap-up visit to Vilna in April 1946, before leaving the USSR. Besides making arrangements with the Bericha to smuggle suitcases of materials across the border, he spent time searching for new troves of hidden books and documents based on a newly received letter from Paris. Its author was the former Vilnius University librarian Ona Šimaite.

Šimaite, an ethnic Lithuanian, had been the guardian angel of several dozen ghetto inmates. She convinced the Germans to allow her into the ghetto under the pretext that she needed to collect overdue library books from inmates. Under this guise, she brought in food, writing materials, and news from the outside world. She gave encouragement and support to writers and artists whom she knew before the war, when they had been readers in the university library. Because her visits to the ghetto were short and tense, Šimaite became an epistolary confidant to inmates. They wrote letters to her, and she collected them during her visits, replied to them while back home, and brought in her replies during her next visit to the ghetto.

But just as important as what Šimaite brought *into* the ghetto was what she took *out*: Shmerke, Sutzkever, and others gave her manuscripts, rare books, and documents, which she removed through the ghetto gate. These were her "overdue library books." She hid the materials at home, at work, and in other locations.

Just before the liquidation of the Vilna ghetto, in September 1943, Šimaite entered the ghetto one last time and took out a sixteen-year-old Jewish girl named Sala Vaksman, hidden under her overcoat. She kept Sala in her home for three weeks and then in a closet in Vilnius University Library. (The girl survived the war and settled in Palestine.)

On April 28, 1944, the Gestapo arrested Šimaite, due to a denunciation by a neighbor. She was tortured but did not reveal any information. The Gestapo deported her to the Dachau concentration camp and, from there, to a camp near the German-French border. After her liberation by the Americans, Šimaite decided to stay in France rather than return to Soviet Lithuania. She was a veteran socialist with a visceral revulsion for Communism.[7]

In February 1946, Šimaite wrote a detailed "Declaration on Vilna Ghetto Documents," which she sent to Sutzkever in Moscow, with copies to other Jewish leaders across the globe. In it, she expressed her hope that "the documents be found and put at the disposal of all Jews interested in historical documentation, regardless of their political views."[8]

First, Šimaite listed the materials that the Germans had seized from her apartment at the time of her arrest. These included two briefcases of YIVO materials. She believed they were in the Rosa Street prison, where the Germans kept confiscated property. Other items taken from her home might be in the Gestapo archive at 16 Ofiarna Vasario Street, she suggested.

Then, she enumerated the materials she had hidden in other locations. The single-most important hiding place was the garret of the Lithuanian Studies Seminar at Vilnius University. That is where she hid the Vilna ghetto diary by Grigorii Shur, a journalist with a crisp style and an eye for telling detail. Unlike other diaries, Shur's covered the period after the ghetto's liquidation, when he and a few hundred other Jews lived in the city's Kailis labor bloc. He was among the last living Jews in German-occupied Vilna.[9]

Šimaite's instructions on how to find the Shur manuscript read like a map for finding buried gold on Treasure Island:

> Enter the gate to house number 11 on Zamkowa Street. Walk across the entire courtyard, enter the final door on the left, and go up the staircase one floor. There, you will find doors to the left and right. Open the door to the left, and you will find yourself in a small corridor. Down the corridor, there will be another door, leading up more stairs. You will reach a small landing and a few steps that lead you to another small corridor that turns to the left, at the end of which you go up one more staircase to the garret.
>
> At the top of the staircase there are three doors: a large door in the center and doors on both sides. Open the door on the left and enter the garret. On the right side of the roof, where it descends, under the roof tiles, there are five packages at varying distances from each other — one large box and four packages. In order to find them, you will need to stand on a chair and use a flashlight.

The "Declaration" went on to describe five other hiding places with ghetto materials: two hundred letters written to her by inmates, stenographic transcripts of speeches by Ghetto representative Jacob Gens, and the diary of a Jewish woman who had worked in the office of Martin Weiss, the German commander in charge of Ponar.[10]

To his great frustration, Sutzkever couldn't find the materials in the garret of the Lithuanian Studies Seminary. Šimaite was sure he didn't follow her directions correctly. "The more I think about the garret, the more I conclude that everything is standing where I put it. The person who searched must have made some kind of mistake."[11] But he did find the texts of Gens's speeches and other materials.

For many years thereafter, Šimaite continued to obsess about the cultural treasures she had hidden. In 1957, she was still writing to friends in Soviet Lithuania and urging them to look in the attic of the Lithuanian Studies Seminar for the materials.[12]

Sutzkever bid farewell to his beloved city, having collected some final documents, and handed over several suitcases to the Bericha. The sadness of saying good-bye must have been mixed with the satisfaction that he had performed his final duties toward the Jerusalem of Lithuania: he had helped bring the murderers to justice, and he had rescued the cultural treasures for posterity.

Sutzkever would never see Vilna again, except in his dreams and his poetry.

The Bust of Tolstoy and Other Russians

"The liveliness and emotional expressiveness of Ilya Gintsburg's best works in the 1890s constitute a new stage in the development of the sculptural portrait in Russia," writes I. M. Schmidt, the preeminent historian of Russian sculpture. Several of Gintsburg's artistic works were held before the war by the An-ski Museum in Vilna and were rescued by Kruk, Shmerke, and Sutzkever.[1]

Ilya Gintsburg (1859–1939) was the poor orphaned son of a rabbi and Talmudist, who liked to chisel the shapes of animals on a household honing stone. The boy's unusual talent came to the attention of the Russian-Jewish master Mark Antokolsky, and the latter invited the eleven-year-old to live and apprentice with him in St. Petersburg. The young Ilya defied the objections of his pious mother and grandfather, a rabbinic judge, and left home for the Russian capital to become an artist. When he embarked on his new life, in 1870, Gintsburg had not received any secular education and couldn't speak or understand Russian.

In St. Petersburg, Gintsburg faced new obstacles. He enrolled in a private school, where classmates ridiculed his Jewish accent, forced him to kiss a crucifix, and beat him up for "killing Christ." When life in the private school became unbearable, he transferred to a state school where the teachers and students were cold but not abusive — except for the geography teacher, who insisted on calling him "little Jew boy."

Gintsburg entered the Imperial Academy of Arts in 1878 and graduated with a gold medal (the equivalent of cum laude). His early statuettes depicted scenes of everyday life drawn from his childhood: a woman churning butter, a mother telling her son a story, and a boy diving into the river. But he soon shifted his focus to portraiture.[2]

The breakthrough in Gintsburg's artistic career occurred in 1891, when his patron, the Russian critic Vladimir Stasov, arranged for him to sculpt a figure of Leo Tolstoy from life. Gintsburg traveled to Tolstoy's four-thousand-acre estate at Yasnaya Polyana, where he spent several days in the company of the great author and produced a statuette of him engaged in writing. The revered Russian classic and young Jewish artist struck up a friendship that lasted until Tolstoy's death in 1910. During that time, Gintsburg produced numerous statuettes, busts, bas-reliefs, and full-blown monuments of Tolstoy standing, walking, sitting, and writing. One of them was exhibited in Vienna in 1897, and another was put on display at the 1900 World's Fair, where it received an award.[3]

At the turn of the twentieth century, Gintsburg sculpted posed figures of numerous Russian cultural personalities: composers Peter Tchaikovsky and Nikolai Rimsky-Korsakov, opera singer Fyodor Chaliapin, philosopher Vladimir Soloviev, landscape artist Ivan Shishkin, scientist Dmitry Mendeleev, and historian Pavel Milyukov. He alternated between plaster and bronze. He also turned to sculpting individuals from the past, such as Ivan the Terrible and Pushkin. One of his signature features was molding full-body dynamic statues that captured his object's gait and gesture.[4]

As Gintsburg's fame grew, his works were purchased by the Hermitage, the Tretyakov Gallery, and the Russian State Museum, where they are held to this day.

Gintsburg was one of the founders of the Jewish Society for the Promotion of Arts in 1915. After the 1917 Bolshevik revolution, he became a professor at the St. Petersburg academy of arts (renamed the Petrograd Free Art Studios) and served as the dean of its sculpture faculty—positions he could never have held under the Tsarist regime, which prohibited Jews from being university professors.

Kruk, Shmerke, and Sutzkever rescued five statues by Gintsburg, including portraits of Tolstoy, Soloviev, Antokolsky, and Ivan the Terrible. But long before they whisked these works away from the Nazis during World War II, they had to survive World War I.

The sculptures were originally acquired by Vilna's Society of Lovers of Jewish Antiquities shortly after its founding in 1913. The society planned to establish a full-fledged Jewish national museum and opened an exhibit in space inside the Vilna Jewish community building in 1914. But then the Great War broke out. The society's board dismantled the exhibit and sent some of its holdings to Moscow, far from the front. It kept other items—including the Gintsburg sculptures—in private homes for the duration of the war, while Imperial Germany occupied the city.[5]

Shortly after the Germans retreated and handed Vilna over to newly formed independent Lithuania, the organization reconstituted itself as the Jewish Historical-Ethnographic Society. In February 1919, it announced that it would create a great Jewish museum in the Jerusalem of Lithuania, subsequently named after author S. An-ski. Little did its leaders know that the next year would prove to be the bloodiest of all, with Lithuania, Poland, and Soviet Russia fighting each other for control of the city. Vilna changed hands five times in a single year. Somehow, the museum collection, including the Gintsburg sculptures, remained intact.[6]

Between the two world wars, the An-ski Museum proudly displayed its Gintsburg sculptures alongside works by Isaak Levitan and Marc Chagall. Today, several of the rescued portraits are held by the Vilna Gaon Jewish State Museum in Vilnius, Lithuania. The location of the rescued bust of Tolstoy is unknown. It seems to have been moved to Russia under the Soviets and is probably held by the Leo Tolstoy Museum in Moscow.[7]

CHAPTER TWENTY-FIVE

Wanderings: Poland and Prague

As soon as Sutzkever arrived in Lodz, Poland, on May 23, 1946, he dispatched a letter to Max Weinreich in New York, to check whether he had received the envelopes he sent him from Moscow and Nuremberg. ("I received nothing in response to my letters, perhaps you didn't write intentionally.") Sutzkever also dropped the bombshell: he had suitcases full of additional materials, numbering several thousand items. He and Shmerke had consulted with each other and were in agreement to send the materials to YIVO in New York.

But in the letter, Sutzkever asked for something in return. He asked Weinreich to arrange for him and Shmerke to come to New York together with the materials and settle there. "I know that it won't be easy for us to be admitted to America. But it would be a great thing for YIVO (not to mention for the two of us), if you brought us over. . . . Without us, the materials—especially the ghetto materials—won't be decipherable in any case. Kalmanovitch's diary needs to have explanatory notes. The same applies to the partisan archive."[1]

From the outset, Shmerke and Sutzkever hoped Poland would be an interim stop. On the one hand, Jewish life there was much freer than in Soviet Lithuania: there were Yiddish newspapers, books, and theater; all the Jewish political movements operated openly (Zionists of all stripes, the Bund and Communists); and an umbrella organization called the Central Union of the Jews in Poland represented the community to domestic and foreign bodies. But antisemitic sentiments and assaults were widespread, just as they had been during the years before the war. The poetic duo wanted to begin a new life. They were interested in settling in either the United States or the Land of Israel. On the same day that Sutzkever wrote to Weinreich, he sent a letter to his brother Moshe in Tel Aviv asking him to try to secure an immigration certificate for British-controlled Palestine.[2]

In Poland, Shmerke embraced socialist Zionism as his new political creed, breaking openly and bitterly with Communism. He created a fracas at a meeting of the Association of Yiddish Writers in Poland, when he declared that Yiddish culture was being systematically per-secuted and liquidated in the Soviet Union and had no future there. Communist members of the association were furious and demanded his dismissal from its governing board. (They failed.) The feisty poet became the editor of the socialist-Zionist newspaper *Our Word* (*Undzer Vort*).

For Shmerke, the struggle for a Jewish state in Palestine was a matter of survival and dignity. It was a continuation of the battle waged by Jewish partisans in the forests, and he wanted to join it.[3] With the fer-vor of a new political convert, he wrote an anthem for Zionist pioneers, which became a hit song among survivors:

> From ghettos and Auschwitz, Ponar and Majdanek,
> From the front and the forest, from the heat and the cold,
> Our rifles stand erect on our shoulders,
> Our hearts are stormy, boiling, and bold.
>
> We will, yes we will, break through the barriers,
> We risk, yes we risk, our lives yet again.
> Halutzim, halutzim* can open the heavens,
> Our struggle has only begun, just begun.
>
> Although we were born to live life fully,
> We still even now at the precipice stand.
> We halutzim have taken a vow to the martyrs,
> To fight for our people's freedom and land.
>
> Shalom fellow Jews, in far-flung places,
> Shalom fellow Jews, in need and sorrow.
> Halutzim call out: come to our homeland.
> To Israel rise up, let us go, let us go![4]

---

*Hebrew for "Zionist pioneers."

But writing and singing songs about pioneers was much easier than actually going to Palestine. Legal migration was tightly restricted by the British, and illegal migration was no less difficult, with the authorities interdicting many of the ships sent by the Bericha and sending their passengers either back to Europe or to internment camps in Cyprus. With an air of uncertainty hovering over Palestine and Poland, Sutzkever and Shmerke considered New York an attractive option, at least in the short term.

Sutzkever was convinced that he had a good chance to obtain an American visa. A recently deceased uncle of his in Boston had left behind a legacy for Sutzkever's mother. He had court papers from Vilnius certifying that he was his mother's son and that she had perished in the Vilna ghetto. He was armed with an English translation of the court papers notarized at the American Embassy in Moscow. Sutzkever hoped that his legal right to inherit an American uncle's legacy would facilitate his receipt of a US visa.[5]

But Sutzkever asked Weinreich to intervene not only on his own behalf but also for Shmerke. "He has an equal part in rescuing these treasures."

Weinreich replied by telegram: "I received your two letters. I also received the previous mailings. I will do everything in my power to help you. Warm regards to the three of you [meaning Sutzkever, his wife, and their one-year-old daughter] and to the Kaczerginskis."[6]

Weinreich's subsequent letters expressed profound gratitude toward his former student and scout, tempered by the emotional restraint that was typical of Litvaks, Lithuanian Jews: "Your latest letter caused me to feel just as much painful joy as all your previous letters," he wrote to Sutzkever in July 1946. "We both work with words, each of us in our own manner, but we don't need any words to express what we feel for each other. And when we will meet face-to-face (and I am sure that we will, sooner or later), we will also need to discuss weightier matters than feelings."[7] There was more than a touch of formality in Weinreich's letters. He opened the letters to Sutzkever "My Dear Friend" but addressed him with the formal pronoun "ir," rather than with the informal "du."

On the matter of immigration visas, Weinreich's initial optimism gradually waned. By August, he was urging patience and realism. "I would do who-knows-what to help you, but my 'who-knows-what' isn't who-knows-what." In a letter addressed to all three Vilna writers then in Poland—Sutzkever, Shmerke, and Chaim Grade—he wrote that Grade had the best chance of being admitted to the United States, because he had half-brothers who were American citizens and who were sponsoring his immigration.[8] The legacy from Sutzkever's uncle would unfortunately not be of much help. Sutzkever's closest friend in America, poet Aaron Glants-Leyeles, was more hopeful and kept reassuring him that receipt of the visa was just a matter of time.[9]

Meanwhile, Sutzkever continued to send sample documents to New York, in dribs and drabs, using various couriers, including staff members of the Joint Distribution Committee's Warsaw office and a visiting delegation of American rabbis.

But then a harrowing pogrom occurred in the town of Kielce, on July 4, 1946, and Sutzkever and Shmerke's lives were turned upside down. Forty-seven Jews were killed and fifty were wounded in the attack, which topped off a year in which more than 350 Polish Jews were killed in antisemitic violence. After Kielce, Polish Jews were thrust into fear and panic, and were overcome with a pressing urge to leave.

Shmerke was the first journalist to arrive in Kielce after the pogrom and published devastating front-page articles in *Our Word* and in the organ of the Central Union of the Jews in Poland, *New Life* (*Dos Naye Lebn*). He reported that almost none of the pogrom victims had been shot dead; they were lynched. Their bodies were either beaten with iron bars or chopped with hatchets. There were no signs that the Polish inhabitants of the city were in sorrow. In fact, many Poles who attended the funeral for the pogrom victims were ordered to do so by their trade union or workplace and wore mocking smiles on their faces. The surviving Jews in Kielce had been relocated to the compound of the state security organs, because their safety was at risk. Shmerke drew the conclusion: the beastly murderers wanted more blood, and most Poles were unmoved by the events. The implication of his articles was clear: it was unsafe for Jews to remain in Poland.[10] Shmerke and Sutzkever drew that conclusion themselves.

Apart from the pogrom and attacks, the poetic duo was also mindful of the fact that the Communists were gradually taking control of the country. Non-Communist political parties were being marginalized, step-by-step, and this did not auger well for the future of Jewish life, or for the smuggled documents they had in their possession. Shmerke and

Sutzkever had fled the Soviet Union, but now the Soviets were catching up with them, as Poland was becoming a Soviet fiefdom.

With no time to spare, and in the absence of American visas or certificates for Palestine, Shmerke, Sutzkever, and Grade did the next best thing —they secured French visas with Weinreich's assistance. On a personal level this was good news: they would get out of Poland. But it also meant that Shmerke and Sutzkever needed to smuggle the suitcases with Jewish cultural treasures across yet another border. Polish customs agents would hardly allow suitcases of books and documents, some of them bearing the stamp of the Vilnius Jewish Museum, to leave the country.

Sutzkever turned again for help to the Bericha. Its central offices were located in Warsaw and Lodz, and were headed by Sutzkever's friend Yitzhak (Antek) Zuckerman, one of the leaders of the Warsaw ghetto uprising. Antek assigned the task of smuggling part of the "Vilna Archive" to David Plonsky ("Jurek"), a fellow Warsaw ghetto fighter. Plonsky's superiors told him that the archive contained valuable documents from the ghetto and annihilation that would eventually be sent on to Eretz Israel.

Crossing the Polish-Czechoslovak border was the easy part of Plonsky's operation. He knew where the gaps in the border patrols were to be found. He also had false Czechoslovak identification papers. But once he was on the other side of the border, Plonsky's faulty language and accent would expose him as a foreigner, in a country where he didn't know his way about very well, and where the Communist regime was intensifying its control and domestic surveillance. The plan he developed was for Sutzkever to take the Warsaw-Paris train on an agreed-upon date, and for Plonsky to meet him at the Prague station during the train's brief stopover. Plonsky would hand over two suitcases through the train-car window. The operation needed to be performed with precision and speed.

Plonsky took the valises across the border, stayed a night in Bratislava, received money from a Bericha commander there, and proceeded by train to Prague. He took many precautions: he got off the train on the outskirts of the city, instead of at the central train station, and he gave his taxi driver an address that wasn't his real destination. And indeed, a few minutes after unloading and hiding on the rooftop of the address where he was dropped off, he saw the taxi driver return—in the company of two policemen.

After spending the night on the rooftop, Plonsky left for the Prague branch of the Young Guard (Shomer Ha-Tza'ir), whose leaders suggested that he hide the suitcases in a synagogue near the train station for a few days. When the appointed date arrived, the station was packed with passengers—and policemen. As the Paris-bound train rolled in from Warsaw, Plonsky spotted Sutzkever's head sticking out of a window. Plonsky approached the train car with the suitcases in hand, ready to stuff them through the window, when a policeman noticed his suspicious activity. An arm grabbed at Plonsky's clothes as he thrust the suitcases over his shoulders. Plonsky shook himself free and jumped into the window himself. He exchanged a few words with Sutzkever and jumped out of a window on the opposite side of the car. He dashed into a transfer tunnel and disappeared into a crowd of passengers standing on another platform. The stunned policeman picked himself up from the ground but had no time to react. The Paris train whistled out of the station, and the culprit was gone. The operation was a success.

When Plonsky returned to the local Bericha safe house that evening, comrades from the movement asked him what he was doing in Prague. He smiled and said, "I've contributed my part to Jewish history."[11]

CHAPTER TWENTY-SIX

Paris

S HMERKE AND SUTZKEVER were delighted to breathe the free
air of Paris. Unlike the bombed-out Polish cities of Lodz and
Warsaw, Paris had many wonders of art and architecture to
offer their sensitive eyes. There was also a dynamic Jewish cultural and
political scene, and an active association of Vilner Jews that offered to
fund the publication of their books. Under the association's auspices,
Sutzkever published his memoir of the Vilna ghetto (which had appeared a year earlier in Moscow), and Shmerke issued his collection
of ghetto songs. The poets' living conditions and wardrobe improved,
thanks to assistance from the Joint Distribution Committee and aid
packages from YIVO. But they both considered Paris to be yet another
transit point. Where they would go next was open and unclear.

Upon arriving in Paris in late November 1946, Sutzkever wrote to
Max Weinreich and reiterated his desire to settle in New York. "I think
that it is important for YIVO, which has become, as you see, a part of
my life." Weinreich urged patience and put Sutzkever in touch with
YIVO's official representative in Paris, Gershon Epshtein. After their
first meeting Epshtein reported back: "He showed me materials that
he rescued—letters from great personalities, lots of treasures from the
Vilna YIVO and Strashun Library, old religious books. . . . He rescued
diaries, and more and more. The materials could fill entire crates."[1]

While he corresponded with Weinreich, Sutzkever also considered
the option of sending the rescued materials to the library of the Hebrew University in Jerusalem. He shared his uncertainty with his closest friend in America, poet Aaron Glants-Leyeles, who discouraged
him from sending the materials to Jerusalem. Leyeles added that the
leading figures in American Yiddish literature, H. Leivick and Joseph
Opatoshu, shared his opinion. "Here the cultural treasures will be lo-

cated among living Jews and will have living value. In the Jerusalem university, they will, under current circumstances, be relics, and the attitude toward them will be far from brotherly and warm."[2] Sutzkever took the warning to heart.

As he had done before, Sutzkever continued to send small packages to Weinreich via various travelers. Traffic between Paris and New York was much greater, making it easy for him to find couriers—so much so that it became difficult for Weinreich to keep track of who was carrying what. Sutzkever didn't always provide exact names; one traveler failed to pick up the materials left for him in the Paris offices of the Joint Distribution Committee (JDC), and another traveler failed to contact Weinreich upon arrival in New York. The system of dispatching material needed to be changed.[3] At the end of January 1947, Weinreich wrote plaintively to Sutzkever: "Communal leaders and journalists are the worst couriers one can imagine, when it comes to reliability and security. Now that you're in a country with a normal postal system, the mail would be the best means. Keep this in mind."[4]

But even better than the mail, Weinreich decided, was to ship materials via Gershon Epshtein, YIVO's Paris representative, who kept a meticulous list of his mailings. Weinreich urged Sutzkever to work closely with the man. "Epshtein is just like YIVO: on bad terms with no one, but in no one's pocket." Between mid-December 1946 and March 19, 1947, YIVO received 360 documents (including books) from Sutzkever via Epshtein.[5] Once the Epshtein channel began functioning, couriers were used rarely and only with his knowledge and approval: the Vilner landsman Leyzer Ran took a suitcase to New York in January 1947, and another suitcase was taken in June by YIVO staff member Moshe Kligsberg who visited Paris.[6]

Shmerke and Sutzkever each had their own stashes of materials that they released to Epshtein at different paces. The two poets were not fully aware what materials were in the other's possession and did not coordinate their actions. Both had sections of Zelig Kalmanovitch's ghetto diary. Shmerke handed over his piece of the diary in February 1947, but Sutzkever held on to his portion until July. When Sutzkever finally gave it to Epshtein, he signed a dedication on the first page: "Dear Max Weinreich, I am sending you the most precious of all the ghetto materials—Kalmanovitch's diary. It is very hard for me to part with it, but it belongs to YIVO, to the people."[7]

Sutzkever was equally reluctant to part with the record book of the Vilna Gaon's kloyz. He promised it to Gershon Epshtein shortly after arriving in Paris, but half a year later, he still hadn't handed it over. The record book, which dated back to the mid-eighteenth century, was the last major relic of the old Jerusalem of Lithuania. The building of the Gaon's kloyz had been severely damaged in the July 1944 battle of Vilnius. Only the record book was intact. Sutzkever finally parted with the folio volume in August, after several reminders from Weinreich. Before relinquishing it, he did something that violated all the rules of manuscript preservation: he wrote his own inscription on the first page, just before its first entry: "Hidden in the bunker at 8 Strashun Street, on the eve of the liquidation of the Vilna ghetto—August 1943, dug up—July 1944. Sutzkever, Paris, July 1947." He signed his named on the first page of Vilna's most revered relic, as if it was his private property.[8]

Weinreich instructed his Paris representative: "Send the record book by airmail, registered. And pack it well, with cardboard. I don't care if postage costs two hundred dollars. The record book is a symbol of Vilna. No matter how frugal we ought to be, it must be sent by airmail."[9]

Besides transferring the rescued cultural treasures, there was another piece of unfinished business that came up unexpectedly: bringing to justice one of the Einsatzstab Reichsleiter Rosenberg plunderers, Herbert Gotthard.

During the ghetto years, Shmerke and Sutzkever never gave any thought to the prospect that the ERR looters would someday pay for their crimes. But an opportunity arose in the summer of 1946, when Sutzkever, then still in Poland, learned that Gotthard, the Nazi Judenforschung "expert" on the ERR team, had been spotted. He was living in a DP camp in Lubeck, Germany, masquerading as a Jew and working in the camp's Jewish committee! Gotthard had invented a new biography for himself, claiming that he was a German-speaking Jew from Mitau, Latvia, who had been an inmate of the Riga ghetto.[10]

Gotthard's cover was blown due to a simple coincidence. A resident of the Lubeck DP camp read Sutzkever's book on the Vilna ghetto and came across the name Herbert Gotthard, which was the name of a somewhat dubious character in the camp. The reader sent off a letter to

Sutzkever in Lodz, with a physical description that matched the short, stout man that Shmerke nicknamed "the little swine."[11]

Sutzkever brought the matter to the attention of the Central Union of Jews in Poland, which it, in turn, submitted a deposition by Sutzkever to the War Crimes Commission of the Supreme Polish Military Court. The man in question, he wrote, was responsible for the destruction of tens of thousands of Jewish cultural treasures in Vilna and for the murder of two prominent Jewish scholars, Nojekh Prylucki and Abraham E. Goldschmidt, in August 1941. The Polish War Crimes Commission contacted the British authorities—the Lubeck camp was in the British zone of occupied Germany—and asked for Gotthard's arrest and extradition to Poland.

Sutzkever also wrote to Weinreich in New York, who fired off a letter to the American military authorities, asking them to intervene with the British to arrest the man whom he called "the liquidator of the Vilna YIVO."

As a result of these efforts, Gotthard was arrested in November 1946. He was held in a British internment camp in Hamburg for more than half a year and then moved to another prison facility. At first, he argued that he was the victim of mistaken identity and that the crimes must have been committed by a different Herbert Gotthard. Later, he changed his story and admitted to having worked for the ERR in Riga and Vilna but said he had been a Jewish slave laborer. He claimed that his assignment consisted solely of translating and conducting research on the Karaites and that he used his position to offer material aid to the other Jewish scholars. Gotthard denied engaging in plunder or being responsible for the murder of Nojekh Prylucki.

The British sent a photograph of Gotthard to Sutzkever, who in the meanwhile relocated to Paris, and Sutzkever confirmed the man's identity: this was the "little swine," the liquidator of the Vilna YIVO.[12]

Shmerke wrote gleefully about Gotthard's arrest and imprisonment. He fantasized that he and the other surviving members of the paper brigade would soon confront him in a Warsaw military courtroom as witnesses. Gotthard's jaw would drop when he would see that several members of the Jewish work brigade had survived and were now his accusers. Shmerke looked forward to the sweet revenge of extradition and justice. Meanwhile, as the bureaucratic wheels turned slowly, Gotthard sat in a British prison cell.

Once Sutzkever and Shmerke were safely in Paris, far from the USSR and the Soviet bloc, a new question arose: how should YIVO inform the public about the rescue and retrieval of the treasures from Vilna? A dramatic event of this magnitude deserved to be publicized; and its heroes, celebrated. But, as Weinreich wrote to the two, "there are weighty reasons not to speak about the matter with complete openness. . . . It is important that the matter be conveyed in a slightly disguised manner."[13]

It isn't hard to figure out Weinreich's concerns: if the full story were publicized, the Soviet government might launch a campaign for the materials' return to Vilnius, on the grounds that they were the stolen property of a Soviet museum. And Jewish Communists would vilify the "partners in crime," Shmerke and Sutzkever, who had stolen the books and documents, and YIVO, the institution that was holding the stolen goods.

Jewish Communists had already begun hurling personal attacks at Sutzkever, portraying him as a thief, not a rescuer. Soon after he arrived in Paris, he heard that there were angry grumblings against his actions back in Poland. A former colleague from the paper brigade, Akiva Gershater, wrote to him from Lodz: "In certain circles, including literary ones, there's been a total reversal of the attitude toward you. They are saying, 'Sutzkever impoverished Vilna,' 'he removed the most precious treasures,' 'we know the whole story,' 'we need to deal with this.'" Gershater warned Sutzkever that the people who were making these accusations had no doubt shared them with their ideological comrades in Paris. He even cautioned him against keeping any museum materials in his Paris apartment, because Communists might organize a break-in.[14]

Angry allegations also emanated directly from Soviet Vilnius: museum staff member Shloime Beilis sent letters to the Association of Vilners in Paris, denouncing Shmerke and Sutzkever as thieves.[15]

Shmerke was never one to shy away from a fight and relished verbal battle with Communists. In Paris, he called them apologists for a murderous regime, and they branded him a traitor and agent of Wall Street.[16] But even Shmerke wasn't eager to wage a public polemic over his decision, as director of the Vilnius Jewish Museum, to remove its treasures and smuggle them out of the USSR. Public disclosure could lead to a clampdown against the museum and to the arrest of his childhood friend, Yankl Gutkowicz. At the very least, further removal of materials would become impossible.

So Shmerke kept silent for several years. When he eventually referred to his smuggling activity in a memoir published in 1949, Jewish Communists released their full fury. "He looted the state museum where he was the responsible custodian. While the USSR paid him a salary to guard the museum materials, he quietly started 'rescuing' them, without the slightest sense of honesty, ethics, and loyalty. He justified his acts by sacrilegiously identifying Sovietness with Nazism. . . . Needless to say, the dishonesty of the Kaczerginskis led the state organs to view with suspicion the potential Shmerkes that might have remained in the country, and this caused serious harm to Soviet Jews."[17]

All of these considerations were behind the mutual agreement that YIVO not publicize the fact that it had received Vilna materials from Shmerke and Sutzkever.[18] In the first half of 1947, *YIVO News* only mentioned in general terms that the institute had in its possession materials from the prewar Vilna YIVO that had been rescued. It didn't explain who had rescued them and how they had reached New York. A large number of Vilna ghetto documents were put on display in YIVO's exhibit "The Jews in Europe 1939–1946," mounted in New York in March–April 1947, but again without explaining how they had been obtained.[19] Weinreich was especially sensitive about the ghetto documents. He knew that YIVO had no legitimate legal claim to them, since the Vilna YIVO no longer existed during the ghetto years. The only rightful owner of the ghetto materials was the Jewish Museum in Vilnius, a Soviet state institution.

By August 1947, YIVO had received the bulk of the materials that Shmerke and Sutzkever had smuggled across Europe, and the YIVO senior administration revisited the question of issuing a news release about their rescue activity.[20] It decided to act cautiously and secured Sutzkever's consent to tell part of the story—in a single sentence.

The lead article of the September 1947 issue of *YIVO News* informed readers that the institute had acquired three extraordinary diaries: Theodor Herzl's diary from the 1880s and the diaries of Zelig Kalmanovitch and Herman Kruk from the Vilna ghetto. The article noted, "How they arrived at YIVO—that is a separate dramatic story that we will relate in detail on another occasion." But on an inside page of the same issue, far from the lead article, *YIVO News* published a photograph of Sutzkever and Shmerke in the Vilna ghetto with a caption in eight-point print: "The two Yiddish poets and a group of cultural activists who worked in the Vilna YIVO under the German regime hid Jewish cultural treasures, including YIVO treasures, in the ghetto, with great risk to their lives. After the war, they dug them up."[21]

The reader who put two and two together (the article on page 1 and the caption on page 7) understood that the diaries had been rescued by Sutzkever and Shmerke.

The caption did not mention the existence of the Jewish Museum, the fact that Sutzkever and Shmerke had been its directors, or that they had smuggled museum holdings (including the three extraordinary diaries) out of the USSR.

The question was so sensitive that discussions ensued on what to call the collection of documents. Naming it the Sutzkever-Kaczerginski Collection would constitute firsthand evidence that they had smuggled the materials out of the USSR. But not naming the collection after its rescuers would have denied them the most basic form of recognition. Shmerke was insistent: "I believe that Weinreich's formulation, 'the Sutzkever-Kaczerginski Archive in YIVO' is the minimum for us. We must not allow ourselves to be terrorized by the Beilises."[22] In the end, the collection was named "Sutzkever-Kaczerginski" but without public fanfare.[23]

While most of the materials were in New York, Shmerke and Sutzkever were still in Paris awaiting their American immigration visas. As the months went by without concrete progress, Sutzkever came to doubt that the coveted visa would ever be forthcoming. Both Weinreich and Glants-Leyeles were silent on the subject, with nothing to report, and Sutzkever's thoughts turned increasingly to Palestine. The idea of settling there had been on his mind for a while.[24]

After attending the World Zionist Congress in Basel in mid-December 1946 as a guest, Sutzkever began mentioning in his letters to New York that he was interested in visiting Palestine before settling in New York. He wanted to see his brother and the *yishuv*, the Jewish community there.[25] By June, he was writing that he had decided to settle in Palestine. He had secured a certificate, with the help of Zionist leaders he met at the Congress. He explained his decision to the Yiddish poet H. Leivick as the only resolution to his personal and creative crisis:

" I find myself in a condition from which only death can rescue me. To put it simply, I have lost the ground underneath my feet. I have never felt so lonely. Even worse, all of my senses have ceased functioning, even the sense of pain. Can you imagine such a person, all the more so—such a poet? It is therefore very possible that I will leave Paris, probably for the Land of Israel. I have a brother there, and life there is on fire. Perhaps there I will find my shadow."

He gave a more prosaic explanation to Weinreich: he was tired of waiting.[26]

Sutzkever left France by ship on September 2, 1947. Upon arriving in Haifa port, he sent one of his first letters to Weinreich: "I am tired, but I am very happy with my journey. I hope to be able to work and study here. . . . I've seen very little of the country and of people. I want to spend a month with myself and gather my thoughts." He then added, "You may be sure, my dear friend, that I will help YIVO from here as well, in any way I can. I will also send you the remaining materials." Yes, Sutzkever still had a large amount material in his personal possession, including parts of Herman Kruk's diary.[27]

Shmerke stayed on in Paris and weighed his options. He was virtually unemployed, living off the advances and sales of his books and a lecture tour of the displaced persons' camps. He came to realize that as a former Communist, his chances of receiving an American visa were dim. He was interested in settling in Palestine, but there was a long line for certificates, and Zionist leaders weren't eager to give preference to a new convert to their cause who had been a Communist for many years.

Shmerke also worried that the negative attitude toward Yiddish in the Hebrew-speaking *yishuv* meant that he would be superfluous there. He wrote to Sutzkever a few months after the latter's arrival in the Land of Israel, to ask him for reassurance and help. "If *you* think that I'll be able to live, find work, and be considered an equal, and if you will really be able to do something in this regard, then I will not only be deeply grateful to you—I will come to Eretz Israel."[28] Sutzkever responded with encouragement but made no concrete promises.

By the end of 1947, the surviving members of the paper brigade had scattered. Shmerke stayed on in Paris, Sutzkever was in Tel Aviv, and Rachela Krinsky was in New York. Other surviving members settled in Israel, Canada, and Australia.

CHAPTER TWENTY-SEVEN

Return from Offenbach,
or Kalmanovitch's Prophecy

MAX WEINREICH had a special place in his heart for the materials that Shmerke Kaczerginski and Abraham Sutzkever had risked their lives—twice—to rescue. But he knew that the bigger prize was the trove of books and documents in Germany, which was fifty times as large. And the thought that the materials were in Germany, land of the murderers and looters, was hard for him to bear.

But securing YIVO's property from the American government that controlled it was proving to be infuriatingly frustrating. The bureaucratic tug of war between the State Department and the War Department was unrelenting. On May 7, 1946, the State Department notified the American Jewish Committee that it had decided to restitute YIVO's collection to New York. And Weinreich celebrated—prematurely, as it turned out. Two and a half weeks later, on May 24, the War Department wrote to nullify that decision. "The advisability of making an exception to the general practice in the case of this collection has been questioned. . . . The policy has been to return looted property of every kind to the country from which it originated."[1]

Meanwhile, the US government began to discuss the entire question of the 1.5 million Jewish books held at Offenbach with a newly formed body called the Commission for European Jewish Cultural Reconstruction, chaired by Columbia University professors Salo Baron and Jerome Michael. The YIVO collection became part of a bigger issue.

The problems in the broader negotiations were complex: There were identifiable books, whose owners could be determined by ex libris and markings, and unidentifiable books, whose owners were unknown. There were books whose owner organizations resumed operation after the war and those owner organizations that no longer existed and had no heirs. There were countries with which the United States had legally binding restitution agreements and those with which it did not.

But beyond the specifics, there was an underlying question: to whom did the Jewish books belong, to their countries of origin, or to the Jewish people? If to the Jewish people, who represented it? There was no Jewish state in 1946. The Commission on European Jewish Cultural Reconstruction—a consortium that included the World Jewish Congress, the American Jewish Committee, the Hebrew University, and many other major groups—claimed that representative role. It asked the US government to recognize it as the trustee, on behalf of the Jewish people, for all Jewish books discovered in the American zone of occupied Germany. The negotiations between the State Department, War Department, and the commission dragged on seemingly endlessly. (They finally reached an agreement in 1949.)[2]

YIVO wanted its case to be dealt with separately from the general question of the 1.5 million Jewish books at Offenbach, as a discrete and straightforward case of returning property to its owner. But the formalists at the War Department would not allow the YIVO case to move forward until the broader issue was resolved.

In one respect, the Commission on European Jewish Cultural Reconstruction ended up being extremely helpful to YIVO. The commission was adamantly opposed to returning Jewish cultural treasures to Poland. It argued that it was inappropriate to send the Jewish books, manuscripts, and ritual objects to a country whose Jewish population had been decimated by 90 percent during the war, and from which surviving Jews were leaving in droves. The Polish-Jewish center was over, finished, wiped out. The cultural treasures should be sent to the major centers of postwar Jewish life: the United States and Palestine.[3]

The State Department took the commission's anti-Polish position to heart, especially since the Polish government didn't express any particular interest in claiming the Jewish material. As a result, the suggestion that YIVO's collections be restituted to Poland was taken off the table.

But the USSR remained a live option, since Vilnius was the capital of the Lithuanian Soviet Socialist Republic and had been a Soviet city for the year immediately before the German invasion. The Offenbach depot cooperated with all countries whose books had been looted, including the Soviet Union, and restituted hundreds of thousands of books to the USSR. In June 1946, a Soviet restitution officer visited the facility, and the Americans authorized him to remove 760 crates—232,100 books in all—for return to their country of origin. They included books from Jewish library collections in Kiev and Odessa looted by Johannes Pohl and the ERR. The subsequent visits to Offenbach by Soviet restitution officers cost Weinreich a great deal of sleep.

Luckily for Weinreich and YIVO, the United States had an interim policy not to recognize the incorporation of Lithuania and the other Baltic states into the Soviet Union and, accordingly, not to restitute property from the Baltics to the USSR. But it was only an interim policy. The topic was under review by the Joint Chiefs of Staff.[4] Meanwhile, the Offenbach depot held on to its Lithuanian books, both Jewish and non-Jewish, and gave them to no one.

The other shoe dropped in early August 1946. The Soviets informed the American authorities that they claimed the Jewish material from Vilnius as their property. Weinreich learned about this through unofficial channels, in a message from Rabbi Judah Nadich, the advisor on Jewish affairs to General Eisenhower. (Nadich telephoned his wife in New York and dictated the letter to YIVO.) Nadich tried to be reassuring. He had talked to General Lucius Clay, the US deputy military governor, about the matter, and Clay had decided to fully support YIVO's claim to its books and papers. He intended to bring the matter to the directorate of Reparation, Deliveries, and Restitution of the Allied Control Council, the body that governed Germany on behalf of the four occupying powers. General Clay promised that if the Allied Control Council didn't agree to return the collection to YIVO in New York, the United States would do so unilaterally.[5]

Weinreich was alarmed and felt that taking the YIVO matter to the council was fraught with danger. The Soviets would oppose shipment to New York, and at the very least, the case would be further delayed as negotiations ensued. Always anticipating the worst-case scenario, he worried that once the topic was the subject of negotiations, the United States might decide to "trade" the YIVO library to the Soviets in exchange for other interests. Weinreich asked John Slawson of the American Jewish Committee to persuade the US government to act unilaterally without bringing the matter to the council.[6]

Meanwhile back in Vilnius, director Yankl Gutkowicz of the Jewish Museum was urging Soviet officials to demand return of the books to his institution. "We have reason to suspect that some groups have set their sights on this Soviet property, first and foremost the YIVO in America. . . . We ask you to take all necessary steps so that Soviet property be returned to its true owners."[7]

Fortunately for YIVO, the onset of the Cold War came to the rescue. Serious tensions soon arose in the Allied Control Council between the representatives of the Soviet Union and the other occupying powers, and by late August 1946, the council was stalemated. It's directorate of Reparation, Deliveries, and Restitution held more than sixty meetings and couldn't even agree on the definition of the word *restitution*, let alone on procedures for processing claims. By the fall of 1946, it became clear that each occupying power would pursue its own restitution policy in the part of Germany that it controlled. General Clay's plan to bring the YIVO restitution matter to the council was moot.[8]

As part of the worsening relations between the United States and Soviet Union, the American interim decision not to restitute books or other property from Lithuania became established policy. The United States did not and would not recognize the Baltics as a legitimate part of the USSR. "No shipments of property to Latvia, and Lithuania, and Estonia are to take place," the US military government in Germany wrote in its annual report, on December 31, 1946.

YIVO's situation was ideal from a political perspective but impossibly frustrating on the ground. The US government had ruled out the alternative restitution options—Poland and the USSR. Everyone agreed that YIVO should receive its property. But no one was willing to take action until the overall agreement between the United States and Jewish Cultural Reconstruction would be finalized. How long that would take no one knew.

In January 1947, YIVO decided to push forward again on its own. Weinreich and YIVO's executive secretary Mark Uveeler visited State Department officials in Washington again, more than eighteen months after their first visit. This time, they had help on the inside. Seymour Pomrenze had since left his position at the Offenbach Archival Depot and worked at the National Archives in Washington. He knew the US government bureaucracy on cultural restitution from top to bottom. He gave Weinreich advice behind the scenes on whom to talk to and what to say. And lo and behold, the wheels of the bureaucracy finally began to move.

On March 11, 1947, the War Department authorized the Office of Military Government, United States (OMGUS) in Germany to release the YIVO collection for transfer to the United States. The order stipulated that the books should be released to the Library of Congress Mission in Germany, which would in turn facilitate their transfer to YIVO. This was done to adhere to the policy of restituting cultural property to states, and not to private individuals or organizations. The Library of Congress, on its part, agreed to YIVO's request that it appoint Pomrenze as a member of its mission, to oversee the transfer.[9]

Besides having a behind-the-scenes advisor in Washington, YIVO also had a "mole" inside the Offenbach depot: Lucy Schildkret, later known as the historian and essayist Lucy Dawidowicz. An employee of the Education Department of the Joint Distribution Committee in Germany, Schildkret was dispatched to Offenbach in February 1947 to select five thousand Yiddish and Hebrew books for use in the displaced persons' camps. She had strong attachments to Weinreich and YIVO, having been a visiting fellow in YIVO's graduate training program in Vilna in 1938–39 and having left Europe just days before the war broke out. While in Vilna, her surrogate parents were Zelig and Riva Kalmanovitch. After returning to New York, she was Max Weinreich's personal secretary from 1943 to 1945. Once in Offenbach, she kept Weinreich fully informed about the goings-on there.

As Lucy Schildkret rummaged through piles of "unidentifiable books" (that is, books whose past owners could not be identified) to select items for the displaced persons' camps, she discovered that many of the "unidentifiables" could in fact be identified—and belonged to YIVO. Some of them had Yiddish-language bibliographic forms inserted in them that she knew from Vilna. Others had accession numbers on double perforated labels, which she recognized. Still others had the handwritten Yiddish signatures of Max Weinreich and other YIVO scholars on the title page (but no stamp or ex libris to be picked up by the German sorters). Schildkret began to set these books aside. And she wrote to Weinreich immediately.

Once the orders came through from the War Department to prepare the transfer of YIVO's books to the United States, the Offenbach depot and the Joint Distribution Committee agreed that Schildkret should shift gears and officially devote her time to finding YIVO books among the "unidentifiables." Joseph Horne, the depot's new director, was eager to wrap up the YIVO matter. By late May, Schildkret had found several thousand items.[10]

In preparation for the transfer, the Offenbach depot made a count of its YIVO holdings:

47 cases of books. 5,457 books (actual count)
47 cases of brochures (not counted, probably about 15,000)
80 cases of archival material (not counted)
8 cases of music (sheet and bound)
15 cases of newspapers
Mathew Strashun Library, not yet boxed. 23,604 books, perhaps
    200 cases.
TOTAL 397 cases.[11]

But thanks to Schildkret's work of identifying YIVO books among the "unidentifiables," the size of the YIVO collection grew to 420 cases.

The Library of Congress Mission, with Colonel Pomrenze at the helm, arrived in Offenbach in mid-June 1947. A master of the US bureaucracy, he came well prepared and performed the giant transfer in under forty-eight hours. Schildkret described the historic event in colorful terms, in a letter to Weinreich:

> The big day has come. Everything worked out beautifully. . . . Pomrenze is, of course, a hard guy to like, but you couldn't have had a better person for the job. He is so crazy about papers, and has so many super-super kinds of orders and stuff, that he can get around anywhere. Saturday morning, Horne told me, "I won't have Pomrenze messing around the depot." Monday afternoon, Horne told him that he could look around and help me, and do any goddamn thing he wanted.
>
> He was simply fantastic on transportation. After all, he came to the depot on Monday morning June 16, and today June 17, by 5:00 p.m. the freight trains were all loaded, [and] arrangements made for them to be attached to the mail train in Frankfurt tomorrow morning. This is the fastest train to Bremen. American MP security guards have been arranged for. The ship to take the books arrives in

Bremerhaven [the port] tomorrow, so they can load as soon as they arrive. Today the receipts were signed.

The liquor store was closed today, so tomorrow or sometime thereafter we drink to all of this.

I asked [Pomrenze] where the hell you would put the books once you had them. But P. seems to have the problem licked with the Matzo factory. . . .

You should be very happy.[12]

The 420 crates left Bremen on June 21 with a ship called the *Pioneer Cove* and arrived in New York port on July 1. Pomrenze "licked" the storage problem with the help of his older brother Chaim, who was an executive at the Manischewitz Matzo Company. The 420 crates were stored in the Manischewitz warehouse in Jersey City, at no cost to YIVO.[13]

The day after the crates arrived, five members of the YIVO leadership set out for Jersey City to examine them. As they opened the first crate and found surviving remnants of the Vilna YIVO, their hands trembled.

There were no public celebrations—too much blood, too many losses. Weinreich rejoiced quietly inside himself, but it was all subdued and restrained. He knew he had accomplished a great thing for Jewish memory and scholarship. He had fulfilled the final wish of his dear friend and colleague, Zelig Kalmanovitch. He recalled the latter's words, while working in the YIVO building as a slave laborer for the ERR: "The Germans won't be able to destroy everything. And whatever they remove will be found at the end of the war and taken from them." At that moment, Weinreich knew that Zelig Kalmanovitch was indeed the prophet of the ghetto.

PART FOUR

From Liquidation to Redemption

CHAPTER TWENTY-EIGHT

The Path to Liquidation

OST OF THE treasures rescued by the paper brigade never left Vilnius. There was no way Shmerke and Sutzkever could take everything with them. The ghetto archive was simply too voluminous, as were the parts of YIVO's archive that were not sent to Frankfurt. Most of the thirty thousand books stayed in the Jewish Museum.

The museum enjoyed a revival in the years after the poetic duo's departure, under its new director Yankl Gutkowicz. Its buildings were repaired by a brigade of German prisoners of war, in an exquisite case of poetic justice. The staff cataloged the collections, and a reading room was opened to the public. The museum mounted a large permanent exhibit on the Holocaust in Lithuania called "Fascism Is Death" and featured smaller short-term exhibitions on Sholem Aleichem and other topics. There were lectures and programs with cultural personalities, including Ilya Ehrenburg and Solomon Mikhoels, the chairman of the Jewish Anti-Fascist Committee.[1]

All of this happened not so much thanks to Gutkowicz's managerial skills but due to the departure of Mikhail Andreievich Suslov from Lithuania. In March 1946, Stalin's grey eminence left Vilnius for a higher position in Moscow. As soon as the arch-enemy of Jewish culture was gone, many obstacles disappeared.

Another contributing factor to the museum's success was its flag-waving Soviet patriotism. Gutkowicz mounted exhibits in honor of the elections to the Supreme Soviet and the third anniversary of Vilnius's liberation. He explained the upshot of the Holocaust exhibit in patriotic terms: "As one walks from room to room . . . you are overcome with a feeling of passionate love and profound gratitude to the Red Army and to Soviet power, which rescued us from destruction and now leads us to a new full-blooded life." The exhibit on Sholem Aleichem marking the thirtieth anniversary of his death culminated with a large portrait of none other than . . . Joseph Stalin, "the man who made it possible for a Jewish museum to be rebuilt in Vilnius."[2] Gutkowicz transformed the Jewish Museum into a truly Soviet institution.

The happy marriage of Jewish identity with Soviet patriotism culminated with the United Nations' vote on the partition of Palestine on Friday, November 29, 1947. The Soviet Union and its allies voted "yes." A few months earlier, the Soviet delegate to the UN, Andrei Gromyko, had expressed his country's support for the establishment of a Jewish state, citing the unspeakable suffering of the Jewish people during the war. (Their main objective was to get the British out.)

Museum staff member Alexander Rindziunsky, a Communist and former FPO fighter, huddled with a group of friends around a radio to listen to the roll-call vote in the General Assembly. When the resolution passed, they were filled with joy—and pride that the USSR was one of the first to declare its support for the Jewish state. Jews in Vilnius celebrated Israel's declaration of independence on May 14, 1948, with parties, toasts, and wishes: "May we have much *nakhes* (joy) from the newborn state." But they were also cautious to keep their joy away from public view. When the Vilnius correspondent for the Moscow Yiddish newspaper *Unity (Eynikayt)* asked people to comment on the founding of the Jewish state, no one was willing say anything on the record for publication. Too much excitement might be seen as an expression of Jewish "nationalism," a dirty word in the Soviet lexicon.[3]

The Jewish Museum and the synagogue were the only public places where Jews could gather to discuss the exhilarating, historic news. And gather they did. The museum was inundated by visitors, some of whom said that they hoped the USSR would form a legion to fight for Israel, just as it had dispatched volunteers to Spain during the Spanish Civil War. A group of visiting Jewish students from Poltava, Ukraine, told Rindziunsky, the staff member, that they were ready to leave for Israel at a moment's notice, by foot if necessary.[4] The first half of 1948 was an emotional high point for the Jews of Soviet Vilnius.

But then everything changed. Joseph Stalin was infuriated by the Jews' outpouring of identification with the new state, including the crowds that greeted the first Israeli ambassador, Golda Meir, in front of the Moscow synagogue. He had wanted to get the British out of Palestine. But for Soviet Jews to declare their affection for a foreign state, let alone one that was increasingly friendly with the United States, was treason in his eyes. He launched a fierce antisemitic campaign in the fall of 1948.

On November 20, the Soviet leadership ordered the dissolution of the Jewish Anti-Fascist Committee, as a "center of anti-Soviet propaganda that regularly provided anti-Soviet information to foreign espionage agencies." The Yiddish newspaper *Unity* (*Eynikayt*) was closed, and the Yiddish publishing house The Truth (Der Emes) was liquidated five days later. The November 20 order stated ominously, "For now, no one is to be arrested."[5]

"For now" lasted one month. Large-scale arrests of Soviet Yiddish writers began in late December 1948. Itzik Feffer, a poet who had been the single-most loyal mouthpiece of Soviet policy, was seized from his home on December 24. So was Benjamin Zuskin, the lead actor of the Moscow State Yiddish Theater, and its director after Solomon Mikhoels died earlier that year under mysterious circumstances. Writers Peretz Markish and Dovid Bergelson, who had been Sutzkever's closest friends in Moscow, were arrested during the last days of January 1949. By February 1949, all the institutions of Yiddish literature had been eliminated, and nearly all its writers were in prison. The most important ones would eventually be executed on August 12, 1952.[6]

According to the new policy, all Jewish culture was branded "nationalist" and "Zionist." Zionism, in turn, was condemned as an agent of American espionage and an enemy of the USSR. It was Suslov's policy on steroids.

While the arrests were not publicized or announced in the press, readers and writers across the globe were alarmed that Yiddish books and periodicals had suddenly ceased publication and that Markish, Bergelson, and so many others had disappeared. Shmerke in Paris and Sutzkever in Tel Aviv feared the worst about their friends in Moscow and knew that they were very lucky to have left just in the nick of time. They didn't know it yet, but they had literally dodged a bullet.

It didn't take long for the assault on Jewish culture to spread from Moscow to Vilnius. The groundwork was set by the Lithuanian minister for state security, Major General Piotr Kapralov, who submitted a top-secret memorandum to the first secretary of the Communist Party, Antanas Snieckus, on January 29, 1949, exposing the danger of Zionism and Jewish nationalism in the Lithuanian ssr.

Kapralov warned that an underground Zionist movement was spreading anti-Soviet propaganda in Lithuania. The movement was closely tied with American espionage and was secretly funded through entities such as the Joint Distribution Committee. Kapralov's memo even charged, outrageously, that the Zionists in Vilnius were cooperating with Lithuanian nationalist guerillas. (In fact, many of the Lithuanian nationalist guerillas were intensely antisemitic. There were a good number of former collaborators with the Nazis in their ranks.)[7]

The memo was essentially a paranoid rant about a Jewish conspiracy that was working on behalf of the main enemies of Soviet power, both foreign and domestic.

Kapralov warned that the Zionists were using legal institutions to spread Jewish chauvinism. Foremost among them was the Jewish Museum. He charged that its permanent exhibit "Fascism Is Death" presented a one-sided picture, as if Jews were the only people to fight the Nazis. The exhibit highlighted the participation of Lithuanian nationalists in the atrocities against the Jews but didn't mention the resistance by Lithuanian Communists. Kapralov's charges were patently false, but that was beside the point. The die was cast.[8]

On April 27, 1949, three months after the Kapralov memo, the state agency in charge of museums formally requested that the Council of Ministers of the Lithuanian ssr "reorganize" the Vilnius Jewish Museum into the Vilnius Local Studies Museum. The request politely avoided using the word "liquidation," but the intention was unmistakable: the Jewish Museum should cease to exist. The Council of Ministers adopted a resolution closing down the museum on June 10, 1949.

The order included detailed instructions on how to dispose of the museum's assets: Its building at 6 Strashun Street should revert to the state agency in charge of museums, and its seven staff positions should be reallocated to the newly established Local Studies Museum. The collections should be divided among Lithuanian repositories: all materials related to local history should be kept in their current location, for the soon-to-be-established Local Studies Museum. Items of broader historical significance should be transferred to the State Historical-Revolutionary Museum. Works of art should be sent to the Administration for the Arts, and the library books should be forwarded to the Book Chamber of the Lithuanian SSR. All other inventory (furniture, equipment, and supplies) and the wing of the museum that led onto Lida Street (the former ghetto prison) were to be handed over to the Vilnius Librarianship College.[9]

The physical closure of the museum was orderly and quiet. Representatives of the NKVD and the censorship agency entered the building, displayed the government resolution, and escorted the staff out of the facility. The officials proceeded to seal the rooms with locks and chains. The liquidation did not come to Gutkowicz and his staff as a surprise. They fully expected it, given that the Jewish Anti-Fascist Committee had been eliminated, and the Jewish cultural elite throughout the USSR had been arrested. Nonetheless, Gutkowicz's eyes filled with tears when the NKVD vehicles arrived.[10]

The Lithuanian Book Chamber was the single-largest "heir" of the liquidated museum's collections: it received 38,560 volumes.[11]

An anonymous letter from Vilnius informed the former museum volunteer Leyzer Ran of the news: "The 'guests' have entered the ghetto again. This time, they came in new Soviet trucks. They dumped all of the museum's materials—artifacts, books, archives—into trucks and took them to Szniadecki Street, to St. George's Church, which is now the Book Chamber. All materials are kept there in excellent condition, except for the Jewish materials, which were dumped into the basement."[12]

"The 'guests' have entered the ghetto again." "We have guests" was the code phrase used by ghetto inmates when Germans entered its territory. In 1949, the museum located in the former ghetto was raided and attacked again by "guests." It was an "Aktion" against Jewish culture, this time by the Soviets.

Quite remarkably, none of the museum's staff members were arrested. Gutkowicz found work as a "haircut norm regulator," who inspected local barber shops to check that they had filled their weekly quota of haircuts, as set by the economic plan. It was a humiliating job for a former museum director, but at least he wasn't in prison. The other staff members found better employment, as writers and editors.[13]

The Jewish school and orphanage soon met the same fate as the museum.[14] The synagogue continued to function, but attendance dropped dramatically—people were afraid to go there.

The surviving members of the paper brigade received the news about the museum's liquidation with anger and sorrow but without surprise. Shmerke had predicted it long ago. He remarked gloomily that geopolitics had defeated him and his colleagues of the paper brigade. Who could have imagined that Stalin's Soviet Union would end up being no better than Hitler's Germany when it came to the treatment of Jewish cultural treasures? He and Sutzkever took solace in the fact that they had smuggled a portion of the materials out of the country before it was too late.

With the last Jewish cultural institutions closed, and the collections of Jewish books and documents seized, all that remained of the Jerusalem of Lithuania were its architectural monuments: the old cemetery and the Great Synagogue. They too were disposed of during the next few years.

The cemetery was bulldozed beginning in 1950, to make way for a sports stadium. Before demolition began, the Jewish religious community managed to transfer the remains of the Vilna Gaon and other historical personalities to the new Jewish cemetery on the outskirts of the city. The bulldozers worked fitfully over the course of several years, and the municipal authorities decided to use some of the extracted tombstones for sidewalks and stairwells on the streets of Vilnius. Their engraved Hebrew letters were visible to those pedestrians who cared to notice on Vokeĉiu Street (formerly Niemiecka), where Jews had first settled in the sixteenth century, and on the steps leading up to the House of Trade Unions.[15]

The Great Synagogue was the last physical remnant of Jewish Vilna to go. For years after the war, its empty shell stood as a haunting presence, reminding passersby that Vilnius had once been the Jerusalem of Lithuania. The roof of the shtot-shul was gone, its window frames were empty cavities, and its interior was covered with mounds of rubble. But the walls remained intact.

The Vilnius municipal architecture commission decided on September 22, 1953, to adopt a reconstruction plan for the part of the Old Town that included the synagogue. It specified that the synagogue be torn down and replaced with residential houses. The plan was not ordered from Moscow. This was a local decision, taken five months after Stalin's death and four months after the Kremlin disavowed Stalin's last great antisemitic campaign. The synagogue was an inconvenient reminder of Vilnius's Jewish past. Only one of the ten members of the commission, Z. S. Budreika, contested the plan and proposed "that the existing synagogue be left as an architectural monument."

The demolition took place over the next year. The stone walls of the edifice were so thick that they required repeated dynamiting. It was as if the synagogue building was putting up resistance.[16] But in the end, the last bastion of the Jerusalem of Lithuania fell and was no more.

The Great Synagogue had averted destruction over many centuries: it withstood the devastation inflicted on the city by the Russian invasion of 1665; it eluded the cannonballs of the Napoleonic War of 1812 and the bombs of World War I. For generations, Vilners believed that the shtot-shul was protected by the Almighty against all harm. God had blessed it and had promised that it would stand until the coming of the Messiah, when it would, in the words of the Talmud, be reconsecrated in the Land of Israel. Survivors of the Vilna ghetto noted with amazement that even the Nazis, who had exterminated Vilna's Jews, did not destroy the Great Synagogue. It was left to the Soviet Lithuanian authorities to dynamite the synagogue and shatter its legend.

CHAPTER TWENTY-NINE

Later Lives

WHILE THE WAR YEARS were the defining moment in the lives of the ERR plunderers and the paper-brigade rescuers, both the villains and surviving heroes lived on for decades, some in fame and some in obscurity.

The men of the Einsatzstab Reichsleiter Rosenberg who looted and destroyed the Jerusalem of Lithuania were never tried or punished for their crimes.

Dr. Johannes Pohl was taken prisoner by the American military on May 31, 1945, in Possneck, East Germany, in his capacity as a staff member of the Nazi propaganda magazine *Welt Dienst*, published by the Institute for the Investigation of the Jewish Question. He admitted to working for the institute and for the ERR, but nonetheless, the Americans released him seventeen months later, after the conclusion of the Nuremberg tribunal.

Pohl was a very lucky man. At Nuremberg, the ERR was branded a criminal organization. Three of Pohl's own memoranda to Alfred Rosenberg, reporting on the ERR's "acquisitions activity," were used as evidence in the trial. Rosenberg was executed, but Pohl, the agency's prime looter of Judaica and Hebraica, was released and never stood trial for anything. The Allies did not dig down to the staff level to prosecute the rank-and-file looters.

After that, Pohl kept a low profile and did not apply for academic or library jobs that would have required a review of his wartime activity. He spent several years in his native Cologne, where he was active in the local parish of the Catholic Church and lived for a time in a church compound on the outskirts of the city.

Pohl published articles in the *Palestina Jahrbuch* of the German Holy Land Society, with which he had been associated since his years as a young priest and vicar. The articles lacked the virulent antisemitism of his previous writings, but occasionally his anti-Jewish animus resurfaced. In an article on the Middle East war of 1948–49, he warned readers that the Arab world now faced a "Russian-Jewish peril." He consistently put the name of the new state, Israel, in quotation marks, to indicate that it was not a legitimate political entity.

Pohl moved to Wiesbaden in 1953 and worked there on the editorial staff of the Steiner publishing house. He was the de facto editor of the Duden German style manual, a standard reference work. But he never returned to the cities of his glory days, Berlin and Frankfurt, and didn't reestablish contact with his former ERR colleagues. By avoiding prominence and social mingling, he eluded arrest. Pohl died in 1960.[1]

The ERR "Judenforschung" expert Herbert Gotthard, the man that Shmerke nicknamed "the little swine," was even luckier. The British had arrested him thanks to Sutzkever's testimony, with support from Max Weinreich, but they ended up releasing him after eighteen months of detention, in late January 1948. The Legal Division of the British Foreign Office ruled that there was "no case for extradition" to Poland and noted that the Polish Military Mission in Germany was "not very interested in the case." The Poles' extradition request was ten lines long, with no accompanying evidence or testimony. Gotthard, for his part, submitted numerous testimonials and lengthy statements in his own defense.

The onset of the Cold War also played a role in Gotthard's release. By January 1948, the British were extraditing very few war criminals to Communist Poland. Gotthard outwaited and outsmarted the system. Shmerke, Sutzkever, and Weinreich were never informed of his release.[2]

Gotthard proceeded to make a career based on a new fictitious biography he concocted. He suppressed any mention of his work for the ERR and claimed he had spent the war years on the faculty of the University of Berlin. This was technically true since he was officially on leave from the university for the two years that he looted and destroyed cultural treasures for the ERR. Gotthard also falsified his academic credentials and asserted that he had received a habilitation degree in October 1946, at the very time when he was masquerading as a Jew in the Lubeck displaced persons' camp. In 1951, he was appointed instructor of Oriental studies at the University of Kiel, north of Hamburg, a position he held for more than twenty years. He taught various Semitic languages, including Hebrew, and gave courses on the Old Testament. Gotthard died in 1983.[3]

Each member of the paper brigade had his or her own fate, with triumphs and tragedies.

Abraham Sutzkever went on to have a long and illustrious literary career. After fighting in Israel's War of Independence, he established a Yiddish literary journal, *The Golden Chain*, with funding from Israel's ruling Labor Party, and it quickly became the most highly regarded organ of Yiddish writing in the world. He fell in love with the Land of Israel but remained faithful to the language of the diaspora. "This country is the face of the Jewish God. . . . I often think that it'll be a Yiddish poet who will truly serenade the Land of Israel. Because the old-new Yiddish language is more biblical than today's modern Hebrew."[4]

Sutzkever carried out his own prediction, by celebrating the beauty of the Sinai Desert, Mount Hermon, and the Galilee in Yiddish verse. But all the while, the ghosts of Vilna remained a powerfully haunting presence in his writing.

Sutzkever published more than thirty volumes of poetry and prose, and counted among his avid readers Israeli president Zalman Shazar and prime minister Golda Meir. He was awarded the Israel Prize, the country's highest honor, in 1985.

While living in Tel Aviv, there was a part of Sutzkever in New York, in the form of YIVO and the collections that he had rescued. He maintained an intimate friendship with director Max Weinreich, and after years of intense correspondence, the two men met face-to-face in 1959, spending two days in seclusion in the Laurentian Mountains, in Canada.[5] Sutzkever never revealed to Weinreich that he had held on to hundreds of documents from the Vilna ghetto archive, taken them to Israel, and kept them in his home. The poet didn't part with those documents for decades. In 1984, he donated this portion of the Vilna ghetto archive to the Hebrew University library—an option he had rejected back in 1946.

Rachela Krinsky settled down with her husband Abraham Melezin and her daughter Sarah, in Neshanic, New Jersey, where the couple ran a chicken farm. The peaceful, rustic surroundings soothed and healed her, after the horrors she had endured in the Stutthof concentration camp. While Rachela's greatest joy was raising Sarah, she still harbored a special love in her heart for Shmerke and wrote to him often. When he visited the United States as a tourist in late 1948, for the founding meeting of the Congress for Jewish Culture, she dropped everything—including her husband—to spend a few days with him.

For several years, Rachela ran a bed and breakfast at her farm that attracted Yiddish writers and intellectuals. In quiet evenings, the visitors recited their poetry to a rapt audience of two: Rachela and Abraham Melezin. She celebrated her daughter's marriage in 1961 and the birth of her granddaughter Alexandra in 1969. Rachela gradually transformed herself from a closed and depressed woman into a warm and giving person, who was active in helping immigrants from the Soviet Union adjust to American life.[6]

Rachela never lost touch with her nanny, Sarah's savior Wikcia Rodziewicz, sending her a never-ending stream of letters, photos, and money. Sarah visited Poland shortly after her wedding and found that Wikcia kept a "shrine" displaying photographs of her that spanned her entire lifetime. (Wikcia's adopted daughter told Sarah quietly, "I've always hated you.") Rachela brought Wikcia to visit the United States in 1970, the only time the two women ever saw each other face-to-face again.[7]

With the passage of time, Rachela found something she never imagined she'd find: contentment in life, surrounded by her husband, daughter, and granddaughter, as well as by her brother and sister who had immigrated to the United States before the war. Her social circle widened after she and her husband relocated to Teaneck, New Jersey, in 1970. In her old age, she wrote to Sutzkever: "We should never forget that we are the lucky few. Who could have imagined fifty years ago that we would survive and live to have a wonderful life?"[8]

Shmerke Kaczerginski never received the American immigration visa he longed for, because of his past history as a Communist. He settled in Argentina in May 1950, with his wife Mary and three-year-old daughter Liba, to direct the South American branch of the Congress for Jewish Culture. At a press conference upon his arrival in Buenos Aires, he declared that his experience smuggling books from the Nazis had instilled in him a deep-set dedication to culture. And he offered a blessing to his newfound home: "May you, the Jewish community of

Buenos Aires, shine with the light of holy devotion to Jewish culture, just as we the brigade of forty writers, educators and cultural activists, did in the Vilna ghetto."[9]

Shmerke kept his charm, his humor, and the knack for making friends. He still loved to belt out tunes at parties and gatherings. He soon became one of the most popular figures in Latin American Jewry and published three books of memoirs and essays—before his premature death.

In April 1954, Shmerke set out for Mendoza, in the Andes, to lead a public Passover celebration on behalf of the Jewish National Fund. After the Passover Seder, the local community asked him to stay on for one more day, to give an impromptu lecture on his years living under the Soviets. Shmerke agreed, saying "even if it's just for ten people or twenty people, it'll be worth it. I want them to hear about the experiences that broke my heart and shattered my youthful dreams."

Eager to return home after his talk, Shmerke took an airplane back from Mendoza to Buenos Aires, even though he had traveled to Mendoza by train. He was in a rush. The night flight on April 23, 1954, crashed into the peak of a mountain in the Andes and burst into flames. There were no survivors.[10]

Shmerke's death, at age forty-six, sent shockwaves through the Jewish world and was front-page news in New York's *Yiddish Daily Forward*. It took a week for the authorities to locate the victims' remains. The fact that only charred portions of his body were discovered evoked the memory of Klooga, where the Germans' set their victims' bodies on fire. Shmerke died as did Herman Kruk and Zelig Kalmanovitch—in flames. When the funeral finally took place on May 4, the book smuggler, ghetto fighter, and partisan was buried next to the newly erected Holocaust memorial on the grounds of the Buenos Aires Jewish cemetery.

Weinreich expressed the upset and anger felt by many: "What an absurdity! To survive everything and then die in those God-forsaken mountains." Sutzkever sent his condolences to the family and community: "Since my mother perished, I have not cried so much. My soul is covered in ashes. Shmerke, I kiss your remains, and I purify your body with my tears." Rachela fell into a deep depression for a year and received psychiatric treatment.[11]

Shmerke's friend and colleague from "Young Vilna" Chaim Grade eulogized him at a memorial program in New York, which was attended by more than five hundred people.

He lived his all-too-short life with song and friendship. He built, created, and struggled. Shmerke's love of his friends knew no bounds and acknowledged no jealousy. When he was faced with deadly danger, he handed over his one and only pistol to Abraham Sutzkever.

An orphan who was literally left on the street, he would have fallen into abandonment and neglect, like so many other children of his kind, were it not for the "school" of modern Jewish culture, which picked him up from the street, washed him, and made him into an independent person. And that is why Shmerke ran to rescue Jewish culture when it was in danger.

Shmerke stayed young in the ghetto, young in the forest, and young in the face of life-threatening dangers and deep disillusionment. And when he, the embodiment of youthfulness, left us, the last sparks of our youth were extinguished. We, his friends, are now all old.[12]

CHAPTER THIRTY

Forty Years in the Wilderness

W HO WOULD HAVE imagined that the Jewish books and documents that remained in Vilnius would spend the next forty years lying in St. George's Church, an eighteenth-century baroque sanctuary, with frescos and portraits of saints staring down at the Hebrew letters? From 1949 to 1989, the treasures had no readers, but they were lucky: they survived intact, escaping paper mills and incinerators during the height of Stalin's antisemitic campaigns.

The books and papers owed their survival to one righteous Gentile —Antanas Ulpis, the director of the Book Chamber of the Lithuanian Soviet Socialist Republic. The Book Chamber was situated in a former Carmelite monastery adjacent to St. George's, and it used the church as its storage facility.

Ulpis was a true book lover who cherished the printed word, regardless of language or author's ethnicity. His institution, the Book Chamber, was charged with preserving a noncirculating copy of everything printed in Lithuania. Mindful that the war had destroyed hundreds of thousands of volumes, he organized excursions across the country soon after hostilities were over, to collect unclaimed printed matter. Ulpis visited paper mills and garbage dumps to rummage through piles of trash in search of books.[1] He was a kindred spirit of the paper brigade.

The tall, stocky, blue-eyed Lithuanian felt an unusual affinity with Jews. He had worked with them before the war in the cultural education society of his hometown of Šiauliai, and he fought alongside them in the XVI Lithuanian Rifle Division of the Soviet partisan movement, where Jews made up 29 percent of the fighters. And once he assumed the position of director of the Book Chamber, he appointed Jews to senior managerial positions, something that wasn't common in Soviet state institutions. Three of his bibliographers were fluent in Hebrew and Yiddish.[2]

Then, in June 1949, the Jewish Museum was liquidated, and Ulpis inherited its library. He vowed to preserve the books, knowing full well that it was a risky, even dangerous, enterprise. The media and state apparatus announced in no uncertain terms that all forms of Jewish culture were anti-Soviet. Letters went out to Soviet state libraries ordering them to remove Yiddish books—both in the original and in translation—from circulation. The Soviet campaign against Jews as "rootless cosmopolitans," "lackeys of the West," and American spies intensified between 1949 and 1953, and most individuals who owned Yiddish books decided to burn their private collections, fearing that ownership would be used as incriminating evidence against them.

In the midst of the mounting hysteria, institutions wanted to get rid of their Jewish collections. Vilnius University Library decided to ship its ten thousand volumes in Hebrew and Yiddish to the trash administration. But Ulpis stepped in, talked to the library administration, and persuaded them to transfer the volumes to the Book Chamber. He placed them in the church, which was filled with enormous mountains of printed matter, the harvests of his book excursions. In some parts of the sanctuary, the mountain nearly reached the fifty-foot-high ceiling.

Following in the footsteps of Vilnius University, the Historical-Revolutionary Museum and the Institute for the History of the Communist Party, which had inherited parts of the Jewish Museum's archive, decided to dispose of their Jewish documents as trash. Why risk being accused of complicity in treason and espionage? Ulpis had no right to claim the archival documents, since his institution dealt only with printed matter, books. But he managed to persuade the directors of the museum and institute to give him their documents. He offered them a creative explanation for his interest: the Book Chamber planned to publish a great retrospective bibliography of all books ever published in Lithuania since the sixteenth century. The Jewish documents contained bibliographic references that would be valuable to the great Lithuanian bibliography.

But just like Shmerke and Sutzkever in 1942 and 1943, Ulpis in 1952 and 1953 needed to have a hiding place for the papers. He wasn't authorized to store archives, even Lithuanian ones, let alone Jewish ones. He decided to bury the documents at the bottom of the mountains of books in St. George's Church, in the middle of the stuffed sanctuary. No one would see them or be able to reach them there. And he told one of his Lithuanian staff members, "We must keep this alive, but we mustn't tell anyone about it."[3]

Ulpis waited until after Stalin's death in March 1953 to do something with the Jewish materials. The atmosphere in the USSR gradually became more relaxed, as Nikita Khrushchev initiated a "thaw" that included a token restoration of Jewish culture. Yiddish writers were released from the gulag (including the Vilnius poet Hirsh Osherovitsh), and amateur Yiddish theater companies appeared in Vilnius and other cities. With posters for the theater popping up on the streets, Ulpis decided it was safe to start cataloging the Yiddish and Hebrew books in his possession.[4]

He instructed a group of his Jewish staff members, including chief bibliographer Solomon Kurliandchik, to spend a few hours a week sorting the Jewish books according to language (Yiddish or Hebrew), type of publication (book or periodical), and place of publication (inside or outside Lithuania). Then he hired a group of Jewish pensioners to work as volunteer catalogers. The senior citizens enjoyed the work; it gave them a chance to read books that were unavailable anywhere in the Soviet Union. Ulpis let them take a few books home for reading, in lieu of payment. That was their reward. Slowly but surely, thousands of volumes left the mountains in St. George's Church for the stacks of the Book Chamber.

Between 1956 and 1965, more than twenty thousand books were cataloged. Occasionally, a writer or the head of the theater ensemble would come to peruse a few volumes. But the general public could not see anything.

Sometime around 1960, while working on sorting the printed matter, Ulpis's deputy and chief bibliographer Kurliandchik came across the boxes of Jewish documents buried at the foot of a book mountain. Ulpis had never told him about them. The bibliographer was stunned to find pages of Yiddish folklore, descriptions of pogroms in Ukraine in 1919, the records of the nineteenth-century Vilna State Rabbinical

Seminary, studies on the history of the Karaites, and . . . reports by the Einsatzstab Reichsleiter Rosenberg. He approached Ulpis, who let him in on the secret: this was the archive of YIVO that he had quietly acquired and hidden away during the final years of Stalin's rule.

Kurliandchik offered to spend a few evenings per week, after working hours, arranging and cataloging the documents. Ulpis agreed. In effect, there was a quiet Judaica department at work in the Book Chamber in the early 1960s. Ulpis even joked with his Jewish staff members that "some day they will erect a monument for me in Israel, for rescuing the remnants of Jewish culture."

But the materials were still in the USSR and subject to the ebb and flow of state antisemitism. When the Central Committee of the Communist Party of Lithuania approved publication of the first volume of Ulpis's great retrospective bibliography, covering all books printed in Lithuania until 1863, it excluded two languages: Hebrew and Yiddish. Ulpis had no choice but to discontinue the cataloging of the Jewish materials. The decision by the Central Committee had undermined his official rationale for the work. The highest political authority in the Lithuanian SSR had spoken.

The sensitivity of the matter was highlighted again in 1967, when two American professors visited Vilnius and asked the Ministry of Culture to view the Judaica collection at the Book Chamber. They asked to see materials on the Karaites and pogroms, topics about which, they had heard through the grapevine, the Book Chamber had documents. Unbeknownst to the professors, the KGB had been trailing them since they entered the Soviet Union in Moscow and knew of their interest. The KGB contacted the Lithuanian minister of culture and instructed him not to share anything with the Americans. The minister, in turn, called in the Book Chamber's acting director Kurliandchik (Ulpis was away on leave) and told him to meet with the professors at the ministry and explain to them that the Book Chamber was closed for repairs. The American professors went home empty-handed.[5]

After the Six-Day War in 1967, there arose a Jewish national movement in the USSR that demanded that Jews have the right to leave for Israel. As the movement's activists staged protests, published underground literature, and studied Hebrew illegally, official Soviet anti-Zionist rhetoric intensified. Jewish culture was suspect again. Ulpis suspended all activity surrounding the Jewish books and papers. They stood in the stacks of the Book Chamber, or lay in St. George's Church, untouched, forlorn, and forgotten.

Ulpis died in 1981. While the Lithuanian had never met Shmerke or Sutzkever, he was the last member of the paper brigade.

CHAPTER THIRTY-ONE

Grains of Wheat

I N NOVEMBER 1988, YIVO's eighty-year-old librarian, Dina Abramowicz, stormed into the director's office. A short, bespectacled woman, whose body was stiff, emotions restrained, and demeanor serious, Dina was a survivor of the Vilna ghetto. She had worked under Herman Kruk in the ghetto library before fleeing with the FPO ghetto fighters to the forest. Dina was the last living link between the New York YIVO, now located at 1048 Fifth Avenue, near the Metropolitan Museum of Art, and the Vilna YIVO on Wiwulskiego Street. Max Weinreich, who had hired her back in 1946, had passed away in 1969. Dina was treated with reverence by YIVO's staff and visitors, because of her erudition, diligence, and age, but most of all because of what she represented—continuity with a lost world. YIVO's new director, Samuel Norich, who was nearly forty years her junior, rose to take her hand whenever she entered the room.

Dina was agitated because of something she had read. The Soviet Yiddish magazine *Sovetish Heymland* had published an article on the fate of Jewish libraries in Vilnius, which mentioned that 20,705 Hebrew and Yiddish books were currently housed in the Book Chamber of the Lithuanian SSR. It was the first time this information was disclosed to the public. Upon reading those words, Dina's jaw dropped and her head felt dizzy. It was the first confirmation that treasures rescued by the paper brigade, and housed in the Jewish Museum, had survived intact in Vilnius. As a friend of Abraham Sutzkever and an avid reader of his poetry, she whispered to herself the words of Sutzkever's poem "Grains of Wheat." The grains had been unearthed—forty-five years later.[1]

The author of the revelatory article was a graduate student of literature at Vilnius University named Emanuel Zingeris. Norich, the new YIVO director, had met him at a conference in Warsaw a few months earlier, and Zingeris had told him that he had found some Jewish books in Vilnius. The young man added cryptically, "I think you'll have occasion to visit our city." But 20,705 volumes was a lot more than "some books."

Norich contacted Zingeris, who invited him to Vilnius to attend the founding conference of the Jewish Culture Society of Lithuania, in March 1989. Under Mikhail Gorbachev's liberalization policy of glasnost, Jews were allowed to establish grassroots societies and organizations, after a forty-year ban on public Jewish life. Zingeris dropped his studies at the university to become the first president of the Jewish Culture Society, as well as director of a newly established Jewish Museum—a revival of the institution that had been liquidated in 1949.[2]

At the opening session of the society's conference, the presiding chairman announced that the director of YIVO, "located in New York City since the war," was in attendance—as if to signal that the spirit of prewar Vilna had returned. YIVO was in Vilna again. Their forty-year nightmare was over.

On the sidelines of the conference, Norich, accompanied by his chief archivist, visited the Book Chamber and met with its director Algimantas Lukosiunas, a disciple of Antanas Ulpis. Just as the two directors finished exchanging pleasantries, a staff member brought in a handcart with five brown paper bags wrapped with string. The staff member unwrapped them and took out documents written in Hebrew letters. Norich and his archivist were speechless. They belonged to YIVO's prewar archive. Many of them bore YIVO's stamp.

Norich was both excited and deeply moved. Zingeris's article had been about books, not about documents. As the staff member unwrapped the packages, Norich experienced a kind of warp-speed time travel. One second, he was with the documents in 1933, when YIVO inaugurated its building on Wiwulskiego Street; the next moment, he was with them in 1943 as they were sorted under the watchful eye of the Germans; then he was with them as they were unearthed after the liberation; and finally he was with them as the security services removed them from the Jewish Museum. He thought of the late Max Weinreich, of Dina Abramowicz back in New York, and of Abraham Sutzkever in Tel Aviv.

After leaving the Book Chamber, Norich went to 18 Wiwulskiego Street, to pay homage to Weinreich and the paper brigade. Once he returned to New York, word about the discovery spread like wildfire. The *New York Times* reported optimistically, "This is a tale of a sundered literary collection finally on the way to a reunification that until recently seemed impossible."[3]

On Norich's second trip to Vilnius, Lukosiunas gave him a tour of the Book Chamber, including St. George's Church, and the YIVO director saw the full scope of the tragedy with his own eyes: abandoned Torah scrolls lying uncovered, mountains of decaying volumes printed on acidic paper, and piles of stray Yiddish newspapers. The scene was a vivid representation of the fate of Jewish life under the Nazis and Soviets. Lukosiunas tried to put a good face on the grim picture and informed Norich that he had established a Judaica Department to catalog the Yiddish and Hebrew materials. It was named after Matityahu Strashun.

But who would do the cataloging? The work required educated people with knowledge of Jewish history and literature, in a country where all forms of Jewish study had been banned for forty years. So Lukosiunas hired a sixty-five-year-old retiree to head the department: Ms. Esfir Bramson, who had graduated from the Sholem Aleichem Yiddish high school in Kaunas, Lithuania, on June 20, 1941 — two days before the Germans invaded. She had just stepped down from her work as a paralegal in the Forestry Ministry and was eager to reconnect with the literature she had read and adored as a young woman. In her stiffness and seriousness, Bramson was quite similar to Dina Abramowicz, except that her health was poorer and her nerves were frayed. Unlike Dina, she had spent her entire adult life as a Jew in the Soviet Union.[4]

Bramson hired a staff of catalogers, all of whom were retirees. It wasn't a case of reverse age discrimination. The only people with knowledge of Jewish languages, history, and literature were senior citizens. Two of them had attended the Sholem Aleichem School with Bramson, one was a native of Vilna, and the fourth had graduated from a Hebrew-language high school. As they segregated and cataloged the documents, memories of the Jewish world of their childhoods, which had been so brutally destroyed, welled up in their minds. There was the joy of recognition, the satisfaction of helping restore Jewish culture, and the pain of recalling murdered friends, family, and an entire culture devastated. Never before was the cataloging work of librarians and archivists accompanied by so many smiles and tears.

Norich began negotiating for the return of YIVO's documents to New York. But Lithuanian Soviet officials were noncommittal. It seemed inconceivable to them that the political leadership in Vilnius, let alone Moscow, would approve the shipment of cultural property to a private organization overseas. And they suspected that if these American Jews wanted the books and papers so badly, they must have tremendous market value. One official suggested that if YIVO found "a Rothschild" to finance the construction of a new Book Chamber building, they would be able strike a deal.

The biggest blow to Norich's hopes came when Zingeris, the man who had first discovered the materials, declared that the Jewish books and documents must remain in Vilnius, because they were Lithuanian cultural heritage. This was part patriotism and part self-interest. He wanted the materials to be transferred to the Jewish Museum that he directed. What's more, Zingeris developed political ambitions and became active in the movement for Lithuanian independence known as Sajudis. He was elected to both the Soviet Congress of People's Deputies and the Lithuanian Supreme Council on the Sajudis list. Some called him the "court Jew" of the Lithuanian nationalist movement. Once the rising politician started proclaiming that the materials were Lithuanian cultural heritage, officials starting repeating the line.

Norich was exasperated. If the materials were Lithuanian heritage, why had Lithuanians left them abandoned in a church? If they were Lithuanian heritage, why was there practically no one left in Lithuania who could read or study them? And what about the matter of ownership? The documents clearly belonged to YIVO.

"Listen," he argued at one meeting,

I was born in a displaced persons' camp in Germany. I have friends a few years older than me, who were children during the war, and who were hidden and rescued by Lithuanians. When the war ended, the rescuers gave the children back to a surviving parent or relative, and if there were no relatives, they returned them to the Jewish community. These documents are our children. We are deeply grateful to the Book Chamber for preserving them, and we are willing to express our gratitude in various ways. But the books and papers that bear YIVO's stamps are our flesh and blood. Please, give them back to us.[5]

Lithuania unilaterally declared its independence from the Soviet Union in March 1990, in a move that strained its relations with Moscow almost to the breaking point. Mikhail Gorbachev refused to recognize the declaration and sent Soviet military reinforcements into the rebel republic. Given the political uncertainty, Norich realized that the question of YIVO's books and papers could only be resolved at the top, by the new Lithuanian head of state, Vytautas Landsbergis. He hoped for a sympathetic reception: Landsbergis's parents had hidden and rescued a Jewish girl from the Germans during the war.

Their first meeting did not go as planned. Norich waited outside Landsbergis's office for an hour, because of an emergency cabinet meeting. As soon as he entered the office, the head of state told him with a bitter smile that he had "good news": Soviet helicopters were about to land in Vilnius. A state of emergency would soon be announced. Landsbergis apologized that the matter of the Jewish books and papers would have to wait for another day.[6]

It took several more years of negotiations. During that time the Soviet Union collapsed, Lithuanian governments came and went, agreements between YIVO and state institutions were signed—and then abrogated by the Lithuanians—and YIVO changed its directors twice. In the midst of all the turmoil, the Book Chamber conducted a cleanup of St. George's Church that led to the discovery of yet another trove of Jewish material.

It was left to YIVO's research director Alan Nadler to finalize a deal in December 1994. It called for the shipment of the documents to New York, where they would be restored, cataloged, copied, and then sent back to Vilnius. This was a great victory for historical memory and scholarship—the documents would see the light of day. But emotionally, it was hard to accept that the members of the paper brigade had risked their lives, and some paid with their lives, so that YIVO could receive photocopies of its own documents. Nadler left open the prospect of renegotiating.

The big day arrived: thirty-five boxes, weighing four hundred pounds, landed at Newark International Airport on February 22, 1995, accompanied by the head of the Lithuanian Central State Archive. When the boxes arrived at YIVO, the staff opened them with the eagerness of children unpacking a much-awaited Chanukah present.

They found inside a panoply of papers: an invitation to the wedding of Rabbi Menachem Mendl Schneerson, the Lubavitcher rebbe; a poster announcing a 1921 performance of "The Dybbuk" by the Vilna Troupe Theater Ensemble; an entrance card to high holiday services in the Vilna Great Synagogue; a child's geometry notebook with Yiddish notes; and a 1937 flyer congratulating the Soviet Union's Jewish Autonomous Region, Birobidzhan, on its third anniversary. Nadler, YIVO's research director, could barely hold back tears as he discovered photographs of the 1919 pogrom in Dubova. Eight members of his grandfather's family had been killed in that pogrom. Dina Abramowicz picked up a letter by Max Weinreich from Copenhagen in 1940 to the YIVO staff. It was like entering a time machine.[7]

As more boxes were opened, archivists and administrators kept calling out, "Oh, my God!" Never had so many "Oh, my Gods" been heard in the walls of this secular research institute.[8]

Amidst the excitement, there was one special guest. Rachela Krinsky-Melezin was there to examine the papers she had helped rescue more than fifty years earlier. "It was so emotional," she said of her first glimpse of the documents. "Back in the ghetto, I saw them every day." Then, after further reflection, she added, "Kalmanovitch always said, 'don't worry, after the war you'll get everything back.'"[9]

YIVO organized a large public celebration to mark the arrival of a second shipment of twenty-eight boxes in January 1996. The institute awarded a prize to the eighty-year-old Abraham Sutzkever, for his rescue of Jewish cultural treasures. It was the public tribute that he and Shmerke Kaczerginski didn't receive back in 1947, because of Cold War considerations—a party almost fifty years late in coming. Sutzkever was too frail to travel to the United States for the event, so Rachela Krinsky accepted the award on his behalf.

Nadler, YIVO's research director and an ordained rabbi, recited the blessing *She-hechianu*: "Blessed are you our God, King of the universe, who has kept us alive, sustained us, and brought us to this day." Veteran Yiddish actor David Rogow, a native of Vilna who knew Shmerke and Sutzkever as teenagers, recited selections from Sutzkever's poetry, including "Grains of Wheat." It was an evening of joy mixed with tears. The chairman of the Vilnius Jewish Community, writer Grigorii Kanovich, said that given the history of the Jewish people in the twentieth century, all truly Jewish celebrations were joy mixed with tears.

While Sutzkever wasn't present, the words he had offered several years earlier, at YIVO's sixtieth anniversary, were hovering in the air. They were his last statement on his work for the paper brigade:

When I first received the invitation by director Samuel Norich to come to YIVO's sixtieth anniversary, I thought to myself, this must be a mistake. YIVO is inside of me, where should I go or come?

But later, I reread the letter of invitation in a different mood, and the following lines latched on to me: "The most important thing we can pass on to American Jews is the treasury of our East European heritage. Our existence is based on our constant effort to secure our cultural continuity. No one alive has done more to secure that continuity than you."

No one alive. I confess that the phrase caused me to feel an earthquake—if it is true that man was created from earth. And I sent a second letter to the YIVO director: I'm coming.

When the evil ones undertook to transform Wiwulskiego 18 into a Ponar for Jewish culture, and they ordered a few dozen Jews from the Vilna ghetto to dig graves for our soul, it was my good fortune, in the midst of our great misfortune, that fate anointed me with a Yellow Star of David to be one of those few dozen Jews.

Only then and there, when I witnessed how the YIVO temple was shaken, could I properly evaluate its architect, Max Weinreich.

I hope Weinreich will forgive me that while wrestling in the paper whirlpool of the YIVO building, I read various documents from his private home archive, which had been transferred there. But reading them encouraged me to rescue a few more things. And rescue meant mainly smuggling them back into the ghetto and burying them. The escaped limbs of YIVO felt safer and more at home amid Jews, in the ghetto soil of the Jerusalem of Lithuania. They waited for the Messiah in the bunker at 6 Shavel Street.

The rescue of YIVO's treasures was performed with a deeply inherited sense of commitment, of performing a *mitzvah*, as if we were rescuing babies.

I wrote many of my poems that are signed "Vilna ghetto" and the date of their decomposition in Weinreich's sinking temple. Perhaps even in his office. The divine presence of Yiddish did not leave me. It protected and inspired me.

To what may I be compared at that moment?

Native Vilners remember the city lunatic Isserson. People once saw the following scene: A painter stood on a ladder in a synagogue in the *shulhoyf* and dipped his paintbrush into a bucket of lime that hung on a ledge, painting the ceiling, back and forth. Suddenly, Isserson came over and shouted up to the painter, "Hold on to your paintbrush, because I'm taking away the ladder."

I may be compared to—I in fact became—that synagogue painter. The ladder underneath me was indeed taken away, but I held on to the paintbrush, which didn't even have a ledge. And lo and behold: I did not fall down. The bucket hung there between heaven and earth.[10]

Rachela Krinsky-Melezin was invited to say a few words as she accepted Sutzkever's award, but she was too overwhelmed and choked up to read her prepared remarks. All she could think about was Shmerke, the book smuggler par excellence who slipped so many books and papers past the ghetto gate; Shmerke, the eternal optimist and the life of every party and gathering; and Shmerke, the love she had and sacrificed for her daughter's sake. If only Shmerke had lived to see this day, he would sing out one of his lively tunes, perhaps the anthem he had written for the ghetto's youth club: "Anyone who wants to can be young . . ."

When the program was over, a young journalist asked Rachela a question. Why had she risked her head to rescue books and manuscripts? Without batting an eye, she answered: "I didn't believe at the time that my head belonged to me. We thought we could do something for the future."[11]

ACKNOWLEDGMENTS

At the end of seven years of intensive research and writing, it's a pleasure to thank the people who helped me take this amazing journey.

Scott Mendel of Mendel Media believed in the importance of this story from the moment I sent him a short e-mail inquiry. Scott urged me to tell the human stories of the book smugglers, not only the history of the books, and thanks to him, the project took on a different shape and direction. Steve Hull of ForeEdge picked up where Scott left off and helped me grasp how narrative history differs from academic prose. It has been a pleasure working with him.

I owe a great debt of gratitude to the YIVO Institute for Jewish Research, which played a great part not only in the book's story but also in my writing it. I was fortunate to have a quiet office at YIVO and to write this book in an atmosphere where the memory of Max Weinreich and Abraham Sutzkever is palpable. I did much intensive work during the semester when I was YIVO's Jacob Kronhill visiting professor. I want to extend special thanks to the library and archival staff who accommodated my every request and whim, even when it involved trips to YIVO's warehouse in New Jersey: Lyudmila Sholokhova, Fruma Mohrer, Gunnar Berg, Vital Zajka, and Rabbi Shmuel Klein.

YIVO's executive director Jonathan Brent not only encouraged me; he has dedicated himself to ensuring that the legacy of the paper brigade endures—by launching a monumental Vilna Collections Project, to digitize the books and documents in Vilnius and New York that are the subject of my book.

I benefitted from the assistance of institutions, researchers, librarians, and archivists in six countries.

At the outset of this project, I spent a very fruitful semester as a visiting scholar at the Leonid Nevzlin Research Center for Russian and East European Jewry, at the Hebrew University in Jerusalem. The Israeli archives were both a goldmine and a pleasant working environment. My special thanks to Rachel Misrati and the staff of the archives department of the National Library of Israel, and Daniela Ozacki of the Moreshet Archive in Givat Haviva. When I wasn't in Jerusalem myself, I could always count on Eliezer Niborski, editor of the Hebrew University's Index to Yiddish Periodicals, to track down articles in rare Yiddish newspapers. Despite my pestering, Eliezer never lost his good cheer and wry sense of humor.

A remarkable group of people supported and assisted my work in Lithuania. My friendship with the late Esfir Bramson, head of the Judaica section of the National Library of Lithuania, inspired me to write this book. As the custodian of the surviving portion of Jewish books and documents in Vilnius, she was a true heir to the tradition of Chaikl Lunski and the paper brigade. I regret that she didn't live to see this book's publication. Her successor, Dr. Larisa Lempert, is a cherished friend who spared no effort to respond to queries and requests. Ruta Puisyte, assistant director of the Vilnius Yiddish Institute, was my devoted and wise research assistant, and Neringa Latvyte of the Vilna Gaon State Jewish Museum provided valuable information.

Vadim Altskan, senior archival projects director at the Mandel Center of the United States Holocaust Memorial Museum is a godsend to scholarship. Parts of the book smugglers' story would have remained unknown to me were it not for his guidance and advice on locating archival resources.

Among the people who provided substantive feedback and saved me from embarrassing mistakes, I want to single out Avraham Novershtern, professor of Yiddish at the Hebrew University, who read and critiqued an earlier draft of the book manuscript. Greg Bradsher of the National Archives and Records Administration in College Park, Maryland, helped me swim in the waters of that mammoth repository. Bret Werb and Justin Cammy graciously shared with me their work and expertise on Shmerke Kaczerginski. Kalman Weiser shared documents from German and Polish archives on the Einsatzstab Reichsleiter Rosenberg looter and Judenforscher (Jewish expert) Herbert Gotthard.

Many scholars and colleagues contributed to this book with their comments and insights: Mordechai Altshuler, Valery Dymshits, Immanuel Etkes, Zvi Gitelman, Samuel Kassow, Dov-Ber Kerler, David G. Roskies, Ismar Schorsch, Nancy Sinkoff, Darius Staliunas, Jeffrey Veidlinger, and Arkadii Zeltser.

I am privileged to have known some of the heroes who participated in this story, and members of their families. Michael Menkin of Fort Lee, New Jersey, the last living member of the paper brigade, is my dear friend and a model of grace, generosity of spirit, and humility. He also explained to me things that I could never have known from any written source. I had illuminating conversations on the Vilna ghetto with Abraham Sutzkever in Tel Aviv in 1999. He remains a giant of literature and culture. Last but not least, Alexandra Wall trusted me with her notes, impressions, and memories about her grandmother Rachela Krinsky-Melezin. Alix is a devoted and proud bearer of the memory of her "babushka," and of her mother, Sarah Wall.

I am fortunate to work in an institution that values what I do. The Jewish Theological Seminary of America has been my academic home and has helped form me as a scholar and person. Chancellor Arnold Eisen and provost Alan Cooper have supported this project and me from the outset.

My heartfelt thanks to the Biblioteca di Economia e Commercio, University of Modena, Italy, for hosting me in the summers and providing a quiet, pleasant space to write.

I am blessed with a loving family, who help me believe in myself: my mother, Gella Fishman, is, at age ninety-one, a powerhouse of energy and insight; my brothers Avi and Monele remind me gently about the importance of family commitments; and my adult children Ahron, Nesanel, Tzivia, and Jacob give me much pride and *nakhes*.

I owe my interest in Jewish Vilna, and therefore my writing this book, to two people who are no longer alive. First, my father, Joshua A. (Shikl) Fishman, who was a disciple of Max Weinreich and collaborated with him on many projects. "Pa" was the first person to tell me as a little boy about a magical place called Vilna and to instill in me a love for Yiddish. I mourn his passing and love him from afar. And second, the great Yiddish novelist Chaim Grade, with whom I developed a close friendship during the final years of his life. Thanks to Grade's writings and conversations with me, prewar Vilna is as alive and vivid today as it was in 1930.

Words fail me in trying to express what I owe to my wife Elissa Bemporad. She has been my first and last reader, my learned critic and advisor. But beyond that, she has brought beauty, love, and poetry into my life. Together with her and our children Elia and Sonia, life is an exciting and joyous adventure.

Introduction

1. Shmerke Kaczerginski, *Ikh bin geven a partisan* (Buenos Aires: Fraynd funem mekhaber, 1952), 53–58; Rachela Krinsky-Melezin, "Mit shmerken in vilner geto," in *Shmerke kaczerginski ondenk-bukh* (Buenos Aires: A komitet 1955), 131.

Chapter 1. Shmerke — The Life of the Party

1. There are two excellent English-language treatments of Kaczerginski. Justin Cammy, *Young Vilna: Yiddish Culture of the Last Generation* (Bloomington: Indiana University Press, forthcoming), chap. 2; and Bret Werb, "Shmerke Kaczerginski: The Partisan Troubadour," *Polin* 20 (2007): 392–412.

2. Yom Tov Levinsky, "Nokh der mite fun mayn talmid," in *Shmerke kaczerginski ondenk-bukh*, 96; Yankl Gutkowicz "Shmerke," *Di Goldene keyt* 101 (1980): 105.

3. Mark Dworzecki, "Der kemfer, der zinger, der zamler," in *Shmerke kaczerginski ondenk-bukh*, 57.

4. B. Terkel, "Der 'fliendiker vilner,'" in *Shmerke kaczerginski ondenk-bukh*, 79–80; the text of Shmerke's first hit song is reproduced in *Shmerke kaczerginski ondenk-bukh*, 229–30.

5. Chaim Grade, "Froyen fun geto," *Tog-morgen zhurnal* (New York), June 30, 1961, 7.

6. Gutkowicz, "Shmerke," 108–9.

7. Grade, "Froyen fun geto," June 30, 1961.

8. Elias Schulman, *Yung vilne* (New York: Getseltn, 1946), 18.

9. Daniel Charney, "Ver zenen di yung vilnianer?" *Literarishe bleter* (Warsaw) 14, February 26, 1937, 135; Schulman, *Yung vilne*, 22.

10. Shmerke Kaczerginski, "Amnestye," *Yung-vilne* (Vilna) 1 (1934), 25–28.

11. Shmerke Kaczerginski, "Mayn khaver sutzkever (tsu zayn 40stn geboyrn-tog)," in *Shmerke kaczerginski ondenk-bukh*, 311–312.

12. See Cammy, *Young vilna*, chap. 2; and Krinsky-Melezin, "Mit shmerken," 131.

13. Shmerke Kaczerginski, "Naye mentshn," *Vilner emes* (Vilnius), December 30, 1940, 3; Shmerke Kaczerginski, "Dos vos iz geven mit bialistok vet zayn mit vilne," *Vilner emes* (Vilnius), December 31, 1940, 3. On his marriage to Barbara Kaufman, see Chaim Grade, "Froyen fun geto," June 30, 1961; and Shmerke Kaczerginski, *Khurbn vilne* (New York: CYCO, 1947) 256.

14. Dov Levin, *Tekufah Be-Sograyim, 1939–1941* (Jerusalem: Hebrew University Institute for Contemporary Jewry and Kibutz Ha-Meuhad, 1989), 139–41.

Chapter 2. The City of the Book

1. Schulman, *Yung vilne*, 17; Lucy Dawidowicz, *From That Time and Place: A Memoir, 1938–1947* (New York: Norton, 1989), 121–22; Krinsky-Melezin, "Mit shmerken," 135.

2. A. I. Grodzenski, "Farvos vilne ruft zikh yerushalayim de-lita," in *Vilner almanakh*, ed. A. I. Grodzenski, 5–10 (Vilna: Ovnt kurier, 1939; 2nd repr. ed., New York: Moriah Offset, 1992).

3. Yitzhak Broides, *Agadot Yerushalayim De-Lita* (Tel Aviv: Igud yotsei vilna ve-ha-sevivah be-yisrael, 1950), 17–22; see also Shloime Bastomski, "Legendes vegn vilne" in Grodzenski, *Vilner almanakh*, 148–50.

4. Zalmen Szyk, *Toyznt yor vilne* (Vilna: Gezelshaft far landkentenish, 1939), 178–85.

5. See Israel Cohen, *Vilna* (Philadelphia: Jewish Publication Society of America, 1st ed.: 1943, 2nd ed.: 1992).

6. Abraham Nisan Ioffe, "Wilna und Wilnauer Klausen," op. 1, file 16, Einsatz-stab Reichsleiter Rosenberg, F. R-633, Lithuanian Central State Archive, Vilnius; Samuel Joseph Fuenn, *Kiryah ne'emanah: korot 'adat yisrael ba-'ir vilna* (Vilna: Funk, 1915), 162–63; Szyk, *Toyznt yor vilne*, 215–17.

7. Chaikl Lunski, "Vilner kloyzn un der shulhoyf," in *Vilner zamlbukh*, ed. Zemach Shabad, vol. 2 (Vilna: N. Rozental, 1918), 100; Szyk, *Toyznt yor vilne*, 217.

8. Shmerke Kaczerginski, "Shtoyb vos frisht: 45 yor in lebn fun a bibliotek," *Undzer tog* (Vilna), June 4, 1937, 5.

9. See Fridah Shor, *Mi-likutei shoshanim 'ad brigadat ha-nyar: sipuro she beit eked ha-sefarim al shem shtrashun ve-vilna* (Ariel, West Bank: Ha-merkaz ha-universitai ariel be-shomron, 2012), and the literature cited there. See also Hirsz Abramowicz, "Khaykl lunski un di strashun bibliotek," in *Farshvundene geshtaltn*, 93–99 (Buenos Aires: Tsentral farband fun poylishe yidn in argentine, 1958).

10. Daniel Charney, *A litvak in poyln* (New York: Congress for Jewish Culture, 1945), 28–29; Dawidowicz, *From That Time*, 121–22; Jonas Turkow, *Farloshene shtern* (Buenos Aires: Tsentral-farband fun poylishe yidn in argentine, 1953), 192–93.

11. See the articles in *Literarishe bleter* (Warsaw) 13, no. 40 (November 27, 1936).

12. See Cecile Kuznitz, *YIVO and the Making of Modern Jewish Culture: Scholarship for the Yiddish Nation* (Cambridge: Cambridge University Press, 2014); *YIVO bleter* 46 (1980); and David E. Fishman, *The Rise of Modern Yiddish Culture* (Pittsburgh: University of Pittsburgh Press, 2005), 93–96, 126–37.

13. Chaikl Lunski, "Der 'seyfer ha-zohov' in der shtrashun-bibliotek," in Grodzenski, *Vilner almanakh*, 43.

Chapter 3. The First Assault

1. See Kalman Weiser, *Jewish People, Yiddish Nation: Noah Prylucki and the Folkists in Poland* (Toronto: University of Toronto Press, 2011), esp. 244–59; Mendl Bal-

beryszski, *Shtarker fun ayzn* (Tel Aviv: Ha-menorah, 1967), 77, 91–93, 104–6, 110; D[ovid] U[mru], "Tsu der derefenung fun der yidishistisher katedre baym vilner universitet," *Vilner emes* (Vilnius), November 2, 1940, 1; Kaczerginski, *Khurbn vilne*, 226.

2. Elhanan Magid, in Tsvika Dror, ed., *Kevutsat ha-ma'avak ha-sheniyah* (Kibutz Lohamei Ha-getaot, Israel: Ghetto Fighters' House, 1987), 142; Balberyszski, *Shtarker fun ayzn*, 110, 112; anonymous letter to M. W. Beckelman, the JDC representative in Vilna, March 20, 1940, file 611.1, Sutzkever-Kaczerginski Collection, RG 223, archives of the YIVO Institute for Jewish Research, New York (hereafter cited as YIVO archives).

3. Balberyszski, *Shtarker fun ayzn*, 112.

4. Ibid., 112, 118–19.

5. Alan E. Steinweis, *Studying the Jew: Scholarly Anti-Semitism in Nazi Germany* (Cambridge, MA: Harvard University Press, 2006).

6. Maria Kühn-Ludewig, *Johannes Pohl (1904–1960): Judaist und Bibliothekar im Dienste Rosenbergs. Eine biographische Dokumentation* (Hanover, Germany: Laurentius, 2000). Regarding his Jerusalem years, see pp. 48–56. Patricia von Papen-Bodek, "Anti-Jewish Research of the Institut zur Erforschung der Judenfrage in Frankfurt am Main between 1939 and 1945," in *Lessons and Legacies VI: New Currents in Holocaust Research*, ed. Jeffry M. Diefendorf, 155–89 (Evanston, IL: Northwestern University Press, 2004).

7. Kühn-Ludewig, *Johannes Pohl*, 160–61, deliberates whether it was Pohl or Gotthard who came to Vilna in July 1941. Sutzkever's various accounts mention both names. Kaczerginski and Balberyszski mention Pohl.

8. Balberyszski, *Shtarker fun ayzn*, 143–47. Balberyszski was a close friend and associate of Prylucki's who visited him and his wife during the period in question. See also Shmerke Kaczerginski, *Partizaner geyen*, 2nd ed. (Buenos Aires: Tsentral farband fun poylishe yidn in argentine, 1947), 65–66; Shmerke Kaczerginski, *Ikh bin geven a partisan* (Buenos Aires: Fraynd funem mekhaber, 1952), 40–41; and Abraham Sutzkever, *Vilner geto* (Paris: Fareyn fun di vilner in frankraykh, 1946), 108.

9. Shmerke Kaczerginski, "Der haknkrayts iber yerushalayim de-lite," *Di Tsukunft* (New York) (September 1946): 639.

10. Balberyszski, *Shtarker fun ayzn*, 180–81.

11. Sutzkever, *Vilner geto*, 108 (Sutzkever reports that the German responsible for their arrest was not Pohl but his lieutenant, Gotthard); Herman Kruk, *Togbukh fun vilner geto*, ed. Mordecai W. Bernstein (New York: YIVO, 1961), 73.

12. Shmerke Kaczerginski manuscript, "Vos di daytshn hobn aroysgefirt un farnikhtet," file 678.2, Sutzkever-Kaczerginski Collection, RG 223, YIVO archives; Kruk, *Togbukh fun vilner geto*, 180.

13. Raphael Mahler, "Emanuel Ringelblum's briv fun varshever geto," *Di Goldene keyt* (Tel Aviv) 46 (1963): 25.

14. ERR collection, op. 1, d. 136, pp. 386, 396, F. 3676, Einsatzsztab Reichsleiter Rosenberg, Central State Archive of Organs of Higher Power (TsDAVO), Kyiv (hereafter cited as TsDAVO).

Chapter 4. Intellectuals in Hell

1. Rokhl Mendelsohn, letter to Pinkhas Schwartz 1959, p. 7, file 770, Sutzkever-Kaczerginski Collection, RG 223, YIVO Institute for Jewish Research, New York; Rachel Margolis, interview by author, Yeruham, Israel, May 6, 2011. See the biography by his brother Pinkhas Schwartz, in Kruk, *Togbukh fun vilner geto*, xi–xlv.

2. Kruk, *Togbukh fun vilner geto*, xxxii–xxxiv.

3. See Samuel Kassow, "Vilna and Warsaw, Two Ghetto Diaries: Herman Kruk and Emanuel Ringelblum," in *Holocaust Chronicles: Individualizing the Holocaust through Diaries and Other Contemporaneous Personal Accounts*, ed. Robert Moses Shapiro, 171–215 (Hoboken, NJ: Ktav, 1999); and Kruk, *Togbukh fun vilner geto*, 294 (June 28, 1942).

4. Kruk, *Togbukh fun vilner geto*, 54–55; Herman Kruk, *The Last Days of the Jerusalem of Lithuania*, trans. Barbara Harshav, ed. Benjamin Harshav (New Haven, CT: Yale University Press and YIVO, 2002), 92.

5. Kruk, *Togbukh fun vilner geto*, 54–55; Kruk, *Last Days*, 92–93.

6. Kruk, *Togbukh fun vilner geto*, 60–63; Kruk, *Last Days*, 97–100.

7. Kruk, *Togbukh fun vilner geto*, 67–69, 77, 80.

8. Kruk, *Togbukh fun vilner geto*, xxxv–xxxvi, 72.

9. Kruk's retrospective report, "A yor arbet in vilner get-bibliotek," October 1942, file 370, pp. 21–22, Sutzkever-Kaczerginski Collection, RG 223, YIVO archives.

10. Kruk, *Togbukh fun vilner geto*, xxxxix, 81–82, 123–24; Balberyszski, *Shtarker fun ayzn*, 443.

11. Grade, "Froyen fun geto," June 30, 1961; Chaim Grade, "Fun unter der erd," *Forverts*, April 1, 1979; Kaczerginski, *Khurbn vilne*, 5.

12. Kaczerginski, *Ikh bin geven*, 19–21; Grade, "Froyen fun geto," June 30, 1961; Grade, "Fun unter der erd," April 1, 1979.

13. Kaczerginski, *Ikh bin geven*, 23–24.

14. Kaczerginski gives conflicting dates for his period outside the Vilna ghetto. In *Khurbn vilne*, the time frame mentioned is September 1941 to April 1942 (see pp. 141, 197, 215); in *Ikh bin geven a partisan*, he mentions winter 1942 to spring 1943. The former dates are corroborated by Kruk, *Togbukh fun vilner geto*, 310.

15. Sutzkever, *Vilner geto*, 26–27, 55–58.

16. Kruk, *Togbukh fun vilner geto*, 92.

Chapter 5. A Haven for Books and People

1. See the monthly library report for October 1941 published in Balberyszski, *Shtarker fun ayzn*, 435–36.

2. Balberyszski, *Shtarker fun ayzn*, 438–39.

3. Inventories of objects in the ghetto library, file 476, Sutzkever-Kaczerginski Collection, RG 223, YIVO archives; on the display cases in the reading room, see

Dina Abramowicz, "Vilner geto bibliotek," in *Lite*, ed. Mendel Sudarsky, Uriah Katsenelboge, and Y. Kisin, 1671–78, vol. 1 (New York: Kultur gezelshaft fun litvishe yidn, 1951), 1675; and Ona Šimaite, "Mayne bagegenishn mit herman kruk," *Undzer shtime* (Paris), August 1–2, 1947, 2.

4. Kruk, *Togbukh fun vilner geto*, 138–40, 162.

5. Abraham Sutzkever, "Tsum kind," in *Lider fun yam ha-moves* (Tel Aviv: Bergen Belzen, 1968), 44–45; English translation in David G. Roskies, ed. and comp., *The Literature of Destruction* (Philadelphia: Jewish Publication Society of America, 1989), 494–95.

6. Sutzkever, *Vilner geto*, 72; Kruk, *Togbukh fun vilner geto*, 157.

7. Herman Kruk, "Geto-bibliotek un geto-leyener, 15.ix.1941–15.ix.1942," file 370, Sutzkever-Kaczerginski Collection, RG 223, YIVO archives; file 295, p. 18, records of Vilnius Ghetto, RG 26.015M, archive of the United States Holocaust Memorial Museum, Washington, D.C. (hereafter cited as USHMM).

8. Abramowicz, "Vilner geto bibliotek."

9. Kruk, "Geto-bibliotek un geto-leyener," 22.

10. Kruk, "Geto-bibliotek un geto-leyener," 22–23; Shloime Beilis, "Kultur unter der hak," in *Portretn un problemen*, 313–416 (Warsaw: Yidish bukh, 1964), 330–31.

11. Zelig Kalmanovitch, "Togbukh fun vilner geto (fragment)," ed. Shalom Luria, with Yiddish translation by Avraham Nowersztern, *YIVO bleter* (New Series) 3 (1997): 82.

12. Kruk, "Geto-bibliotek un geto-leyener," 23–25.

13. Kruk, "Geto-bibliotek un geto-leyener," 14, 17, 18, 27–28.

14. op. 1, d. 256, records of Vilnius Ghetto, F. R-1421, Lithuanian Central State Archive, Vilnius (hereafter cited as F. R-1421 records).

15. op. 1, d. 246, F. R-1421 records.

16. op. 1, d. 304, 340, 341, F. R-1421 records.

17. "Di sotsyal-psikhologishe rol fun bukh in geto," op. 1, d. 230, F. R-1421 records.

18. Mark Dworzecki, *Yerushalayim de-lite in kamf un umkum* (Paris: Yidish-natsionaler arbeter farband in amerike un yidisher folksfarband in frankraykh, 1948), 241; Kruk, "Geto-bibliotek un geto-leyener," 6; letter to all building superintendents in ghetto no. 1 (evidently from late September or October 1941), file 450, Sutzkever-Kaczerginski Collection, RG 223, YIVO archives.

19. Kruk, *Togbukh fun vilner geto*, 99; Kruk, *Last Days*, 140 (with modifications).

20. Balberyszski, *Shtarker fun ayzn*, 439; file 15, F. R-1421 records. The order was dated November 27, 1941.

21. Kruk, *Togbukh fun vilner geto*, 97, 116, 129 (January 4, and January 7, 1942).

22. Bebe Epshtein, "A bazukh in der groyser shul. Derinerung fun geto," file 223, Sutzkever-Kaczerginski Collection, RG 223, YIVO archives. In a subsequent clandestine visit, Dr. Daniel Feinshtein discovered the private library of Rabbi Chaim Ozer Grodzensky in a corner of the women's gallery of the Great Synagogue. Kruk, *Togbukh fun vilner geto*, 150 (January 27, 1942), 152 (January 29, 1942), 161 (February 9, 1942).

23. Kruk, *Togbukh fun vilner geto*, 126–28 (January 7, 1942).

24. Acquisition cards of the Vilna ghetto museum, file 283, pp. 4–5, file 366, nos. 1 and 67, F. R-1421 records.

25. On these institutions, see the library reports for September and October 1941, in Balberyszski, *Shtarker fun ayzn*, 435–38; and later reports in the Sutzkever-Kaczerginski Collection, RG 223, files 367 and 368, YIVO archives. On the museum, see files 453 and 472 in the same Sutzkever-Kaczerginski Collection; and files 265, 266, 349, 354, F. R-1421 records.

26. See the photo in the insert.

A Rescued Gem: The Record Book of the Vilna Gaon's Synagogue

1. Shelomo Zalman Havlin, "Pinkas kloyz ha-gra be-vilna," *Yeshurun* 16 (2005): 748.

2. Ibid., 750.

3. Endowment fund established by Moshe Dinershtein, 5th of Sivan 5673 (June 10, 1913), file 184.11, pp. 56–58, Sutzkever-Kaczerginski Collection, RG 223, part 2, YIVO archives.

4. "Bet Midrash shel maran Ha-Gra zatsal, Vilna, Yetso," dated 1st of Tamuz, 5686 (July 2, 1916), file 184.11, Sutzkever-Kaczerginski Collection, RG 223, part 2, YIVO archives.

5. "Lezikaron olam," dated Hodesh Menahem Av 5682 (August 1922), file 184,11 Sutzkever-Kaczerginski Collection, RG 223, part 2, YIVO archives.

Chapter 6. Accomplices or Saviors?

1. Kruk, *Togbukh fun vilner geto*, 163 (February 11, 1942); Kruk, *Last Days*, 198. The names of the ERR team members are based on Abraham Sutzkever's manuscript "Tsu der geshikhte fun rozenberg shtab," file 678.1, and the anonymous account on the ERR, file 678, pp. 1–2, Sutzkever-Kaczerginski Collection, RG 223, YIVO archives.

2. Kruk, *Togbukh fun vilner geto*, 178–79 (February 19, 1942), Kruk, *Last Days*, 212 (with modifications).

3. Kruk, *Togbukh fun vilner geto*, 180; Kruk, *Last Days*, 213.

4. Kruk, *Togbukh fun vilner geto*, 183.

5. Kruk, *Togbukh fun vilner geto*, 178–81.

6. Šimaite, "Mayne bagegenishn," 3.

7. Kruk, *Togbukh fun vilner geto*, 182–83, 188.

8. Herman Kruk manuscript, "Ikh gey iber kvorim," D. 2.32, Moreshet Archive, Givat Haviva, Israel. See also Kruk, *Togbukh fun vilner geto*, 190–91, and Kruk's report of activities for July and August 1942, d. 501, F. R-1421 records.

9. Kruk, *Togbukh fun vilner geto*, 190; Kruk, *Last Days*, 222.

10. Work at 3 Uniwersytecka Street continued sporadically until August 1943.

See Zelig Kalmanovitch, *Yoman be-geto vilna u-ketavim min ha-'izavon she-nimtsa' ba-harisot* (Tel Aviv: Moreshet-Sifriat Poalim, 1977), 101, 103.

11. Kruk, *Togbukh fun vilner geto*, 200, 272; Sutzkever, "Tsu der geshikhte," 2–3; Kaczerginski, "Vos di daytshn," 1–2; Rachela Pupko-Krinsky, "Mayn arbet in YIVO unter di daytshn," *YIVO bleter* 30 (1947): 214–23. Kaczerginski estimated that twenty-four thousand books were destroyed by the Luftwaffe unit. These accounts are corroborated by Johannes Pohl's report to the ERR in Berlin dated April 28, 1942: ERR collection, op. 1, d. 128, pp. 182–83, TsDAVO.

12. Kruk, *Togbukh fun vilner geto*, 200.

Chapter 7. The Nazi, the Bard, and the Teacher

1. Kruk, *Togbukh fun vilner geto*, 240 (April 23, 1942); Kruk, *Last Days*, 268 (with modifications).

2. Kühn-Ludewig, *Johannes Pohl*, 189. Himpel claimed, in an account written in 1959, that he persuaded Pohl to catalog the materials in situ, using qualified Jewish forced laborers.

3. Staff figures are taken from Kaczerginski, *Partizaner geyen*, 66; Kalmanovitch, "Togbukh fun vilner geto," 87 (June 4, 1942); and I. Kowalski, *A Secret Press in Nazi Europe: The Story of a Jewish United Partisan Organization* (New York: Central Guide Publishers, 1969), 99.

4. Kruk, *Togbukh fun vilner geto*, 21 (March 20, 1942).

5. Sutzkever, "Tsu der geshikhte," 9–10; and Pohl, letter to Berlin, April 2, 1942, ERR collection, op. 1, d. 128, pp. 163–64, TsDAVO.

6. ERR collection, op. 1 d. 128, pp. 193; 330–33, TsDAVO.

7. Sutzkever, "Tsu der geshikhte," 9; Kaczerginski, "Vos di daytshn," 3. Kaczerginski states that Pohl's estimate was $250,000; Pohl's April 28, 1942, report to Berlin, ERR collection, op. 1, d. 128, p. 187, TsDAVO.

8. Pohl divided his time between Berlin (the ERR's headquarters), Frankfurt (the Institute for Investigation of the Jewish Question), and the field. In May 1942, he was in Kovna (45,778 volumes in the synagogue library); in June, he was in Kiev (90,000 volumes); and in early November, he was in Kharkov, where forty thousand volumes of Hebraica and Judaica were found. He visited Vilna on the way to and from his trips to Ukraine. See ERR collection, op. 1, d. 50a, d. 119, pp. 220–21, TsDAVO.

9. Kaczerginski, *Ikh bin geven*, 17.

10. Ibid., 100–101.

11. The English translation is based on Roskies, *Literature of Destruction*, 479–82, with my own modifications.

12. Kaczerginski, *Khurbn vilne*, 179, 182–83, 197, 205, 239, 240, 244; Association of Jews from Vilna and Vicinity in Israel, accessed January 26, 2017, http://www.vilna.co.il/89223/ברנשטיין; YIVO Institute, "Yizker," *YIVO-bleter* 26, no. 1 (June–September 1945): 5; K. S. Kazdan, ed., *Lerer yizker-bukh: di umgekumene lerer*

fun tsisho shuln in poyln (New York: Komitet, 1954), 242; Kruk, *Togbukh fun vilner geto*, 211; Sutzkever, "Tsu der geshikhte," 2–3.

13. Yehuda Tubin, ed., *Ruzhka: Lehimata, Haguta, Demuta* (Tel Aviv: Moreshet, 1988); Kaczerginski, *Khurbn vilne*, 307; "Biographies: Avram Zeleznikow (1924–)," Monash University, accessed January 5, 2017, http://future.arts.monash.edu /yiddish-melbourne/biographies-avram-zeleznikow.

14. This portrait is based on Rachela Krinsky's handwritten answers to questions submitted by her granddaughter Alexandra Wall written in 1997, "Answers to the Questionnaire," and the memoirs of Rachela's postwar husband Abraham Melezin, especially chapter 37, "Rachela," in boxes 1 and 6 of the Abraham Melezin Collection, RG 1872, YIVO archives. Additional information was provided by Rachela's granddaughter Alexandra Wall.

Chapter 8. Ponar for Books

1. Dworzecki, *Yerushalayim de-lite*, 167; Reizl (Ruzhka) Korczak, *Lehavot ba-efer*, 3rd ed. (Merhavia, Israel: Sifriyat Po'alim, 1965), 76; Kruk, *Togbukh fun vilner geto*, 238 (April 20, 1942).

2. Kruk, *Togbukh fun vilner geto*, 242–43 (April 25, 1942).

3. On Sporket, see his ERR personnel file, op. 1, d. 223, p. 233, TsDAVO; Kruk, *Togbukh fun vilner geto*, 267 (May 15, 1942); Kalmanovitch, "Togbukh fun vilner geto," 81 (May 17 and May 19, 1942); Kalmanovitch, *Yoman be-geto vilna*, 93 (December 1, 1942); Sutzkever, "Tsu der geshikhte," 3–4; and Kaczerginski, *Ikh bin geven*, 41. On Gotthard, see the ERR collection, op. 1, d. 128, p. 138, d. 145, p. 167, TsDAVO.

4. Pupko-Krinsky, "Mayn arbet," 216; Kalmanovitch, "Togbukh fun vilner geto," 92 (June 12, 1942).

5. Sutzkever, "Tsu der geshikhte," 3, 8, 9; Sutzkever, letter to Ilya Ehrenburg, July 1944, in "Ehrenburg," Abraham Sutzkever Collection, Arc 4° 1565, National Library of Israel, Archives Department, Jerusalem (hereafter cited as Sutzkever Collection); Sutzkever, *Vilner geto*, 110.

6. "Aufgabenstellung des Einsatzstabes Reichsleiter Rosenberg," cited in Kühn-Ludewig, *Johannes Pohl*, 184.

7. Memo by Dr. Wunder on "Generisches Schrifttum," Riga, May 27, 1942, op. 1, d. 233, pp. 276–78, TsDAVO.

8. Kruk, *Togbukh fun vilner geto*, 282 (June 5, 1942); Kaczerginski, "Vos di daytshn," 4, 6; Kalmanovitch, *Yoman be-geto vilna*, 76 (August 10, 1942), 78 (August 21, 1942).

9. Kaczerginski, *Partizaner geyen*, 68.

10. Kalmanovitch, "Togbukh fun vilner geto," 88.

11. Kruk, *Togbukh fun vilner geto*, 282 (June 5, 1942), 300 (June 9, 1942).

12. ERR collection, op. 1, d. 128, pp. 330–31, TsDAVO.

13. Kaczerginski, "Vos di daytshn," 4; "Nirenberger protses," file 124, "Tezn tsu mayn eydes zogn," pp. 5–7, Sutzkever Collection. The disposal of the Torah

scrolls to a leather factory is corroborated by Sporket's correspondence with his superiors in Berlin; ERR collection, op. 1, d. 119, p. 189 (September 26, 1942), p. 191 (September 16, 1942), TsDAVO.

14. Kalmanovitch, "Togbukh fun vilner geto," 93.

15. Kalmanovitch, *Yoman be-geto vilna*, 89 (November 15, 1942).

16. Sutzkever, "Tsu der geshikhte," 4–5. The work reports of the Polish Department of the Rosenberg Detail for July 5–10 and 12–17, 1943, signed by Nadezhda (Dina) Jaffe, document the transfer of the Zawadzki Publishing House, d. 507, F. R-1421 records.

17. Memo dated May 21, 1942, op. 1, d. 119, p. 215, TsDAVO.

18. Kaczerginski, "Vos di daytshn," 5; A. Malatkov, "Geratevete kultur-oytsres," *Eynikayt* (Moscow), August 17, 1944.

19. Sutzkever, "Tsu der geshikhte," pp. 7–8. Pohl's layout in his October 15, 1942, report describes the use of rooms prior to the influx of Russian and Polish collections. ERR collection, op. 1, d. 128, pp. 330–31, TsDAVO.

20. Kalmanovitch, "Togbukh fun vilner geto," 88 (June 7, 1942); Kalmanovitch, *Yoman be-geto vilna*, 109 (July 5, 1943).

21. Kruk, *Togbukh fun vilner geto*, 282 (June 5, 1942); Kalmanovitch, "Togbukh fun vilner geto," 90 (June 8, 1942), 91 (June 10, 1942), 92 (June 12, and June 15, 1942), 95 (June 18, 1942), 103 (July 19, 1942).

22. Kalmanovitch, *Yoman be-geto vilna*, 82 (October 11, 1942), 85 (October 25, 1942), 91 (November 16, 1942); Kruk, *Togbukh fun vilner geto*, 457 (February 13, 1943); file 179, p. 1, collection of documents on Vilna (Vilnius) Ghetto, Arc 4° 1703, National Library of Israel, Archives Department, Jerusalem (hereafter cited as documents on Vilna Ghetto); Kaczerginski, "Vos di daytshn," 3.

Chapter 9. The Paper Brigade

1. Kalmanovitch, "Togbukh fun vilner geto," 100; Kalmanovitch, *Yoman be-geto vilna*, 87 (November 1, 1942); file 497, p. 1, file 499, pp. 4, 6, records of Vilnius Ghetto, USHMM.

2. Kaczerginski, *Ikh bin geven*, 41–42.

3. Pupko-Krinsky, "Mayn arbet," 215; Kruk, *Togbukh fun vilner geto*, 401–2 (November 10, 1942); Kruk, *Last Days*, 408.

4. Pupko-Krinsky, "Mayn arbet," 215.

5. Kaczerginski diary, file 615, pp. 34–35, Sutzkever-Kaczerginski Collection, RG 223, YIVO archives.

6. Ibid., 35.

7. Pupko-Krinsky, "Mayn arbet," 217.

8. Ibid. 216–19; Abraham Sutzkever, "A vort tsum zekhtsiktn yoiyl fun YIVO," in *Baym leyenen penimer* (Jerusalem: Magnes, 1993), 206–7; Kaczerginski, *Ikh bin geven*, 53.

9. Kaczerginski, *Ikh bin geven*, 43–44; Pupko-Krinsky, "Mayn arbet," 221.

10. Krinsky-Melezin, "Mit Shmerken," 129.

11. Pupko-Krinsky, "Mayn arbet," 216.

12. Alexandra Wall, notes of interview with her grandfather, Abraham Melezin, November 2007, in possession of the author.

13. Szmerke Kaczerginski, "Dos elnte kind," in *Lider fun di getos un lagern*, ed. Szmerke Kaczerginski (New York: Tsiko bikher farlag, 1948), 90–91.

14. Pupko-Krinsky, "Mayn arbet," 221; Ona Šimaite, letter to Abraham Sutzkever, August 23, 1947, "Shimaite, Anna," file 1, Sutzkever Collection.

15. Dworzecki, *Yerushalayim de-lite*, 263.

16. Korczak, *Lehavot ba-efer*, 115–16; Tubin, *Ruzhka*, 194.

Chapter 10. The Art of Book Smuggling

1. Michael Menkin (Minkovitch), interview by author, Fort Lee, New Jersey, February 13, 2014. Menkin worked in the YIVO worksite in the spring and summer of 1942. He now lives in Fort Lee, New Jersey.

2. Kruk, *Togbukh fun vilner geto*, 300–301; Kruk, *Last Days*, 322 (with modifications). Kruk gave a partial list of documents they rescued. "Documents from the Ukrainian People's Republic, of the People's Republic's Ministry of Jewish Affairs [from 1918–19]; materials from the archives of Nojekh Prylucki, Simon Dubnow, Ber Borokhov; a portfolio of materials about Isaac Meir Dick, consisting of a bibliography of his publications and material for his biography; a portfolio of proverbs from various countries and places. And there was an enormous amount of letters: letters from Sholem Aleichem and several of his manuscripts; manuscripts by David Einhorn, David Pinsky, and S. L. Citron; materials from Dr. Alfred Landau's [Yiddish] linguistic treasures; photographs from YIVO's Yiddish theater museum; letters by Moyshe Kulbak, Sh[muel] Niger, D[aniel] Charney, Chaim Zhitlowsky, Joseph Opatoshu, A. Leyeles, Zalmen Reisen, Leon Kobrin, Moyshe Nadir, Marc Chagall, H. Leivick, Dr. Nathan Birnbaum, Yaakov Fichman." On September 24, 1942, Kruk added, "Recently the Rosenberg Task Force employees work with a new energy. Scores of books and documents are brought into the ghetto every day. The brigade of porters [i.e., smugglers] has grown by several times." Kruk, *Togbukh fun vilner geto*, 351.

3. Pupko-Krinsky, "Mayn arbet," 217. For examples of denunciations by the caretaker, see Kalmanovitch, *Yoman be-geto vilna*, 110 (July 9, 1943), 112 (July 13, 1943).

4. Korczak, *Lehavot ba-efer*, 82–83.

5. Pupko-Krinsky, "Mayn arbet," 217–19; Kaczerginski, *Ikh bin geven*, 53–57.

6. Krinsky-Melezin, "Mit Shmerken," 130–31.

7. Answers to questions by her granddaughter Alexandra Wall, box 1, Abraham Melezin Collection, RG 1872, YIVO archives.

8. Sutzkever, *Vilner geto*, 111–12.

9. Kalmanovitch, *Yoman be-geto vilna*, 94 (December 9, 1942), 110 (July 9, 1943), 112 (July 13, 1943).

10. Pupko-Krinsky, "Mayn arbet," 217–18.

11. Kalmanovitch, *Yoman be-geto vilna*, 74 (August 2, 1942). Kaczerginski, *Khurbn vilne*, 209, states that Kalmanovitch opposed hiding books from the Germans and believed it was preferable to cooperate in the shipment of books to Germany, because the materials would be retrieved after the war. This is a simplification of Kalmanovitch's view. As his ghetto diary indicates, Kalmanovitch supported both the smuggling of books into the ghetto and the shipment of books to Germany, to minimize the third option—their destruction in the paper mills.

12. Kaczerginski, *Partizaner geyen*, 69; Kaczerginski, *Ikh bin geven*, 41–42; Avraham Zheleznikov, interview by author, Melbourne, Australia, July 8, 2012; Korczak, *Lehavot ba-efer*, 110.

13. File 330, p. 9, and file 366, pp. 68, 73, 115, records of Vilnius Ghetto, RG-26.015M, USHMM.

14. Sutzkever note, "Gefunen dem togbukh fun dokter hertsl," file 770 and part 2, file 184, Sutzkever-Kaczerginski Collection, RG 223, YIVO archives.

15. Kazys Boruta, *Skambėkit vėtroje, beržai* (Vilnius: Vaga, 1975), 341–42.

16. Sutzkever, *Vilner geto*, 112.

17. Pupko-Krinsky, "Mayn arbet," 219–20.

18. Abraham Sutzkever, "Kerndlekh veyts," in *Yidishe gas*, 32–33 (New York: Matones, 1947); English translation: Abraham Sutzkever, "Grains of Wheat," in *A. Sutzkever: Selected Poetry and Prose*, trans. and ed. Barbara Harshav and Benjamin Harshav, 156–58 (Berkeley: University of California Press, 1991).

19. Kruk, *Togbukh fun vilner geto*, 575–76 (June 18, 1943); Kruk, *Last Days*, 567–68 (with modifications). Abraham Sutzkever, letter to Max Weinreich, Paris, January 12, 1947, foreign correspondence, 1947, YIVO Administration, RG 100, YIVO archives. Kalmanovitch wrote about this event, "I blessed God for granting me the privilege to hear good tidings. . . . I told the news to a number of people who were close to the institution. All are rejoicing. There are no words to express the emotions that are stirring." Kalmanovitch, *Yoman be-geto vilna*, 107.

A Rescued Gem: Herzl's Diary

1. Ilse Sternberger, *Princes without a Home: Modern Zionism and the Strange Fate of Theodor Herzl's Children, 1900–1945* (San Francisco: International Scholars Publications, 1994); "Hans Herzl, Son of Theodor Herzl, Commits Suicide after Funeral of Sister Paulina," *Jewish Telegraphic Agency Bulletin*, September 18, 1930; "Hans Herzl's Wish Comes True—76 Years Later," *Haaretz*, September 19, 2006.

2. Zalmen Rejzen, "Doktor Teodor Herzl's umbakanter togbukh," *Morgenzhurnal*, April 10, 1932; Max Weinreich, memo to Abraham Cahan, June 7, 1933, "Teodor hertsl's togbukh fun di yorn 1882–1887," Bund Collection, RG 1400, YIVO archives.

3. Weinreich, memo to Cahan.

Chapter 11. The Book and the Sword

1. Korczak, *Lehavot ba-efer*, 54.

2. Ibid., 95.

3. Ibid., 95–96.

4. Ibid., 90–92.

5. Korczak, *Lehavot ba-efer*; Dworzecki, *Yerushalayim de-lite*, 395; Michael Menkin (Minkovitch), interview by author, Fort Lee, New Jersey, August 19, 2013.

6. Sutzkever, *Vilner geto*, 122–25, 229.

7. Aba Kovner, "Flekn af der moyer," *Yidishe kultur* (New York) (May 1947): 26; Rokhl Mendelsohn-Kowarski, letter to Pinkhas Schwartz, undated, file 770, pp. 1–2, 5, Sutzkever-Kaczerginski Collection, RG 223, YIVO archives.

8. Shmerke Kaczerginski, "Mayn ershter pulemiot," *Epokhe* (New York), nos. 31–32 (August–October 1947): 52–56.

9. Korczak, *Lehavot ba-efer*, 96–97; Leon Bernstein, *Ha-derekh ha-ahronah* (Tel Aviv: Va'ad Tsiburi, 1990), 184.

10. Korczak, *Lehavot ba-efer*, 96. Isaac Kowalski, who worked in the YIVO building for three months, also smuggled munitions manuals and arms into the ghetto on behalf of the FPO; Kowalski, *Secret Press*, 96–101.

11. Kowalski, *Secret Press*, 100.

12. Abraham Sutzkever, "Di blayene platn fun roms drukeray," in *Lider fun yam ha-moves*, 94; in English, Abraham Sutzkever, "The Lead Plates of the Rom Printers," in *A. Sutzkever*, 168–70.

13. Kaczerginski, "Mayn ershter pulemiot," 57–58.

14. There are three versions of this incident, with slight variations: Sutzkever, *Vilner geto*, 220; Kaczerginski, *Ikh bin geven*, 45–52 (and in Kaczerginski, "Mayn ershter pulemiot," 57–59); and Pupko-Krinsky, "Mayn arbet," 220–21. I have followed the Pupko-Krinsky and Kaczerginski versions, which are fully compatible.

15. Kaczerginski, *Ikh bin geven*, 11.

Chapter 12. Slave-Labor Curators and Scholars

1. This detail is mentioned in the study by Ioffe, "Wilna und Wilnauer Klausen," 10, 14–15.

2. Sutzkever, "Tsu der geshikhte," 13–15; Kaczerginski, *Partizaner geyen*, 69–71. See also Bernstein, *Ha-derekh ha-ahronah*, 169. On the Karaite question, see below.

3. Kruk, *Togbukh fun vilner geto*, 327 (July 30, 1942); Kruk, *Last Days*, 340 (with modifications); Kalmanovitch, *Yoman be-geto vilna*, 73–75 (July 31, 1942), 75–76 (August 13).

4. W.K., "Die Einstige des Judentums, eine wertvolle Sonderschau des 'Einsatzstabes Rosenberg' in Wilna," *Wilnaer Zeitung*, no. 194, August 20, 1942.

5. Kalmanovitch, *Yoman be-geto vilna*, 75.

6. Sutzkever, "Tsu der geshikhte," 15; Sutzkever, *Vilner geto*, 178; Kaczerginski, *Partizaner geyen*, 69.

7. Kalmanovitch, "Togbukh fun vilner geto," 94.

8. Kiril Feferman, "Nazi Germany and the Karaites in 1938–1944: Between Racial Theory and Realpolitik," *Nationalities Papers* 39, no. 2 (2011): 277–94; Shmuel Spektor, "Ha-kara'im be-eyropah she-bi-shlitat ha-natsim be-re'i mismakhim germani'im," *Pe'amim* 29 (1986): 90–108.

9. Feferman, "Nazi Germany"; Spektor, "Ha-kara'im be-eyropah."

10. Gerhard Wunder in Berlin, letter to ERR in Riga, for forwarding to Vilna, October 28, 1942, ERR collection, op. 1, d. 118, pp. 146–47, TsDAVO.

11. The translations, bibliography, and essay are found in the YIVO archives, Karaites, RG 40; and in op. 1, files 18, 22, Einsatzstab Reichsleiter Rosenberg, F. R-633, Lithuanian Central State Archive, Vilnius.

12. ERR collection, op. 1, d. 233, p. 122; d. 118, pp. 118, 146–47, TsDAVO; Kalmanovitch, *Yoman be-geto vilna*, 82 (October 11, 1942); quote from Kalmanovitch, *Yoman be-geto vilna*, 90 (November 15, 1942). On Szapszal, see Mikhail Kizilov, *Sons of Scripture: The Karaites in Poland and Lithuania in the Twentieth Century* (Berlin: De Gruyter, 2015), 216–83 and passim.

13. On the visits, see Kalmanovitch *Yoman be-geto vilna*, 105 (April 30, 1943); and Akiva Gershater, "Af yener zayt geto," in *Bleter vegn vilne: zamlbukh*, 41–45 (Lodz, Poland: Farband fun vilner yidn in poyln, 1947), 44–45. On Szapszal's honorarium and plans to disseminate his study, see ERR collection, op. 1, d. 170, pp. 204–5, d. 118, pp. 146–47, TsDAVO; slave labor salary, ERR collection, op. 1, d. 147, p. 383, TsDAVO. On Kalmanovitch's extra loaf of bread, see Kalmanovitch, *Yoman be-geto vilna*, 87.

14. Sutzkever, "Tsu der geshikhte," 11; Gershater, "Af yener zayt geto," 44–45; and similarly Dworzecki, *Yerushalayim de-lite*, 332.

15. Dworzecki, *Yerushalayim de-lite*, 332. This account is confirmed by the ERR collection, op. 1, d. 128, pp. 309, 329, TsDAVO.

16. ERR collection, op. 1, d. 233, pp. 220–21, d. 118, pp. 341–42, TsDAVO; Kalmanovitch, *Yoman be-geto vilna*, 76 (August 9, 1942), 78 (August 21, 1942).

17. The studies are found in files 9, 15–17, 26, Einsatzstab Reichsleiter Rosenberg, F. R-633, and files 233, 494, 504, 505, records of Vilnius Ghetto, F. R-1421, both in the Lithuanian Central State Archive, Vilnius. See my article, "Slave Labor Jewish Scholarship in the Vilna Ghetto," in *There Is a Jewish Way of Saying Things: Studies in Jewish Literature in Honor of David G. Roskies* (Bloomington: Indiana University Press, forthcoming).

18. "Die Juden im historischen Littauen," file 16, p. 10, Einsatzstab Reichsleiter Rosenberg, F. R-633, Lithuanian Central State Archive, Vilnius.

19. Ibid., p. 12.

20. "Friedhofe und Grabsteine der Juden in Wilna," file 9, Einsatzstab Reichsleiter Rosenberg, F. R-633, Lithuanian Central State Archive, Vilnius.

21. ERR collection, d. 118, p. 315, TsDAVO.

22. Kalmanovitch, *Yoman be-geto vilna*, 93 (December 7, 1942), and 103 (April 25, 1943); ERR collection, d. 118, p. 379, TsDAVO.

23. Kruk, *Togbukh fun vilner geto*, 469 (March 8, 1943); Kruk's final report for the ERR, covering the period February 18, 1942–July 10, 1943, op. 1, d. 5, pp. 37–39, Einsatzstab Reichsleiter Rosenberg, F. R-633, Lithuanian Central State Archive, Vilnius.

Chapter 13. From the Ghetto to the Forest

1. Kaczerginski, *Lider fun di getos*, 341–41.

2. An excerpt of this document is presented in David E. Fishman, *Embers Plucked from the Fire: The Rescue of Jewish Cultural Treasures in Vilna*, 2nd expanded ed. (New York: YIVO, 2009), 19–20.

3. Kaczerginski, *Ikh bin geven*, 53–55.

4. Pupko-Krinsky, "Mayn arbet," 221–22; Abraham Sutzkever, "A tfile tsum nes," in *Lider fun yam ha-moves*, 38. The translation is my own.

5. Mark Dworzecki, "Der novi fun geto (Zelig Hirsh Kalmanovitsh)," *Yidisher kemfer* (New York), September 24, 1948, 4–5.

6. Bernstein, *Ha-derekh ha-ahronah*, 245; Kalmanovitch, *Yoman be-geto vilna*, 119 (August 2–3, 1943).

7. Kruk, *Togbukh fun vilner geto*, xxxviii–xxxix; Dworzecki, *Yerushalayim de-lite*, 269; Kaczerginski, *Khurbn vilne*, 211.

8. Kalmanovitch, *Yoman be-geto vilna*, 126.

9. Kaczerginski, *Ikh bin geven*, 87–87.

10. Kaczerginski, *Ikh bin geven*, 90, 95; Korczak, *Lehavot ba-efer*, 180–90.

11. Kaczerginski, *Ikh bin geven*, 99.

12. Kaczerginski, *Ikh bin geven*, 113, 119–21.

13. Kaczerginski, *Ikh bin geven*, 127–51.

14. Kaczerginski, *Ikh bin geven*, 152–59.

15. Moshe Grossman, "Shemaryahu Kaczerginski," *Davar* (Tel Aviv), May 14, 1954, 4; Chaim Grade, "Eykh noflu giboyrim," in *Shmerke kaczerginski ondenk-bukh*, 44–45.

16. Kaczerginski, *Ikh bin geven*, 172; Sutzkever, "Tsu der efenung fun der oysshtelung lekoved mayn vern a ben-shivim," in *Baym leyenen penimer*, 213–14.

17. Kaczerginski, *Ikh bin geven*, 194–96; Moshe Kalcheim, ed., *Mitn shtoltsn gang, 1939–1945: kapitlen geshikhte fun partizaner kamf in di narotsher velder* (Tel Aviv: Farband fun partizan, untergrunt-kemfers un geto-ufshtendlers in yisroel, 1992), 149, 283.

18. Kaczerginski, *Ikh bin geven*, 212–17.

19. Kaczerginski, *Partizaner geyen*.

20. Shmerke Kaczerginski, "Yid, du partizaner," in *Shmerke kaczerginski ondenk-bukh*, 253.

Chapter 14. Death in Estonia

1. On Kalmanovitch's decision, see Kaczerginski, *Ikh bin geven*, 118–19; Kaczerginski, "Der haknkrayts," 641; on Kruk's decision, see letters by Liola Klitschko, 1946, and Rachel Mendelsohn-Kowarski to Pinkhas Schwartz, 1959, in file 770, Sutzkever-Kaczerginski Collection, RG 223, YIVO archives.

2. Kaczerginski, *Khurbn vilne*, 109; Mark Dworzecki, *Vayse nekht un shvartse teg: yidn-lagern in estonye* (Tel Aviv: I. L. Peretz, 1970), 305.

3. See Dov Levin, "Tsvishn hamer un serp: tsu der geshikhte fun yidishn visnshaftlekhn institut in vilne unter der sovetisher memshole," *YIVO bleter* 46 (1980): 78–97.

4. Abraham Sutzkever, "Vi Z. Kalmanovitch iz umgekumen," *Yidishe kultur* (New York), no. 10 (October 1945): 52.

5. Yudl Mark, "Zelig Kalmanovitch," *Di Goldene keyt* (Tel Aviv), 93 (1977): 143. Similarly, see Dworzecki, *Vayse nekht*. For a detailed account by inmate Aryeh Sheftel, see Kalmanovitch, *Yoman be-geto vilna*, 55–57.

6. Kaczerginski, *Khurbn vilne*, 109–10; Kalmanovitch, *Yoman be-geto vilna*, 58.

7. Based on Maria Rolnikaite, "Ya dolzhna raskazat," in *I vse eto pravda*, 123–35 (St. Petersburg: Zoltoi Vek, 2002); Grigorii Shur, *Evrei v Vil'no: Khronika, 1941–1944 gg.* (St. Petersburg: Obrazovanie-Kul'tura, 2000), 181–87; Dworzecki, *Yerushalayim de-lite*, 481–84.

8. Kaczerginski, *Khurbn vilne*, 291.

9. Kaczerginski, *Khurbn vilne*, 75.

10. Kruk, *Last Days*, 674–55; Dworzecki, *Vayse nekht*, 133–34, 141.

11. Dworzecki, *Vayse nekht*, 224, 308, 324.

12. Borukh Merin, *Fun rakev biz klooga* (New York: CYCO, 1969), 136, 142.

13. Kruk, *Last Days*, 685–86.

14. Kruk, *Last Days*, 693–94.

15. See Dworzecki, *Vayse nekht*, 138, 161–63, 189, 287, 302, 305, 377–79; Kruk, *Last Days*, 704.

16. Kruk, *Last Days*, v.

Chapter 15. Miracle from Moscow

1. "Undzer batsiung tsum ratnfarnand: aroyszogunugen fun yidishe shrayber," *Dos naye lebn* (Lodz, Poland), November 6, 1946, 3; Sutzkever, *Baym leyenen penimer*, 66.

2. See Sutzkever's biographical portrait of Paleckis in file 1008.2, Sutzkever Collection.

3. See Sutzkever, *Baym leyenen penimer*, 131; Boris Grin, "Mit sutzkevern in otriad 'nekome,'" *Oystralishe yidishe nayes* (Melbourne), October 13, 1961, 7.

4. Sutzkever, *Baym leyenen penimer*, 67.

5. Abraham Sutzkever, "Rede fun sutzkever," *Eynikayt* (Moscow), April 6, 1944;

Dos yidishe folk in kamf kegn fashizm (Moscow: Ogiz, 1945); Sutzkever, *Baym leyenen penimer*, 139–40.

6. Ilya Ehrenburg, "Torzhestvo cheloveka," *Pravda* (Moscow), April 27, 1944, 4.

7. Leon Leneman, "Ven boris pasternak shenkt avek zayn lid avrom sutskevern," *Di tsionistishe shtime* (Paris), January 31, 1958.

8. Kaczerginski, *Ikh bin geven*, 282.

9. Ibid., 291–303.

10. Ibid., 312.

11. Ibid., 346, 372, 380–83, quote from 383.

Chapter 16. From under the Ground

1. According to Kaczerginski, in "Vos di daytshn," the Germans detonated the building before retreating from Vilna.

2. Kaczerginski, *Ikh bin geven*, 386–87.

3. Ilya Ehrenburg, *Liudi, godi, zhizn: Vospominanie v triekh tomakh* (Moscow: Sovetskii pisatel, 1990), 2:339–40; Aba Kovner, "Reshita shel ha-beriha ke-tenuat hamonim," *Yalkut Moreshet* 37 (June 1984): 7–31.

4. Shmerke Kaczerginski, *Tsvishn hamer un serp: tsu der geshikhte fun der likvidatsye fun der yidisher kultur in sovetn-rusland*, 2nd expanded ed. (Buenos Aires: Der Emes, 1950), 15–41.

5. Abraham Sutzkever, "Ilya Ehrenburg," in *Baym leyenen penimer*, 142–43; notes by Sutzkever (undated), file 219, documents on Vilna Ghetto.

6. Kaczerginski, "Vos di daytshn," 7.

7. Kaczerginski, *Khurbn vilne*, 179, 183, 205.

8. Ibid., 197, 239, 240.

9. Ibid., 218, 244.

10. Kaczerginski, *Ikh bin geven*, 184.

11. Kaczerginski, *Khurbn vilne*, 307.

12. Sutzkever, *Vilner geto*, 229.

13. Kaczerginski, *Tsvishn hamer un serp*, 41 (diary entry dated July 20, 1944).

14. Kaczerginski files, no. 11, Sutzkever Collection.

15. File 47, Shmerke Kaczerginski Collection, RG P-18, Yad Vashem Archives, Jerusalem, Israel.

16. "Ershte zitsung," in "Protokoln fun zitsungen fun der initsiativ grupe," file 757, p. 1 (unpaginated), Sutzkever-Kaczerginski Collection, RG 223, YIVO archives.

17. Kaczerginsky, *Tsvishn hamer un serp*, 43 (entry dated August 5, 1944); Abraham Sutzkever, "Vos mir hobn geratevet in vilne," *Eynikayt* (Moscow), October 12, 1944.

18. Sutzkever, "Vos mir hobn."

19. Kovner, "Flekn af der moyer," *Yidishe kultur* (New York) (April 1947): 18; on other FPO materials discovered by Kovner, see "Flekn af der moyer," *Yidishe kultur* (New York) (May 1947): 27, (June 1947): 25, 27.

20. Malatkov, "Geratevete kultur-oytsres."

Chapter 17. A Museum Like No Other

1. Grade, "Fun unter der erd," April 1, 1979; see Kaczerginski, "Vilner yidisher gezelshaftlekher yizker-leksikon," in *Khurbn vilne*, 173–314.

2. "Zitsung fun presidium fun yidishn muzey," August 1, 1944, in "Protokoln fun zitsungen fun der initsiativ grupe," file 757, pp. 3–7 (unpaginated), Sutzkever-Kaczerginski Collection, RG 223, YIVO archives; Kaczerginski, *Tsvishn hamer un serp*; Sutzkever, "Vos mir hobn."

3. "Protokol fun baratung fun partizaner aktivistn bam muzey fun yidisher kultur un kunst," in "Protokoln fun zitsungen fun der initsiativ grupe," file 757, pp. 9–11 (unpaginated), Sutzkever-Kaczerginski Collection, RG 223, YIVO archives.

4. Untitled document, Kaczerginski, file 11, Sutzkever Collection; in English translation: Fishman, *Embers Plucked*, 20.

5. Leyzer Engelshtern, *Mit di vegn fun der sheyris ha-pleyte* (Tel Aviv: Igud yotsei vilna ve-ha-sevivah be-yisrael, 1976), 71–72, 83.

6. Engelshtern, *Mit di vegn*, 101–2; Grade, "Fun unter der erd," March 15, 1979. Merchandise was still being wrapped in the pages of Hebrew books in 1945. Nesia Orlovitz-Reznik, *Ima, Ha-mutar kvar livkot?* (Tel Aviv: Moreshet, n.d.), 9.

7. The original letter is found in file 743, Sutzkever-Kaczerginski Collection, RG 223, YIVO archives. (A photograph of the original is found in D. 1.4.94, Moreshet Archive, Givat Haviva, Israel.) The Jewish Museum made a Russian translation and submitted it in February 1946 to the Extraordinary State Commission for Investigating the Atrocities of the German-Fascist Invaders and Their Accomplices, file 726, Sutzkever-Kaczerginski Collection, RG 223, YIVO archives. Kaczerginski published a Yiddish translation (with deletions) in *Khurbn vilne*, 55–57.

8. Aba Kovner note dated July 5, 1962, to "A Plea to Our Jewish Brothers and Sisters," D. 1.4.94, Moreshet Archive, Givat Haviva, Israel. Alexander Rindziunsky, a partisan who participated in the liberation of Vilnius, notes, "Only when we were certain, and we had eyewitnesses that someone handed over Jews to the Gestapo, did we act differently: we liquidated them without waiting for judicial procedures." *Hurban vilna* (Lohamei ha-geta'ot, Israel: Beit lohamei ha-geta'ot, 1987), 197.

9. Minutes of meeting on August 8 and September 3, 1944, in "Protokoln fun zitsungen fun der initsiativ grupe," file 757, Sutzkever-Kaczerginski Collection, RG 223, YIVO archives.

10. Kaczerginski, *Khurbn vilne*, 61. A large part of *Khurbn vilne* consists of testimony collected by the museum in the months immediately after Vilna's liberation. Sutzkever, "Vos mir hobn."

11. Korczak, *Lehavot ba-efer*, 311–14.

12. For instance, see files 200, 223, 234, and 253, documents on Vilna Ghetto; and file 712, Sutzkever-Kaczerginski Collection, RG 223, YIVO archives.

13. "Ershte zitsung," in "Protokoln fun zitsungen fun der initsiativ grupe," file 757, p. 1 (unpaginated), Sutzkever-Kaczerginski Collection, RG 223, YIVO archives.; Kaczerginski, *Tsvishn hamer un serp*, 44.

14. See the photo in the insert.

15. Kaczerginski, *Tsvishn hamer un serp*, 44–45; M. Gutkowicz, "Der yidisher muzey in vilne," *Eynikayt* (Moscow), March 28, 1946; Beilis, "Kultur unter der hak," *Portretn un problemen*, 315–18; Hirsh Osherovitsh, unpublished memoirs, no. 370, box 3608, pp. 159–61, Hirsh Osherovitsh Collection, RG 370, Genazim Institute, Tel Aviv. All descriptions of the museum refer to the prison cells and their inscriptions.

16. Leyzer Ran, *Ash fun yerushalayim de-lite* (New York: Vilner farlag, 1959), 166. On the state of the buildings, see Osherovitsh, unpublished memoirs, no. 370, box 3608, pp. 159–61, Hirsh Osherovitsh Collection, RG 370, Genazim Institute, Tel Aviv.

17. Kaczerginski, *Tsvishn hamer un serp*, 46; "Protkol fun der zitsung fun di mitarbeter fun der yidisher opteylung bay der visnshaft akademie in lite," August 9 and August 21, 1944, in "Protokoln fun zitsungen fun der initsiativ grupe," file 757, pp. 12–19 (unpaginated), Sutzkever-Kaczerginski Collection, RG 223, YIVO archives.

18. Entry dated August 25, 1944, Aba Kovner notebook, D. 1.6028, Moreshet Archive, Givat Haviva, Israel.

19. Kaczerginski, *Tsvishn hamer un serp*, 46; op. 6, d. 1, p. 27, Ministry of People's Education of the Lithuanian Soviet Socialist Republic, F. R-762, Lithuanian Central State Archive, Vilnius; certificate from the People's Commissariat for Education to Sutzkever, August 26, 1944, Kaczerginski, file 11; Sutzkever Collection.

20. Testimony of Alexander Rindziunsky, A 1175, pp. 9–11, Moreshet Archive, Givat Haviva, Israel; Kaczerginski, *Tsvishn hamer un serp*, 47–48.

21. Kaczerginski, *Tsvishn hamer un serp*, 49–50.

22. Dovid Bergelson, letter to Abraham Sutzkever, undated, "Dovid Bergelson," Sutzkever Collection; Shakhna Epshtein, letter to Abraham Sutzkever, September 7, 1944, Shakhna Epshtein, Sutzkever Collection.

A Rescued Gem: Sholem Aleichem's Letters

1. Nakhmen Mayzel, "Sholem aleykhem's briv tsu yankev dinezon," *YIVO bleter* 1 (1931): 387.

2. See ibid., 385–88; and M.W., "Draysik nit publikirte briv fun sholem-aleykhemen," *Filologishe shriftn fun yivo* 3 (1929): 153–72.

3. Sholem Aleichem, letter to an unnamed friend, February 1906, file 88.1, Sutzkever-Kaczerginski Collection, RG 223, YIVO archives. It was presumably addressed to the Warsaw Yiddish writer Jacob Dinesohn, who was his close friend and confidant.

Chapter 18. Struggling under the Soviets

1. Kaczerginski, *Tsvishn hamer un serp*, 45–46; Leyzer Ran, ed. *Yerushalayim de-lite ilustrirt un dokumentirt* (New York: Vilner albom komitet, 1974), 2:526.

2. Kaczerginski, *Tsvishn hamer un serp*, 51, 53; Leah Tsari, *Mi-tofet el tofet: Sipura shel tzivia vildshtein* (Tel Aviv: Tarbut ve-hinukh, 1971), 67; Rindziunsky, *Hurban vilna*, 60.

3. Kaczerginski, *Tsvishn hamer un serp*, 49, 58–60. Tsari, *Mi-tofet el tofet*, 65–77. On the history of the school, see Dov Levin, "Ha-perek ha-aharon shel bate ha-sefer ha-yehudiim ha-mamlakhtiim be-vrit ha-moatsot," in *Yahadut Mizrah Eiropa bein shoah le-tekumah*, ed. Benjamin Pinkus, 88–110 (Beersheba, Israel: Ben Gurion University Press, 1987).

4. On the ban on philanthropy, see Engelshtern, *Mit di vegn*, 97–100; on the travails of the schools, see Tsari, *Mi-tofet el tofet*, 73–76.

5. Kaczerginski, *Tsvishn hamer un serp*, 51–52.

6. Ibid., passim; Osherovitsh, unpublished memoirs, no. 370, box 3608, p. 152, Hirsh Osherovitsh Collection, RG 370, Genazim Institute, Tel Aviv.

7. The draft manuscript of the collection is held in op. 1, file 50, Jewish Museum, Vilnius, F. 1390, Lithuanian Central State Archive, Vilnius. Kaczerginski signed a contract with the Moscow "Der Emes" publishing house in 1945 to publish part of his collection under the title *Songs of the Vilna Ghetto*, but the Moscow edition never appeared (Kaczerginski, *Tsvishn hamer un serp*, 68). He published the book two years later, in 1947, when he resided in Paris. Kaczerginski's *Dos gezang fun vilner geto* was followed by a fuller work, *Lider fun di getos un lagern*, published in New York in 1948.

8. The portrait is based on Chaim Grade's novella "Froyen fun geto."

9. Freydke Sutzkever, letter to Abraham Sutzkever, August 25, 1944, file 1286.2, "Freydke Sutzkever," Sutzkever Collection.

10. Shmerke Kaczerginski, letter to Rachela Krinsky, July 4, 1945, box 11, p. 2, letters by Yiddish writers, RG 107, YIVO archives.

11. Shmerke Kaczerginski, file 11, Sutzkever Collection; English translation in Fishman, *Embers Plucked*, 20.

12. Kaczerginski, *Tsvishn hamer un serp*, 45; "Gefunen dem togbukh fun dokter hertsl," file 770, Sutzkever-Kaczerginski Collection, RG 223, YIVO archives.

13. Offhand negative comments about each other arise in Shmerke's and Kovner's letters to Sutzkever in September through November 1944, "Shmerke Kaczerginski" and "Aba Kovner" files, Sutzkever Collection.

14. While Sutzkever found a bit of the diary, Kaczerginski found the bulk of it. Shmerke Kaczerginski, letter to Abraham Sutzkever, undated [March–April 1945], Kaczerginski letters, file 9, Sutzkever Collection; cf. Pinkhas Schwartz, "Biografye fun herman kruk," in Kruk, *Togbukh fun vilner geto*, xiii–xlv. See also Sutzkever's letter to Pinkhas Schwartz, June 1, 1960, file 770, Sutzkever-Kaczerginski Collection, RG 223, YIVO archives. The discovery was made public in a Jewish Telegraphic Agency report, published in *Forverts* and *Morgen-zhurnal*, February 27, 1945.

15. Y. Mayers, "2,000 yidishe froyen bafrayt fun prison-lager in poyln; 4,000 yidn itst do in Vilne," *Forverts* (New York), February 27, 1945, 1.

16. See Jan T. Gross, "Witness for the Prosecution," *Los Angeles Times Book Re-*

view, September 22, 2002, 1; and Kruk, *Last Days*, http://yalebooks.com/book /9780300044942/last-days-jerusalem-lithuania.

17. Aba Kovner, letter to Abraham Sutzkever, October 27, 1944, file 312, documents on Vilna Ghetto.

18. The original Lithuanian text of Kovner's memorandum is in D. 1.433, in the Moreshet Archive, Givat Haviva, Israel; and in Hebrew translation in Korczak, *Lehavot ba-efer*, 387–89. Kovner was either misinformed or disingenuous. After the war, the Jewish academic structure in Kiev was a tiny Cabinet for Jewish Culture, not an institute.

19. Aba Kovner, letter to Abraham Sutzkever, November 8, 1944, file 312, documents on Vilna Ghetto.

20. Dr. Benjamin Bliudz, interview by Dov Levin, Oral History Division, Hebrew University, January 26, 1972, interview no. 12 (234), p. 18.

21. Gennady Kostyrchenko, ed., *Gosudarstvenyïı antisemitizm v SSSR: Ot nachala do kulminatsïı, 1938–1953* (Moscow: Mezhdunarodnyi Fond Demokratia, Makerik, 2005), 44–45.

22. Korczak, *Lehavot ba-efer*, 387–89.

23. Order renewing the activity of museums in the Lithuanian SSR, op. 1, file 7, p. 5, Committee on Cultural Educational Institutions of the Council of Ministers of the Lithuanian Soviet Socialist Republic, F. 476, Lithuanian Archives of Literature and Art, Vilnius.

24. Ekaterina Makhotina, *Erinnerung an den Krieg—Krieg der Erinnerungen: Litauen und der Zweite Weltkrieg* (Göttingen: Vanderhoeck and Ruprecht, 2016).

25. Shmerke Kaczerginski, letter to Abraham Sutzkever, November 17, 1944, undated, Kaczerginski letters, file 9, Sutzkever Collection.

26. Shmerke Kaczerginski, letter to Abraham Sutzkever, November 20, 1944, file 3, Kaczerginski letters, Sutzkever Collection.

27. Ibid.

Chapter 19. Tears in New York

1. See YIVO Institute, *Yediyes fun amopteyl* 87–88, nos. 1–2 (March–April 1940).

2. Shloime Mendelsohn, "Vi azoy lebn di poylishe yidn in di getos," *YIVO bleter* 19, no. 1 (January 1942): 1–28.

3. YIVO Institute, *Fun di arkhiv- un muzey-obyektn vos der yivo hot geratevet fun eyrope* (New York: Author, 1943), 2.

4. "Petitsye fun amerikaner gelernte tsu president ruzvelt vegn shkhites af yidn in eyrope," *Yediyes fun YIVO*, no. 1 (September 1943): 4, 5.

5. "Azkore nokh sh. dubnov in yivo," *YIVO bleter* 22, no. 1 (September–October 1943): 119.

6. Emanuel Ringelblum, *Kapitlen geshikhte fun amolikn yidishn lebn in poyln*, ed. Jacob Shatzky (Buenos Aires: Tsentral fareyn fun poylishe yidn in argentine, 1953), 548–49.

7. Albert Clattenburg Jr., assistant chief, Special War Problems Division, US

Department of State, letter to Max Weinreich, August 28, 1944, and Max Weinreich, letter to Albert Clattenburg Jr., September 29, 1944, box 1, "Restitution of YIVO Property, 1945–1949," YIVO archives; John Walker, letter to Max Weinreich, September 14, 1944, and Max Weinreich, letter to John Walker, September 29, 1944, pp. 12, 19, "Roberts Commission" correspondence, RG 239, National Archives, College Park, MD.

8. Aba Kovner, letter to Abraham Sutzkever, September 25, 1944, file 312, collection of documents on Vilna (Vilnius) Ghetto, Arc 4° 1703, National Library of Israel, Archives Department, Jerusalem. Sutzkever may also have used some of the materials to write his article on Lithuania for *The Black Book*, the great compendium on the Holocaust in the USSR.

9. Sutzkever, "A vort tsum," 208–9.

10. Abraham Sutzkever, letter to Max Weinreich, December 12, 1944, file 546, held in "Restitution of YIVO Property, 1945–1949," box 2, Max Weinreich Collection, RG 584, YIVO archives.

11. See the biography of Stefania Shabad in Kazdan, *Lerer yizker-bukh*, 417–19.

12. YIVO Institute, "Yizker," selections taken from pp. 4, 5, 6, 8, 19.

13. Ran, *Ash fun yerushalayim*, 205–7.

14. See Gabriel Weinreich's memoirs on his father: "Zikhroynes vegn d'"r maks vaynraykh," in *YIVO bleter* (New Series) 3 (1997): 343–46; Max Weinreich, *Hitler's Professors: The Part of Scholarship in Germany's Crimes against the Jewish People* (New York: YIVO, 1946). Weinreich's tense relationship with German linguistics after the war is the subject of a forthcoming study by Professor Kalman Weiser of York University.

Chapter 20. The Decision to Leave

1. Korczak, *Lehavot ba-efer*, 306–7; Shmerke Kaczerginski, letter to Abraham Sutzkever, Kaczerginski undated letters, file 9, pp. 2–3, Sutzkever Collection.

2. Kovner, "Reshita shel ha-beriha," 27; Perets Alufi, ed., *Eyshishok: Koroteha ve-hurbana* (Jerusalem: Va'ad nitsole eyshishok be-yisrael, 1950), 84–86, 119–22; Tsari, *Mi-tofet el tofet*, 83.

3. Aba Kovner, interview by Yehuda Bauer, March 5, 1962, A 350, p. 9, Moreshet Archive, Givat Haviva, Israel; Aba Kovner, Vitka Kempner Kovner, and Ruzhka Korczak, interview by Yehuda Bauer, May 10, 1964, A 350, p. 13, Moreshet Archive, Givat Haviva, Israel.

4. Shmerke Kaczerginski, letter to Abraham Sutzkever, January 12, 1945, file 9, p. 2, Kaczerginski undated letters, Sutzkever Collection.

5. Kaczerginski, *Tsvishn hamer un serp*, 111–12.

6. Aba Kovner, letter to Abraham Sutzkever, February 1, 1945, file 312, documents on Vilna Ghetto.

7. See her memoir: Noemi Markele-Frumer, *Bein ha-kirot ve-anahnu tse'irim* (Lohamei ha-geta'ot, Israel: Beit lohamei ha-geta'ot, 2005).

8. Shloime Beilis, *Leksikon fun der nayer yidisher literatur*, vol. 1, ed. Shmuel Niger

and Jacob Shatzky (New York: Congress for Jewish Culture, 1956), 289–90; Shloime Beilis, letter to Abraham Sutzkever, February 24, 1987, Beilis, file 5, Sutzkever Collection; Hirsh Osherovitsh, "Tsu zibetsik—nokh blond, bay di ful shaferishe koykhes un . . . elnt" (unpublished manuscript on Shloime Beilis), Hirsh Osherovitsh, file 1, Sutzkever Collection.

9. Kaczerginski, *Khurbn vilne*, 256, 277; Grade, *Froyen fun geto*, passim.

10. See Maria Rolnikaite, "Eto bylo potom," in *I vse eto pravda*, 312.

11. Kaczerginski, *Tsvishn hamer un serp*, 94–96.

12. Shmerke Kaczerginski, letter to the Jewish Anti-Fascist Committee, April 22, 1945, file 47, p. 4, Shmerke Kaczerginski Collection, RG P-18, Yad Vashem Archives, Jerusalem, Israel; Shmerke Kaczerginski, letter to Abraham Sutzkever, undated, Kaczerginski letters, file 9, Sutzkever Collection; Shmerke Kaczerginski, letter to Ilya Ehrenburg, in Kaczerginski, *Tsvishn hamer un serp*, 99–101.

13. Kaczerginski, *Tsvishn hamer un serp*, 103–4.

14. Ibid., 57, 60–61, 108. For population figures, see Mayers, "2,000 yidishe," 1; "Number of Jews in Vilna Grows to 4,000," *Jewish Telegraphic Agency Bulletin*, April 12, 1945.

15. Kaczerginski, *Tsvishn hamer un serp*, 105–8.

16. Ibid., 110–11.

Chapter 21. The Art of Book Smuggling—Again

1. Shmerke Kaczerginski, letter to Abraham Sutzkever, undated (from context, late April 1945), Kaczerginski undated letters, file 9, Sutzkever Collection. Similarly, Aba Kovner, letter to Abraham Sutzkever, September 25, 1944: "Abrasha, you must help Vitke leave for Lola. She was supposed to travel, but there are difficulties." Aba Kovner, file 2, Sutzkever Collection.

2. Osherovitsh, unpublished memoirs, box 3608, p. 161, Hirsh Osherovitsh Collection, RG 370, Genazim Institute, Tel Aviv.

3. Yankl Gutkowicz, "Shmerke," 110; the document transferring the directorship of the Jewish Museum, dated July 31, 1945, is found in file 47, p. 2, Shmerke Kaczerginski Collection, RG P-18, Yad Vashem Archives, Jerusalem, Israel. For more on Gutkowicz, see Shloime Beilis, "A vertfuler mentsh: Tsum toyt fun Yankl Gutkowicz," *Folks-shtime* (Warsaw), August 7, 1982, 5–6.

4. Zvi Rajak, "Di groyse folks-levaye far di geshendte toyres fun di vilner shuln un botei-midroshim," *Der Tog* (New York), April 6, 1947, 6. Rabbi Ausband left Vilna in February 1946; see the interview with him at "David P. Boder Interviews Isaac Ostland; September 13, 1946; Hénonville, France," Voices of the Holocaust, accessed January 10, 2017, http://voices.iit.edu/audio.php?doc=ostlandI.

5. Chaim Grade, "Froyen fun geto," January 12, 1962, 6. In the novella, the characters' names were Gordon (Gutkowicz) and Merinsky (Shmerke).

6. The text of the school play is in file 45; the book contract, in file 47; and the letter from Feffer, in file 9, Shmerke Kaczerginski Collection, RG P-18, Yad Vashem Archives, Jerusalem, Israel.

7. Grade, "Froyen fun geto," January 12 and January 19, 1962.

8. Shmerke Kaczerginski, letter to Rachela Krinsky, July 4, 1945, box 11, pp. 9–11, letters by Yiddish writers, RG 107, YIVO archives.

9. Grade, "Froyen fun geto," January 19, 1962. Kaczerginski sent his first letter to Sutzkever from Poland on November 28, 1945, file 312, documents on Vilna Ghetto.

10. The visits were in January and April 1946. For traces of the January visit, see the identification card he was issued by Gutkowicz on January 23, 1946, Documents in Russian-Lithuanian, file 38, Sutzkever Collection; and Abraham Sutzkever, "Mayn eydes zogn baym nirebererger tribunal," in *Baym leyenen penimer*, 150. During the last visit, Sutzkever gave a public lecture on his impressions of the Nuremburg trial to a packed audience at the Vilnius dramatic theater, on April 19, 1946. A copy of the placard for the lecture is found in "Nirenberger Protses," file 10, Sutzkever Collection. Sutzkever mentions his April visit in his first letter to Weinreich from Poland.

11. Shmerke Kaczerginski, letter to Abraham Sutzkever, November 28, 1945, file 312, documents on Vilna Ghetto.

12. Kaczerginski, *Tsvishn hamer un serp*, 113.

13. Gershon Epshtein, YIVO's Paris representative, wrote to YIVO in New York, on November 26, 1946: "Sutzkever left very important materials in Warsaw and Berlin, weighing 20–25 kilograms." Box 46-3, file: "France," YIVO Administration, RG 100, YIVO archives.

14. Ya'akov Yanai, *Mulka* (Tel Aviv: 'Am oved, 1988); Sima Ycikas, "Zionist Activity in Post-War Lithuania," *Jews in Eastern Europe* (Jerusalem) 3, no. 34 (Winter 1997): 28–50.

Chapter 22. Rachela's Choice

1. Rachela Krinsky-Melezin, "Answers to the Questionnaire, the First and Rough Draft," box 3, pp. 15–20, Abraham Melezin Collection, RG 1872, YIVO archives.

2. Rachela Krinsky, letters to Abraham Sutzkever, June 15 and June 26, 1945, file 1, Rokhl Krinsky, Sutzkever Collection.

3. Rachela Krinsky, letter to Abraham Sutzkever, from Lodz, Poland, January 12, 1946, file 1, Rokhl Krinsky, Sutzkever Collection; Rachela Krinsky, letter to family in America, from Lodz, Poland, October 1945, box 1, Abraham Melezin Collection, RG 1872, YIVO archives.

4. Abraham Sutzkever, letter to Rachela Krinsky, August 8, 1945, file 10, Rokhl Krinsky, Sutzkever Collection.

5. Shmerke Kaczerginski, letter to Rachela Krinsky, July 4, 1945, box 11, letters by Yiddish writers, RG 107, YIVO archives.

6. Abraham Melezin, "My Memoirs," memo 37, "Rachela," box 5, pp. 23–24, 26, Abraham Melezin Collection, RG 1872, YIVO archives.

7. Rachela Krinsky, letter to Abraham Sutzkever, January 12, 1946, file 1728.2, Rokhl Krinsky, Sutzkever Collection.

8. Rachela Krinsky, letter to Abraham Sutzkever, undated (probably December 1945), file 1728.1, Rokhl Krinsky, Sutzkever Collection.

9. The poem is dated March 27, 1946. Abraham and Rachela Melezin Collection, RG 1995.A.0819, USHMM.

10. Abraham Melezin, "My Memoirs," memo 37, "Rachela," box 5, esp. pp. 23–28, 41, Abraham Melezin Collection, RG 1872, YIVO archives; Alexandra Wall, notes of 2007 interview with Abraham Melezin; Krinsky-Melezin, "Answers to the Questionnaire," 21–26. See Moshe Grossman, "Shmerke!" in *Shmerke kaczerginski ondenk-bukh*, 48.

Chapter 23. The German Discovery

1. Max Weinreich, letter to assistant secretary Archibald MacLeish, April 4, 1945, box 1, "Restitution of YIVO Property, 1945–1949," YIVO archives.

2. Max Weinreich, "Protokol fun der bagegenish in steyt-departament un komerts-departament vegn yivo-farmegn in eyrope," confidential memo, May 9, 1945, "Restitution of YIVO Property, 1945–1949," YIVO archives; J. H. Hilldring, letter to Lt. General Lucius Clay, June 6, 1945, M1949, p. 100, general records of US military government in Germany, RG 260, National Archives, College Park, MD.

3. Report by J. H. Buchman to Mason Hammond, June 23, 1945, and memorandum from Mason Hammond to the director of Reparations, Deliveries and Restitution Division, US Army Group C, June 23, 1945, M1949, pp. 97–98, general records of US military government in Germany, RG 260, National Archives, College Park, MD.

4. Abraham Aaroni, letter to Celia Aaroni Hochst, June 20, 1945, "Restitution of YIVO Property, 1945–1949," YIVO archives.

5. Max Weinreich, letter to George W. Baker, assistant chief, Division of Economic Security Controls, Department of State, July 6, 1945, box 2, "Restitution of YIVO Property, 1945–1949," YIVO archives.

6. Glenn Goodman, "Rosenberg—Institut fur Judenforschung: Repositories in Hungen, Oberhessen," undated, M1949, p. 81, general records of US military government in Germany, RG 260, National Archives, College Park, MD.

7. Abraham Aaroni, letter to Shlomo Noble, August 9 1945, box 1, "Restitution of YIVO Property, 1945–1949," YIVO archives; Abraham Aaroni, memo on "Jewish libraries," October 10, 1945, M1949, p. 100, general records of US military government in Germany, RG 260, National Archives, College Park, MD.

8. J. H. Hilldring, director, Civil Affairs Division, Department of War, letter to Rabbi Judah Nadich, advisor to General Eisenhower on Jewish Affairs, February 20, 1946, box 1, "Restitution of YIVO Property, 1945–1949," YIVO archives.

9. Letters in box 1, "Restitution of YIVO Property, 1945–1949," YIVO archives.

10. Offenbach Archival Depot (OAD) report, May 3, 1946, box 2, folder 2, p. 5, Seymour Pomrenze Papers, RG P-933, American Jewish Historical Society, New York.

11. OAD report, March 31, 1946, p. 6, April 30, 1946, p. 6, August 31, 1946, p. 9, December 31, 1946, p. 6, box 2, folder 1, Seymour Pomrenze Papers, RG P-933, American Jewish Historical Society, New York.

12. Professor Samuel C. Kohs, letter to Philip Schiff, Washington representative of the Jewish Welfare Board, March 14, 1946, "Restitution of YIVO Property, 1945–1949," YIVO archives; Report of Offenbach Depot, March 1, 1946, box 2, folder 1, Seymour Pomrenze Papers, RG P-933, American Jewish Historical Society, New York.

13. Max Weinreich, letter to Seymour Pomrenze, March 19, 1946, box 1, "Restitution of YIVO Property, 1945–1949," YIVO archives; on the Dubnow collection, see Max Weinreich, letter to Offenbach depot director Joseph Horne, July 11, 1946, box 1, "Restitution of YIVO Property, 1945–1949," YIVO archives; on Strashun and other "YIVO Associated Libraries," see memo "YIVO's Associated Libraries," submitted to Seymour Pomrenze, June 5, 1947, box 1, "Restitution of YIVO Property, 1945–1949," YIVO archives, and in "YIVO OAD 18," pp. 26–35, general records of US military government in Germany, RG 260, National Archives, College Park, MD.

14. Robert Murphy, political advisor to US Military Government in Germany, cable to the secretary of state, April 12, 1946, Department of State, RG 59, 800.414/4-1246, National Archives, College Park, MD.

15. L. B. LaFarge, letter to Max Weinreich, April 23, 1946, "Restitution of YIVO Property, 1945–1949," YIVO archive. "Disposition of YIWO library, taken from Poland, but wanted in US, awaiting State Department Decision," OMGUS, Economics Division, Restitution Branch, "Memorandum on Current Status of Archives and Library Activity," July 15, 1946, box 5, folder 10, Seymour Pomrenze Papers, RG P-933, American Jewish Historical Society, New York.

Chapter 24. Parting Duties

1. See the published stenographic transcript of Sutzkever's testimony (in French), "Nirenberger Protses," file 4, Sutzkever Collection.

2. "Tezn fun mayn eydes-zogn in nirnberg," file 14, "Nirnberger protses," Abraham Sutzkever Collection, Arc 4° 1565, National Library of Israel, Archives Department, Jerusalem.

3. French stenographic transcript of testimony, pp. 309–10, "Nirenberger Protses," file 4, Sutzkever Collection.

4. Abraham Sutzkever, letter from Nuremberg to colleagues in Moscow, file 13, "Nirnberger protses," Abraham Sutzkever Collection, Arc 4° 1565, National Library of Israel, Archives Department, Jerusalem; similarly, see Sutzkever, "Mayn eydes zogn," 163–64. Sutzkever's testimony was covered by *Pravda* on February 28, 1946, p. 4, and was discussed in an article by B. Polevoi, "Ot imeni chelovechestva," *Pravda*, March 4, 1946, 4.

5. Abraham Sutzkever to Max Weinreich, February 17, 1946, file 19, Weinreich letters, Sutzkever Collection.

6. Abraham Sutzkever, "Mit Shloyme Mikhoels," in *Baym leyenen penimer*, 108–11; Moshe Knapheis, "Di Sutzkever teg in buenos ayres," *Di prese* (Buenos Aires), June 10, 1953, 5.

7. See her article "Mayn korespondents mit mentshn fun vilner geto," *Di Goldene keyt* 8 (1951): 203–11; Philip Friedman, *Their Brothers' Keepers* (New York: Crown, 1957), 21–25; Julija Šukys, *Epistophilia: Writing the Life of Ona Simate* (Lincoln: University of Nebraska Press, 2012); Julija Šukys, *And I Burned with Shame: The Testimony of Ona Šimaite, Righteous among the Nations* (Jerusalem: Yad Vashem, 2007). Šimaite was awarded the title of "Righteous among the Nations" by Yad Vashem in 1966.

8. Ona Šimaite, "Declaration on Vilna Ghetto Documents," file 334, p. 1, collection of documents on the Vilna (Vilnius) Ghetto, Arc 4° 1703, National Library of Israel, Archives Department, Jerusalem.

9. The diary was first published in the original Russian; Shur, *Evrei v Vilno*. It has since been published in Dutch, German, Italian, Lithuanian, and other languages.

10. Šimaite, "Declaration on Vilna Ghetto Documents," 3–6.

11. Ona Šimaite, letter to Abraham Sutzkever, January 10, 1947, file 1, Šimaite letters, Sutzkever Collection.

12. Šukys, *Epistophilia*, 24, 26.

A Rescued Gem: The Bust of Tolstoy and Other Russians

1. I. M. Schmidt, *Russkaia skulptura vtoroi poloviny XIX–nachala XX veka* (Moscow: Iskusstvo, 1989), 78.

2. I. Ya. Ginzburg, "Kak ya stal skulptorom," in *Iz proshlogo: vospominania*, 9–86 (Leningrad: Gosudarstvennoe izdatelstvo, 1924). His early works are discussed and published in *Evreiskaia entsiklopedia* (St. Petersburg: Brokgaus and Efron, 1906–1913), 6:534–36.

3. Galina Eliasberg, Galina Evtushenko, and Anna Evtushenko, "Obraz tol'stogo v skulpture i memuaristike I. Ya. Gintsburga (k problem khudozhestvennogo vospriatie)," *Vestnik VGU, Seria Filologia, Zhurnalistika* 1 (2013): 124–31.

4. E. N. Maslova, ed., *Skul'ptor Ilia Gintsburg* (Leningrad: Khudozhnik RFSFR, 1964).

5. "Fun der vilner gezelshaft 'libhober fun yidishn altertum,'" *Vilner vokhnblat* 44 (November 1, 1913): 2; 47 (November 15, 1913): 2; Chaikl Lunski, "Di yidishe historish-etnografishe gezelshaft," in *Pinkes far der geshikhte fun vilne in di yorn fun milkhome un okupatsye*, ed. Zalmen Rejzen, 855–64 (Vilna: Historish-etnografishe gezelshaf a"n sh. an-ski, 1922); E. I. Goldschmidt, "Di vilner historish-etnografishe gezelshaft un ir muzey," in Grodzenski, *Vilner almanakh*, 189–94.

6. "Fun der yidisher historish etnografisher gezelshaft," *Undzer tog* (Vilna), January 9, 1920, 3; February 4, 1920, 5.

7. Information supplied by Neringa Latvyte, director of the Vilna Gaon Museum's Historical Department; see "Priglashaem na vystavku skul'pturnikh portre-

tov tol'stogo, raboty il'ii gintsburga," Tolstoy Museum, Moscow, accessed January 29, 2017, http://tolstoymuseum.ru/exhibitions/1705/?sphrase_id=2147.

Chapter 25. Wanderings: Poland and Prague

1. Abraham Sutzkever, letter to Max Weinreich, May 23, 1946, file 546, Max Weinreich Collection, RG 584, YIVO archives (copy in file 19, Weinreich letters, Sutzkever Collection).

2. Abraham Sutzkever, letter from Lodz to Moshe Savir (Sutzkever), October 18, 1946, and again from Paris, November 20, 1946, file 1266.3, "Moshe Savir," Sutzkever Collection.

3. Grossman, "Shmerke!" 48–50. Shmerke expressed his desire to move to Palestine in a letter to American Yiddish poet H. Leivick: Shmerke Kaczerginski to H. Leivick, August 4, 1946, box 38, H. Leivick Collection, RG 315, YIVO archives.

4. Shmerke Kaczerginski, "Khalutsim lid," in *Shmerke kaczerginski ondenk-bukh*, 257–58.

5. Abraham Sutzkever, letter to Max Weinreich, May 25, 1946, Max Weinreich Collection, RG 584, YIVO archives.

6. The text is cited in Max Weinreich's June 5, 1946, follow-up letter, file 1, Weinreich letters, Sutzkever Collection.

7. Max Weinreich, letter to Abraham Sutzkever, July 17, 1946, in "Briv fun maks vaynraykh tsu avrom sutzkever" (ed. Avraham Nowersztern), *Di Goldene keyt*, nos. 95–96 (1978): 171–72.

8. Max Weinreich, letter to Abraham Sutzkever, Shmerke Kaczerginski, and Chaim Grade, August 15, 1946, file 1, Weinreich letters, Sutzkever Collection.

9. See Aaron Glants-Leyeles letters to Abraham Sutzkever from June 15, 1946, July 26, 1946, August 13, 1946, and September 10, 1946, file 1, Leyeles, Sutzkever Collection.

10. Shmerke Kaczerginski, "Vos ikh hob gezen un gehert in kielts," *Undzer vort* (Lodz, Poland), no. 5 (July 1946): 1–2; Shmerke Kaczerginski, "Di levaye fun di kieltser kdoyshim, fun undzer spetsyeln sheliekh, Sh. Kaczerginski," *Dos naye lebn* (Lodz, Poland), July 12, 1946, 1.

11. Richard Walewski, *Jurek* (Tel Aviv: Moreshet/Sifriyat Hapoalim, 1976), 204–6.

Chapter 26. Paris

1. Gershon Epshtein, letter to YIVO, November 26, 1946, box 46-3, file: "France," YIVO Administration, RG 100, YIVO archives.

2. Aaron Glants-Leyeles, letter to Abraham Sutzkever, December 1, 1946, file 1, Leyeles, Sutzkever Collection.

3. Abraham Sutzkever, letter to Max Weinreich, November 28, 1946; file 546,

Max Weinreich Collection, RG 584, YIVO archives; Max Weinreich, letter to Abraham Sutzkever, December 12, 1946, and January 9, 1947, in Nowersztern, "Briv fun maks vaynraykh," 173.

4. Max Weinreich, letter to Abraham Sutzkever, January 30, 1946, in Nowersztern, "Briv fun maks vaynraykh," 177. (Similarly, Shmerke Kaczerginski, letter to Abraham Sutzkever, October 21, 1947, file 3, Kaczerginski letters, Sutzkever Collection.)

5. Max Weinreich, letter to Abraham Sutzkever, November 21, 1946, file 1, Weinreich, Sutzkever Collection; Max Weinreich, letter to Abraham Sutzkever, May 1, 1947, in Nowersztern, "Briv fun maks vaynraykh," 178.

6. Max Weinreich, letter to Gershon Epshtein, February 3, 1947, box 47-8, file: "Epshtein," YIVO Administration, RG 100, YIVO archives; Max Weinreich, letter to Shmerke Kaczerginski and Abraham Sutzkever, July 10, 1947, file 2, Max Weinreich, Sutzkever Collection.

7. Max Weinreich, letter to Abraham Sutzkever, July 10, 1947, file 2, "Max Weinreich," Abraham Sutzkever Collection, Arc 4° 1565, National Library of Israel, Archives Department, Jerusalem; Max Weinreich, letter to Abraham Sutzkever, July 12, 1947, in Nowersztern, "Briv fun maks vaynraykh," 179; Max Weinreich, letter to Abraham Sutzkever, July 17, 1947, in Nowersztern, "Briv fun maks vaynraykh," 180. Inscription is recorded in RG 223, file 8, YIVO archives.

8. Max Weinreich, letter to Abraham Sutzkever, August 5, 1947, in Nowersztern, "Briv fun maks vaynraykh," 181; the *pinkas* is in part 2, file 184, Sutzkever-Kaczerginski Collection, RG 223, YIVO archives.

9. Max Weinreich, letter to Gershon Epshtein, July 25, 1947; box 47-8, "Epshtein," YIVO Administration, RG 100, YIVO archives.

10. Herbert Gotthard, letter to Professor Gotthold Eljakim Weil, Hebrew University, September 7, 1945, "Korrespondenz . . . über die Auslieferung der ehemaligen Mitarbeiters in Arbeitsstab Rosenberg, Dr. Gotthard, an Polen, 1945–1947, file 77, "Zentralkomitee der befreiten Juden in der Britische Zone," RG B 1/28, Zentralarchiv zur Erforschung der Geschichte der Juden in Deutschland, Heidelberg.

11. Shmerke Kaczerginski, "Men hot arestirt dos khazerl," *Unzer moment* (Regensburg, Germany), July 14, 1947, 6; Abraham Sutzkever, letter to Rokhl Krinsky, November 19, 1946, file 10, Krinsky letters, Sutzkever Collection.

12. "Gekhapt likvidator fun vilner yivo," *Yediyes fun YIVO*, no. 22 (September 1947): 6 (citing *Dos naye lebn*, May 18, 1947); Max Weinreich, letter to Abraham Sutzkever, April 18, 1947, file 2, Weinreich letters, Sutzkever Collection; "Gestapo Agent Who Liquidated Vilna YIVO Captured; Was Masquerading as Jewish DP," *Jewish Telegraphic Agency Bulletin*, May 21, 1947. Weinreich wrote to American officials about Gotthard soon after the latter was discovered, on September 4, 1946, and urged that the matter be investigated. Box 4, folder 6, Territorial Collection, RG 116, YIVO archives.

13. Max Weinreich, letter to Abraham Sutzkever and Shmerke Kaczerginski, December 30, 1946, box 47-2, "1947 correspondence," YIVO Administration, RG 100, YIVO archives.

14. Akiva Gershater, letter to Abraham Sutzkever, December 12, 1946, file 1, Gershater, Sutzkever Collection.

15. Shmerke Kaczerginski, letter to Elias Schulman, February 6, 1948, box 3, file 54, Elias Schulman papers, ARC MS15, Katz Center for Advanced Judaic Studies, University of Pennsylvania, Philadelphia.

16. See Shmerke Kaczerginski, letter to H. Leivick, January 21, 1947, box 38, H. Leivick Collection, RG 315, YIVO archives; and Grossman, "Shmerke!" 48–50.

17. Tsalel Blits, "Vegn an altn pashkvil fun a yidishn kravchenko," *Undzer Shtime* (São Paulo, Brazil), December 20, 1951, 3.

18. Weinreich says that nondisclosure was requested by Sutzkever, in his letter to the latter on July 10, 1947, file 2, Max Weinreich, Sutzkever Collection. In a September 1, 1947, letter from Paris, Sutzkever wrote to Weinreich, "I totally agree with the idea not to publicize the names. As you probably recall, that was my opinion from the beginning." Box 47-2, "1947 correspondence," YIVO Administration, RG 100, YIVO archives.

19. "A symbol fun vilner yivo in New York," *Yediyes fun YIVO*, no. 19 (February 1947): 5; "Di yidishe katastrofe in bilder un dokumentn, vos men zet af der oysshtelung 'yidn in eyrope 1939–1946,'" *Yediyes fun YIVO*, no. 20 (April 1947): 1–2.

20. Nowersztern, "Briv fun maks vaynraykh," August 25, 1947, 182.

21. "Dray dokumentn fun yidisher geshikhte: togbikher fun teodor hertsl, zelig kalmanovitsh un herman kruk in yivo," *Yediyes fun YIVO*, no. 22 (September 1947): 1; "A sutskever un sh. katsherginski in vilner geto," *Yediyes fun YIVO*, no. 22 (September 1947): 7.

22. Shmerke Kaczerginski, letter to Abraham Sutzkever, December 8, 1947, file 3, Kaczerginski letters, Sutzkever Collection.

23. "Fun di vilner arkhiv oytsres," *Yediyes fun YIVO*, no. 27 (June 1948): 5; "Vilner kolektsye in arkhiv fun YIVO gevorn katologirt," *Yediyes fun YIVO*, no. 33 (June 1949): 3.

24. Abraham Sutzkever, letter from Lodz to Moshe Savir (Sutzkever), October 18, 1946, and again from Paris, November 20, 1946, file 1266.3, "Moshe Savir," Sutzkever Collection.

25. Aaron Glants-Leyeles, letter to Abraham Sutzkever, December 1, 1946, file 1, Leyeles letters, Sutzkever Collection; Max Weinreich, letter to Abraham Sutzkever, April 4, 1947, file 1, Weinreich letters, Sutzkever Collection.

26. Abraham Sutzkever, letter to H. Leivick, June 4, 1947, file 1, Leivick letters, Sutzkever Collection; Abraham Sutzkever, letter to Max Weinreich, July 12, 1947, box 47-2, "1947 correspondence," YIVO Administration, RG 100, YIVO archives.

27. Abraham Sutzkever, letter to Max Weinreich, September 21, 1947, file 562,

Max Weinreich Collection, RG 584, YIVO archives. On the remaining pages of the Kruk diary, see the letters from Pinkhas Schwartz and Z. Szajkowski to Abraham Sutzkever, October 28, 1955, and January 16, 1956, file 1, YIVO letters, Sutzkever Collection. Sutzkever donated a large addendum of materials to YIVO in 1956.

28. Shmerke Kaczerginski, letter to Abraham Sutzkever, December 8, 1947, file 3, Kaczerginski letters, Sutzkever Collection. See also Max Weinreich's letter to Shmerke Kaczerginski, September 8, 1948, file 8, Shmerke Kaczerginski Collection, RG P-18, Yad Vashem Archives, Jerusalem, Israel.

Chapter 27. Return from Offenbach, or Kalmanovitch's Prophecy

1. Charles Kindleberger, chief of Division of German and Austrian Economic Affairs, Department of State, letter to John Slawson, executive vice president, American Jewish Committee, May 7, 1946, box 2, "Restitution of YIVO Property, 1945–1949," YIVO archives; O. P. Echols, director, Civil Affairs Division, War Department, letter to John Slawson, May 24, 1946, box 2, "Restitution of YIVO Property, 1945–1949," YIVO archives. See also Paul Vanderbilt, assistant archives and libraries officer, Restitution Branch, OMGUS, June 28, 1946, letter to Luther Evans, Librarian of Congress, file 457, p. 457, general records of US military government in Germany, RG 260, National Archives, College Park, MD.

2. See Dana Herman, "Hashavat Avedah: A History of Jewish Cultural Reconstruction Inc." (PhD diss., McGill University, 2008).

3. Jerome Michael, letter to J. H. Hilldring, assistant secretary of state, August 21, 1946, esp. pp. 1, 5, box 2, "Restitution of YIVO property, 1945–1949," Yivo archives.

4. Cable from Dean Acheson to Political Affairs Department, Berlin, April 30, 1946, 440.00119 EW/4–146, Department of State, RG 59, National Archives, College Park, MD; War Department, cable to OMGUS, May 2, 1946, Restitution: Religious and Cultural (Jewish), general records of US military government in Germany, RG 260, National Archives, College Park, MD.

5. Hadassah M. Ribalow, letter to Max Weinreich, August 8, 1946, box 2, "Restitution of YIVO Property, 1945–1949," YIVO archives.

6. Max Weinreich, letter to John Slawson, August 13, 1946, box 2, "Restitution Box of YIVO Property, 1945–1949," YIVO archives.

7. Yankl Gutkowicz, letter to the Jewish Anti-Fascist Committee, September 17, 1947, op. 1, d. 923, pp. 49–50, Jewish Anti-Fascist Committee, F. 8114, State Archive of the Russian Federation (GARF), Moscow; see also Gutkowicz's later appeal to the chairman of the State Committee on Cultural Educational Institutions, August 2, 1948, d. 10, Committee on Cultural Educational Institutions of the Council of Ministers of the Lithuanian Soviet Socialist Republic, F. 476, Lithuanian Archives of Literature and Art, Vilnius.

8. Michael Kurtz, "The Allied Struggle over Cultural Restitution, 1942–1947," *International Journal of Cultural Property* 17, no. 2 (May 2010): 177–94; and, more

generally, Michael Kurtz, *America and the Return of Nazi Contraband* (Cambridge: Cambridge University Press, 2009).

9. Luther Evans, Librarian of Congress, letter to assistant secretary of state John H. Hilldring, February 25, 1947, and John H. Hilldring, letter to Luther Evans, March 11, 1947, both in "Restitution of YIVO Property, 1945–1949," YIVO archives.

10. Nancy Sinkoff, "From the Archives: Lucy S. Dawidowicz and the Restitution of Jewish Cultural Property," *American Jewish History* 100, no. 1 (January 2016): 117–47; Lucy Schildkret, letter to Max Weinreich, February 16, 1947, "Restitution of YIVO Property, 1945–1949," YIVO archives.

11. "Summary of YIVO collections," March 31, 1947, YIVO OAD 18, p. 44, general records of US military government in Germany, RG 260, National Archives, College Park, MD.

12. Lucy Schildkret, letter to Max Weinreich, June 17, 1947, box 2, "Restitution of YIVO Property, 1945–1949," YIVO archives.

13. Handwritten chronology of restitution, letter from Harborside Warehouse Company to YIVO, box 2, "Restitution of YIVO Property, 1945–1949," YIVO archives ; Mark Uveeler, letter to Lucy Schildkret, July 2, 1947, box 47-8, file "Germany," YIVO Administration, RG 100, YIVO archives.

Chapter 28. The Path to Liquidation

1. See David E. Fishman, "Evreiskii muzei v vilniuse, 1944–1949," in *Sovietica Judaica*, 193–211 (Jerusalem: Gesharim Press, 2017).

2. Gutkowicz, "Der yidisher," 3; H[irsh] O[sherovitsh], "A sholem aleichem oysshtelung in vilnius," *Eynikayt* (Moscow), June 8, 1946, 3.

3. Alexander Rindziunsky, *Hurban vilna*, 219; Osherovitsh, unpublished memoirs, no. 370, box 3608, p. 206, Hirsh Osherovitsh Collection, RG 370, Genazim Institute, Tel Aviv.

4. Rindziunsky, *Hurban vilna*, 219–20.

5. See Kostyrchenko, *Gosudarstvenyii antisemitizm*, 138, 147; Gennady Kostyrchenko, *Tainaia politika Stalina: Vlast' i antisemitizm* (Moscow: Mezhdunarodnie Otnoshenia, 2003), 352.

6. Joshua Rubinstein, "introduction," in *Stalin's Secret Pogrom: The Post-War Inquisition of the Jewish Anti-Fascist Committee* (New Haven, CT: Yale University Press, 2001), 41–44; Kostyrchenko, *Gosudarstvenyii antisemitizm*, 234, 287–88; Kostyrchenko, *Tainaia politika Stalina*, 478.

7. Vytautas Tininis, *Komunistinio Režimo Nusikaltimai Lietuvoje, 1944–1953*, vol. 2 (Vilnius: International Commission for the Evaluation of the Crimes of the Nazi and Soviet Occupation Regimes in Lithuania, 2003), 239–44.

8. Ibid., 247–49.

9. "O reorganizatsii evreiskogo muzeia v. gorod vilnius v vilniusskii kraevecheskii muzei," op. 2, d. 133, pp. 117–26, Council of Ministers of the Lithuanian Soviet Socialist Republic, F. R-754, Lithuanian Central State Archive, Vilnius;

see Yu Rozina, "K voprosu ob unichtozhenii pamiatnikov istorii i kultury Vilniusa v poslevoenyi period," in *Evrei v rossii: Istoria i kultura, sbornik trudov*, ed. Dmitry Eliashevich, 246–52 (St. Petersburg: St. Petersburg Jewish University, 1998), 250–51.

10. Rindziunsky, *Hurban vilna*, 213, Alexander Rindziunsky, interview by Dov Levin, A 529, 118–19, Oral History Division, Hebrew University; Akiva Yankivsky, interview by author, Lod, Israel (via telephone), February 3, 2010.

11. E. Račkovska, "Respublikinės spaudinių saugyklos suformavimas," in *Iš bibliografijos aruodų*, 13–20 (Vilnius: Knygų rūmai, 1985).

12. "Di likvidatsye fun vilner yidishn muzey," *Nusekh vilne buletin* (New York), no. 2 (August–September 1957): 4; Ran, *Ash fun yerushalayim*, 196.

13. Beilis, "A vertfuler mentsh," 5; Shloime Beilis, letter to Abraham Sutzkever, February 24, 1987, Beilis, file 5, Sutzkever Collection; Rindziunsky, *Hurban vilna*, 225; anonymous obituary in *Folks-Shtime* (Warsaw), July 29, 1988.

14. Levin, "Ha-perek ha-aharon," 94; Genrikh Agranovskii and Irina Guzenberg, *Vilnius: po sledam litovskogo yerusalima* (Vilnius: Vilna Gaon State Museum, 2011), 228; Y. Bekerman and Z. Livneh, eds., *Ka-zot hayta ha-morah zehava* (Tel Aviv: Igud yotsei vilna ve-ha-sevivah be-yisrael, 1982), 198, 200.

15. Agranovskii and Guzenberg, *Vilnius*, 559–60.

16. Ibid., 77–78; minutes of meeting of Vilnius municipal architecture commission, op. 11, file 158, pp. 58–59, Institute for Projecting of Urban Construction, F. 1036, Vilnius District Archive, Vilnius.

Chapter 29. Later Lives

1. Kühn-Ludewig, *Johannes Pohl*, 273–85.

2. Herbert Gotthard file, file 14, pp. 82–86, United Nations War Crimes Commission, RG 67.041M, USHMM.

3. Ludmila Hanisch, *Die Nachfolger der Exegeten: Deutschsprachige Erforschung des Vorderen Orients in der ersten Hälfte des 20. Jahrhunderts* (Wiesbaden, Germany: Harasowitz Verlag, 2003), 187; *Christian Albrechts Universität, Kiel: Personal- und Vorlesungsverzeichnis, Sommersemester, 1959* (Kiel, Germany: Walter G. Muhlau Verlag, 1959), 29, 44, 79.

4. Abraham Sutzkever, letters to Chaim Grade, November 17, 1947, February 12, 1948, file 252, YIVO archives, RG 566.

5. See Ruth Wisse, "The Poet from Vilna," *Jewish Review of Books* (Summer 2010): 10–14.

6. Krinsky-Melezin, "Answers to the Questionnaire," box 1; Abraham Melezin memoirs, "Making a New Life in America," box 1, Abraham Melezin Collection, RG 1872, YIVO archives.

7. Alexandra Wall, communication to author, e-mail, August 3, 2016.

8. Rachela Krinsky-Melezin, letter to Abraham Sutzkever, September 11, 1991, file 1728.8, Sutzkever Collection.

9. "Ershter zhurnalistisher tsuzamentref mitn dikhter-partizan Sh. Kaczerginski," *Idishe tsaytung* (Buenos Aires), June 7, 1950, 5.

10. Preface, in *Shmerke kaczerginski ondenk-bukh*, 13; Jeanne Joffen, "Shmerke kaczerginski's letste teg," in *Shmerke kaczerginski ondenk-bukh*, 92.

11. "A. Sutzkever baveynt dem toyt fun Sh. Kaczerginski," *Idishe tsaytung* (Buenos Aires), May 11, 1954, 3; Max Weinreich, letter to Abraham Sutzkever, May 6, 1954, file 552c, Max Weinreich Collection, RG 584, YIVO archives.

12. Chaim Grade, "Eykh noflu giboyrim," *Shmerke kaczerginski ondenk-bukh*, 43–45.

Chapter 30. Forty Years in the Wilderness

1. Račkovska, "Respublikinės spaudinių," 13–20; Fishman, "Tsu der geshikhte," 293–98.

2. Shulamith and Victor Lirov, interview by author, Israel, December 23, 1997; Rivka Charney, interview with author, January 2, 1998.

3. Meile Urnieziute, unpublished interview by unknown interviewer, 1; Almone Sirijus Giriene, unpublished interview by unknown interviewer, 3, both interviews in author's possession.

4. Chaim Shoshkes, "Mayne ershte bagegenishn mit yidn in vilne," *Tog-morgn zhurnal* (New York), October 21, 1956.

5. Fishman, "Tsu der geshikhte"; Shlomo Kurlianchik, interview by author, Natanya, Israel, December 16, 1997.

Chapter 31. Grains of Wheat

1. Emanuel Zingeris, "Bikher un mentshn (vegn dem goyrl fun yidishe un hebreyishe bikher-fondn in lite)," *Sovetish heymland* (Moscow) (July 1988): 70–73; Dina Abramowicz, memo to Samuel Norich, box 1, uncataloged collection, YIVO Vilna Transfer, 1989–, YIVO archives.

2. Samuel Norich, interview by author, Manhattan, New York, April 18, 2016.

3. Richard Shephard, "Rejoining the Chapters of Yiddish Life's Story," *New York Times*, August 30, 1989.

4. See Hirsh Smoliakov, "Far di kumendike doyres," *Yerusholayim de-lite* (Vilnius), June 1990, 4.

5. I was present at that meeting, in the offices of the State Committee on Printed Matter of the Lithuanian SSR, June 1989.

6. Jonathan Mark, "Soviet Crackdown in Lithuania Clouds Jewish Archive's Fate," *Jewish Week* (New York), January 18, 1991; Norich, interview.

7. "Yivo Unpacks Treasure-Trove of Documents Lost since World War II," *Jewish Telegraphic Agency Bulletin*, February 28, 1995; Jeffrey Goldberg, "The Shtetl Is Sleeping," *New York Times Magazine*, June 18, 1995; YIVO Institute, "YIVO Institute Recovers Lost Vilna Archives," *YIVO News* (Fall 1995): 1. "Report on the Work Completed on the YIVO-Vilnius Documents," January 30, 1996, box 2, YIVO Vilna Transfer, 1989–, YIVO archives.

8. Masha Leon, "How Jewish It All Was: A Peek at YIVO's Lost World," *Forward*, March 3, 1995, 1.

9. Larry Yudelson, "YIVO Unpacks Documents Lost since War," *Jewish Telegraphic Agency Bulletin*, February 28, 1995; Steve Lipman, "Paper Trail," *Jewish Week* (New York), March 3, 1995, 1.

10. Sutzkever, *Baym leyenen penimer*, 205–8 (selections from these pages).

11. Yudelson, "YIVO Unpacks Documents"; similarly, Alexandra Wall, "Babushka and the Paper Brigade," *Jewish Standard* (Teaneck, NJ), February 9, 1996, 6.

GLOSSARY

Aktion. A German raid or operation to round up, deport, or murder Jews.

Bericha. Underground operation after the Holocaust to move Jews from Europe to the Land of Israel, largely by illegal immigration.

Bimah. The platform in the synagogue from which the Torah is read.

Bund. The main Jewish socialist party in Imperial Russia and Poland, founded in Vilna in 1897. Its adherents, called Bundists, were democratic socialists who opposed Bolshevism and supported secular Yiddish culture.

Chanukah. Jewish winter holiday, commemorating the rededication of the Temple in 165 BC. It is marked by the kindling of lights.

combine. Soviet term for a group of industrial enterprises that work in close association with each other.

commissariat. A ministry of Soviet government.

displaced persons. Term used after World War II for Holocaust survivors who could not or would not return to their home country. The allies and United Nations administered displaced persons' camps in Germany, Austria, and Italy.

Einsatzstab Reichsleiter Rosenberg (ERR). Nazi party organization dedicated to the looting of cultural property. It was headed by Nazi ideologist Alfred Rosenberg.

Eretz Israel. The Land of Israel (in Hebrew and Yiddish).

FPO. Abbreviated named of the Fareynikte Partizaner Organizatsye, the underground armed resistance organization in the Vilna ghetto.

Galicia. Region of southern Poland that belonged to the Austro-Hungarian Empire before World War I.

Gebietskommissar. Highest regional administrator in the occupied eastern territories under the control of Nazi Germany.

Haggadah. Text read on the holiday of Passover, recounting the liberation of the Israelites from slavery in Egypt.

Hasidism. Jewish religious movement in Eastern Europe, characterized by a theology of divine immanence, enthusiastic prayer, and reverence of holy men called *Rebbes*.

Joint Distribution Committee (JDC). American Jewish relief organization founded during World War I. It served as a major support for Jewish social welfare and educational programs in interwar Poland and aided Holocaust survivors after the war.

Judenrat. Nazi-imposed council responsible for administering the affairs of the Jewish population in a city or ghetto.

kaddish. Hymn in praise of God recited by mourners at burial and during periods of mourning.

kiddush. Prayer and blessing over wine recited on the Sabbath and holidays.

kloyz (**Yiddish**). House of prayer and study, usually smaller and less decorous than a synagogue.

malina (**Yiddish**). Hiding place in the ghetto, to avoid discovery by the Germans.

menorah. A sacred candelabrum lit by priests in the ancient Temple in Jerusalem.

mitzvah. A good deed done out of a sense of religious duty.

Monuments Men. Men and women who served in the Monuments, Fine Arts, and Archives Department of the American military to locate and protect cultural property, including art and books that had been stolen by the Nazis.

NKVD. Soviet law enforcement agency known for mass executions and political repression during the rule of Joseph Stalin. Predecessor to the KGB.

pinkas. Traditional record-book of a synagogue or Jewish religious association.

pogrom. Violent riot directed against Jews.

Ponar (Yiddish; in Polish: Ponary, Lithuanian: Paneriai). Mass-murder site on the outskirts of Vilna.

Purim. Holiday celebrating the rescue of the Jews from annihilation in ancient Persia, as recounted in the biblical book of Esther.

Revisionist Zionism. Movement led by Vladimir (Ze'ev) Jabotinsky that called for the establishment of a Jewish state in all of the historical Land of Israel, including Transjordan, and advocated armed action against British rule in Palestine.

Rosh Hashanah. The Jewish New Year's festival, which usually occurs in September.

Seder. Ritual recounting and reenacting the Israelites' liberation from Egyptian slavery, in celebration of the holiday of Passover.

shiva. Seven-day period of mourning, during which one sits on a low chair near the floor.

Shomer Ha-Tza'ir. Secular socialist-Zionist youth movement; Shomer Ha-Tza'ir was a scouting movement that stressed agricultural training, collectivism, and study of Hebrew.

shtot-shul (Yiddish). The Great Synagogue of Vilna, founded in 1573.

shulhoyf **(Yiddish).** The synagogue courtyard, which housed the Great Synagogue, Strashun Library, the synagogue of the Vilna Gaon, and other institutions. The historic heart of Jewish Vilna.

Talmud. The central text of postbiblical Judaism, completed in Babylonia in the sixth century.

yeshiva. Religious academy for study of the Talmud.

Yiddish. The language spoken by East European Jews. A Germanic language with Hebrew and Slavic components.

yishuv. The Jewish community in pre–State of Israel Palestine.

YIVO (Yiddish acronym for Yiddish Scientific Institute). Research academy for the study of Yiddish language and literature, Jewish history, and the social science study of the Jews. YIVO was founded in Vilna in 1925.

Yom Kippur. The fast of the Day of Atonement, the holiest day of the year on the Jewish calendar.

zhid. Derogatory word for Jew in Russian.

BIBLIOGRAPHY

Interviews

Most of the following individuals interviewed were either inmates of the Vilna ghetto or inhabitants of postwar Vilnius.

Rivka Charney, Cholon, Israel
Shlomo Kurlianchik, Natanya, Israel
Shulamith and Victor Lirov, Israel
Rachel Margolis, Yeruham, Israel
Michael Menkin, Fort Lee, New Jersey
Samuel Norich, Manhattan, New York
Chaya Palevsky, Bronx, New York
Maria Rolnikaite, St. Petersburg, Russia
Alexandra Wall, Berkeley, California
Akiva Yankivsky, Lod, Israel (via telephone)
Avraham Zheleznikov, Melbourne, Australia

Archives

ISRAEL
Genazim Institute, Tel Aviv
    RG 370, Hirsh Osherovitsh Collection
Moreshet Archive, Givat Haviva, Israel
    A 350, Yehuda Bauer interview with Aba Kovner; Yehuda Bauer interview with Aba Kovner, Vitka Kempner Kovner, and Ruzhka Korczak
    A 1175, testimony of Alexander Rindziunsky
    D. 1.433, Kovner memorandum on the creation of an institute for Jewish culture
    D. 1.4.94, "A Plea to Our Jewish Brothers and Sisters" with explanatory notes
    D. 1.6028, Aba Kovner notebook
    D. 2.32, Herman Kruk manuscript, "Ikh gey iber kvorim"
National Library of Israel, Archives Department, Jerusalem
    Arc 4° 1565, Abraham Sutzkever Collection
    Arc 4° 1703, collection of documents on Vilna (Vilnius) Ghetto
Oral History Division, Hebrew University, Jerusalem
    12 (234), interview with Dr. Benjamin Bliudz
    A 529, interview with Alexander Rindziunsky
Yad Vashem Archives, Jerusalem, Israel
    RG P-18, Shmerke Kaczerginski Collection

GERMANY
Zentralarchiv zur Erforschung der Geschichte der Juden in Deutschland,
    Heidelberg
    RG B 1/28, Zentralkomitee der befreiten Juden in der Britische Zone

LITHUANIA
Lithuanian Archives of Literature and Art, Vilnius
    F. 476, Committee on Cultural-Educational Institutions of the Council of
        Ministers of the Lithuanian Soviet Socialist Republic
Lithuanian Central State Archive, Vilnius
    F. R-633, Einsatzstab Reichsleiter Rosenberg
    F. R-754, Council of Ministers of the Lithuanian Soviet Socialist Republic
    F. R-762, Ministry of People's Education of the Lithuanian Soviet Socialist
        Republic
    F. 1390, Jewish Museum, Vilnius
    F. R-1421, records of Vilnius Ghetto
Vilnius District Archive, Vilnius
    F. 1036, Institute for Projecting of Urban Construction

RUSSIA
State Archive of the Russian Federation (GARF), Moscow
    F. 8114, Jewish Anti-Fascist Committee

UKRAINE
Central State Archive of Organs of Higher Power (TsDAVO), Kyiv
    F. 3676, Einsatzsztab Reichsleiter Rosenberg (http://err.tsdavo.gov.ua)

UNITED STATES
American Jewish Historical Society, New York
    RG P-933, Seymour Pomrenze Papers
Katz Center for Advanced Judaic Studies, University of Pennsylvania,
        Philadelphia
    ARC MS15, Elias Schulman papers
National Archives, College Park, MD
    RG 59, Department of State
    RG 239, "Roberts Commission"
    RG 260, general records of US military government in Germany
United States Holocaust Memorial Museum, Washington, D.C.
    RG 26.01M, selected records from the Central State Archives of Lithuania
    RG-26.015M, records of Vilnius Ghetto
    RG 26.021M, Fonds of Einsatzstab Reichsleiter Rosenberg
    RG 67.041M, United Nations War Crimes Commission
    RG 1995.A.0819, Abraham and Rachela Melezin Collection

YIVO Institute for Jewish Research, New York
    RG 40, Karaites
    RG 100, YIVO Administration
    RG 107, letters by Yiddish writers
    RG 116, Territorial Collection
    RG 223, Sutzkever-Kaczerginski Collection
    RG 315, H. Leivick Collection
    RG 566, Chaim Grade Collection
    RG 584, Max Weinreich Collection
    RG 1400, Bund Collection
    RG 1872, Abraham Melezin Collection
    Uncataloged collection "Restitution of YIVO Property"
    Uncataloged collection, "YIVO Vilna Transfer, 1989–"

Published

Abramowicz, Dina. "Vilner geto bibliotek." In *Lite*, edited by Mendel Sudarsky, Uriah Katsenelboge, and Y. Kisin, 1671–78. Vol. 1. New York: Kultur gezelshaft fun litvishe yidn, 1951.

Abramowicz, Hirsz. "Khaykl lunski un di strashun bibliotek." In *Farshvundene geshtaltn*, 93–99. Buenos Aires: Tsentral farband fun poylishe yidn in argentine, 1958.

Agranovskii, Genrikh, and Irina Guzenberg. *Vilnius: po sledam litovskogo yerusalima*. Vilnius: Vilna Gaon State Museum, 2011.

Alufi, Perets, ed. *Eyshishok: Koroteha ve-hurbana.* Jerusalem: Va'ad nitsole eyshishok be-yisrael, 1950.

Arad, Yitzhak. *Ghetto in Flames: The Struggle and Destruction of the Jews in Vilna in the Holocaust*. New York: Holocaust Library, 1982.

"Azkore nokh sh. dubnov in yivo." *YIVO bleter* 22, no. 1 (September–October 1943): 119.

Balberyszski, Mendl. *Shtarker fun ayzn*. Tel Aviv: Ha-menorah, 1967.

Bekerman, Y., and Z. Livneh, eds. *Ka-zot hayta ha-morah zehava*. Tel Aviv: Igud yotsei vilna ve-ha-sevivah be-yisrael, 1982.

Beilis, Shloime. "Kultur unter der hak." In *Portretn un problemen*, 313–416. Warsaw: Yidish bukh, 1964.

———. "A vertfuler mentsh: tsum toyt fun Yankl Gutkowicz." *Folks-shtime* (Warsaw), August 7, 1982, 5–6.

Bernstein, Leon. *Ha-derekh ha-ahronah*. Tel Aviv: Va'ad Tsiburi, 1990.

Blits, Tsalel. "Vegn an altn pashkvil fun a yidishn kravchenko." *Undzer Shtime* (São Paulo, Brazil), December 20, 1951, 3.

Boruta, Kazys. *Skambėkit vėtroje, beržai*. Vilnius: Vaga, 1975.

Broides, Yitzhak. *Agadot yerushalayim de-lita*. Tel Aviv: Igud yotsei vilna ve-ha-sevivah be-yisrael, 1950.

Cammy, Justin. *Young Vilna: Yiddish Culture of the Last Generation*. Bloomington: Indiana University Press, forthcoming.

Charney, Daniel. *A litvak in poyln*. New York: Congress for Jewish Culture, 1945.

———. "Ver zenen di yung vilnianer?" *Literarishe bleter* (Warsaw) 14, February 26, 1937, 134–35.

Christian Albrechts Universität, Kiel: Personal- und Vorlesungsverzeichnis, Sommersemester, 1959. Kiel, Germany: Walter G. Muhlau Verlag, 1959.

Cohen, Israel. *Vilna*. Philadelphia: Jewish Publication Society of America, 1st ed.: 1943, 2nd ed.: 1992.

Dawidowicz, Lucy. *From That Time and Place: A Memoir, 1938–1947*. New York: Norton, 1989.

"Di likvidatsye fun vilner yidishn muzey." *Nusekh vilne buletin* (New York), no. 2 (August–September 1957): 4.

Dos naye lebn (Lodz, Poland). "Undzer batsiung tsum ratnfarnand: aroyszogunugen fun yidishe shrayber." November 6, 1946, 3.

Dror, Tsvika, ed. *Kevutsat ha-ma'avak ha-sheniyah*. Kibutz Lohamei Ha-getaot, Israel: Ghetto Fighters' House, 1987.

Dworzecki, Mark. "Der novi fun geto (Zelig Hirsh Kalmanovitsh)." *Yidisher kemfer* (New York), September 24, 1948, 4–5.

———. *Vayse nekht un shvartse teg: yidn-lagern in estonye*. Tel Aviv: I. L. Peretz, 1970.

———. *Yerushalayim de-lite in kamf un umkum*. Paris: Yidish-natsionaler arbeter farband in amerike un yidisher folksfarband in frankraykh, 1948.

Ehrenburg, Ilya. *Liudi, godi, zhizn: Vospominanie v triekh tomakh*. Moscow: Sovetskii pisatel, 1990.

———. "Torzhestvo cheloveka." *Pravda* (Moscow), April 27, 1944.

Eliasberg, Galina, Galina Evtushenko, and Anna Evtushenko. "Obraz tol'stogo v skulpture i memuaristike I. Ya. Gintsburga (k problem khudozhestvennogo vospriatie)." *Vestnik VGU, Seria Filologia, Zhurnalistika* 1 (2013): 124–31.

Engelshtern, Leyzer. *Mit di vegn fun der sheyris ha-pleyte*. Tel Aviv: Igud yotsei vilna ve-ha-sevivah be-yisrael, 1976.

Evreiskaia entsiklopedia. St. Petersburg: Brokgaus and Efron, 1906–1913.

Feferman, Kiril. "Nazi Germany and the Karaites in 1938–1944: Between Racial Theory and Realpolitik." *Nationalities Papers* 39, no. 2 (2011): 277–94.

Fishman, David E. *Embers Plucked from the Fire: The Rescue of Jewish Cultural Treasures in Vilna*. 2nd expanded ed. New York: YIVO, 2009.

———. "Evreiskii muzei v vilniuse, 1944–1949." In *Sovietica Judaica*, 193–211. Jerusalem: Gesharim Press, 2017.

———. *The Rise of Modern Yiddish Culture*. Pittsburgh: University of Pittsburgh Press, 2005.

———. "Slave Labor Jewish Scholarship in the Vilna Ghetto." In *There Is a Jewish Way of Saying Things: Studies in Jewish Literature in Honor of David G. Roskies*. Bloomington: Indiana University Press, forthcoming.

———. "Tsu der geshikhte fun di yidishe zamlungen in der litvisher melukhisher bikher-kamer." *YIVO bleter* (New Series) 1 (1991): 293–98.

Friedman, Philip. *Their Brothers' Keepers*. New York: Crown Publishers, 1957.

Fuenn, Samuel Joseph. *Kiryah ne'emanah: korot 'adat yisrael ba-'ir vilna*. Vilna: Funk, 1915.

"Fun der vilner gezelshaft 'libhober fun yidishn altertum.'" *Vilner vokhnblat* 44 (November 1, 1913): 2; 47 (November 15, 1913): 2.

Gershater, Akiva. "Af yener zayt geto." In *Bleter vegn vilne: zamlbukh*, 41–45. Lodz, Poland: Farband fun vilner yidn in poyln, 1947.

Ginzburg, I. Ya. "Kak ya stal skulptorom." In *Iz proshlogo: vospominania*, 9–86. Leningrad: Gosudarstvennoe izdatelstvo, 1924.

Goldberg, Jeffrey. "The Shtetl Is Sleeping." *New York Times Magazine*, June 18, 1995.

Grade, Chaim. "Froyen fun geto." *Tog-morgn zhurnal* (New York), June 30, 1961, January 12, 1962, January 19, 1962.

———. "Fun unter der erd." *Forverts*, March 15, 1979, April 1, 1979.

Grin, Boris. "Mit sutzkevern in otriad 'nekome.'" *Oystralishe yidishe nayes* (Melbourne), October 13, 1961.

Grodzenski, A. I., ed. *Vilner almanakh*. Vilna: Ovnt kurier, 1939. 2nd reprint ed., New York: Moriah Offset, 1992.

Gross, Jan T. "Witness for the Prosecution." *Los Angeles Times Book Review*, September 22, 2002.

Grossman, Moshe. "Shemaryahu Kaczerginski." *Davar* (Tel Aviv), May 14, 1954, 4.

Gutkowicz, M. "Der yidisher muzey in vilne." *Eynikayt* (Moscow), March 28, 1946.

Gutkowicz, Yankl. "Shmerke." *Di Goldene keyt* 101 (1980): 105–10.

Haaretz. "Hans Herzl's Wish Comes True—76 Years Later." September 19, 2006.

Hanisch, Ludmila. *Die Nachfolger der Exegeten: Deutschsprachige Erforschung des Vorderen Orients in der ersten Hälfte des 20. Jahrhunderts*. Wiesbaden, Germany: Harasowitz Verlag, 2003.

Havlin, Shelomo Zalman. "Pinkas kloyz ha-gra be-vilna." *Yeshurun* 16 (2005): 746–60.

Herman, Dana. "Hashavat Avedah: A History of Jewish Cultural Reconstruction Inc." PhD diss., McGill University, 2008.

Idishe tsaytung (Buenos Aires). "A. Sutzkever baveynt dem toyt fun Sh. Kaczerginski." May 11, 1954.

———. "Ershter zhurnalistisher tsuzamentref mitn dikhter-partizan Sh. Kaczerginski." June 7, 1950.

Jewish Telegraphic Agency Bulletin. "Gestapo Agent Who Liquidated Vilna YIVO Captured; Was Masquerading as Jewish DP." May 21, 1947.

———. "Hans Herzl, Son of Theodor Herzl, Commits Suicide after Funeral of Sister Paulina." September 18, 1930.

———. "Number of Jews in Vilna Grows to 4,000." April 12, 1945.

———. "Yivo Unpacks Treasure-Trove of Documents Lost since World War II." February 28, 1995.

Kaczerginski, Shmerke. "Amnestye." *Yung-vilne* (Vilna) 1 (1934): 25–28.

———. "Der haknkrayts iber yerushalayim de-lite." *Di Tsukunft* (New York) (September 1946): 638–41.

———. "Di levaye fun di kieltser kdoyshim, fun undzer spetsyeln sheliekh, Sh, Kaczerginski." *Dos naye lebn* (Lodz, Poland), July 12, 1946, 1.

———. "Dos vos iz geven mit bialistok vet zayn mit vilne." *Vilner emes* (Vilnius), December 31, 1940, 3.

———. *Ikh bin geven a partisan.* Buenos Aires: Fraynd funem mekhaber, 1952.

———. *Khurbn vilne.* New York: CYCO, 1947.

———, ed. *Lider fun di getos un lagern.* New York: Tsiko bikher farlag, 1948.

———. "Mayn ershter pulemiot." *Epokhe* (New York), nos. 31–32 (August– October 1947): 52–59.

———. "Men hot arestirt dos khazerl." *Unzer moment* (Regensburg, Germany), July 14, 1947, 6.

———. "Naye mentshn." *Vilner emes* (Vilnius), December 30, 1940, 3.

———. *Partizaner geyen.* 2nd ed. Buenos Aires: Tsentral farband fun poylishe yidn in argentine, 1947.

———. "Shtoyb vos frisht: 45 yor in lebn fun a bibliotek." *Undzer tog* (Vilna), June 4, 1937, 5.

———. *Tsvishn hamer un serp: tsu der geshikhte fun der likvidatsye fun der yidisher kultur in sovetn-rusland.* 2nd expanded ed. Buenos Aires: Der Emes, 1950.

———. "Vos ikh hob gezen un gehert in kielts." *Undzer vort* (Lodz, Poland), no. 5 (July 1946): 1–2.

Kalcheim, Moshe, ed. *Mitn shtoltsn gang, 1939–1945: kapitlen geshikhte fun partizaner kamf in di narotsher velder.* Tel Aviv: Farband fun partizan, untergrunt-kemfers un geto-ufshtendlers in yisroel, 1992.

Kalmanovitch, Zelig. "Togbukh fun vilner geto (fragment)." Edited by Shalom Luria, with Yiddish translation by Avraham Nowersztern. *YIVO bleter* (New Series) 3 (1997): 43–113.

———. *Yoman be-geto vilna u-ketavim min ha-'izavon she-nimtsa' ba-harisot.* Tel Aviv: Moreshet-Sifriat Poalim, 1977.

Kassow, Samuel. "Vilna and Warsaw, Two Ghetto Diaries: Herman Kruk and Emanuel Ringelblum." In *Holocaust Chronicles: Individualizing the Holocaust through Diaries and Other Contemporaneous Personal Accounts*, edited by Robert Moses Shapiro, 171–215. Hoboken, NJ: Ktav, 1999.

Kazdan, K. S., ed. *Lerer yizker-bukh: di umgekumene lerer fun tsisho shuln in poyln.* New York: Komitet, 1954.

Kizilov, Mikhail. *Sons of Scripture: The Karaites in Poland and Lithuania in the Twentieth Century.* Berlin: De Gruyter, 2015.

Knapheis, Moshe. "Di Sutzkever teg in buenos ayres." *Di prese* (Buenos Aires), June 10, 1953, 5.

Korczak, Reizl (Ruzhka). *Lehavot ba-efer.* 3rd ed. Merhavia, Israel: Sifriyat Po'alim, 1965.

Kostyrchenko, Gennady, ed. *Gosudarstvenyii antisemitizm v SSSR: Ot nachala do kul-*

minatsii, 1938–1953. Moscow: Mezhdunarodnyi Fond Demokratia, Makerik, 2005.

———. *Tainaia politika Stalina: Vlast' i antisemitizm.* Moscow: Mezhdunarodnie Otnoshenia, 2003.

Kovner, Aba. "Flekn af der moyer." *Yidishe kultur* (New York) (April 1947): 18–21; (May 1947): 25–28; (June 1947): 24–28.

———. "Reshita shel ha-beriha ke-tenuat hamonim." *Yalkut Moreshet* 37 (June 1984): 7–31.

Kowalski, I. *A Secret Press in Nazi Europe: The Story of a Jewish United Partisan Organization.* New York: Central Guide Publishers, 1969.

Kruk, Herman. *The Last Days of the Jerusalem of Lithuania.* Translated by Barbara Harshav. Edited by Benjamin Harshav. New Haven, CT: Yale University Press and YIVO, 2002.

———. *Togbukh fun vilner geto.* Edited by Mordecai W. Bernstein. New York: YIVO, 1961.

Kühn-Ludewig, Maria. *Johannes Pohl (1904–1960): Judaist und Bibliothekar im Dienste Rosenbergs. Eine biographische Dokumentation.* Hanover, Germany: Laurentius, 2000.

Kurtz, Michael. "The Allied Struggle over Cultural Restitution, 1942–1947." *International Journal of Cultural Property* 17, no. 2 (May 2010): 177–94.

———. *America and the Return of Nazi Contraband.* Cambridge: Cambridge University Press, 2009.

Kuznitz, Cecile. *YIVO and the Making of Modern Jewish Culture: Scholarship for the Yiddish Nation.* Cambridge: Cambridge University Press, 2014.

Leneman, Leon. "Ven boris pasternak shenkt avek zayn lid avrom sutskevern." *Di tsionistishe shtime* (Paris), January 31, 1958.

Leon, Masha. "How Jewish It All Was: A Peek at YIVO's Lost World." *Forward,* March 3, 1995, 1.

Levin, Dov. "Ha-perek ha-aharon shel bate ha-sefer ha-yehudiim ha-mamlakhtiim be-vrit ha-moatsot." In *Yahadut mizrah eiropa bein shoah le-tekumah,* edited by Benjamin Pinkus, 88–110. Beersheba, Israel: Ben Gurion University Press, 1987.

———. *Tekufah Be-Sograyim, 1939–1941.* Jerusalem: Hebrew University Institute for Contemporary Jewry and Kibutz Ha-Meuhad, 1989.

———. "Tsvishn hamer un serp: tsu der geshikhte fun yidishn visnshaftlekhn institute in vilne unter der sovetisher memshole." *YIVO bleter* 46 (1980): 78–97.

Lipman, Steve. "Paper Trail." *Jewish Week* (New York), March 3, 1995, 1.

Lunski, Chaikl. "Der 'seyfer ha-zohov' in der shtrashun-bibliotek." In *Vilner almanakh,* edited by A. I. Grodzenski, 37–46. Vilna: Ovnt kurier, 1939. 2nd reprint ed., New York: Moriah Offset, 1992.

———. "Di yidishe historish-etnografishe gezelshaft." In *Pinkes far der geshikhte fun vilne in di yorn fun milkhome un okupatsye,* edited by Zalmen Rejzen, 855–64. Vilna: Historish-etnografishe gezelshaf a"n sh. an-ski, 1922.

———. "Vilner kloyzn un der shulhoyf." In *Vilner zamlbukh*, edited by Zemach Shabad, 97–112. Vol. 2. Vilna: N. Rozental, 1918.

Mahler, Raphael. "Emanuel Ringelblum's briv fun varshever geto." *Di Goldene keyt* (Tel Aviv) 46 (1963): 10–28.

Makhotina, Ekaterina. *Erinnerung an den Krieg — Krieg der Erinnerungen: Litauen und der Zweite Weltkrieg*. Göttingen: Vanderhoeck and Ruprecht, 2016.

Malatkov, A. "Geratevete kultur-oytsres." *Eynikayt* (Moscow), August 17, 1944.

Mark, Jonathan. "Soviet Crackdown in Lithuania Clouds Jewish Archive's Fate." *Jewish Week* (New York), January 18, 1991.

Mark, Yudl. "Zelig Kalmanovitsh." *Di Goldene keyt* (Tel Aviv) 93 (1977): 127–43.

Markeles-Frumer, Noemi. *Bein ha-kirot ve-anahnu tse'irim*. Lohamei ha-geta'ot, Israel: Beit lohamei ha-geta'ot, 2005.

Mayers, Y. "2,000 yidishe froyen bafrayt fun prison-lager in poyln; 4,000 yidn itst do in Vilne." *Forverts* (New York), February 27, 1945.

Mayzel, Nakhmen. "Sholem aleykhem's briv tsu yankev dinezon." *YIVO bleter* 1 (1931): 385–403.

Mendelsohn, Shloime. "Vi azoy lebn di poylishe yidn in di getos." *YIVO bleter* 19, no. 1 (January 1942): 1–28.

Merin, Borukh. *Fun rakev biz klooga*. New York: CYCO, 1969.

Monash University. "Biographies: Avram Zeleznikow (1924–)." Accessed January 5, 2017. http://future.arts.monash.edu.

M.W. "Draysik nit publikirte briv fun sholem-aleykhemen." *Filologishe shriftn fun yivo* 3 (1929): 153–72.

Nowersztern, Avraham. *Avraham sutskever bi-mlo'ot lo shiv'im ta'arukha/avrom sutskever tsum vern a ben shivim, oysshtelung*. Jerusalem: Jewish National and University Library, 1983.

———. *Avrom sutskever bibliografye*. Tel Aviv: Yisroel bukh, 1976.

———, ed. "Briv fun maks vaynraykh tsu avrom sutzkever." *Di Goldene keyt*, nos. 95–96 (1978): 171–203.

Orlovitz-Reznik, Nesia. *Ima, Ha-mutar kvar livkot?* Tel Aviv: Moreshet, n.d.

O[sherovitsh], H[irsh]. "A sholem aleichem oysshtelung in vilnius." *Eynikayt* (Moscow), June 8, 1946, 3.

Polevoi, B. "Ot imeni chelovechestva." *Pravda*, March 4, 1946, 4.

Pupko-Krinsky, Rachela. "Mayn arbet in YIVO unter di daytshn." *YIVO bleter* 30 (1947): 214–23.

Račkovska, E. "Respublikinės spaudinių saugyklos suformavimas." In *Iš bibliografijos aruodų*, 13–20. Vilnius: Knygų rūmai, 1985.

Rajak, Zevi. "Di groyse folks-levaye far di geshendte toyres fun di vilner shuln un botei-midroshim." *Der Tog* (New York), April 6, 1947, 6.

Ran, Leyzer. *Ash fun yerushalayim de-lite*. New York: Vilner farlag, 1959.

———, ed. *Yerushalayim de-lite ilustrirt un dokumentirt*. New York: Vilner albom komitet, 1974.

Rejzen, Zalmen. "Doktor Teodor Herzl's umbakanter togbukh." *Morgen-zhurnal*, April 10, 1932.

Rindziunsky, Alexander. *Hurban vilna.* Lohamei ha-geta'ot, Israel: Beit lohamei ha-geta'ot, 1987.

Ringelblum, Emanuel. *Kapitlen geshikhte fun amolikn yidishn lebn in poyln.* Edited by Jacob Shatzky. Buenos Aires: Tsentral fareyn fun poylishe yidn in argentine, 1953.

Rolnikaite, Maria. *I vse eto pravda.* St. Petersburg: Zolotoi Vek, 2002.

Roskies, David G., ed. and comp. *The Literature of Destruction.* Philadelphia: Jewish Publication Society of America, 1989.

Rozina, Yu. "K voprosu ob unichtozhenii pamiatnikov istorii i kultury Vilniusa v poslevoenyi period." In *Evrei v rossii: Istoria i kultura, sbornik trudov,* edited by Dmitry Eliashevich, 246–52. St. Petersburg: St. Petersburg Jewish University, 1998.

Rubinstein, Joshua, ed. *Stalin's Secret Pogrom: The Post-War Inquisition of the Jewish Anti-Fascist Committee.* New Haven, CT: Yale University Press, 2001.

Schmidt, I. M. *Russkaia skulptura vtoroi poloviny XIX–nachala XX veka.* Moscow: Iskusstvo, 1989.

Schwartz, Pinkhas. "Biografye fun herman kruk." In *Togbukh fun vilner geto,* by Herman Kruk, edited by Mordecai W. Bernstein, xiii–xlv. New York: YIVO, 1961.

Schulman, Elias. *Yung vilne.* New York: Getseltn, 1946.

Shephard, Richard. "Rejoining the Chapters of Yiddish Life's Story." *New York Times,* August 30, 1989.

Shmerke kaczerginski ondenk-bukh. Buenos Aires: A komitet, 1955.

Shor, Fridah. *Mi-likutei shoshanim 'ad brigadat ha-nyar: sipuro she beit eked ha-sefarim al shem shtrashun ve-vilna.* Ariel, West Bank: Ha-merkaz ha-universitai ariel be-shomron, 2012.

Shoshkes, Chaim. "Mayne ershte bagegenishn mit yidn in vilne." *Tog-morgn zhurnal* (New York), October 21, 1956.

Shur, Grigorii. *Evrei v Vil'no: Khronika, 1941–1944 gg.* St. Petersburg: Obrazovanie-Kul'tura, 2000.

Šimaite, Ona. "Mayne bagegenishn mit herman kruk." *Undzer shtime* (Paris), August 1–2, 1947.

———. "Mayn korespondents mit mentshn fun vilner geto." *Di Goldene keyt* 8 (1951): 203–11.

Sinkoff, Nancy. "From the Archives: Lucy S. Dawidowicz and the Restitution of Jewish Cultural Property." *American Jewish History* 100, no. 1 (January 2016): 117–47.

Smoliakov, Hirsh. "Far di kumendike doyres." *Yerusholayim de-lite* (Vilnius), June 1990, 4.

Spektor, Shmuel. "Ha-kara'im be-eyropah she-bi-shlitat ha-natsim be-re'i mismakhim germani'im." *Pe'amim* 29 (1986): 90–108.

Steinweis, Alan E. *Studying the Jew: Scholarly Anti-Semitism in Nazi Germany.* Cambridge, MA: Harvard University Press, 2006.

Sternberger, Ilse. *Princes without a Home: Modern Zionism and the Strange Fate of*

Theodore Herzl's Children, 1900–1945. San Francisco: International Scholars Publications, 1994.

Šukys, Julija. *And I Burned with Shame: The Testimony of Ona Šimaite, Righteous among the Nations.* Jerusalem: Yad Vashem, 2007.

———. *Epistophilia: Writing the Life of Ona Simate.* Lincoln: University of Nebraska Press, 2012.

Sutzkever, Abraham. *Baym leyenen penimer.* Jerusalem: Magnes, 1993.

———. "Kerndlekh veyts." In *Yidishe gas,* 32–33. New York: Matones, 1947.

———. *Lider fun yam ha-moves.* Tel Aviv: Bergen Belzen, 1968.

———. "Rede fun sutzkever." *Eynikayt* (Moscow), April 6, 1944.

———. *A. Sutzkever: Selected Poetry and Prose.* Translated and edited by Barbara Harshav and Benjamin Harshav. Berkeley: University of California Press, 1991.

———. *Vilner geto.* Paris: Fareyn fun di vilner in frankraykh, 1946.

———. "Vi Z. Kalmanovitch iz umgekumen." *Yidishe kultur* (New York), no. 10 (October 1945): 52–53.

———. "Vos mir hobn geratevet in vilne." *Eynikayt* (Moscow), October 12, 1944.

Szyk, Zalmen. *Toyznt yor vilne.* Vilna: Gezelshaft far landkentenish, 1939.

Tininis, Vytautas. *Komunistinio Režimo Nusikaltimai Lietuvoje, 1944–1953.* Vol. 2. Vilnius: International Commission for the Evaluation of the Crimes of the Nazi and Soviet Occupation Regimes in Lithuania, 2003.

Tsari, Leah. *Mi-tofet el tofet: Sipura shel tzivia vildshtein.* Tel Aviv: Tarbut ve-hinukh, 1971.

Tubin, Yehuda, ed. *Ruzhka: Lehimata, Haguta, Demuta.* Tel Aviv: Moreshet, 1988.

Turkow, Jonas. *Farloshene shtern.* Buenos Aires: Tsentral-farband fun poylishe yidn in argentine, 1953.

U[mru], D[ovid]. "Tsu der derefenung fun der yidishistisher katedre baym vilner universitet." *Vilner emes* (Vilnius), November 2, 1940, 1.

Undzer tog (Vilna). "Fun der yidisher historish etnografisher gezelshaft." January 9, 1920, 3; February 4, 1920, 5.

Von Papen-Bodek, Patricia. "Anti-Jewish Research of the Institut zur Erforschung der Judefrage in Frankfurt am Main between 1939 and 1945." In *Lessons and Legacies VI: New Currents in Holocaust Research,* edited by Jeffry M. Diefendorf, 155–89. Evanston, IL: Northwestern University Press, 2004.

Walewski, Richard. *Jurek.* Tel Aviv: Moreshet/Sifriyat Hapoalim, 1976.

Wall, Alexandra. "Babushka and the Paper Brigade." *Jewish Standard* (Teaneck, NJ), February 9, 1996, 6.

Weinreich, Gabriel. "Zikhroynes vegn d"r maks vaynraykh." *YIVO bleter* (New Series) 3 (1997): 343–46.

Weinreich, Max. *Hitler's Professors: The Part of Scholarship in Germany's Crimes against the Jewish People.* New York: YIVO, 1946.

Weiser, Kalman. *Jewish People, Yiddish Nation: Noah Prylucki and the Folkists in Poland.* Toronto: University of Toronto Press, 2011.

Werb, Bret. "Shmerke Kaczerginski: The Partisan Troubadour." *Polin* 20 (2007): 392–412.

Wisse, Ruth. "The Poet from Vilna." *Jewish Review of Books* (Summer 2010): 10–14.

W.K. "Die Einstige des Judentums, eine wertvolle Sonderschau des 'Einsatzstabes Rosenberg' in Wilna." *Wilnaer Zeitung*, no. 194, August 20, 1942.

Yanai, Ya'akov. *Mulka.* Tel Aviv: 'Am oved, 1988.

Ycikas, Sima. "Zionist Activity in Post-War Lithuania." *Jews in Eastern Europe* (Jerusalem) 3, no. 34 (Winter 1997): 28–50.

YIVO Institute. *Fun di arkhiv- un muzey-obyektn vos der yivo hot geratevet fun eyrope.* New York: Author, 1943.

———. *Yediyes fun amopteyl* 87–88, nos. 1–2 (March–April 1940).

———. *Yediyes fun YIVO.* 1943–1948.

———. "YIVO Institute Recovers Lost Vilna Archives." *YIVO News* (Fall 1995): 1.

———. "Yizker." *YIVO bleter* 26, no. 1 (June–September 1945): 3–19.

Yudelson, Larry. "YIVO Unpacks Documents Lost since War." *Jewish Telegraphic Agency Bulletin*, February 28, 1995.

Zingeris, Emanuel. "Bikher un mentshn (vegn dem goyrl fun yidishe un hebreyishe bikher-fondn in lite)." *Sovetish heymland* (Moscow) (July 1988): 70–73.